D1520129

Confucianisms for a Changing World Cultural Order

CONFUCIAN CULTURES

Roger T. Ames and Peter D. Hershock, series editors

Confucianism: Its Roots and Global Significance
Ming-huei Lee, edited by David Jones

Confucianisms for a Changing World Cultural Order
Edited by Roger T. Ames and Peter D. Hershock

Confucianisms for a Changing World Cultural Order

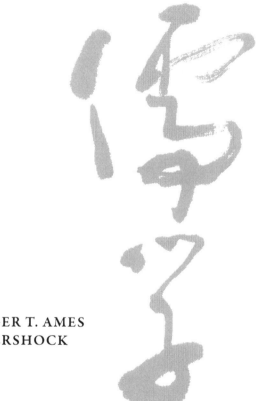

EDITED BY ROGER T. AMES
and PETER D. HERSHOCK

University of Hawai'i Press
Honolulu

East-West Center
Honolulu

© 2018 University of Hawai'i Press

All rights reserved

Printed in the United States of America

23 22 21 20 19 18   6 5 4 3 2 1

Library of Congress Cataloging-in-Publication Data

Names: Ames, Roger T., editor. | Hershock, Peter D., editor.
Title: Confucianisms for a changing world cultural order / edited by Roger T.
   Ames and Peter D. Hershock.
Other titles: Confucian cultures.
Description: Honolulu : University of Hawai'i Press : East-West Center,
   [2018] | Series: Confucian cultures | Includes bibliographical references
   and index.
Identifiers: LCCN 2017024231 | ISBN 9780824872588 (cloth alk. paper)
Subjects: LCSH: Confucianism.
Classification: LCC BL1853 .C75 2017 | DDC 181/.112 —dc23
LC record available at https://lccn.loc.gov/2017024231

University of Hawai'i Press books are printed on acid-free paper
and meet the guidelines for permanence and durability of
the Council on Library Resources.

Composition by Wanda China
Calligraphy by Peimin Ni

Contents

Introduction

Roger T. AMES and Peter D. HERSHOCK

THE LAST QUARTER CENTURY has brought remarkable progress across a broad spectrum of domains. The recent worldwide recession notwithstanding, global wealth has increased at historically unprecedented rates. Medical advances have made life expectancies around the world the highest in history. The Internet and smartphone revolutions have made information almost miraculously accessible to an ever-increasing portion of the world's people. And democracy movements across North Africa and the Middle East have raised hopes for the ideals of universal suffrage and human rights.

Yet alongside these undeniably positive effects of the contemporary processes of industrialization and globalization there have come widening gaps of wealth, income, resource use, and risk. Recognition has dawned that human activity is capable of adversely affecting such planetary-scale phenomena as the climate, amplifying the conditions for opportunity migration, and causing potentially catastrophic economic disruption. The manufacturing and consumption booms that are fueling global economic growth have accelerated environmental degradation, including urban environments; transportation advances have accentuated the likelihood of global pandemics; development-heightened appetites for energy have made recourse to high-risk fuel extraction and power-generating technologies matters of perceived national necessity; and the conditions for continued economic and political vitality have become ever more intimately keyed to those for volatility.

This "perfect storm" comprised of successes mixed with ever-amplifying challenges has several underlying conditions that encourage us to view our current situation as marking an era-defining shift from prioritizing the technical to giving privilege to what is ethical. First, human beings and our ways of being in the world are complicit in some immediate way for the predicaments we are facing. Second, these predicaments are not constrained by national or social

1

boundaries. Crises such as pandemics and global warming have global reach and affect everyone regardless of nationality or status. Third, an organic relationship obtains among this set of pressing challenges, rendering them zero-sum—we either address them all or we can resolve none of them. This means that these challenges cannot be met seriatim by individual players. Rather, we are facing largely human-precipitated predicaments that can only be engaged wholesale by a world community acting in concert. Finally, the predicaments with which we find ourselves ever more powerfully confronted can only be resolved by effecting a radical change in human intentions, values, and practices.

At the same time, however, the growth dynamics of the "network society" and "global informational capitalism" are fueled by the multiplication and magnification of differences. In combination with the near ubiquitous embrace of democratic ideals that urge respect for individual voices, there is a glaring absence of a robust global culture of respectful and open deliberation. The stage is thus set for intensifying confrontations among groups and value systems, each claiming rights to sovereign conduct—conditions that are ill-suited to global predicament resolution. A signal result is the growing awareness of the limits of liberalism writ at global scale in a world of increasingly complex interdependencies. Corollary to this is a growing recognition of the need to consider alternatives to the bifurcation of the liberal and illiberal approaches to world order that framed the conflicts of the Cold War era and that continues to inform much of contemporary national policy-making and international relations.

In a single generation, the rise of Asia, and particularly the rise of China, has precipitated a sea change in the prevailing economic and political order of the world. In the quarter century since 1989, the Asia Pacific Economic Cooperation (APEC) forum has grown to include twenty-one Asia-Pacific nations with 40 percent of the world's population, the GDP in the Asia-Pacific region has more than tripled, and trade in and with the region has increased by over 400 percent. The Chinese economy has grown at annual double-digit rates to overtake Japan as the second largest economy in the world, and is predicted to become the world's largest economy at some time in the 2020s.

Asian development generally and the global impact of China's growth more specifically are producing seismic changes in the world's economic order and international relations. To date, these changes have remained largely entrained with the troubling dynamics of the "perfect storm" noted above. But this reconfiguration of economic and political dominance nevertheless opens possibilities for cultural changes of the sort required to challenge a world cultural order that has long been dominated by a powerful liberalism, especially since this liberalism has proven impotent with respect to the global predicaments and equity issues that promise to shape the course of the twenty-first century. Challenges might be posed, for example, from the perspectives of indigenous peoples, or from religious traditions like Christianity, Islam, and Buddhism. But there is much to recommend considering the cultural resources offered by what Robert Bellah referred to as "secular religions" like Confucianism.

When we look for the cultural resources necessary to respond to global predicaments, primary among them are resources suited to replacing the familiar competitive pattern of single actors pursuing their own self-interest with a collaborative pattern of players strengthening possibilities for coordination across national, ethnic, and religious boundaries. As is now widely appreciated, Confucian cultures celebrate the relational values of deference and interdependence. That is, relationally constituted persons are to be understood as embedded in and nurtured by unique, transactional patterns of relations—a conception of person that contrasts rather starkly with the more familiar model of discrete, self-determining individuals that is an artifact of eighteenth- and nineteenth-century Western European approaches to modernization and nation-state building and that has become closely associated with liberal democracy. Might a contemporary Confucian ethic that locates moral conduct within a thick and richly textured pattern of family, community, and natural relations be a force for challenging and changing the international cultural order?

James P. Carse provides us with a distinction between finite and infinite games that might be useful in beginning to think through how Confucian values could make a difference in a newly emerging cultural order.[1] Using the "game" as an analogy for purposeful human endeavors, James Carse distiguishes between finite games that are played to win by single actors according to a finite set of rules over a finite period of time. Finite games thus have specifiable beginnings and ends, and result in both winners and losers. The pervasiveness of what has become an ideology of individualism and rational-choice theory makes finite games a familiar model of the way in which we are inclined to think about our daily transactions as particular persons, as corporations, and as sovereign states, across a range of activities that entail competition, including sports, business, education, and foreign affairs.

Infinite games are different. They are not played to win, but rather to enhance the quality of play. Infinite games thus have no discernible beginnings or endings, and rather than focusing on competition among single actors, they focus attention on strengthening relationships with the ultimate goal of sharing in advancing human flourishing, not sorting out winners from losers. The relationship among family members might be a good example of the infinite games we play, where parents are resolutely committed to continuing to strengthen the relationship they have with their children so that together they can respond productively to whatever increasingly complex problems their lives lived together might present. In the case of infinite games, the interdependence of relationships means that the success and prosperity of parents and children are coterminous and mutually entailing—they either succeed or fail together. Infinite games are always win-win or lose-lose.

What is Confucianism? In English this tradition takes its name from "Confucius," but not so in Chinese. "Confucianism" as *ruxue* 儒學 does not appeal to the person of Confucius; it is rather the learning of the *ru* class of intellectuals dating back to the Shang dynasty who are responsible for inheriting the tradition, reforming and reauthorizing it for their own time and place, and then passing it on to the succeeding generation with the recommendation that they do the same. It is for this reason that we have argued for a *narrative* rather than an *analytical* understanding of Confucianism.[2] Confucian philosophies are not finite games playing in hope of winning argumentative victories, but rather as infinite games of continually enhancing relational quality in response to always changing circumstances.

In short, framing our question as "What is Confucianism?" in analytical terms tends to essentialize Confucianism as a specific ideology—a technical philosophy—that can be stipulated with varying degrees of detail and accuracy. "What" is a question that is perhaps more successfully directed at attempts at systematic philosophy where through analysis one can seek to abstract the formal, cognitive structure in the language of principles, theories, and concepts. However, the "what" question is at best a first step in evaluating the content and worth of a holistic and thus fundamentally aesthetic tradition that takes as its basic premise the uniqueness of each and every situation, and in which the goal of ritualized living is to redirect attention back to the level of concrete feeling. Beyond the "what" question, we need to ask more importantly after the always transforming and reforming content of a still persistent tradition; that is, we need to address Confucian *practice*. Thus, our central question is: *how* has "Confucianism" functioned historically generation after generation within the specific conditions of an evolving Chinese culture to try to make the most of its circumstances?

However we might choose to characterize "Confucianism," it is more than any particular set of precepts or potted ideology identified post hoc within different phases or epochs of China's cultural narrative. Confucianism is not so much an isolatable doctrine or a commitment to a certain belief structure as it is the continuing narrative of a community of people—the center of an ongoing "way" or *dao* of thinking and living. Approaching the story of Confucianism as a continuing cultural narrative presents us with a rolling, continuous, and always contingent tradition out of which emerges its own values and its own logic. A *narrative* understanding of Confucianism is made available to us by drawing relevant correlations among specific historical figures and events. Confucianism is importantly biographical and genealogical—the stories of formative models. And in reflecting on the lives of Chinese *philosophers*—a survey of often passionate, sometimes courageous intellectuals who as heirs to the tradition of the "scholar-official" (*shi* 士) advance their own programs of human values and social order—we become immediately aware that any account of the existential, practical, and resolutely historical nature of this tradition makes it more (and certainly less) than what would be defined as "philosophers" doing "philosophy" within the contemporary Western context.

Over time, this intergenerational embodiment and transmission of an aggregating Confucian culture spread throughout the East Asian world of Korea, Japan, and Vietnam to become a pan-Asian phenomenon that over the centuries has shaped and been shaped by this family of distinctive and yet interrelated cultures. And, the evidence today is that many in Asia feel that Confucian culture can make valuable contributions to the articulation of a new world cultural order. Enormous resources are being invested in China and other Asian cultural spheres to renew traditional Confucian learning as a repository of values and conceptual resources that can be drawn upon to shape their own responses to contemporary dynamics. Within China, we have over the past two decades witnessed a dramatic rise of "Schools of Canonical Learning" (*guoxueyuan* 國學院) across college campuses. And internationally, at the best institutions of higher learning across America and the globe, we have seen the proliferation of now almost four hundred Chinese government-funded "Confucius Institutes" (*Kongzi xueyuan* 孔子學院). It is clear that Confucian philosophy is being actively promoted both domestically and internationally by a collaboration of academic and political forces within China itself.

In July 2013 academic representatives from the traditional Confucian cultures—China, Korea, Japan, and Vietnam—together with other international scholars held a preparatory meeting at Sungkyunkwan University in Korea and agreed to establish a World Consortium for Research in Confucian Cultures. This initial meeting was followed by the inaugural conference of this Consortium at the University of Hawai'i and the East-West Center in October 2014. The conference sought to explore critically the meaning and value of Confucian cultures in a newly emerging world cultural order by asking the following questions: What are Confucian values within the context of the disparate Confucian cultures of China, Japan, Korea, and Vietnam? What relevance do Confucian values have for a changing world cultural order? What are the limits and the historical failings of Confucian culture and how are these weaknesses to be critically addressed? How must Confucian culture be reformed in our generation if it is to become an international resource for positive change? This volume of essays aims at opening intercultural prospects on answering these questions, but also on responding to the distinctive ethical and moral challenges of flourishing together in an increasingly interdependent and predicament-rich world.

This book is divided into four parts: "Confucianisms in a Changing World Cultural Order," "Different Confucianisms," "Clarifying Confucian Values," and "Limitations and the Critical Reform of Confucian Cultures." The four chapters in Part I, "Confucianisms in a Changing World Cultural Order," argue that Confucian traditions are not merely of historical interest, but also offer resources that have significant and growing contemporary relevance. Part II, "Different Confucianisms," addresses the historically and culturally complex nature of Confucianism. The five chapters in this section explore how differences among Chinese, Korean, Japanese, and Vietnamese engagements with Confucian texts and practices open up spaces for mutual contribution—opportunities for "growing" Confucian thought through intercultural comparison.

Part III, "Clarifying Confucian Values," includes two chapters that seek to bring key Confucian values into high-resolution focus: contingency and loyalty. Whereas a main stream of Western philosophy has focused on the search for epistemic certainty and the derivation of universal principles in accordance with which to organize the moral life, the evolution of Confucian thought has been rooted in bringing the concrete and particular roles and relationships that are constitutive of personal and communal identity into ever higher *resolution* and then deepening the *resolve* with which one strives to enhance relational quality. Examining the concepts of contingency and loyalty makes usefully concrete how Confucian commitments structure the moral life. Finally, the four chapters in Part IV, "Limitations and the Critical Reform of Confucian Cultures," acknowledge the open nature of Confucian traditions and the importance therein of reflexive critique—a readiness to revise and reform the constellation of values that shape the emergence and evolution of Confucian cultures. It is only a vital and critical Confucianism that will have real relevance for a new and emerging world cultural order.

Notes

1. James Carse, *Finite and Infinite Games* (New York: Ballantine, 1987).
2. "New Confucianism: A Native Response to Western Philosophy," in *Chinese Political Culture,* ed. Hua Shiping (Armonk, NY: M. E. Sharpe, 2001).

PART I

Confucianisms in a Changing World Cultural Order

CHAPTER 1

Rethinking Confucianism's Relationship to Global Capitalism

Some Philosophical Reflections for a Confucian Critique of Global Capitalism

Sor-hoon TAN

IN A PAPER that I presented at the 2011 East-West Philosophers Conference, I argued that while the highest Confucian ideal requires that one enjoy an ethical life even in poverty, there is a second best option that combines Confucian ethical values with the pursuit of material wealth—exemplified by Confucius' student Zigong and taken up by twentieth-century *rushang* 儒商 (Confucian merchants)—that "fits better with the pressures of contemporary life in capitalist societies."[1] In retrospect, this seems too accepting of the current capitalist system, despite my repeated caution in the same paper and elsewhere that Confucians today have strong reasons to criticize, inter alia, the increasing inequalities of global capitalism, and that instead of instrumentalizing Confucian values to aid capitalism Confucians should provide critical perspectives to constrain and reform capitalism to serve Confucian ethical life.[2] The present chapter attempts to contribute to a Confucian critique of global capitalism. It may not be enough to convince those who see the Confucian revival in the twentieth century as a postcolonial discourse providing ideological support for the very power relations of global capitalism that Confucianism purports to criticize.[3] Nor will it satisfy radicals who seek nothing less than the complete overthrow of the capitalist system.[4] Furthermore, a Confucian critique of global capitalism is not a task for philosophers alone, but will require multidisciplinary and multi-sector collaboration. What I offer here are merely some philosophical reflections that I hope will contribute to that larger project.

Confucianism and Capitalism: A Century of Debate

The relationship between Confucianism and capitalism has long been the subject of debate. At the beginning of the last century, Max Weber had extended his theory about the connection between the Protestant ethic and "the spirit of capitalism" to the study of the religions of China, suggesting that Confucianism, with its very different values, was among the reasons why modern capitalism did not develop endogenously in China, despite its long history of domestic and international commerce and trade.[5] The "Weberian thesis" had its critics from the beginning, and revisions have been proposed, especially since East Asian societies perceived in some ways as "Confucian"—Hong Kong, Singapore, South Korea, and Taiwan—have achieved impressive economic growth within the post–World War II capitalist system.[6] The same cultural-economic dynamic is assumed to be at work in the rise of China in the world economy over the last few decades. Even though Confucianism failed to bring about capitalism, it has proven conducive to capitalism once countries enter that system. According to the proponents of the "Post-Confucian thesis," not only has Confucian ethics, with "the belief in thrift, hard work, filial piety, and loyalty in the extended family, and most of all, the respect for scholarship and learning," contributed to East Asia's impressive economic growth, overtaking European and North American capitalist economies; it also offers an alternative development model for modernization.[7] Its cultural resources have enabled Confucian East Asia to achieve modern societies that are less adversarial, less individualistic, and less self-interested than their Western counterparts.[8] Confucianism has inspired criticism and rejection of the liberal-democratic models of Western Europe and North America both in the "Asian values" debate of the eighties and nineties and in the continuing discussions of China's future and its role in a globalizing world.[9]

Some blame the 1997 Asian financial crisis on crony capitalism associated with Asian values, including Confucian values, suggesting they belonged to "the dustbin of history."[10] Others place the blame on the current capitalist system itself, particularly the excessively rapid rate of liberalization in markets and financial arrangements, and other policies of the U.S. Treasury and International Monetary Fund.[11] The crisis probably had relatively less impact on the Chinese economy because China had more financial controls than other more open economies in East Asia, and the key difference separating Asian countries that were devastated by the crisis and those that managed to weather it better was not their values but the nature and degree of their international exposure to highly mobile capital.[12] The more recent 2008 financial crisis, which began in the United States, could not be blamed on "Asian values," and the "Beijing consensus" is now challenging the "Washington consensus" as an alternative global economic model.[13] While the leaders of the Chinese Communist Party present the aim of their economic reforms in terms of a market economy that supports "socialism with Chinese characteristics," recent studies of the Chinese economy and society predominantly reveal a transition to some form of capitalism, albeit with significant differences from the mature capitalist economies of Western Europe and North America.[14] Assessments of these differences vary as to whether they are strengths or weaknesses. Among those who promote Confucianism as a source of strength in China's development, Daniel A. Bell identifies the features of East Asian capitalism that are more salient in "East Asian countries informed by the Legalistic Confucian heritage"—Hong Kong, Singapore, South Korea, Taiwan, and the PRC—"than in developed societies in North America and Western Europe" as evidence that Confucianism offers an alternative model that promotes economic productivity while securing the welfare of those most vulnerable to the negative effects of capitalism.[15]

My own approach to the relation between Confucianism and global capitalism will be from a different angle, offering some preliminary reflections on the philosophical ideals of the early Confucian texts and tentative suggestions on how they might contribute to a critique of global capitalism.

The Early Confucian Approach to Economic Problems as Ethical Problems

Early Confucians considered the material welfare of the people to be a central responsibility of government, and this introduced economic concerns into their teachings. Just as these teachings approached political problems by advocating virtuous government as an ethical solution, the *Analects,* the *Mencius,* and the *Xunzi* approached economic problems pertaining to the satisfaction of human wants with finite resources from an ethical perspective. *Analects* 13.9 recommends that governments make those who live in their territories prosperous and then educate them. For Confucius, in order to provide for the people's material welfare, equitable distribution is more important than a constant increase in production (16.1). Confucius believed in "helping the needy" instead of "making the rich richer" (6.4).[16] The indiscriminate gratification of every desire has no inherent value, as Confucians distinguish between ethical and unethical desires and believe that unethical desires should be restrained or eliminated through self-cultivation—the highest ethical ideal is to be able to delight in the virtuous life even in the midst of poverty (4.5, 6.11).[17] Confucius would not endorse the obsessive, unrestrained pursuit of income and wealth by individual persons, of profit by businesses, and of GDP growth by countries. Solutions to economic problems must not just seek the most efficient way to maximize production and accumulation, but rather should ethically aim to improve people's lives.

Early Confucians were realistic enough to accommodate people's materialistic pursuits, since their highest ideal of enjoying virtue in the midst of poverty was beyond the reach of the average person, and certainly not the starting point for personal cultivation. Mencius, who in some ways is even more uncompromising than Confucius when it comes to the conflict between materialistic and ethical pursuits, nevertheless points out that for most people economic security is a precondition for the pursuit of the ethical life. He argues that physical deprivation is demoralizing and drives people to do wrong, so in order to lead people to live an ethical life, a government must first take care of the people's livelihood:

> Only an exemplary person can have a constant heart in spite of a lack of constant means of support. The people, on the other hand, will not have constant hearts if they are without constant means. Lacking constant hearts, they go astray and fall into excesses, stopping at nothing.... Hence, when determining what means of support the people should have, a clear-sighted ruler ensures that these are sufficient for the care of parents on the one hand and for the support of wife and children on the other, so that people always have sufficient food in good years and escape starvation in bad; only then does he drive them toward goodness. In this way the people find it easy to follow him.[18]

The task of a humane government is to ensure that everyone has the means to maintain a minimum level of material welfare, and this begins with assisting those who are worst off because of their relative lack of productive ability and social support (*Mencius* 1B5). Confucian humaneness (*ren* 仁) constrains competition and the pursuit of efficiency.

The *Mencius* gives priority to ethical considerations over economic productivity and efficiency:

> When wasteland is not brought under cultivation and wealth is not accumulated, this, too, is no disaster for the state. But when those above ignore the rites, those below ignore learning, and lawless people arise, then the end of the state is at hand. (*Mencius* 4A1)

Mencius thus condemns those who "open up wasteland and increase the yield of the land" as deserving of punishment. Increasing economic productivity by exploiting more natural resources and increasing factor efficiency are not ethically wrong in themselves—quite the contrary; the context of the passage shows that Mencius rejects such activities only when they impose severe hardship on the majority for the gain of a minority.[19]

Mencius adopts an ethical rather than an economic approach when considering the various taxation practices known to the early Chinese. Mencius criticizes the *gong* 貢 method practiced during the Xia dynasty, on the basis of its impact on the welfare of the people, instead of encouraging economic productivity or efficiency. The taxation method that Mencius prefers is called *zhu* 助, which means "to give help." According to Mencius, it does not differ from the other methods in quantum ("all three amounted to a taxation of one in ten"). Mencius justifies his choice by the ethical effect of this method, which involves the communal cultivation of "public land" in the "well-field system" (*jingdi* 井地):

> If those who own land within each *jing* befriend one another both at home and abroad, help each other to keep watch, and succor each other in illness, they will live in love and harmony. A *jing* is a piece of land measuring one *li* square, and each *jing* consists of 900 *mu*. Of these, the central plot of 100 *mu* belongs to the state, while the other eight plots of 100 *mu* each are held by eight families who share the duty of caring for the plot owned by the state. Only when they have done this duty dare they turn to their own affairs. (*Mencius* 3A3)[20]

The cultivation of the central plot of "public land" educates the people to give priority to what is shared over what is privately owned, and working together on the public land also nurtures relationships of cooperation and mutual help and contributes to communal harmony.

Other than the state's attention to economic matters, we find early Confucian texts referring to ordinary people exchanging goods in markets, and mentioning merchants and traders.[21] In defending Confucianism against rival teachings, Mencius rejects Xu Xing's idea of "one price in the market" by defending price differences for different goods (*Mencius* 3A4). While Mencius might seem to understand better how market transactions work and is more friendly to a "market economy," one should not jump to the unwarranted conclusion that Mencius shares the modern view that the price mechanism is always the best way of allocating resources for production or infer from this that he is a supporter of "free markets" in the contemporary sense. While he recognizes the usefulness of markets, he does not approve of profit maximization:

> In antiquity, the market was for the exchange of what one had for what one lacked. The authorities merely supervised it. There was, however, a

despicable fellow who always looked for a vantage point and, going up on it, gazed into the distance to the left and to the right in order to secure for himself all the profit there was in the market (*wang shili* 罔市利). The people all thought him despicable, and, as a result, they taxed him. The taxing of traders began with this despicable fellow. (*Mencius* 2B10)

Disapproval of those who leave the land or abandon their craft for more profitable trade and commerce is probably behind Xunzi's inclusion of "reducing the number of merchants and traders" among policies that will "allow people to make a generous living."[22]

Whereas the *Analects* and the *Mencius* address economic issues in passing when discussing various aspects of good government as an ethical problem, in the *Xunzi* economics is arguably the topic of book 10, "Enriching the State." Taking up such a topic, unusual for a Confucian, was a response to historical circumstances: states such as Qi and Qin had reorganized both their structure and their economy to become powerful and wealthy, and Mozi, whose philosophy Mencius considered a key rival to Confucianism, had examined the relation between the nature of government and a country's prosperity and argued the need for economic incentives and proper resource management as essential for good government. There were various theories on how to make a state rich and powerful, most of which implicitly or explicitly challenge Confucius' ethical emphasis in his teachings about good government.[23] To have a chance of being adopted by rulers, Confucian teachings had to address their economic and political aspirations; Xunzi tries to do this while advancing the cause of Confucian ethics in opposition to rival schools. Even as Xunzi focuses on the fundamental economic problem of scarcity, his solution is typically Confucian: a state will prosper if the government adopts Confucian ethical practices—which for Xunzi is encapsulated in "ritual and appropriateness" (*liyi* 禮義)—on the personal as well as the policy level. Any other way of pursuing wealth will eventually fail.

Mozi criticizes Confucian ritual practices as wasteful of resources, and recommends "moderation of use" as the way for a state to be self-sufficient. Xunzi rejects this proposal as self-defeating and exaggerating the problem of "inadequacy" of resources. Mozi's solution permits a standard of living that is barely above survival and provides insufficient incentive to mobilize the people to produce economically or serve the state in any way, and "will result in a decreasing population, a diminishing number of office holders, and the elevation of toilsome and bitter efforts, with each member of the Hundred Clans having equal responsibilities and tasks and equivalent efforts and toils." This deprived state undermines authority and exacerbates "social anarchy," which is the "misfortune truly common to the whole world" rather than the problem of inadequacy (*Xunzi* 10.8). Xunzi believes that nature is bountiful enough that human beings can satisfy, beyond the needs of survival, those desires the pursuit of which produces the refinements and accomplishments of civilization highly valued by Confucians. He sees human beings and nature in a relation of interdependence, where humans should be careful of the power and resources of nature—neither completely at its mercy nor seeking to control it completely.[24] While the production of an agricultural society owes much to the vicissitudes of nature, it is the responsibility of governments to ensure that the people "do not suffer the misfortune of cold and hunger, even though the year has been marked by calamities, natural disasters, floods and droughts" (*Xunzi* 10.7).

The use of resources not only translates into expenditure but may also be productive. How many desires can be satisfied depends not just on how much there is in terms of natural resources but also on how human beings manage and employ these resources in economic production and other productive activities. Central to the productive activities that support human civilization are the division of labor and cooperation, both of which require what Xunzi calls *fen* 分 ("differentiation"—also translated as "class divisions"), instituted in the rituals that define relational roles and regulate social interactions, including the distribution of burdens and benefits (*Xunzi* 10.1).[25] A society governed by Confucian ethical norms is economically productive because it is harmonious.

Although Xunzi rejects Mozi's anti–ritual-and-music philosophy, he adopts the latter's idea of "moderation of use" (*jieyong* 節用), but insists that moderation must be effected "by means of ritual" and, in addition, that it is necessary to "let the people make a generous living through the exercise of government" (*Xunzi* 10.2). Xunzi advocates that governments adopt policies that encourage people's economic productivity by allowing them to devote more efforts to their own livelihood and allowing them to keep more of what they produce. Endorsing the satisfaction of desires beyond meeting survival needs does not turn Xunzi into a hedonist, nor would he go along with rampant consumerism, given his disapproval of "reckless extravagance" and his belief that "desires given free rein without limitation" would be impossible to satisfy and destroy any hope of social order (*Xunzi* 10.1). He would undoubtedly view governments who pursue GNP growth to the exclusion of all else as practicing the "thieving way" of pandering to the people and weakening them the way spoiling a child ruins her future (*Xunzi* 10.10). Confucian rituals moderate use by regulating the satisfaction of desires according to ethical norms that set out what is due to people occupying different positions in society, each of which should be occupied by one whose virtues match the position. Unlike Confucius and Mencius, Xunzi may be seen as explicitly advocating meritocracy in going beyond just appointing the person most suited for any position to also matching the person's salary or reward to their contribution. "His emolument [*lu* 祿] must match his services to the state" (*Xunzi* 10.3a).[26] Although Xunzi is thinking mainly in terms of official appointments in government, such meritocracy also benefits economic organizations.

Xunzi is very conscious that meritocracy implies inequality, "sharp divisions and graded differences," which are not merely economic. These serve as incentives that, together with penalties, change people's behavior, including their economic productivity (*Xunzi* 10.9). Xunzi emphasizes, however, that such inequality is not intended to gratify the "reckless extravagance or boastful fondness for elegance" of the ruling or upper classes, but rather is ethical in purpose, "to brightly illuminate the forms and patterns of humaneness and to make comprehensible the obedience and accord required by humane principles" and "to nurture virtue and to differentiate the trivial from the important" (*Xunzi* 10.4). Inequality is valued only when it contributes to the flourishing of the community and benefits all members. It is acceptable to those who receive less only when they believe that the inequality is justified because those who receive more contribute to the security and well-being of those who receive less and moreover deserve respect for exemplary conduct (*Xunzi* 10.5).

Thus, people find an exemplary ruler who is "loyal, honest, fair, and impartial…more pleasing to them than incentives and commendations," and one who leads by example is "more awe-inspiring than punishments and penalties" (*Xunzi* 10.10). While incentives are important when appropriately employed, the ethical power of virtuous rulers—who lead and nurture the people "as though they were watching over an infant"—is more important in unifying the people in harmonious cooperation and industrious striving, both of which will contribute to wealth. When those with power appropriate riches unethically by oppressing and stealing from those they govern or employ, such unjustified inequality will lead to "the greatest dangers and ruination" (*Xunzi* 10.6). From Xunzi's perspective, economic production is a cooperative enterprise the success of which depends on ethical conduct on the part of all, but especially those who govern or who hold power, be it political or economic, and the distribution of the products should be according to the ethical criteria of sustaining a harmonious community rather than according to principles of economic competitiveness. Xunzi's book 10, "Enriching the State," ostensibly concerned with economics, aims to establish the priority of ethical concerns.

The Ethical Critique of Global Capitalism

According to Deepak Lal, the basic human instinct to trade that archeologists trace to the Stone Age was disruptive of settled agricultural society and threatened the communal bonds that all agrarian civilizations tried to foster. Xunzi's recommendation to "reduce the number of merchants and traders" is typical of what Lal calls the "communalist ethics" of premodern agrarian societies, before the divergence between communalism and individualism led to the development of capitalism and the economic rise of the West.[27] Although he dismisses most ethical complaints against global capitalism as "atavistic, harking back to the material beliefs of the old agrarian civilizations," Lal concedes that "morality is needed to rein in opportunistic behavior."[28] Lal maintains that morality that has played a role in controlling transaction costs throughout human history is found in local traditions and works better when it is part of such practices than when the state tries to enforce behavioral norms, although such morality can be influenced by the behavior of governments, NGOs, or supranational institutions.[29]

Confucianism is among Lal's "local traditions." However, instead of a Confucian critique of global capitalism, adopting Lal's framework would merely offer a capitalist Confucian ethics that fosters selected virtues, such as frugality, diligence, honesty, and trustworthiness, which increase productivity and enhance cooperation and efficiency by reducing the costs of transaction in various economic activities, from the factory floor to management to customer relations to international finance and trade. Such an ethics would condemn cases where businesses profit by deceiving consumers, sometimes at the cost of lives, of CEOs escaping with their golden parachutes while ordinary people lose their jobs and life savings, or of taxpayers ending up with the bill for the reckless and downright irresponsible behavior of greedy bankers. Although not without critical perspectives, this approach is inadequate because it diagnoses the problems as arising from ethical failure on the part of individual persons; it assumes that global capitalism itself is not fundamentally flawed or in need of systemic constraints. Furthermore, it is doubtful whether Confucianism is still able to "socialize children through the moral emotions of shame and guilt to 'be good'" to the extent of reining in the worst misconduct of global capitalists even in East Asian societies.

South Korea is probably among the most likely candidates for the effectiveness of Confucianism in such socialization, and yet the recent tragedy of the Sewol ferry sinking casts doubt on the ability of local traditions to check unscrupulous quests for profit that are endemic to capitalism. An investigation of the accident on April 16, 2014, with a death toll of nearly three hundred, mostly high school students, revealed that the ferry operator, who ignored repeated warnings about stability issues in the retrofitted vessel and, in order to cut costs, disregarded safety requirements by not properly securing cargo, overloaded the ferry more than three times the legal limit despite feedback from worried staff, who were mostly on term contracts or were temporary hires with little say in the operation.[30] Ample evidence points to global capitalism eroding local traditions and the moral fabric of societies, instead of the latter effectively constraining the former.

A Confucian critique of global capitalism cannot be limited to recommending a personal virtue ethic to capitalists; even implementing it through comprehensive ethical education in schools or exhorting families to foster Confucian virtues in their young members may not be enough. Such "moral education" programs may not even be viable if global capitalism itself creates a pervasive environment that undermines the values that a Confucian ethics purports to inculcate. Instead we need to understand the problems of global capitalism from systemic perspectives. Capitalism is by nature expansionary and constantly seeks new sources of cheap labor, land, and raw materials, and new markets in order to survive and maximize profits. The spread of capitalism throughout the world predates what we call global capitalism today. Previously this worldwide expansion took the form of separate national economies becoming capitalist and then forming networks of international trade and finance. Global capitalism is the project of creating a single universal free market with "neoliberal" policies of liberalization, stabilization, and privatization—often referred to as "the Washington consensus"—that transnational organizations such as the World Trade Organization, the International Monetary Fund, and the Organization for Economic Cooperation and Development have been prescribing for the last two decades.[31]

Today, the global economy is distinguished from the earlier "world economy" by transnational capital with mobility no longer being hampered by material and political obstacles. The production processes themselves have become global, with decentralization and transnational integration around the world on an unprecedented scale through the use of new technologies and organizational innovations. The mobility of capital increases its ability to generate profit by taking advantage of low-cost materials and factors of production wherever they are located, including relatively less mobile labor. The mobility of unskilled labor in global capitalism results in an underclass of migrant workers in many rich developed countries, while a minority mobile professional-managerial class becomes incorporated into what William Robinson calls the "transnational capitalist class." The globalization of the production process is accompanied by "unprecedented concentration and centralization of worldwide economic management, control and decision-making power in transnational capital and its agent."[32]

The creation of the global free market aims to free economic life from social and political control on a global scale.[33] It is not just an economic project, but involves transformation of the very nature of human relationships. How do the new global capital-labor relation, business-consumer relation, government-business relation, and other new forms of human interactions created in global capitalism fit into a Confucian worldview? Could they fit at all? Confucianism advocates a relational ethics centered in five basic relationships: "love between father and son, duty between ruler and minister, distinction between husband and wife, precedence between elder and younger brothers, and faith between friends" (*Mencius* 3A4). Other human relationships are modeled on these, so that the more general political relationship between government and governed may be considered a combination of the parent-child relation and the ruler-minister relation so that the government has an ethical responsibility for the welfare of the people and for leading them in maintaining the security of the polity, seeking the prosperity and flourishing of the community. Relations between fellow citizens may be seen as requiring friendship as well as functional differentiation in cooperation, combining the basic relationships between friends and spouses.

Traditionally, the larger community is compared with the family in the Confucian understanding of human organizations in relational terms. One would expect the same analogy to hold in the case of business organizations—CEOs should care for and lead other members of a company as a virtuous Confucian ruler would relate to his minister, and functional differentiation, mutual respect, and support in spousal relations and trust between friends would serve as analogies for the cooperative working relationship among all members of the company. Insofar as seniority is considered, the "precedence between elder and younger brothers" would provide a model of how to show deference and the reciprocal demand on the senior to reciprocate by caring and setting an example for the junior members of an organization. From this Confucian perspective, the relationship that comes closest to that between businesses and their customers is probably that of friends, requiring mutual benefit, good will, and trustworthiness.

Instead of merely providing a guide for how to be virtuous in the new economic environment, the relational framework of Confucian ethics should generate a critique of global capitalist relations by questioning whether there are systemic obstacles to participants relating to one another virtuously in ways that would promote personal cultivation and nurture harmonious communities. If global capitalism is driven by relentless competition and the pursuit of profit, it would have no place for Confucian relational virtues. When labor is a commodity, workers can bear no resemblance to family members. If maximizing profit is the only consideration, customers are not friends. For the sake of profit, if they can get away with it, businesses will sell inferior goods at high prices, using advertisements to persuade consumers to purchase commodities that not only do not benefit them but quite possibly will harm them. To describe such unscrupulous conduct as "unfriendly" is a gross understatement. In other words, success in global capitalism drives one to relate to others by thinking of profit first and disregarding what is ethically appropriate to a particular relationship, the very opposite of Confucius' admonition to "think of appropriate conduct (*yi* 義) on seeing a chance to profit" (*Analects* 14.12).

When people fail to extend the virtuous quality of family relations to social relations outside the family in capitalist societies, the reverse dynamics take over, so that even family relations become infected with the obsession with material gains, as is evident in litigation among family members fighting over inheritances, and other similar cases. Relentless competition is not limited to the accumulation of capital but pervades the whole society—we see this even in competition for grades and limited university spaces in disciplines that are popular usually because they are "marketable." Instead of personal cultivation, we find education turned into a means of making money.[34] Even the much admired emphasis in East Asian societies on education that is attributed to Confucian influence becomes perverted: parents concerned over their children's economic future put so much pressure on them to do well in the increasingly competitive economic environment that this undermines the family relationship and fails to cultivate a Confucian ethical character in their children.[35]

Cultivating virtuous Confucian relationships has never been easy, but there are forces in global capitalism that make it even more difficult, if not impossible. The most important human relationships in traditional societies are face-to-face relationships of embodied interactions, but globalization connects people located in various parts of the world who often never meet in person, and decisions and actions in one part of the world affect many in faraway places. The valued qualities of various human relationships in the Confucian understanding are cultivated through everyday interaction at close quarters through ritual practice; such cultivation is not possible in the type of remote interactions that characterize many relationships in global capitalism. A Confucian sage-king's virtue can embrace the whole world, at least in theory, but it is rooted in the humaneness (*ren* 仁) of person-to-person interaction, "establishing others in seeking to establish oneself, promoting others in seeking to promote oneself" (*Analects* 6.30). And humaneness begins with filial and fraternal responsibility in the family (1.2). It is much more difficult to disregard the effect of one's actions on those whom one encounters every day than on those who live half the world away; their humanity and the reality of harm to them and their suffering impinges less on one's consciousness with increased physical distance. Even though new technologies give access to information about what is happening in other parts of the world, not everyone has equal access. For those with access, selectivity is necessary, and too many choose to ignore unpleasant information.

Unlike immediate experience, overexposure through the media can also breed indifference to people's sufferings. Global capitalism allows investors to become wealthy without ever having to give a thought to whether the same economic processes keep millions working for low wages in conditions injurious to their health, destroy local communities by putting people out of work when factories are moved overseas, or contribute to the degradation of the environment.

Those at the front lines of exploitative and other unethical practices—factory supervisors, middle management, or sales staff, for example—if they have any doubts about the ethics of the businesses they work for, salve their conscience by pushing the responsibility on to the decision makers higher up the chain. When questioned about their failure to protect their people (whether as workers or consumers) and the environment, governments cite the need to provide a "business friendly" regulatory environment in the competition for transnational capital to promote economic growth. Global capitalism attests to the adage "If one's aim is wealth, one cannot be humane" (*Mencius* 3A3).

According to the neoliberal ideology, market freedoms are natural and desirable and conducive to economic growth, while government intervention should be limited to maintaining macro-stability to facilitate the workings of the free market. Critics such as Polanyi and Gray point out that the free market is in fact an artificial creation of state power and is maintained by a collusion of economic and political interests.[36] Neoliberal ideology has been challenged, and many East Asian societies have followed different development paths, with the government often playing a much more interventionist role than prescribed by neoliberals. This has been interpreted as a Confucian legacy since the Confucian idea of a good government is one that takes care of the people's livelihood, which in today's world means reducing poverty by increasing GDP through various policies and state actions. The Confucian requirement that governments give priority to the worst off in society may also have resulted in policies that help reduce inequalities and ensure a more egalitarian distribution of economic growth, at least in the initial years of development. However, after a period of falling inequality, East Asian economies also began to display the pattern of increasing inequalities that dominates capitalist economies. Excessive inequalities are socially divisive and destabilizing. The worst excesses of capitalism in the nineteenth and early twentieth centuries were curbed by the state stepping in to regulate the market and redistribute wealth and income, as well as to relieve poverty and promote social welfare through public spending. Confucianism could provide justification for such policies, but this is unlikely to be enough to halt, let alone reverse, the trend of increasing inequalities even if governments professed to be Confucian (and in reality few do so unequivocally).

Economic management has become the most important task for governments, in some cases determining a governing party's ability to stay in power. Even without succumbing to neoliberal free market ideology, governments in the global capitalist environment have little leverage over transnational capital, and increasing the GDP often means "playing the game" of global capitalists, who are also able to use their wealth to lobby politicians of their home country to apply political pressure on developing countries that resist their entry or wish to restrict their freedoms. The prevalent relationship between economic power and political power in global capitalism is incompatible with a Confucian ethical worldview. Economic power and political power have been entangled throughout human history. Political power has been used to amass wealth at all levels, and in order to serve their interests the rich who are not part of the ruling class have used wealth to influence those who hold political power. When the politically powerful were not also the wealthiest due to historical circumstances, occasionally economic power and political power held each other in check. Early Confucians were very conscious that avarice on the part of rulers was often the cause of bad government, leading the rulers to enrich themselves at the expense of the people, or to engage in acquisitive conquests at the cost of their people's lives. The Confucians objected strongly to socioeconomic inequalities that caused the people to suffer.[37] Confucianism seeks to break the collusion of economic power and political power by insisting that it is the virtuous who should rule, and the virtuous are those who, "on seeing the chance to profit, think of appropriate conduct" (*Analects* 14.2).

From a Confucian perspective, it is important that those who govern are not motivated by the desire for material gain, for fear that this would undermine virtue and government for the people. This is why I have questioned recent attempts to equate Confucian government with meritocracy, as an alternative to liberal democracy.[38] The way meritocracy works in global capitalism is likely to result in treating government like any other profession that "purchases" talents and expertise. While this does not mean that every politician will then be motivated only by material gain, politics would attract more who are thus motivated and moreover legitimize such motivation. It might be argued that, even without "Confucian meritocracy," many are already attracted to politics because of the potential for material gain through the use of political influence; Confucian meritocracy is certainly preferable to any corrupt political system that neither delivers competent government nor prevents those in power from enriching themselves at the expense of the people. However, without assurance that a meritocracy would rule with virtue, Confucians should worry more about the incentives and opportunities in global capitalism to generate profits for the few at the expense of the many—what is to prevent "meritorious" elites from appropriating the larger share of economic growth as reward for their "merit"?

Simply insisting on rule by the virtuous is not likely to solve any contemporary problems. There still exists no viable mechanism by which we could ensure that only the virtuous attain power, and attempts to reform existing governments the way Confucians tried to do with the rulers of their times are impractical. Confucians need to turn away from the historical elitist tendency of Confucianism to focus on reforming the ruling elite and learn from the practical experience of societies that have achieved some limited success curbing the polarizing excesses of capitalism. In mature capitalist societies, such as England

and the United States, state intervention to regulate the market and temper the social ills of capitalism came about mostly because of the extension of the democratic franchise. This is not surprising: as Aristotle pointed out, the poor in any society always constitute the many, and democracy gives power to them. The tendency of capitalism to increase socioeconomic inequality has to some extent been kept in check by the (albeit imperfect) political equality of democracy, although the increasing infiltration of economic interests and power into the political process has been undermining democracy in many countries. Nevertheless, reformist critiques of global capitalism focus on the need for more effective national as well as transnational governance, including some form of global democracy.[39] Confucianism could contribute to such reformist critiques by offering a conception of Confucian global democracy that transforms the relationship of global economic transactions into cooperative interactions, imbuing them with the qualities of basic Confucian relationships.

Radical critics would insist that a capitalism that is not exploitative and dehumanizing is an oxymoron. If so, the Confucian alternative (whether constructed out of a modernized Confucianism itself or preferred by Confucians after comparing available alternatives) may end up replacing rather than reforming capitalism. I do not foreclose the more radical outcome. However, the transformation will not be achieved by a violent overthrow of the status quo justified by the belief in some utopia. Confucians would advocate transforming the existing human relationships in all domains from the bottom up, and, most importantly, subordinating the economic and political relationships to Confucian ethical constraints.

Notes

1. Sor-hoon Tan, "Materialistic Desires and Ethical Life in the Analects and the Mencius," in *Moral Cultivation and Confucian Character: Engaging Joel J. Kupperman,* ed. Chenyang Li and Peimin Ni (Albany: State University of New York Press, 2014), p. 209.

2. Ibid., p. 208; see also "Limiting Confucian Meritocracy," in *Resolution of Conflict in Korea, East Asia and Beyond: Humanistic Approach,* ed. Center for International Affairs (Seoul: Academy of Korean Studies Press, 2012), p. 142.

3. Arif Dirlik, "Confucius in the Borderlands: Global Capitalism and the Reinvention of Confucianism," *Boundary 2* 22, no. 3 (1995): 229–273.

4. I remember well Henry Rosemont's comment at the 2011 East-West Conference that capitalism is "rotten to the core." For examples of arguments that global capitalism can and should be replaced, see William I. Robinson, *A Theory of Global Capitalism* (Baltimore: Johns Hopkins University Press, 2004); Alex Callinicos, *An Anti-Capitalist Manifesto* (Cambridge, UK: Polity, 2003); Ulrich Duchrow, *Alternatives to Global Capitalism: Drawn from Biblical History, Designed for Political Action,* trans. Elaine Griffiths (Utrecht: International Books, 1995).

5. Max Weber, *The Religion of China: Confucianism and Taoism,* trans. Hans Gerth (New York: Free Press, 1951) (translation of "Konfuzianismus und Taoismus," part 1 of *Die Wirtschaftsethik der Weltreligionen,* in *Archiv für Sozialwissenschaft,* 1916); *The Protestant Ethic and the Spirit of Capitalism,* trans. Talcott Parsons (New York: Scribner, 1930) (translation of "Die protestantische Ethik und der Geist des Kapitalismus," *Archiv für Sozialwissenschaft,* 1904–1905).

6. Weiming Tu, ed., *The Triadic Chord: Confucian Ethics, Industrial East Asia and Max Weber* (Singapore: Institute of East Asian Philosophies, 1991). Dixin Xu and Chengming Wu, eds., in *Chinese Capitalism, 1522–1840* (New York: St Martin's Press, 2000), argue that capitalism did develop in China before the twentieth century.

7. Fareed Zakaria, "Culture Is Destiny: A Conversation with Lee Kuan Yew," *Foreign Affairs* 73, no. 2 (1994). On the "post-Confucian thesis," see Herman Kahn, *World Economic Development: 1979 and Beyond* (Boulder: Westview Press, 1979), pp. 117–123, 329–383; Roderick MacFarquar, "The Post-Confucian Challenge," *The Economist,* February 9, 1980; Joan Connell, "Revival of Confucianism Fuels East Asia's Economic Miracle," *Houston Chronicle,* March 15, 1992 (cf. Richard Gwyn, "Beloved Confucius Didn't Spark Pacific Rim's Growth," *Toronto Star,* March 27, 1994); Peter L. Berger and Hsin-Huang Michael Hsiao, eds., *In Search of an East Asian Development Model* (New Brunswick, NJ: Transaction Books, 1988); Hung-chao Tai, ed., *Confucianism and Economic Development: An Oriental Alternative?* (Washington D.C.: Washington Institute, 1989).

8. Tu Wei-ming, "Multiple Modernities: A Preliminary Inquiry into the Implications of East Asian Modernity," in *Culture Matters: How Values Shape Human Progress,* ed. Samuel P. Huntington and Lawrence E. Harrison (New York: Basic Books, 2000).

9. Kishore Mahbabuni, "The West and the Rest," *National Interest* 28 (1992); Bilahari Kausikan, "Asia's Different Standard," *Foreign Policy* 92 (Autumn 1993); Margaret Ng, Bilahari Kausikan, and Joseph Chan, "Hong Kong, Singapore, and Asian Values," *Journal of Democracy* 8, no. 2 (1997); Josiane Cauquelin, Paul Lim, and Birgit Mayer-Konig, eds., *Asian Values: An Encounter with Diversity* (Richmond, Surrey: Curzon, 1998); Wm. Theodore de Bary, *Asian Values and Human Rights* (Cambridge, MA: Harvard University Press, 1998); Michael Hill, "'Asian Values' as Reverse Orientalism: The Case of Singapore," Department of Sociology Working Paper 150 (Singapore: National University of Singapore, 2000); Michael D. Barr, *Cultural Politics and Asian Values: The Tepid War* (New York: Routledge, 2002). See also Daniel Bell, *Beyond Liberal Democracy: Political Thinking for an East Asian Context* (Princeton: Princeton University Press, 2006); Daniel A. Bell and Jiang Qing, "A Confucian Constitution for China," *New York Times,* July 10, 2012.

10. Joshua Moravchik and Fareed Zakaria, "The Dustbin of History," *Foreign Affairs* 34 (November 2002); cf. "Singapore Leader Lee Says Asian Crisis Will Not Erode Confucian Values…," *Agence France-Presse,* December 15, 1997. For the questions raised by the Asian financial crisis concerning "Asian values," see Lucian Pye, "'Asian Values': From Dynamos to Dominoes?" in *Culture Matters: How Values Shape Human Progress,* ed. Samuel P. Huntington and Lawrence E. Harrison (New York: Basic Books, 2000), and special feature, "What Would Confucius Say Now?" *The Economist,* July 25, 1998.

11. Jason Furman and Joseph E. Stiglitz, "Economic Crises: Evidence and Insights from East Asia," *Brookings Papers on Economic Activity* 2 (1998); Robert Wade and Frank

Veneroso, "The Asian Crisis: The High Debt Model Versus the Wall-Street-Treasury-IMF Complex," *New Left Review* 228 (March/April 1998): 5; Richard Greb, "Analyzing Asia," *Northwestern* (January/February 1999); Joseph E. Stiglitz, *Globalization and Its Discontents* (New York: Norton, 2003), chap. 4; Callinicos, *An Anti-Capitalist Manifesto*, pp. 40–41. For various views on the Asian financial crisis, see also William C. Hunter, George G. Kaufman, and Thomas H. Krueger, eds., *The Asian Financial Crisis: Origins, Implications and Solutions* (London: Kluwer Academic Publishers, 1999); Gregory W. Noble and John Ravenhill, eds., *The Asian Financial Crisis and the Architecture of Global Finance* (Cambridge, UK: Cambridge University Press, 2000); Richard Robison et al., eds., *Politics and Markets in the Wake of the Asian Crisis,* Asian Capitalisms series (New York: Routledge, 2000); Wing Thye Woo, Jeffrey D. Sachs, and Klaus Schwab, eds., *The Asian Financial Crisis: Lessons for a Resilient Asia* (Cambridge, MA: MIT Press, 2000); Arvid John Lukauskas and Francisco L. Rivera-Batiz, eds., *The Political Economy of the East Asian Crisis and Its Aftermath* (Cheltenham, UK: Edward Elgar, 2001).

12. Yu Yongding, "China: The Case for Capital Controls," in *Global Finance: New Thinking on Regulating Speculative Capital Markets,* ed. Walden Bello, Nicola Bullard, and Kamal Malhotra (New York: Zed Books, 2000), pp. 177–187; Jeffrey Winters, "The Financial Crisis in Southeast Asia," in *Politics and Markets in the Wake of the Asian Crisis,* ed. Robison et al., p. 37.

13. Joshua Cooper Ramo, *The Beijing Consensus* (London: Foreign Policy Center, 2004); Ping Huang, ed., *China and Globalization: Beijing Consensus, Washington Consensus, or What?* (Beijing: Social Science Texts Press, 2005); Wei Pan, ed., *China Model: A New Developmental Model from the Sixty Years of the People's Republic* (Beijing: Central Compilation and Translation Press, 2009); Stefan A. Halper, *Beijing Consensus: Legitimizing Authoritarianism in Our Time* (New York: Basic Books, 2012); Edward K. Y. Chen, "Asian Capitalism: Beijing Consensus as an Economic Development Model for the Twenty-First Century," in *Asian Responses to the Global Financial Crisis: The Impact of Regionalism and the Role of the G20,* ed. Jehoon Park, T. J. Pempel, and Geng Xiao (Cheltenham, UK: Edward Elgar, 2012); cf. S. Philip Hsu, Suisheng Zhao, and Yu-shan Wu, eds., *In Search of China's Development Model: Beyond the Beijing Consensus* (New York: Routledge, 2011). Joseph Stiglitz argues that both the 1997 Asian crisis and the 2008 crisis are due to "fundamental flaws" in the capitalist system driven by "market fundamentalism," the belief that markets are self-regulating; see Joseph E. Stiglitz, *Freefall: America, Free Markets, and the Sinking of the World Economy* (London: Allen Lane/Penguin, 2006; New York and London: W. W. Norton, 2010).

14. George C. S. Lin, *Red Capitalism in South China: Growth and Development of the Pearl River Delta* (Vancouver: University of British Columbia Press, 1997); Doug Guthrie, *Dragon in a Three-Piece Suit: The Emergence of Capitalism in China* (Princeton: Princeton University Press, 1999); Mary Elizabeth Gallagher, *Contagious Capitalism: Globalization and the Politics of Labor in China* (Princeton: Princeton University Press, 2005); Kellee S. Tsai, *Capitalism without Democracy: The Private Sector in Contemporary China* (Ithaca: Cornell University Press, 2007); Scott Kennedy, ed., *Beyond the Middle Kingdom: Comparative Perspectives on China's Capitalist Development,* Contemporary Issues in Asia and the Pacific series (Stanford: Stanford University Press, 2011); Carl E. Walter and Fraser J. T.

Howie, *Red Capitalism: The Fragile Foundation of China's Extraordinary Rise* (London: Wiley, 2011); Michael Webber, *Making Capitalism in Rural China* (Cheltenham, UK, and Northampton, MA: Edward Elgar, 2012); Victor Nee and Sonja Opper, *Capitalism from Below: Markets and Institutional Change in China* (Cambridge, MA: Harvard University Press, 2012); Michael Keith et al., *China Constructing Capitalism* (Abingdon, Oxon: Routledge, 2014).

15. Bell, in *Beyond Liberal Democracy,* p. 259 (cf. Halper, *Beijing Consensus,* p. 70), recognizes the Beijing consensus as a refinement of the growth model pioneered by the Asian tigers, but does not emphasize their common Confucian legacy in examining the challenge that China's authoritarian model poses to the United States.

16. Unless otherwise stated, translations of the *Analects* are from *The Analects of Confucius: A Philosophical Translation,* trans. Roger T. Ames and Henry Rosemont, Jr. (New York: Ballantine, 1998); references give the traditional book and chapter numbering.

17. See Tan, "Materialistic Desires," p. 195, for the Confucian understanding of competition between ethical and unethical desires.

18. *Mencius* 1A7; translation modified from D. C. Lau, *Mencius* (Harmondsworth: Penguin, 1970). Unless otherwise stated, all citations from the *Mencius* are from this translation.

19. Cf. *Mencius* 6B7; the Son of Heaven rewards feudal lords who "open up land and cultivate the fields well." According to the *Xunzi* (10.14), the humane person "would open up wilderness lands to cultivation and fill the granaries and storehouses, and provide useful instruments."

20. A plot divided into nine with one subdivided plot in the center surrounded by the other eight has been described as *jing* 井, literally meaning "a well," because the character is composed of two vertical lines intersecting two horizontal lines, which is how the division is done.

21. Archeologists trace the human instinct to engage in "truck and barter," the basis of economic activity, to the stone age; see John Richard Hicks, *Causality in Economics* (Oxford: Blackwell, 1979), p. 43.

22. *Xunzi* 10.3b. References are to book and section numbers in John Knoblock, trans., *Xunzi: A Translation and Study of the Complete Works,* 3 vols. (Stanford: Stanford University Press, 1990), vol. 2.

23. Knoblock's introduction to book 10, in his *Xunzi,* vol. 2, pp. 113–114.

24. Book 17, "Discourse on Nature."

25. Cf. *Mencius* 3A4, the rejection of Xu Xing's philosophy that everyone should aim to be self-sufficient by growing their own food and Mencius' argument for a division of labor where economic surplus produced by "those who use their muscles" supports "those who use their minds," i.e., those who contribute to economic production by ruling well.

26. According to Knoblock, in *Xunzi,* vol. 2, p. 303n. 22, this is a cardinal teaching of Mozi that Xunzi adopted. I believe that Xunzi actually modified the meritocratic doctrine in this passage by explicating *yong* 用 not only as "services to the state" but also what people "use" to satisfy their needs, turning the "matching" requirement into a needs-based distribution. However, for the purpose of this chapter, I am willing to go along with the more common interpretation.

27. Deepak Lal, "Private Morality and Capitalism: Learning from the Past," in *Making Glaobzalition Good: The Moral Challenges of Global Capitalism,* ed. John H. Dunning (Oxford: Oxford University Press, 2003). See also Deepak Lal, *Unintended Consequences: The Impact of Factor Endowments, Culture, and Politics on Long-Run Economic Performance* (Cambridge, MA: MIT Press, 1998). While I find his basic thesis persuasive, Lal's philosophically superficial account of the "communalism" of "Sinic civilization" is misleading.

28. Lal, "Private Morality and Capitalism," pp. 52, 57.

29. Ibid., p. 57; cf. other views of the need for ethical constraints on global capitalism in the same edited volume.

30. In-Soo Nam, Min-Jeong Lee, and Jeyup S. Kwaak, "Korean Ferry Carrying Triple the Allowed Load," *Wall Street Journal,* Asia Edition, April 24, 2014; Jeyup S. Kwaak, "Ferry's Captain Warned about Stability Issue," ibid., May 1.

31. This term was coined by John Williamson, in his *Latin American Adjustment: How Much Has Happened?* (Washington D.C.: Institute for International Economics, 1990), to describe the reforms undertaken by South American economies in the 1980s, but over time came to signify a set of "neoliberal" policy prescriptions thought to be necessary and sufficient for economic development.

32. Robinson, *A Theory of Global Capitalism,* p. 11. See the rest of the work for a detailed Marxist theory of global capitalism advocating a democratic socialist alternative.

33. John Gray, in his *False Dawn: The Delusions of Global Capitalism* (New York: New Press, 1998), compares this to the experiment of social engineering in mid-nineteenth-century England that created the free-market economy, a process that Karl Polanyi calls the Great Transformation, in his *The Great Transformation: The Political and Economic Origins of Our Times* (Boston: Beacon Press, 1944).

34. Other critics have argued that commodification corrupts the intrinsic value of certain goods and services when no limit is set on spreading marketization. See Steven Lukes, "Invasions of the Market," in *Worlds of Capitalism: Institutions, Governance and Economic Change in the Era of Globalization,* ed. Max Miller (New York: Routledge, 2005).

35. A Singapore mother laments that she "raised a lawyer but lost a son" because their relationship throughout his growing years was dominated by her pushing him to do well academically, to the exclusion of more holistic caring, understanding, and communicating. Her son became a successful lawyer, but they have little to say to each other, let alone any kind of close relationship that could qualify for Confucian filiality.

36. Polanyi, *The Great Transformation;* Gray, *False Dawn.*

37. *Analects* 12.9, 16.1; *Mencius* 1A2, 1A4; *Xunzi* 9.5, 10.11, 10.13.

38. Bell, *Beyond Liberal Democracy,* chap. 6; Sor-hoon Tan, "Beyond Elitism: A Community Ideal for a Modern East Asia," *Philosophy East and West* 59, no. 4 (2009). See also Daniel A. Bell and Chenyang Li, eds., *The East Asian Challenge for Democracy: Political Meritocracy in Comparative Perspective* (New York: Cambridge University Press, 2013).

39. For examples of reformist proposals, see Mahbub ul Haq, Inge Kaul, and Isabelle Grunberg, eds., *The Tobin Tax: Coping with Financial Volatility* (New York: Oxford University Press, 1996); Kamal Malhotra, "Renewing the Governance of the Global Economy," in Bello, Bullard, and Malhotra, *Global Finance,* pp. 42–60; Susan George, "Clusters of Crisis and a Planetary Contract," http://www.tni.org/archives/archives_george_clusters (2001);

Anthony Giddens, ed., *The Global Third Way Debate* (Cambridge, UK: Polity, 2001); Joseph E. Stiglitz, *Making Globalization Work* (London: Allen Lane/Penguin, 2006; New York and London: W. W. Norton, 2006); Narcis Serra and Joseph E. Stiglitz, *The Washington Consensus Reconsidered: Towards a New Global Governance* (New York: Oxford University Press, 2008), part 3; Jose Miguel Andreu and Rita Dulci Rahman, *Global Democracy for Sustaining Global Capitalism* (New Delhi: Academic Foundations, 2009); Helmut Willke and Gerhard Willke, *Political Governance of Capitalism: A Reassessment beyond the Global Crisis* (Cheltenham, UK: Edward Elgar, 2012); Joseph E. Stiglitz and Mary Kaldor, eds., *The Quest for Security: Protection without Protectionism and the Challenge of Global Governance* (New York: Columbia University Press, 2013).

CHAPTER 2

Confucianism as an Antidote for Liberal Self-Centeredness

A Dialogue between Confucianism and Liberalism

LEE Seung-Hwan

Premodern, Modern, and Postmodern Conditions in Asia and the Need for a Confucian-Liberal Dialogue

Today's Asian society is a dynamic melting pot in which premodern, modern, and postmodern elements coexist without having undergone any orderly process. In the West, modernization has proceeded gradually over a span of three hundred years. But most Asian countries have rushed to catch up with the West in a mere few decades, and rapid cultural change has brought confusion over cultural values and social norms. Some parts of Asian society still harbor premodern values such as patriarchal authority, family-centrism, and the preference for male offspring, while other parts are increasingly embracing modern values such as equality, individualism, and liberalism. Not only do premodern and modern elements coexist, but postmodern voices are also appearing through various channels to speak up for the environment, nature, and community.

Amid this whirlwind of frenzied modernization, Asians have had no time for dispassionate reflection on their long-term social ideal, and this has ultimately resulted in a confusion of values and a loss of cultural identity. This current confusion of values that is felt among Asians can be attributed to two interrelated processes. On the one hand, under the sweeping tide of modernization, traditional values have been altered, distorted, or applied to purely utilitarian ends. On the other hand, modern values introduced from the West have taken root in unhealthy ways. For instance, the traditional Confucian value placed on community has been seriously distorted under the modernization process into the practices of nepotism and personal connections. Among the various values relating to tradition and modernity, Asian people have been driven to choose only those that were able to promote material profit and selfish desires, and have pursued them blindly without principled reflection. Accordingly, it is now important that Asian society leave behind its tangled strands of distorted tradition and modernity and be reborn through a creative fusion of strong ideas drawn from both tradition and modernity. Only through this kind of reflexive synthesis can Asian countries achieve modernity while preserving their cultural identity, and accept the benefits of Western civilization while overcoming the limits of modernity.

In this chapter, by employing the method of socio-philosophical comparison and mutual critique between the mainstay of the Asian traditional value system (especially Confucianism) and the central tenet of modern values (i.e., liberalism), I will try to formulate a blueprint for a new social ideal suited to the Asian society of the future. This kind of remapping project of social ideals not only will be helpful for Asian society itself, but also can shed light on other developing countries that face similar problems.

Positive Liberty and Negative Liberty

Needless to say, the most important social ideal pursued by the modern West is liberty. Liberty is the condition in which an individual is able to determine her/his own actions autonomously without interference from others. In the liberal tradition, individual liberty is set above any other normative value, to the extent that laws and norms are founded upon the principle of noninterference. One can do anything one wants to do, as long as one does not interfere with the liberty of others. The grounds for the imposition of limits upon the liberty of an individual by law are known as liberty-limiting principles. While radical liberals admit no such grounds except the harm principle,[1] those liberals who are less radical (or moderate) hold that, in addition to the harm principle, an offense principle can also be a legitimate basis for limiting individual liberty.[2]

The ultimate goals of the pursuit of liberty are to free an individual from the unjust interference of others and to maximize the scope of autonomous choice. Thus, the liberty pursued by liberalism is not a positive liberty, but a negative one that seeks only to avoid external interference. In this context, as Charles Taylor defines it, the liberty sought by liberalism is an opportunity concept, in the sense that it promises increased opportunities for autonomous choice.[3]

Liberalism stresses individual liberty over other normative values. In this respect, it can be clearly distinguished from perfectionism, which takes individual self-perfection as its ultimate goal, and also from utilitarianism, where the highest goal is to maximize utility or efficiency. Liberals recognize the "presumption in favor of liberty," which holds that unless there is a sufficient rational basis for limiting the liberty of an individual, the law and the state should allow the individual to make a free choice. It is from this principle that liberals deduce the principle of noninterference.

John Stuart Mill considered individual liberty and autonomy so important that he believed that the only reason for the law or the state to limit individual liberty was to prevent individuals from harming each other. He argued that, even with the intention of producing better and happier individuals, the law and the state must not intervene against individuals without their consent:

> [T]he only purpose for which power can be rightfully exercised over any member of a civilized community, against his will, is to prevent harm to others. His own good, either physical or moral, is not a sufficient warrant. He cannot rightfully be compelled to do or forbear because it will be better for him to do so, because it will make him happier, because, in the opinions of others, to do so would be wise, or even right.... Over himself, over his body and mind, the individual is sovereign.[4]

Unlike the negative liberty sought by liberalism, the liberty sought by Confucianism is a positive one. The Confucian utopia is not a society in which everyone is free from the interference of others, but one in which one's inner moral sense is in perfect accord with the objective norms of the community without the slightest alienation between the two. Thus, in contrast to the negative liberty that liberalism emphasizes, Confucianism pursues what might be called positive liberty. In describing the attainment of perfect harmony between the inner moral sense and the objective norms of community, Confucius confessed, "at seventy I followed my heart's desire without overstepping the line."[5]

The Confucian project of self-cultivation aims ultimately at mastering one's own heart to bring it into line with the norms of community. This Confucian concern with positive liberty is aptly expressed in many texts. For instance, "I neither complain to Heaven nor blame my fellow people,"[6] and "To return to the observance of the rites through overcoming the self constitutes benevolence (仁)."[7]

As Confucianism values positive over negative liberty, it focuses more on internal than external constraints when addressing the issue of removing the constraints that constitute barriers to individual freedom. For instance, Confucius praised his follower Yan Hui for preserving a sense of inner peace despite the poverty of his housing, food, clothing, and other living conditions: "How admirable Hui is! Living in a mean dwelling on a bowlful of rice and a ladleful of water is a hardship most men would find intolerable, but Hui does not allow this to affect his joy. How admirable Hui is!"[8] Of course, Confucius here did not imply a rejection of the basic needs of life. Rather, he meant that the true sense of freedom was to be attained by liberating oneself from internal constraints, not merely from external ones. The *Zhongyong* (Doctrine of the Mean) illustrates this with an example from archery: "In archery we have something like the way of the superior man. When the archer misses the center of the target, he turns round and seeks for the cause of his failure in himself."[9]

Thus, the ideal state of the individual sought by Confucianism is not a negative liberty attained when an individual is free from the interference of others, but a positive one that can be attained by overcoming one's uncontrolled first-order desires. From the standpoint of the Confucian theory of self-cultivation, liberalism's 'free from the interference of others' does not guarantee a true sense of freedom. No matter how much an individual is free from external interference, as long as one remains a slave to one's inner desires, one is not truly free.

Conversely, from a Confucian perspective, one who correctly understands her/his own character and can manage her/his first-order desire is free regardless of external constraints. Mencius says,

> Some parts of the body are noble, and some ignoble; some great, and some small. The great must not be injured for the small, nor the noble for the ignoble. He who nourishes the little belonging to him is a little man, and he who nourishes the great is a great man.[10]

The "ignoble part" or "small part" of which Mencius speaks is a first-order desire unfiltered by "second-order reflection," and to follow this kind of first-order desire alone is to be reduced to being a slave to one's own desires.

According to Confucianism, freedom in a genuine sense cannot be attained just on the condition of noninterference, but can be fully attained on the condition of unity without alienation between the inner and outer realms. This kind of condition can be achieved when one correctly understands one's own inner nature and controls one's first-order desires. From this we can see why, in the Confucian tradition, there has been less emphasis on individual rights than on such virtues as reciprocity, benevolence, and modesty.

Human Dignity, Rights, and Virtues

In the liberal tradition, every human being possesses equal dignity from birth. Kant spelled out our duty to respect the dignity of human beings in this way: "Do not suffer your rights to be trampled underfoot by others with impunity."[11]

This notion of human dignity is founded on rational autonomy, the unique aspect of human beings to become, in Kant's famous phrase, "free and rational sovereigns in the kingdom of ends." Like Kant, Alan Gewirth also finds the basis of human dignity in the rational and autonomous capacities of humans as goal-pursuing agents.[12] Even in the utilitarian side of the liberal tradition, as set forth by John Stuart Mill in *On Liberty,* the concept of human dignity is also closely related to the rational and autonomous ability of an individual as a goal-seeking agent.[13]

In Confucianism, on the other hand, the basis of human dignity is not found in the autonomy of the human being, but in the potential of each individual to become an authentic person through self-cultivation. Confucianism seeks to dissolve the status distinctions between high and low prevailing in the class-based society through the equal potential to become an authentic person. Confucius and Mencius replaced the class-based society's hierarchical distinction between the noble and the humble with the axiological distinction between the virtuous and the un-virtuous. Mencius also taught that everyone was equal in her/his inherent possession of the potential to achieve moral perfection.

In the liberal tradition, every human being is regarded as equal from birth, regardless of social or personal distinctions. According to liberalism, having a high or low character, an elevated or vulgar personality, is just a private matter in which no one has a right to interfere. Thus, a contemporary liberal philosopher like Joel Feinberg insists that if a couple chooses to have sex in a bar, or even commit incest (providing both parties are consenting and the act is not committed in public), unless their behavior violates the liberty of others there are no grounds for preventing it. If the state attempts to prevent their behavior, it is violating the rights of the individual.[14]

In contrast to liberalism's non-moral equality, Confucianism tends to grant each individual a different degree of rights according to the quality of the person's character. Just as a sword should not be put in the hand of a man of bad character, the moral weapon of rights should not be given to someone whose character is unworthy. Commenting on the ancient story of King Wu punishing the tyrant Zhou, Mencius supported Wu's coup d'état, explaining, "Although I heard that King Wu had punished a wicked villain, I did not hear him to have assassinated his lord." This meant that a tyrant like Zhou had little value as a man of character, and that he should not be granted an amount of rights equal to what others have received.

The difference between Confucianism and liberalism in their view of human dignity produces a concomitant difference in the assertion of the means by which human dignity is to be ensured. In the liberal tradition, the device for ensuring human dignity is "rights." Only when all individuals respect each other's rights can human dignity be firmly guaranteed. As long as no one violates the rights of another, no state power or legal institution can restrict the right of the individual to act freely.

While liberalism relies on rights as a guarantor of human dignity, Confucianism focuses on providing the conditions of welfare that make it possible for each individual to achieve moral perfection within the community to which s/he belongs. Confucius clearly expressed this concern with welfare when he said that the privilege of education should be extended to everyone regardless of birth, and that the wealth of a state was less important than the equitable distribution of the wealth. Mencius also stated that only when the basic means of subsistence have been secured can morals and rites be taught.[15] In other words, to promote character building and moral self-perfection, the basic conditions of welfare must first be satisfied.

In some cases, the Confucian concept of welfare appears in the form of paternalism. In many Confucian writings, a ruler's concern for the welfare of his people is compared with parents' love for their children. For instance, the *Shujing* (Book of Documents) states, "A ruler should always treat the people like a newborn baby." This concept of welfare with its emphasis on care for the people is a positive expression of the rule of virtue, but when the people are compared with a baby incapable of autonomous judgment, there is the risk of losing all checks on the power of despotic rulers. When the people are treated as children, their free will is denied, and those in power may use virtues as a disguise for tyranny. Due to this danger, liberals hold that paternalism, no matter how benevolent its motivation is, cannot be justified unless accompanied by respect for the rights of the individual person. As Feinberg states, "If adults are treated as children they will come in time to be like children. Deprived of the right to choose for themselves, they will soon lose the power of rational self-decision."[16]

Confucian welfarism, which finds the highest responsibility of the state in welfare and well-being founded on benevolence, stands in marked contrast to the liberal view of the state as responsible primarily for respecting the rights of the individual. From an impartial point of view, there are both good and bad aspects of liberalism's exclusive stress on individual rights on the one hand and in Confucianism's stress on paternalistic caring on the other. Liberalism's excessive emphasis on individual rights may have such undesirable consequences as economic disparity, rampant materialism, fetishism, and moral decay. Meanwhile, Confucianism's emphasis on paternalistic caring may have an undue effect on an individual's free will and capacity for autonomous decision making. From this perspective, a social ideal that respects nothing but individual liberty is liable to neglect the equitable distribution of wealth, while one that stresses the common good alone runs the risk of authoritarianism.[17]

Self-interest and the Common Good

Even if liberalism cannot be directly equated with individualism, the condition in which liberalism is fostered and can flourish is surely to be a society in which individualism prevails. Society as imagined by liberals is a gathering of individuals autonomously and independently pursuing their own interests free from the interference of others. Thus, liberalism perceives human nature as fundamentally self-centered, interested solely in personal ends and indifferent to the welfare of others. Inevitably, in a society of individuals indifferent to each other and concerned only with their own self-interest, the ethical norms most in demand are fairness, procedural justice, noninterference, and respect for rights. John Locke argues that in order for these self-centered beings to live together without conflict, they establish and grant their provisional assent to the institution known as the state, using it to prevent clashes of interest or to provide compensation when such clashes do arise. Robert Nozick similarly insists that in a society in a state of nature, a proxy institution is necessary to prevent the violation of the rights of the weaker by the stronger, or to compensate for such a violation when it does occur. Thomas Hobbes goes even further than Locke in viewing society in a state of nature, considering it to be not just an assembly of selfish individuals but a battleground in which everyone is at war with everyone else. John Rawls differs from the classical liberals in his emphasis on equitable distribution and the search for a solution to the problem of the cleavages between the wealthy and the poor, but still assumes a view of human nature and society little different from that of classical liberalism. For Rawls, the original condition of human beings in need of social justice is a gathering of rational individuals each pursuing his/her own self-interest without regard for others.

Following the spread of political and economic liberty, the pursuit of individual self-interest ceased to be regarded as immoral and, on the contrary, came to be regarded as legitimate and proper. In particular, with the change of social conditions, the notion of negative liberty, which had served as a starting point for protecting the individual from the tyranny of feudal rulers (whether monarchs and aristocrats or clergy), gradually drifted away from communal concerns such as the pursuit of a common good or the welfare of society as a whole.

In contrast to the atomistic view of the self and the individual as portrayed by liberalism, Confucianism envisages humans as relational beings inseparable from the community to which they belong. In Confucianism, the identity of an individual is not to be found by separating and isolating the self from others, but by understanding one's position in relation to others. From the Confucian point of view, the abstract, atomistic, and solipsistic self imagined by modern Western philosophy (particularly in the Cartesian tradition) is a phantasmagoric being that could never exist in this real world. In the Confucian tradition, an individual is always understood through human relationships as someone's father, someone's husband, or someone's neighbor. The "rectification of names" that Confucius speaks of can also be more clearly understood in this context. Confucius said, "Let the ruler be a ruler, the subject a subject, the father a father, the son a son."[18] The standard by which the ruler acts as a ruler is not to be found in an abstract concept like Plato's idea of the Good, but in a concrete reality such as the relationship between ruler and subject or father and son. Similarly, the "five basic human relationships" (*wu-lun* 五倫) that form the backbone of Confucian relationship-oriented morality derive their justificatory basis from the communitarian understanding of "the self in a context."[19] This relationship-based view of humans within the Confucian tradition contrasts sharply with liberalism's self-centered view of human beings.

Within the liberal social system with its atomistic view of human beings, it is accepted as proper that each individual pursues solely his own interest without regard to others. But in Confucianism, which discredits an individual existence isolated from the community to which an individual belongs, the exclusive pursuit of one's own self-interest can hardly be justified. The ideal society sought by Confucianism is a community comprised of virtuous people who care for one another and support each other's welfare. In Confucianism, a loving and well-ordered family (which in ancient times referred to the extended relations of a clan society rather than the modern nuclear family) was regarded as the model for an ideal society, and the ideal state should be modeled on the family. The social gradation of "self-cultivation, loving family, well-ordered country, peaceful world" that appears in the *Daxue* (Great Learning) also supports the Confucian concept of a communitarian society, which regards society as an expansion of caring relationships.

Mencius described the ideal society pursued by Confucianism as follows:

> Farmers share the same well harmoniously, come and go to each other freely, pool their strength to ward off thieves or misfortunes, and when their neighbor is sick, they help and nurse each other kindly. Moreover, only after tilling the communal land dare they work in their private fields.[20]

In the ideal community described by Mencius, distinctions between yours and mine are not so clear-cut, and any behavior that deviates from the communal norms embraced by the community is unacceptable. In a communal society such as this, a man who pursues his own self-interest alone will become an object of blame, while someone who cares for another's misery before asserting his own due and supports the welfare of others will be admired as a virtuous person. The distinction made by Confucius and Mencius between the virtuous (or great person) and the mean (or small person) can be understood from a socio-philosophical standpoint as a contrast between two human types: the person who pursues his interests but with consideration for the well-being of others, and the person who pursues his interests in order to satisfy his selfish desire alone. Confucius says, "Of neighborhoods benevolence is the most beautiful. How can the man be wise who, when he has the choice, does not settle in benevolence?"[21] A benevolent village is a community composed of people who are caring for each other. From a Confucian perspective, any individual engaged solely in the pursuit of self-interest without caring for others, or who sticks to his own way of living without regard for the common good of the community, is not an ideal human type.

The idea that one sometimes needs to restrain one's own self-interest for the sake of the common good leads naturally to the view that an individual's rights sometimes need to be waived for the sake of the common good, if necessary. This community-based view of rights explains clearly why the excessive claim of individual rights has not taken root in Confucian soil. In the Confucian tradition, which puts the common good above self-interest, when a conflict of interests arises it is not to be resolved through the aggressive claims of one's rights, but through a yielding of self-interest by the parties concerned, for the sake of their reconciliation and the harmony of the community. Thus, in legal terms, the ideal of Confucian society was to make an effort to resolve conflict not through an in-court system of justice administered by trials but through an extra-court system of justice that was dependent on negotiation and mediation.

The Ethics of Harmony versus the Ethics of Self-assertion

According to Feinberg, rights are valid claims that an individual may make "against" others who have a duty to satisfy those claims.[22] As the use of the word "against" suggests, rights claims would not arise unless two individuals or groups stand in confrontation. For instance, between a couple in love, as long as their love lasts there is no need for the assertion of rights. Only when they cease to love each other and compete for a limited pool of assets, or stand in confrontation over the cost of raising their children, does the discourse of rights become necessary.

Assertions of rights are necessarily founded on confrontation between two individuals or groups. In this context, Karl Marx was correct in saying that "rights-talk" is based on an antagonistic relationship in which each human being is alienated from the others. He attacked "rights" as the exclusive and selfish possession of the bourgeoisie.[23] To Marx, "rights" in capitalist society were nothing but a self-justification on the part of the "haves," a necessary evil that is bound to exist within the capitalist social order. Marx criticized the liberal watchwords of "rights" and "negative liberty" for reducing warm and concrete human relationships to undifferentiated exchange values.[24] By converting what should be warm relationships into economic exchange values, "rights-talk" committed the error of converting human character and personhood into monetary value. Finally, Marx condemned "rights-talk" for being based on a principle of isolation that seeks to separate people from each other instead of pursuing harmony.

The Confucian emphasis on placing the common good before self-interest, and communal harmony before individual rights, has much in common with Marx's criticism of bourgeois "rights-talk." The ideal of a loving community that Confucianism pursues advocates yielding and reconciliation as a way of resolving conflicts of interest, and takes a dim view of greedy demands for one's own portion. The root of this Confucian strategy of conflict resolution through yielding and compromise can be traced back to the spirit of harmony emphasized throughout the history of Confucianism. Harmony is regarded as an important ideal to aspire to in every sphere of human life. Within each person, emphasis is put on harmony between one's words and behavior, and between personal desires and communal norms. In family relationships, great importance is attached to harmony between parents and children, between husband and wife, and between siblings themselves. Beyond the family, harmony between neighbor and neighbor, and between the individual and the community, is seen as the key to creating a community of *ren* 仁. Even the relationship between human beings and Nature should be one of harmony and coexistence without the intrusion of excessive human chauvinism. Preoccupied with harmony, social ideals attributed to Confucian culture have regarded self-righteous rights claims as an obstacle to communal harmony, and have admired the virtues of modesty and yielding instead of self-assertion in the pursuit of self-interest. The disapproval of rapacious self-assertion was expressed by Confucius as follows:

> A virtuous person, even when confronted by another, does not fight back.[25]

> A virtuous person has strong self-respect but does not dispute; he lives harmoniously in his community but does not form factions.[26]

> A virtuous person never squabbles.[27]

As we can see from these passages, the Confucian tradition disapproves of aggressive self-righteous claims. In contrast to the Confucian attitude, the representative twentieth-century liberal philosopher Feinberg says, "Not to claim in the appropriate circumstances that one has a right is to be spiritless or foolish," and again, "Having rights enables us to stand up like a man."[28] While the liberal camp, to which Feinberg belongs, sees individual rights as a minimum condition for securing human dignity, Confucianism holds that in some circumstances it is better that the assertion of rights be restrained for the sake of harmony in the community.

Toward a Reconciliation of Liberalism and Confucianism

The foregoing comparison between the social ideals of Confucianism and liberalism can be summarized as follows. First, while liberalism aims to secure a space for autonomous choice through mutual noninterference, Confucianism emphasizes the achievement of harmonious accord by individuals for the common good of the community through the overcoming of self-centeredness. As a result, Confucianism accentuates positive rather than negative liberty, and embraces a communitarian ethic that is more concerned with caring and harmony than with exclusive claims to one's own rights. Second, the liberal conception of human dignity is founded on the rational capacity of human beings as autonomous and independent individuals, in contrast to the Confucian view of human beings as relationship-based, interdependent, and mutually caring. In terms of ethical norms, the Confucian belief in the ability of human beings to become more virtuous by overcoming selfishness leads to an emphasis on self-cultivation and self-restraint rather than antagonistic rights claims. Accordingly, it is the cultivation of virtues that is considered essential in the pursuit of authentic personhood and harmonious coexistence within the community. Third, the Confucian ideal of harmony leads naturally to a virtue-centered morality that emphasizes caring and modesty rather than self-righteous claims.

While liberalism seeks to secure the maximum scope for autonomous choice through providing a normative shield of noninterference, Confucianism seeks to achieve an ideal community through the overcoming of selfishness and the cultivation of virtues. Each social ideal has its own historical and cultural background. Within the traditional context of patriarchal family structure, agricultural mode of production, and monarchical system, Confucianism held its position in politics as a double-edged sword that served both to uphold the existing order and to restrain the monarchical power of the ruling class. Admittedly, criticisms of Confucianism as a government-patronized state ideology that served the interest of the ruling class are not without foundation from a macrohistorical standpoint, but the contribution of Confucian literati in their persistent effort to remonstrate and restrain the ruling class should not be neglected either. The historical significance of Confucianism can be found in its effort to prevent the abuse of power and the excessive pursuit of self-interest by presenting the ruling class with a blueprint for achieving an authentic personhood.

The society in which we live today no longer replicates the historical condition in which Confucianism once prevailed. The transition from a pre-dominantly extended family to a nuclear family structure, from an agricultural economy to industrial capitalism, and from an absolute monarchy to a liberal democracy has created a wide gulf between tradition and modernity. Conspicuous among the phenomena that arose as a result of these changes is the advent of individualism, the justification of self-interest, and the assertion of autonomy, liberty, and rights. These new values often clash with the traditional values that Asians have inherited from the past, creating serious confusion and conflict. The current situation in Asia, especially in Korea, is reminiscent of the times of turmoil and disorder when liberalism arose in the West. As human liberty and autonomy came to be valued, people abandoned their faith in the beliefs (whether moral, customary, religious, or political) that they had inherited from the past, and, under the banner of "rights," individuals secured their own space, free from interference. The historical achievement of liberalism was the freeing of people from religious constraints, political oppression, and the chains of feudal morality. However, by taking the notion of self-centeredness as its theoretical foundation, liberalism left itself ill equipped to deal with issues such as social welfare, the pursuit of the common good, and the elevation of human character.

In the case of contemporary Korea, where liberalism and capitalism have been grafted onto a five-hundred-year-old tradition of Confucianism, contrasting values are jumbled together in confusion: virtue and rights, individual and community, self-interest and the common good, et cetera. Koreans now seem to be faced with a choice between two paths. Their dilemma is whether to choose the liberal (and neoliberal) path with its disproportionate stress on individual rights, or to revive the Confucian virtue ethic with its focus on caring and harmony.

Or might there not be a third way that avoids both extremes? We have already seen that both social ideals have their strong and weak points. If we opt for negative liberty alone, we can secure an autonomous sphere free from interference, but we are liable to neglect the welfare of those in need and the establishment of a desirable community. On the other hand, if we put too much emphasis on positive liberty, we can pursue the improvement of our character and the harmony of community, but we run the risk of lapsing into totalitarianism. If we insist on rights alone, we are apt to become overnight millionaires full of selfishness and lacking humaneness, while if we emphasize virtues alone we can easily sink into spineless compliance and obedient slavery. Is there no way to discard the weak points in both value systems and combine their strong points into a new system of values?

Liberty, in an ideal sense, must be a total freedom comprising both positive and negative liberty. No matter how free an individual may be from external interference, so long as one remains a slave to one's internal desires, one is not truly free. Conversely, no matter how well one may control one's internal desires, so long as one is bound by chains or suffers from suppression and oppression, one is not actually free. Thus, freedom in a total sense means a state in which an individual is free not only from external interference but also from internal restraints. When we define the ideal sense of freedom in this way, we are one step closer to relieving the anomie of values that currently envelops Korea and other Asian countries. Just as freedom in a total sense requires both positive and negative liberty, true human liberation means not only economic and political liberation, but also moral and spiritual liberation to deliver us from unbridled internal desires and inward constraints.

The ideal of total freedom cannot be attained solely through the insistence on negative liberty or individual rights. Rights surely perform a necessary social function, protecting innocent people from unjust power and ensuring their just share. But at times, rights can also become a powerful self-defensive measure bolstering the greedy claim of possession for the "haves." Rights serve as a normative device for defining the minimal morality by coercively extracting a minimum of duty from an opponent. But minimal morality is not enough to achieve an authentic personhood and harmony in the society. We need liberty and rights to protect us from unjust power, while at the same time we also need the virtues of caring and benevolence for the harmony of the society. We need both rights and virtues, liberty and caring, justice and benevolence. Finally, we need a reconciliation of liberalism and Confucianism. In this sense, I believe that Confucius' old teaching of self-cultivation, authentic personhood, and a community of *ren* 仁 can function as a new antidote for the cultural illness of liberal self-centeredness.

Notes

1. According to the harm principle (the only liberty-limiting principle accepted by classical liberals), the state may restrict the liberty of an individual only if that individual harms the liberty of another individual, and in no other case may the state interfere with individual liberty. See John Stuart Mill, *On Liberty,* ed. David Spitz (London: Norton, 1975), pp. 10–11.

2. An example is Joel Feinberg; see his *Harm to Others* (Oxford: Oxford University Press, 1985), p. 9. In addition, the whole of Feinberg's *Offense to Other*s (Oxford: Oxford University Press, 1985) is devoted to debating the validity of the offense principle.

3. Charles Taylor, "What's Wrong with Negative Liberty," in *Philosophy and the Human Sciences,* Philosophical Papers, vol. 2 (Cambridge: Cambridge University Press, 1985).

4. Mill, *On Liberty,* p. 11.

5. *Analects* 2.4, in Confucius, *The Analects* (Lun yü), trans. D. C. Lau (Harmondsworth, UK: Penguin Books, 1979), p. 63.

6. *Doctrine of the Mean* 14.3; author's translation.

7. *Analects* 12.1, in Confucius, *The Analects,* trans. Lau, p. 112.

8. *Analects* 6.11, in Confucius, *The Analects,* trans. Lau, p. 82.

9. *Doctrine of the Mean* 14.5, in Confucius, *Confucian Analects, The Great Learning and The Doctrine of the Mean,* trans. James Legge, 2nd rev. ed. (Oxford: Clarendon Press, 1893), p. 396.

10. *Mencius* 6A14, in *The Works of Mencius,* trans. James Legge (Oxford: Clarendon Press, 1895).

11. Immanuel Kant, *The Metaphysical Principles of Virtue* (1797), trans. J. W. Ellington (Indianapolis: Hackett, 1983), pp. 98–99.

12. See Alan Gewirth, "The Basis and Content of Human Rights," in *Human Rights* (Chicago: University of Chicago Press, 1982).

13. Mill, *On Liberty,* pp. 10–11.

14. See Joel Feinberg, *Harmless Wrongdoing* (Oxford: Oxford University Press, 1988), p. 166.

15. *Mencius* 3A4, in Legge, *The Works of Mencius.*

16. Joel Feinberg, "Legal Paternalism," in *Paternalism,* ed. Rolf Sartorius (Minneapolis: University of Minnesota Press, 1983), p. 3.

17. John Rawls' *A Theory of Justice* may be read as an attempt to overcome the drawbacks of both extremes (classical liberalism and welfarism) and combine their strong points into a single consistent system.

18. *Analects* 12.11, in Confucius, *The Analects,* trans. Lau, p. 114.

19. David L. Hall and Roger T. Ames, *Thinking Through Confucius* (Albany: State University of New York Press, 1987), p. 16.

20. *Mencius* 3A3.

21. *Analects* 4.1, in Confucius, *The Analects,* trans. Lau, p. 72.

22. See Joel Feinberg, *Social Philosophy* (Englewood Cliffs, NJ: Prentice-Hall, 1973), pp. 66–67.

23. See Karl Marx, "On the Jewish Question," in Karl Marx and Frederick Engels, *Collected Works,* vol. 3, *1843–1844* (London: Lawrence and Wishart, 1975), p. 162.

24. See *Grundrisse,* in ibid., p. 42.

25. *Analects* 8.5.

26. *Analects* 15.21.

27. *Analects* 3.7.

28. Joel Feinberg, "The Nature and Value of Rights," *Journal of Value Inquiry* 4 (1970): 252.

CHAPTER 3

Toward Religious Harmony

A Confucian Contribution

Peter Y. J. WONG

LET ME BEGIN by appropriating John Dewey's distinction regarding three forms of the term "religion":

> There is a difference between religion, *a* religion, and the religious; between anything that may be denoted by a noun substantive and the quality of experience that is designated by an adjective.[1]

Despite Dewey's dismissal of the use of the singular "religion" in view of the diversity of religions that one encounters, I would like to retain the term, and suggest we use it in the upper case—that is, Religion[2]—as it involves a sense that goes well beyond the objective sense of the term. On the most obvious level, "Religion" and "a religion" differ according to the perspective one adopts, and according to the presence or absence of allegiance to particular religions. For the committed adherent, the path one follows is always "Religion," while, in contrast, those paths that are significantly different from one's own we may call "religions" (or "a religion"). Religion, in the uppercase, is not to be understood as a reified, absolute entity but as an all-embracing framework that mediates one's access to the world. As such, one's religious sentiment is understood as a feeling that is borne within Religion. A similar parallel can be drawn with regard to language, in that one's access to concepts is always mediated by Language, and there is a qualitative difference between the language that one speaks and those languages of which one speaks.[3] There was a time, and it may still exist in some circles (such as the philosophy of religion in Western analytic philosophy), when one's field of study almost always operated under the auspices of Religion[4] and was not concerned about the religions, such that other religions and religious traditions were not the proper subject of study.[5] We note that for at least a millennium in the West, Religion has been identified with Christianity or monotheism.

Yet, is Religion necessarily to be identified with a religion? Could Religion be sufficiently broad such that it supports a variety of religions, include both theistic and non-theistic religions, and accommodate religious experiences that are not based on an affiliation to particular religions? For surely we need Religion to be broad in order that religious sentiments and experiences be shareable across the divide of religions.

For there to be Religion that is accommodating, the common understanding of religions in terms of belief is inadequate. It is no wonder that Dewey sought to do away with religion altogether and emancipate the "religious."[6] This chapter does not go as far as Dewey, but takes the view that we can't divorce descriptions of Religion and religions from the religious. But we take the lesson from Dewey that key to our understanding of religion is the religious in its adjectival sense, and not belief.

A possible elaboration on the difference between "religions" and "religious" could be found in the writings of Wilfred Cantwell Smith, regarding which he draws a distinction between a public and institutional aspect, one that Smith calls "cumulative traditions" (religions), and a personal but not individualist aspect, called "faith" (religious). As the latter aspect is closely related to the phenomena of religious experiences, he—like Dewey—takes this to be the more primary aspect of religion. It is a point that we will return to later. To anticipate, we will claim that "religion" and "religious" cannot be so neatly separated. And while a proper account of religion needs to include the religious, the reverse is also true.

According to Smith, to the extent that a tradition could be called "religion," a certain degree of self-consciousness is needed. Thus, Smith thinks that many indigenous traditions and practices ought not to be called "religion," precisely because they are not self-reflexive about their own practices as practices, and they have not self-consciously sought to systematize or formalize the religious aspect of their way of life.[7] For the foregoing reasons, he calls into question the use of reified terms in reference to certain traditions such as "Daoism" or "Confucianism."[8] Accordingly, we also take Smith to imply that such traditions ought not to be called "religions."

That is not all. Smith goes on to question the very meaningfulness of the term "religion," including "Christianity," "Judaism," and "Islam": although they are reified terms, in reality they do not refer to any identifiable, abstractable essence.[9] For Smith, when we take a closer look at "religion," or for that matter "Christianity," "Islam," or "Judaism," we find only the institutional "cumulative traditions" and personal "faiths."[10]

The question is, should we forgo the use of the term "religion" and instead speak only of "traditions"?

Smith's argument with forgoing the use of the term "religion" is not so straightforward. It seems that there is a confusion on Smith's part over the reality of religion that relies on an essentialistic approach to settle the issue. While religion, and we agree, does not correspond to any isolable entity, this does not mean that religions do not exist. Religions exist as complexes and are dependent upon the contexts of human activity. Currency and economy, for instance, do not fully identify with specific things in the world, yet we normally agree that they exist; that is, they exist within the context of human society, which recognizes, among other things, property and the practices of human commerce, but not in the sense of an entity or that they are metaphysically real.[11]

A large part of the problem regarding the term "religion" seems to be the objectification of alien others, whose means of showing reverence and piety is not shared by the observer.[12] In the current literature on the study of religions, there is the objection that "religion" is a colonial imposition, used as a means to control colonies.[13] Thus, perhaps the term "religion" ought to be abandoned or restricted to the Western context. While it is the case that "religion" as a category is modern, originating in the West,[14] and susceptible to becoming an instrument of domination, the alternative of refraining from identifying certain traditions and practices with "religion," or as "religious," would also be susceptible to other kinds of discriminations: for example, the perverse view that cultures different from the West do not have practices or traditions worthy of the term "religion." It seems that the politics of proprietorship of the term "religion" is an issue that we need to be vigilant about, yet seeking to do away with the term "religion" is not necessarily a remedy either.

In view of the various critiques, perhaps our understanding of "religion" could be rehabilitated and modified to accommodate non-theistic sensibilities. We begin with the Chinese case of referring to religions as *zongjiao*, a translation that is borrowed from the Japanese.[15] While the term is intended to be a translation of the Western term "religion," it nevertheless represents an attempt to express the meaning of "religion" from within the resources available to Sino-Japanese culture. Therefore, the original uses of the term that have been recruited for the translation are not irrelevant details.

The term *zongjiao* 宗教, as a bound compound, made its first appearance in Chinese Buddhist writings and refers to Buddhist teachings in general; that is, the teachings of the Buddha called *jiao,* and those of his followers called *zong.*[16] However, unlike its current usage, which tends to suggest "theistic religion," it was still closely associated with the traditional usage of the term *jiao* 教, which is commonly rendered as "teaching." In addition, Wu Rujun 吳汝鈞 locates the term in other writings of Chinese Buddhism, in which *zong* refers to the schools or sects of Buddhism, and *jiao* to the dissemination of their teachings. Furthermore, Wu also identifies other usages, in which *zong* refers to that which cannot be spoken (*prasiddhi*); and *jiao* as the attempts at communicating the unsayable.[17]

Even within the non-Buddhist Chinese world, the use of the term *jiao* seems to overlap with the modern use of *zongjiao*. Reference to the Confucian tradition in conjunction with the term *jiao* occurred as early as the beginning of the Han 漢 dynasty, in Sima Qian's 司馬遷 epic work on Chinese history, the *Shiji* 史記.[18] Possibly as early as after the end of the Han (the Tang at the latest), Confucianism, Daoism, and Buddhism were already jointly referred to as the three teachings (*sanjiao* 三教).[19] In this case, the term *sanjiao* implies established traditions and lineages that are authoritative and state-sanctioned; it is also interesting to note that they are ranked in terms of their eminence, which comes close to Smith's notion of self-conscious organization as a mark of religion.

However, the appellation of *jiao* is not strictly limited to such identifiable schools or movements. The work *Jingjie* 經解, collected in the *Book of Rites* (*Liji* 禮記), when referring to different aspects of Confucian teaching, speaks also of the teaching of the rituals (*Lijiao* 禮教), the teaching of the songs (*Shijiao* 詩教), and the teaching of music (*Yuejiao* 樂教).

In common Chinese usage, *jiao* 教 literally means "to teach." According to the *Analects,* Confucius is said to have taught four things: culture, conduct, doing one's utmost, and making good on one's words.[20] From this, we see that what is implied is not only the idea of the straightforward imparting of knowledge (*jiaoshou* 教授), but also transformative teaching (*jiaohua* 教化). For example, the *Jingjie* refers to the transformative influence of the rites as *jiaohua*:

> The transformative teaching of *li* (禮之教化) is subtle. Its curbing of bad actions takes place before the event. And it is capable of influencing people to become good and stay away from wrongdoing without their being aware of it.[21]

Jiao also connotes *jiaoyu* 教育, usually translated as "education." However, the term can also be translated as "teaching and nurturing."[22] Thus, education is concerned not only with the transmission of knowledge but also the formation of the person in all aspects—social, cultural, and interpersonal. Finally, as indicated by its radical, *pu* 攴, *jiao* is also authoritative in connotation; therefore, it is associated with various terms that mean both teaching and actions typically associated with authoritative conduct: to give guidance (*jiaodao* 教導), to admonish (*jiaohui* 教誨), and to instruct or to reprimand (*jiaoxun* 教訓), all of which are reflected in the teaching activities of Confucius.

The foregoing considerations suggest that there may be resources within the Chinese tradition for coming to a different understanding of religion. Cai Renhou 蔡仁厚, in his work on the Mohist School (墨家), initially takes his understanding of religion from a Western theistic perspective. In this work, he sought to assess the Mohist sense of religiousness in theistic terms centered on the Mohist understanding of the heavens (or perhaps "Heaven") (*tian* 天), demon (*gui* 鬼), and divine (*shen* 神). He concluded that while there is an understanding of a transcendent and benevolent deity that is associated with the Mohist view of *tian,* the Mohist School ought not to be viewed as a religion because it lacks a certain sensibility that problematizes existence (as is found in notions such as sin or suffering in other traditions), nor is there a view about the helplessness of the human condition, nor a sense of the mystical—characteristics he takes to be essential marks of a religion.[23] By the same yardstick, we may conclude that Confucianism—because of a much vaguer sense of *tian*—is even farther away from a theistic construal of religion.

Interestingly, Cai Renhou apparently changed his mind regarding the notion of religiousness that is operative in Chinese traditions. In remarks later appended to his discussions just mentioned, rather than a religiousness characterized as a belief in a deity, he offers an alternative understanding of religion based on functional terms, as follows:

> A religion (*zongjiao* 宗教) must be the inspirational source of cultural life and creativity. First, it must lay down for the people "a path for their daily living," and second, it must open up "a way for their spiritual life." ... People of today take any talk about the Confucian Religion (*Rujiao* 儒教) to be a taboo subject.[24] This is because of the current fashion that unconsciously adopts Western religion as the standard. They do not understand the East, especially the significance of the term "*jiao*" (教) for the Chinese. I wonder how many people in this age have considered that the Chinese cultural system also constitutes another standard.[25]

In the alternative that Cai Renhou adumbrates—in contrast to the efforts of Kang Youwei and others—he avoids the theistic construal of religion. The suggestion seems to be that rather than being dictated by a theistic understanding of religiousness, which tends to distort our understanding of the meaning of the term *jiao* in Confucian teaching, we should seek to re-describe it from the Chinese perspective.

In view of the foregoing considerations, "religion," when construed broadly in terms of *jiao,* can be thought of as an authoritative way (*dao* 道) that imparts wisdom, facilitates transformation, and nurtures the formation of the total person. This is in good agreement with the *Zhongyong,* which states, "Practicing the way is called *jiao*" (修道之謂教). And we can add to this Cai Renhou's notion of the way as one that provides meaning for daily living and guidance for the spiritual life.

Yet, such characterizations of *a* religion will always remain unsatisfactory to those who hold allegiance to specific traditions, for whom an almost unbridgeable gap exists between the objective "a religion," even when construed as *jiao,* and the all-involving "Religion." And the difference between the two may be located in the term "religious." J. L. Schellenberg, drawing upon Smith, speaks of the latter term as the personal aspect of religion that includes religiousness, piety, and spirituality.[26] One thinks of Religion as providing the space within which one makes sense of the world. For example, my colleague Patrick Hutchings writes, "Why should I be, and why should I be in such a world? My adherence to the Christian faith suggests an answer....Why should you be in the world? If it was good enough for the Son of God, then it's good enough for the likes of you."[27] In such responses, one can't help but be personal, and the language of one's religion features ineluctably in the articulation of one's religious sentiments.

The foregoing involves the aspect that Smith calls "faith." While Smith clearly takes the holding of specific beliefs to be an aspect of faith, he also has a broader understanding of it that includes art and music. Despite Smith's broader interpretation, he still describes the religious in terms of transcendence.[28] Smith's understanding of transcendence as that which is greater than oneself[29] draws inspiration from the theistic religions. And as such, Smith's description of "faith" tends to exclude non-theistic traditions, such as the majority of Buddhist and Confucian teachings.[30] While the failure is partly due to the limitation of Smith's conception of faith, one understands that he could not remain silent—he needed to say something about what it means to be religious. The question is how do we find a way of discussing the religious aspect of experience without falling into sectarian particularity? Or, rather, how do we come to some agreement about the religious aspect of experience despite our diverging articulations of such? I would suggest that even "secular" people cannot escape this difficulty, as they would still need to resort to some kind of particular articulation in order to differentiate the religious experience from that of the superficial sort. It would seem that a functional description of religion might be more promising. And Confucianism in the Chinese world can offer an example for our consideration.

Rather than a notion of "religious" that is understood with reference to a transcendent deity, the *Zhongyong* speaks of the possibility of achieving sublime action for the person who walks the path according to Confucian teaching. In the *Zhongyong, jiao* is also described as the process of leading a person from "understanding" or "clarity" (*ming* 明) to "authenticity," "integrity," or "whole-hearted engagement" (*cheng* 誠).[31] Ultimately, the culmination of such a process allows the person who is fully human to participate in, and realize the transformative and nurturing work of, the heavens and the earth (the paired imageries that evoke the natural world) expressed in the following manner:

> Only those who are wholeheartedly engaged (*cheng* 誠) to the utmost … can participate in the transforming and nurturing action of heaven (*tian* 天) and earth.… [Only then] can they form a triad together with heaven and earth.[32]

Here we see the breadth and depth of *jiao* expressed in Confucian terms; it begins with teachings that invite practice, promote understanding (*ming*), sincerity of purpose (*cheng*), luminosity (*ming*) in conduct,[33] and authentic engagement. Moreover, the teachings facilitate creative realizations that shape entire communities and beyond. To be, and become, fully human in the Confucian tradition is then a religious project, one that begins within the simple and ordinary circumstances of inherited traits and familial relationships, gradually expanding and developing such connections and circumstances to the point of becoming influential, and eventually arriving at the tremendous deeds of transforming and enhancing one's world, to match—and to collaborate—with the works of the natural world.[34] The vision is to realize a humanized world that improves upon the natural world in a way that facilitates the growth and transformation of everything within it.[35]

Thus, from the perspective of the Confucian tradition, to think of *jiao* simply in terms of the modern usage of teaching, as the imparting of knowledge, would be reductionistic. At the same time, we note how the discussion has proceeded seamlessly from the understanding that "cultivating the way is called *jiao*" to "leading one from clarity to wholehearted engagement is called *jiao*." Regarding the term *jiao,* the former phrase corresponds to the aspect of "religion" in Smith, and the latter to that of "religious" in Dewey. We might say that for the *Zhongyong*'s understanding of *jiao,* the "religious" and "religion" are intimately bound together.

Even Smith's articulation of the public aspect of religion as "cumulative traditions" necessarily involves saying what these traditions are cumulative of—namely experiences having to do with transcendence. It would seem that attempts to strictly separate the religious from religion might be difficult if not impossible. Similarly, when Dewey attempts to emancipate religious experiences while at the same time he eschews religions, he wishes to retain the possibility that religious experience be understood as one that brings about a "better, deeper enduring adjustment in life."[36] Yet, how would one recognize experience to be religious without further elaboration as to what counts as better and deeper?

For similar reasons, it is problematic with societies that seek to maintain religious harmony by attempting to apply to religions a secular framework—its sheer neutrality leaves out an account of the religious dimension of the traditions it seeks to accommodate, which therefore diminishes those very traditions and renders them impotent and irrelevant. It is not surprising that religions tend to resist such attempts; even a non-theistic tradition such as Confucianism, which seems to be closest to a secular perspective, requires that "religion," understood as *jiao,* be expressive of particular values.

It seems that attempts at reconciling religions in terms of beliefs are doomed to failure because of competing and mutually exclusive claims that are irreconcilable. Moreover, as discussed, mere description of "belief" is insufficient to reveal the religious character of Religion. We suggest that a functional approach offers the best chance of success.

When Religion is understood in functional terms, then the borders between religions can become more permeable. The Chinese notion that "the three *jiao* are continuous" (*sanjiao heyi* 三教合一) realizes the possibility of moving from one tradition to another without insurmountable differences and barriers.[37] It allows one to find new ways of being religious when circumstances change. (Does this understanding require the confessional religions to alter their claim of exclusiveness? One supposes it must.) When our understanding of Religion expands beyond identification with a particular religion, then we can begin to explore the kind of religiousness of the ordinary that Dewey so desired. Perhaps what we are looking for is the development of a religious culture that is accommodating enough to include most religions, which are themselves in turn open enough. The Chinese experience shows that such a change can be done without damaging the integrity of the respective traditions, and it need not lead to confusion or chaos.

Notes

1. John Dewey, *A Common Faith* (New Haven: Yale University Press, 1934), p. 3.

2. At the same time, a more vague and undifferentiated sense of "religion" in the lower case is also used in this chapter.

3. My thanks to Arindam Chakrabarti for suggesting this point in his comments on this chapter.

4. For example, the problem of evil is always a present concern.

5. This is mainly because "religions" do not motivate philosophical problems.

6. For Dewey, being religious is a quality that can be found in the most ordinary of experiences and does not require any explicit connection with religion: "I am not proposing a religion, but rather the emancipation of elements and outlooks that may be called religious" (Dewey, *A Common Faith,* p. 15). "Any activity pursued in behalf of an ideal end against obstacles and in spite of threats of personal loss because of conviction of its general and enduring value is religious in quality. Many a person, inquirer, artist, philanthropist, citizen, men and women in the humblest walks of life, have achieved, without presumption and without display, such unification of themselves and of their relations to the conditions of existence" (ibid., p. 27).

7. See Wilfred Cantwell Smith, chapter 3, "Other Cultures: The Religions," in *The Meaning and End of Religion* (Minneapolis: Fortress Press, 1991 [1962]), pp. 51–79.

8. See ibid., pp. 62ff.

9. Islam is treated as a special case by Smith, as the religion is self-consciously named "Islam" and shares a similar understanding of religion with the West.

10. Smith speaks of the Abrahamic traditions as more predisposed to reification because of the way they saw themselves as a system or a formalized way of life, and because of the ideal that there be a unique and singular articulation. But, ultimately, he concludes later in his book that "the concept of a religion is recent, Western-and-Islamic, and unstable" (ibid., p. 120).

11. See J. L. Schellenberg, *Prolegomena to a Philosophy of Religion* (Ithaca and London: Cornell University Press, 2005), and Kevin Schilbrack, *Philosophy and the Study of Religions: A Manifesto* (Chichester, West Sussex: Wiley Blackwell, 2014), as projects aiming at rehabilitating "religion" as a viable category.

12. Furthermore, such acts of objectification tend to provoke yet more objectified points of view. Smith says, "A dialectic ensues. . . . If one's own 'religion' is attacked, by unbelievers who necessarily conceptualize it schematically, or all religion is, by the indifferent, one tends to leap to the defence of what is attacked, so that presently participants of a faith— especially those most involved in argument—are using the term in the same externalist and theoretical sense as are their opponents" (Smith, *The Meaning and End of Religion,* p. 43).

13. See Schilbrack, *Philosophy and the Study of Religions,* pp. 86–89.

14. Smith gives an account of how the notion of "religion(s)" came about through abstraction and objectification in seventeenth- and eighteenth-century Europe (Smith, *The Meaning and End of Religion,* p. 43).

15. See Anna Sun, *Confucianism as a World Religion: Contested Histories and Contemporary Realities* (Princeton and Oxford: Princeton University Press, 2013), pp. 23ff.

16. 「佛教以佛所說為教，佛弟子所說為宗，宗為教的分派，合稱宗教，指佛教的教理。《景德傳燈錄》十三〈圭峰宗密禪師答史山人十問〉之九：『（佛）滅度後，委付迦葉，展轉相承一人者，此亦蓋論當代為宗教主，如土無二王，非得度者唯爾數也。』」《辭源·宗教》. Anna Sun records a slightly different account by citing T. H. Barrett and Francesca Tarocco, who "suggest that the two words, *zong* and *jiao,* have in fact 'been brought together in the sixth century by one or two scholar-monks who differentiated strand[s] in Buddhist thought as different 'principle-teachings' " (T. H. Barrett and Francesca Tarocco, "Terminology and Religious Identity: Buddhism and the Genealogy of the Term *Zongjiao,*" in *Dynamics in the History of Religions between Asia and Europe:*

Encounters, Notions, and Comparative Perspectives, ed. Vokharde Krech and Marion Steineke [Leiden and Boston: Brill, 2012], p. 311, cited in Sun, *Confucianism as a World Religion,* p. 23). It is also interesting to note the source that Barrett and Tarocco themselves draw from: the writings of Fazang 法藏: *Huayan yicheng jiao yi fen qi zhang* 華嚴一乘教義分齊章, 1, 480c–481b, Taishō, vol. 45, no. 1866. Perhaps there is a sense of understanding *zong* 宗 as "sect," in which *zongjiao* means the teachings of the sects. Moreover, it is interesting to note that the work also distinguishes different classifications of teachings (*jiao*) in Buddhism.

17. Wu Rujun 吳汝鈞, *Fojiao sixiang da cidian, "Zongjiao"* 佛教思想大辭典、「宗教」 (Dictionary of Buddhist thought, "religion") (Taibei: Taiwan Shangwu Yinshuguan 臺灣商務印書館 [Taiwan Commercial Press], 1992), pp. 284, 285. It is interesting to note that the Venerable Jing Kong 淨空, a contemporary Chinese monk, recently provided a creative interpretation of the term *zongjiao* in which he suggests that *zong* refers to that which is dominant, important, and respectable, and *jiao* to education, teaching, and transformation (「宗教」這一名詞, 其在中文的釋義為:「宗」具有:主要的、重要的、尊崇的;三種意義;「教」具有:教育、教學、教化三重含義). And thus, the work of Buddhist interpretation of the term continues. See http://www.amtb.org.tw/jkfs/jkfs .asp?web_choice=7&web_amtb_index=31; accessed 23/9/14.

18. See *Shiji*, "Zhujiachuan" 史記、朱家傳:「魯人皆以儒教、而朱家用俠聞。」. Here, the term *jiao* is used as a verb.

19. 北史、卷十周本紀下 *Bei shi*, "Juan shi zhou benji xia":「十二月癸巳、集群臣及沙門道士等、帝[高祖武皇帝]升高座、辨釋三教先後、以儒教為先、道教為次、佛教為後。」.

20. *Analects* 7.25.

21. 禮記、經解 *Liji*, "Jingjie":「故禮之教化也微、其止邪也於未形、使人日徙善遠罪而不自知也。」. Here we have a recurring theme in Confucian and Daoist philosophy: the valuing of subtlety. It venerates that which is effective but the influence of which is undetectable, i.e., *shen* 神. If the term is to be construed as divine, then the tendency is to be functional in its approach: anyone who is able similarly to exert undetectable influences of consequence, they, too, are considered *shen.*

22. See *Mencius* 7A20: "The noble person has three delights…to have the talents of the world and nurture them is the third delight" (君子有三樂…得天下英才而教育之, 三樂也).

23. This is required in order to motivate soteriology. Perhaps this aspect is absent in Chinese religiosity.

24. This is probably in reference to the movement in modern China to transform Confucianism into a modern religion, after the fashion of Christianity, that was led by personages such as Kang Youwei 康有為; that and other similar attempts ultimately failed with the fall of the first Republic. The names proposed by those movements for the Confucian religion were Rujiao 儒教, Kongjiao 孔教, and Kongjiaohui 孔教會. See Sun, *Confucianism as a World Religion,* pp. 42ff. Moreover, the question of whether Confucianism is a religion continues to be a controversial subject in contemporary China; see Anna Sun, "The Confucianism as a Religion Controversy in Contemporary China," in Sun, *Confucianism as a World Religion,* pp. 77–93.

25. 「凡宗教、必須是文化生活與文化創造之靈感的泉源。第一、它須為生民安排『日常生活之軌道』，第二、它須開出『精神生活之途徑』。 時下人忌諱說儒教，那是由於時風之勳染，不自覺以『西方宗教』為標準，所以不了解東方、特別是中國自己的『教』義。試問當今之世，有幾個人曾經想到，中國自己的文化系統，亦同樣是一個標準？」 (Cai Renhou 蔡仁厚, *Mojia zhexue* 墨家哲學, 3rd ed. [Taibei: Dongda Tushu Gongsi 東大圖書公司, 1993; 1st ed. 1978], p. 97).

26. Schellenberg, *Prolegomena to a Philosophy of Religion,* p. 6.

27. Patrick Hutchings, "Religious Belief" (forthcoming).

28. "We speak of the life of religious man seeming to be somehow in two worlds, the mundane realm of limiting and observable and changing actuality and a realm transcending this. What is the nature of that transcendent sphere and what is the nature of its relation to this mundane one are questions on which, to put it mildly, there is no general agreement" (Smith, *The Meaning and End of Religion,* p. 154).

29. "[M]en's involvement with them is an involvement through them with something greater than they"—i.e., in "words, both prose and poetry; in patterns of deeds, both ritual and morality; in art, in institutions, in law, in community, in character" (Smith, *The Meaning and End of Religion,* p. 171).

30. Roger Ames argues for a sense of religiousness in Confucianism that is not to do with something that is beyond (that transcends) the human. Rather, it is a "human-centered religiousness." (See Roger T. Ames, "Confucian Human-Centered Religiousness," in Ames, *Confucian Role Ethics: A Vocabulary* [Honolulu: University of Hawai'i Press, and Hong Kong: Chinese University Press, 2011], pp. 211–255.) According to Ames, "for the Confucian, it is the creative possibility within the inspired human life to enchant the cosmos that is the more important meaning of 'religiousness.' This enchantment in the 'thoughtful' feelings of family and friends emerges in their mutual and reciprocated sensitivity and awareness" (ibid., p. 239).

31. *Zhongyong,* chapter 21: 「自明誠謂之教」. The meaning of *cheng* 誠 is complex and too broadly construed to be encapsulated in a single translation; the possible meanings of the term range from being sincere to being wholehearted in one's commitment, and from being candid to being unimpeded. Furthermore, there is also the recent thought-provoking and novel interpretation of *cheng* as "creativity"; see Roger T. Ames and David L. Hall, *Focusing the Familiar: A Translation and Philosophical Interpretation of the Zhongyong* (Honolulu: University of Hawai'i Press, 2001).

32. *Zhongyong,* chapter 22: 「唯天下至誠…可以贊天地之化育…可以與天地參矣」.

33. "The way of the great learning consists in clarifying the luminous excellences…" 「大學之道，在明明德…」 (*Daxue* 大學).

34. This sense of progressing from the incipient to the profound is found in the *Zhongyong,* and is articulated even more explicitly in the *Daxue.*

35. Roger Ames puts it this way: "I will argue that Confucian religiousness is precisely this sense of co-creativity of self and world, and in fact that such co-creativity is the only kind of real creativity. Indeed, in this Confucian cosmology, nothing happens by itself.…I will invoke the Confucian notion of the "three capacities" (*sancai* 三才) and the claim that human creativity is an ingredient integral and necessary to further inspire the heavens and the earth in the evolving process of generating cosmic spirituality" (Ames, *Confucian Role Ethics,* p. 241).

36. See Dewey, *A Common Faith,* p. 14.

37. Contrast this with a solution on the level of "religions"—e.g., those popular religious movements that tend to be full-on syncretic, what Anna Sun calls "redemptive societies"; they seek to amalgamate the different religions and maintain the theistic model: Yiguandao 一貫道 (and, not mentioned in Sun's book, the Vietnamese Cao Đài). See Sun, *Confucianism as a World Religion,* p. 43.

CHAPTER 4

The Special District of Confucian Culture, the Amish Community, and the Confucian Pre-Qin Political Heritage

ZHANG Xianglong

IT SEEMS COMMON SENSE to a Western mind that a theory of the state should present a potentially optimal mode of political design. Correspondingly, Plato, Aristotle, and modern philosophers propose various political doctrines, each of which takes one type of state as the best. In political reality, every political party, insofar as its political power allows, wants to establish its own ideal state and dismiss all others. It rarely, if ever, occurs to such parties that the best political structure may go beyond one mode of state or be composed of various types of states.

Several years ago when I proposed the notion of a protective district, a Special District of Confucian Culture or SDC,[1] my main objective was not to set up an ideal mode of ruling but to deal with the predicament faced by Confucians that, on the one hand, the revival of Confucianism requires an authentic experience of community life based on family and lineage, but that, on the other hand, the globalized as well as individualized factuality of a ruling society denies such a life. This set of circumstances strongly urges, therefore, that we build a binary structure consisting of both the current political-economic-technological system and the *other* system, that is, the Confucian one. Without the current one, the *other* one cannot possess an actual footing; without the *other* one, the current one finds no way to have a feasible future or to be moral in an integrated sense. This chapter will try to outline a possible "other one" by explaining the concept of the SDC and, moreover, by making comparisons of it with the Amish in order to state some concrete arguments for its necessity and feasibility. Finally, it will attempt to identify an even further reason for the establishment of the SDC that relates to a pre-Qin Confucian political heritage. *Gongyang* 公羊 Confucians refer to this as "opening up three traditions" (*tong santong* 通三统, discussed below).

Why a Special District of Confucian Culture?

We all know the reasons for setting up a nature reserve: maintaining biodiversity, protecting the original environment and rare species, maintaining ecological balance, and so forth. Almost all of these can also apply to a cultural reserve or protected cultural district to a certain degree, if the "bio" is altered to "cultural." However, a special cultural district is inhabited by human beings with cultural traditions, and so there must be additional considerations involved in its establishment.

Confucianism has its roots in the family, especially in the parent-child relation. To extend this relation into communities, states, and "land under heaven" through an education in the arts and its exemplars is one of the primary functions of a Confucian authority. Due to these two features—its family orientation and its transformation of human society through education—Confucianism did not feel the need to form itself into a religion with an independent and clear organization. Consequently, when the great tide of Westernization came—the so-called "dramatic change never seen in three thousand years"—the old family-education-society system was destroyed or seriously damaged, and Confucianism found no refuge in churches and temples as had other non-Western religions such as Buddhism and Daoism. That was one reason for the sharp and radical decline in the twentieth century of this once so successful cultural body. Up until about fifteen years ago, therefore, we saw no authentic Confucian living experience in almost any major aspect of life in mainland China, and in this sense Confucianism had become a "wandering soul without a body."

In the last two decades, there has been a growing interest in Confucianism in Chinese academic circles and among Confucian sympathizers and even some young people. However, this phenomenon looks to belong chiefly to a cultural nostalgia movement and has not penetrated into the mainstream, whether political, economic, educational, or technological. The anti-Confucian ideology fostered by the May Fourth "New Culture" movement and further fueled by the Cultural Revolution still prevails. One of its manifestations was the withdrawing of the statue of Confucius from the side quadrant of Tiananmen Square in April of 2011, following the combined efforts of both the political left and right. Although the Chinese government has set up quite a few "Confucius Institutes" in foreign countries, these institutes seem to be Confucian in name only.

In this unfavorable environment, Confucians have offered two notable responses. One is from the rightist side, represented by Mou Zongsan, which claims that in modern times Confucianism must "be self-restricted" to its moral base so as to let its own political and cognitive traditions be superseded by Western democracy and science, for these are the "universal truth" and the "common ideal."[2] The other is the leftist position advocated most famously by Jiang Qing, which insists that Confucianism must sustain its political dimension in the contemporary era, and that, therefore, a Confucian religion in the strict sense should be formed with the goal of becoming the state religion of China.[3]

The rightist line undermines the vitality of Confucianism by forcing it to adopt a Westernized political and cognitive framework. The leftist line in contrast tries to reform Confucianism into a church-like national religion. In an anti-Confucian atmosphere, however, it risks leaving Confucianism hanging in the air and losing its vitality as well. Both lines pay little attention to the importance to Confucianism of family and community, or to the Confucian focus on *xiaodao* 孝道 (the Way of family reverence, or filial piety). Admittedly, it is extremely difficult in this era of globalization to revive the traditional family and display its advantages. But this does not mean that the Confucian struggle for survival today can afford to neglect its family-*xiaodao* keystone. Without it, no form of Confucianism can be genuine and alive.

For these reasons, the establishment of an SDC makes very good sense, insofar as it enables Confucianism to seek a new way of maintaining its vitality today. It meets the requirements of both compromising with contemporary globalization and regenerating Confucianism. The SDC is marginal, and will therefore not negatively affect what is going on in mainstream society. Because it permits a small but authentic Confucian community to exist, it satisfies the need to sustain a true Confucian life-world in an environment of adversity.

What Is an SDC?[4]

An SDC is a small autonomous region in which Confucian communities prevail. More specifically, it is grounded in the family and guided by a renewal of the traditional Confucian arts and principles. This kind of region requires a land grant for the establishment of limited self-governing communities that only an authoritative institution such as the state can provide. As much as possible the land should be geographically marginal or isolated, for two reasons: the effort to set up an SDC should not interfere with anyone's livelihood, and the district should be secluded from the ruling society so that it can maintain the necessary space for a free and independent existence. After the initial wave of settlers makes improvements to the environment, the land should be made ready for farming and habitation by a small community.

Without question, this community must be grounded in a family- or lineage-based social structure. Therefore, what directs its establishment is neither liberal nor autocratic principles, but rather the familial rudiments enhanced by the Confucian arts. The family on various levels supplies the organic structure of the small society, in which many problems are dealt with, such as construction and repair, agricultural production, insurance, public welfare, conflict resolution, and basic education. Accordingly, one of the major tasks of an SDC is, on the one hand, to improve family structure by retrieving both a familial prototype and the traditional Confucian refinement of this prototype and, on the other hand, learning as well as creating new family structures. The family should provide a meaning-generating context for human life rather than a rigid hierarchical system that diminishes the natural free spaces of the living. In this respect, the thought of the peasant thinker Wang Fengyi (1864–1937) may be quite illuminating.[5] He criticized the dogmatic and corrupt aspects of the family culture of his time: for instance, the discrimination against women, the overemphasis on the material aspects of marriage (such as claiming a bride-price), and the insufficient care provided by families to their elders. But unlike the May Fourth radicals, he wanted to preserve and revitalize the inner life of the family, in particular the family ethics that takes *xiao,* family reverence or filial piety, as the foremost virtue. The numerous schools he created for the education of women, for instance, were not intend to reshape the females of society into no-family-care individuals, but to emphasize the "roots of the family" (家 之本)—the mother and daughter-in-law, who help the whole family to achieve harmony, moral rectitude, and prosperity.

The political edifice of the SDC would not be a hereditary system like that of a monarchy, for such a system would not be the best concretization of family-configured morality. The ideal of Confucian politics is "to make the world harmonious" (平天下), which depends on "regulating the state," "coordinating the family," and "cultivating oneself."[6] Its superb manifestation is the Yao-Shun model of transferring authority according to virtue and wisdom, rather than through a hereditary system within one family. In other words, the family and its "role ethics"[7] are deeper than the political system. It can serve as the latter's origin and spiritual guide, but its makeup cannot be fully objectified into an inherited form of politics. Therefore, the SDC's authority should come from and be curbed by the common people (*baixing* 百姓) grounded in the traditional family and in a Confucian wisdom that surpasses that of a monarchical system.

There may be two houses or congresses: a *baixing* house (百姓院) and a Confucian house (通儒院). The representatives of the *baixing* house are elected by family-based *baixing* or common people. Everyone in the SDC can vote for the representatives, but the votes coming from the family as a whole hold greater weight than those from individuals. In this way, family formation acquires certain advantages, but individuals are also allowed to speak out. To avoid the monopoly of big family lineages, there should be a regulatory system to enforce the division of lineages over a certain size. The Confucian house should be composed of esteemed and tested Confucians. The administrative leader of the SDC, the director of the district, would be nominated by the *baixing* house and approved by the Confucian house. The civil-service examination system (科举制) would be revived for the selection of officers and promising Confucians. The procedure and content of the examination should be adapted according to what the SDC's long-term existence requires.

The primary form of economic production should be agriculture, for it is the form most agreeable to family health, but family-based industry and commerce would be permitted. In brief, this is a natural, family-centered, humanistic economy. It guarantees the basic needs of every family and individual, but also encourages as well as assists everyone to display their own talents, and to conduct their own life with happiness and decency. In this society, the "lowest" people in terms of wealth or social status should be guaranteed a life that allows them to maintain themselves, as well as a hopeful outlook. On the other hand, the "higher" the people rise in wealth or status, the more their contributions to the district should be substantially larger. There is no rigid economic or social stratification. Privileged status is not admitted except that which comes from embodying morality and wisdom.

The district will use clean and family-friendly technologies *only*. That means it will reapply the traditional technologies but at same time improve them, and will try its best to learn and invent smarter green technologies. Fossil fuels for driving engines are to be prohibited, and electricity—especially public-grid electricity—is with a few exceptions banned in general. Traditional medicine such as Chinese medicine will be the cornerstone of healthcare, but the "green" parts of Western and other types of medicine are to be absorbed. *Laodong* 劳动 (work/labor in a wholesome sense) with the aid of such technology will allow labor to regain dignity through craftsmanship in a spirit of joyfulness.

Education will help secure a sustainable and comfortable future for the community by "going back to the past and renewing the present." The Confucian classics and arts are essential, but certain techniques and approaches to thinking developed by Western and other societies beyond China must be taken in, particularly those related to green living and technology. In other words, exchanges between the Confucian and other traditions are encouraged as far as the preconditions that they be clean and sustainable are met. Institutions of higher learning should be introduced for the pursuit of advanced knowledge. The SDC will be a place where a youthful enthusiasm for learning and new discovery can flourish. Here the moral philosophy of the family will be both conservative and creative, since it will emphasize both continuity of tradition and the capacity to deal with unforeseen changes.

The SDC naturally will take Confucianism as its basic belief system and keep it alive through the program described above. However, due to its dependence on a natural family ethics, rather than on dogmatic creeds, the SDC will have the confidence to leave room for other beliefs as far as they are in harmony with the fundamental principles and rules of this society.

What will the SDC look like? One passage from *The Peach Blossom Spring* by Tao Yuanming 陶渊明 (365–427) may give us a sense of its outlook:

> The fisherman left his boat and entered the cave, which at first was extremely narrow, barely admitting his body; after a few dozen steps it suddenly opened out onto a broad and level plain where well-built houses were surrounded by rich fields and pretty ponds. Mulberry, bamboos and other trees and plants grew there, and criss-cross paths skirted the fields. The sounds of cocks crowing and dogs barking could be heard from one courtyard to the next. Men and women were coming and going about their work in the fields. The clothes they wore were like those of ordinary people. Old men and boys were carefree and happy.[8]

The spirit of an SDC community will be poetic in the sense of the harmony realized in "poem, song, music, and temperament" (诗, 歌, 声, 律), as rendered by the "Yaodian" 尧典 section of *The Book of History* (*Shujing* 书经).[9] And the lifestyle depicted there also shares remarkable similarities with the Amish community in the United States.[10]

A Comparison with the Amish Community

The Amish are a special Anabaptist Protestant Christian group that formed in the middle of the seventeenth century in Europe. Persecuted heavily there, the Amish emigrated to North America between the 1730s and 1850s, and they now live in the United States and Canada.[11] They believe that true Christians should in every way separate themselves from an immoral world in the pursuit of power. Thus, the Amish have resisted uniformity and control over their rural communities by any alien institution, whether that institution is in the form of a united church system, a state authority, mandatory education, modern technology, or modern rational thought. What the Amish cherish most are a sincere religious faith, a healthy family, and a vital and active community. For these reasons, some significant comparisons may be drawn between the Amish and the proposed SDC.

First, both pay strong attention to family and combine religious beliefs with family morality. For both groups, love of deity essentially cannot be disconnected from love of family members. The Amish resist such code expressions as "eternal salvation," and prefer to speak of a "living hope" that demands their ethical practice.[12] "[I]t makes no sense to them to separate ethics from salvation or to speak of one dimension and not the other."[13] The "ethics" here relates to the conviction that family morality comes first. So they reject a formal bureaucratic church and hold church services in their homes every other Sunday:

> The district's twenty to forty families live near each other. A single four-letter word, *Gmay*—a [German] dialect shorthand for *Gemeinde* (community)—refers to this local church-community, both its members and its worship services.[14]

These families are to a great extent related to each other and "provide care, support, and wisdom for all stages of life."[15] Therefore, "[t]he family [rather than the individual or an institution] is the primary social unit in Amish society.... The family is the church in microcosm.... It is difficult to exaggerate the importance of the extended family in Amish society."[16] It is the family orientation of their community and Christian faith that distinguish the Amish from other Christian groups and allows a closer comparison to the Confucian community in the SDC.

Consequently, we find that *xiaodao* or filial piety, which features strongly in Confucian culture, is also encouraged and practiced to a certain degree in Amish society: "The words of the fifth commandment, 'Honor thy father and thy mother,' are heard frequently in Amish circles."[17] When parents become old, they move to an apartment adjacent to the house of one of their married children where they receive care from their children when needed.[18] As a result, among the Amish one hardly hears of anyone applying to live in a retirement center or nursing home.

In order to sustain their family-based religious beliefs in the midst of a hostile environment, both find it necessary to uphold some level of separation from the mainstream society. In 1954 an Amish man named Levi living in Pennsylvania was arrested and imprisoned five times within four months because he refused to send his fourteen-year-old son to the ninth grade of middle school.[19] The same thing happened around that time to one hundred other Amish people who, together with Levi, insisted that it was their own community that should take responsibility for their youngsters' education and that their children should stop their school education by the eighth grade. Such efforts at keeping a substantial distance from the mainstream have characterized the entire history of the Amish. Since the twentieth century, the Amish have striven to hold on to "the right not to be modern"[20] and to continue their "Ordnung" (divine order of life tested by tradition)[21] in all aspects of their lives. They well understand that the outcome of this non-modernization struggle will decide the destiny of their community. "Within two generations, the progress-seeking churches would surrender their distinctive Amish identity and merge with neighboring Mennonites."[22] As already mentioned, the SDC community will be aware of the unconditional requirement for isolation from modern society under the present circumstances, and therefore will much appreciate the valuable knowledge gained from the Amish experience. The Amish have shown that without this kind of separation—or *"Absonderung"* in Amish German—no authentic and energetic Confucian community is possible today. In spite of some obvious differences between China and the United States, the two groups are similar in their antipathy to modernity, advanced technology, and "the will to power."

Furthermore, both sides are composed of small communities with "a high-context culture" (Edward T. Hall's term) "in which people are deeply involved with one another...[and] are integrated, for members are skilled in thinking comprehensively according to a system of the common good. Loyalties are concrete and individuals work together to settle their problems."[23] Finding effective ways to attract young people of the next generation—and to persuade them to choose to stay in the "backward" community—is the key to Amish survival. This requires a high level of social intimacy, and a corresponding low level of mobility:

> By limiting mobility, horse-drawn transportation supports this small-scale, face-to-face community. In addition, a horse-based culture requires rural environs and keeps Amish communities outside urban areas, which threaten Amish sensibilities.[24]

"Old Order [the conservative Ordnung] authority rested on informal oral tradition in each local community."[25] Therefore, "[i]n general, the more conservative the Ordnung, the higher the retention [of young people]."[26] Contrary to quite a few pessimistic predictions made by researchers, the Amish population had increased from six thousand in 1900 to 275,000 by 2012.

In order to sustain their faith, family, and community, both the Amish and SDC consider it imperative to resist the overwhelming domination of modern technology and to choose technology appropriate to their way of life. They clearly know that the actual consequences of technology are not unrelated to moral standards and their way of thinking. An Amish leader says: "The moral decay of these last days has gone hand in hand with lifestyle changes made possible by modern technology."[27] When we use technology to achieve what we want, technology in turn uses our lives to realize its own goal and thus transform us to fit its flattening framework. The Amish people "recognized the way mechanization displaced family and local communities in favor of distant sources of production and influence."[28] You may use your cell phone to call your parents, but by using the mobile phone system you are actually being put into a situation where family members are distancing themselves from each other and community interaction is no longer face-to-face. You may bring your high-tech harvest machine to help your neighbor, but when almost everyone has a machine, mutual assistance becomes an unusual phenomenon. Within the web of modern technology, where even individualized service can be essentially uniform, a community is reduced to single families, families to individuals, and individuals to manipulated desires. The result of all this is that we need commercial media and state institutions to form any kind of group consciousness, and we require crises, enemies, or sometimes even war to provoke in us a sense of solidarity.

That is why the Amish, especially the Old Order Amish, have been resisting the universal impact of modern technology. Some progressive Amish communities have tried to accept certain new technologies in order to adapt to a changing world. But, "Diversity has its limits." If they did not "negotiate" with the technology by following the rules of the Old Order, the result was a disaster. "Although Beachy Amish members have continued to dress somewhat plainly and even retained the Pennsylvania Dutch dialect for a generation or so, their embrace of the car, along with other technological and doctrinal innovations, put them outside the Old Order fence."[29] One of the reasons for rejecting car ownership, according to one Amish leader, is that "they bring moral decay as people work and live away from their families," and one Amish publication gives as the reason the fact that "the car pulls families apart, increases the temptation to travel into cities, and detaches families from their local churches."[30] From these statements, we can observe what kinds of morals are treasured by the Amish and why they consider cars, telephones, television, grid-supplied electricity, and so forth to be serious threats.

To maintain family, faith, and community, the most suitable profession for both the Amish and SDC is agriculture. "Over the generations, the Amish have developed a strong conviction that the small family farm is the best place to raise children in the faith."[31] However, since the 1950s, especially during the latter part of the twentieth century, Amish farming has encountered significant difficulties, and the households engaged in farming have decreased considerably. Some farmers have adopted relatively high-technology equipment such as vacuum milkers and bulk cooling tanks for milk production.[32] Fortunately, early in the twenty-first century, in addition to the traditional way of farming, which is still practiced by the most conservative groups, a number of new agricultural practices, such as cheese making, the auctioning of produce, organic farming, intensive grazing, and the use of greenhouses, have emerged, or in some ways have been revived, in Amish communities.[33] The Amish experience seems to show that the prosperity of the family and community is largely affected by the technology that is used. The SDC needs to make agriculture and traditional green technology its foundation.

With heartfelt admiration for the Amish people and their culture as described above, it is proper here to reflect on some lessons that SDC thinkers can learn from the Amish.

First, although the Amish have been astute enough to recognize the moral consequences of adopting modern technology, and have engaged in resistance to it and chosen to accept only parts of it and negotiate with it cautiously, their approach to dealing with the issue of technology in general may at times seem to be too *passive*. There is no organized, long-term practice to establish an indigenous system for appropriating technology that can satisfy the overall needs of the Amish today and in the future. For example, it is a smart negotiation or compromise to adapt a commercial computer run by grid electricity so that a battery-powered word processor can be used—and as long as "e-mail, Internet access, video games, or other interactive media" are disabled.[34] However, it would be much better and safer for the Amish to develop their own processor (on the model, say, of an improved *suanpan* 算盘 or traditional Chinese abacus). The Amish strategies of dealing with modern technology up to now have been partially successful, but new dangers have appeared in some communities such as the acceptance of cell phones and solar electricity,[35] which may become more insidious threats. So the future success of the Amish in their attempt to tame modern technology is seen as "uncertain."[36]

Second, the Amish need to develop their *own* advanced education and research projects so that they may achieve the capacity to create and sustain their own technology network. Historically, Confucianism had its own effective education and examination system, but these did not cover practical technology relating to farming and industry, a gap that the SDC must fill.

Third and most fundamentally, it will be necessary to establish a clearer boundary between the Amish and SDC communities and their respective surrounding mainstream societies so that the principle of separation can be fully realized. This means that the Amish and the SDC should each have their own special district where their own lifestyles prevail exclusively. Although the Amish have tried to interpret this separation in terms of the dichotomy between religious life and the worldly life, or between church and state,[37] they are nevertheless living in the world and hence must constantly confront the politics of the worldly life, if only because it heavily influences the quality of the separation. In other words, they should live on the land run autonomously by them, so that they can have independent forms of social organization, economy, and technology networks. While it is good to avoid the alienating influence of bureaucratic institutions, they badly need institutions of their own that are not alienated from their family- and community-oriented lifestyles, while at the same time they can organize the dispersed Amish communities into a self-ruling body. It is not a state, but rather a self-run community in the same sense that Hong Kong is (that is, if the Special District's leader is actually selected by its people).

This would allow the Amish people to avoid directly facing the outside world as single-family units or as individuals, and to avoid the economic pressure to modernize their technology. For instance, in the 1950s and 1960s, state health regulations requiring that Grade A milk be distinguished from Grade B milk pushed some Amish farms to accept mechanical milkers and cooling tanks.[38] In 2002 "Some farmers complained that an inflexible farming Ordnung was actually pushing young families into nonfarm employment and suggested that, if church leaders wanted to save the family farm, the Ordnung would need to be relaxed."[39] Why did the Ordnung hinder Amish agriculture at this point when it had not done so before? Because the external economic environment had changed: "Escalating prices for hybrid seeds, fertilizer, equipment, and veterinary bills all conspired to make farming an expensive enterprise, even on a small scale."[40] Considering the mutual reinforcement between the modern economy and modern technology, if the Amish want to resist, by separation, the moral-decay brought on by modern technology, the separation should also extend to economic life—and therefore to political life. From this perspective, establishing an autonomous SDC or SDA (i.e., a Special District for Amish Culture) would seem necessary.

How Is the SDC Different from a Reserve?

One difference between the SDC and a nature reserve is that the SDC is less a place for protecting rare species and more a way to preserve a potential way of life for future humanity. It is, in fact, a way, or perhaps even *the* way, of engendering the full essence or possibilities of Confucianism, thereby making it "become itself" in the future.

Confucianism's forte lies not in the building of a power structure or a church system with a prominent form, whether that form be individualistic, governmental, or religious, but in constituting an attractive lifestyle that is characterized by humaneness, harmony, artistic creativity, spontaneity, and durability. This lifestyle must have its primary grounding in a sound family and community structure that takes *xiaodao* 孝道 (loving, serving, respecting, and honoring the memory of one's parents) as its foundation and extends it through the Confucian arts to the whole community. The family relation and the practice of *xiaodao,* however, have been established in the temporal existence of peoples down through the generations, as I have described elsewhere.[41] Due to the fact that, for Confucianism, all political entities such as the state have their roots in the family and its rituals, this temporality is necessarily embodied in Confucian political philosophy, and therefore makes it different from the Platonic way of seeking the best state in an Ideal that is independent of time.

Because *tiandao* 天道, or the Way of Heaven, is ever changing, no actual political regime, however it may be shaped according to some Ideal, can avoid ultimate deterioration and decline. New regimes must emerge to replace the present one to fulfill the demands of *tiandao.* Here the key to political "replacement" is the actualization of timely virtue rather than a resort to violence, trickery, or some absolutist ideology. This is what distinguishes a legitimate replacement or *ge* 革 (revolution) from an illegitimate one or *cuan* 篡 (usurpation). The *Book of Changes* states:

> Heaven and earth effectuate four seasons by revolutions. The revolutions of Tang [the first king of the Xia dynasty] and Wu [the first king of the Zhou dynasty] complied with heaven and were responsive to the will of the people (顺乎天而应乎人). How great was the timeliness of the revolution [hexagram] (革之时大矣哉)![42]

Alternatively:

> Heaven and earth bring about revolution, and the four seasons complete themselves thereby.
> Tang and Wu brought about political revolutions because they were submissive toward heaven and in accord with men. The time of revolution is truly great.[43]

The legitimization of the revolutions of Tang and Wu, and indeed the evidence of their complementarity with both Heaven and humanity, lie in their timely way of replacing the preceding dynasty, similar to the way Spring replaces Winter. It is a natural way of following the *dao* and of opportunely fulfilling the needs of Heaven and humanity.

A Confucian revolution is therefore necessary for Confucianism to achieve its political objectives. In addition, to prove itself to be a revolution rather than a usurpation is to *show* how it complies with heaven and is responsive to the will of the people. "Showing" cannot, however, be limited to presenting arguments, apologies, or even facts, all of which are subject to interpretations and can be potentially attacked by critics, but instead must demand a real community life that demonstrates how a self-evident and morally glamorous Confucian life-world can actually function. This community life, however, first requires a grant of land to sustain itself.

Before the Qin (221–207 B.C.E.), there were quite a few autonomous lands in the empire ruled by nobles, which sometimes provided the necessary material basis for such "showing." Confucius said: "The Zhou's Wen and Wu arose from the small districts of Feng and Hao, but finally achieved the great kingship" (周文武起丰镐而王).[44] Here, "Wen" refers to King Wen, who was then the duke of Zhou, and after his death received the posthumous title of Wen Wang or King Wen. He was the father of "Wu" in this quotation (or King Wu). Wen set up the small district of Feng, where he led Zhou's people in building a fabulous "SDC"; and the same thing happened to Wu in Hao. In this way they were able to *show* the virtuousness of their politics and won over the hearts of most of the people at the fall of the Shang empire. Thus, even before the brief war against the cruel Shang emperor, the Zhou had gained the new legitimacy of heaven by demonstrating their timely morality. This is the very meaning of "kingship" (*wang* 王)—obtaining and sustaining rule by lively virtue rather than by power.

The Amish experience demonstrates how a small minority community through its vitality and humanity can exert a substantial sociocultural influence on mainstream society over time. Before the middle of the twentieth century, the social mainstream did not have a very positive view of the Amish. "A queer religious sect," "drab," "odd in many ways: they are a strange people" were the usual comments.[45] Since the 1960s, however, their image in the public mind has seen a steady improvement, despite some minor setbacks, and they "now have become objects of public interest and admiration."[46] "One of the greatest ironies of Amish life is that a people committed to remaining separate from the world have attracted so much attention from it."[47] The more curious thing is that, although the Amish reject most of the things that typical Americans cherish—individualism, science, modern technology, and freedom of personal choice—many Americans still feel attracted to the Amish way of life. "Why are we so intrigued by the Amish?" it is asked.[48] Eventually, the answer is found in the high quality of the Amish lifestyle, which bears certain similarities to how Sima Qian described the district of Feng, where King Wen ruled:

> Widows and orphans, the destitute and the disabled, receive respect and care within their community.... [V]iolent crime is virtually nil. Divorce is unheard of, and the elderly grow old within a caring circle of family and friends.... Work pulses with meaning, human dignity, and a delight in artisanship. Extended family networks provide care throughout the life cycle.[49]

"[A]ll things considered, Amish quality-of-life indicators are remarkably robust.... It seems that in some uncanny way the Amish may have outwitted us—or perhaps even outwitted modernity itself."[50] It is apparent from the Amish example that living the community life itself is more persuasive and self-evident than any prevailing values and standards, because it *is* the direct manifestation of *tiandao* or the Way of Heaven.

According to Confucian political philosophy, if someone receives his life's calling from *tiandao* and touches the deepest parts of the people's hearts, that person will win the kingship. In the terms of the "SDC" built by Wen and Wu, the Zhou achieved such a calling. This did not mean, however, that the Zhou could claim either legitimacy or kingship forever. Sooner or later, a new dynasty would be born in another small place that had been cultivated with virtue, and in due time it would go on to replace the Zhou. Moreover, this does not mean that the dynasty replaced by the Zhou would forever lose *its* legitimacy. Like the seasons, dynasties complete the circle at least in a formal sense, constituting the political *tiandao,* or Way of Heaven. Therefore, Confucians proposed the idea of *tong santong* 通三统 or "connecting three systems," which holds that when a new kingship or political system comes to power, it should retain the cultural and political system of its predecessors in a measured way. A specific example: the new ruler must assign a piece of land to each of the remaining inhabitants of the previous two dynasties and permit them to keep their cultures and traditions on the land. Moreover, compared to other feudal subjects, the owners of these lands would carry additional privileges, such as being able to come before the ruler holding the status of guests rather than subjects.[51] In this way, the three systems are "connected" in a circle, implying that, one by one, the old will return in the future.

The current SDC can be seen as the manifestation of a preceding system, and is part of the "circle." Moving beyond the current PRC government and the Republican government in Taiwan, the SDC stands for the old dynasties, which took Confucianism as their dominant cultural and political direction. It therefore points to the past but also embraces the future in the circle of the "three connecting systems." More crucially, its existence will make the *tong santong* truly possible today, and allow the current political structure to move from a dependence on power to a dependence on virtue. In the United States—if a speculative comparison is allowed here—there could be an interconnected three-part system there as well: it would be composed of the current U.S. government; the way of life in the nineteenth-century, now represented by the Amish (if they can establish themselves in a special district); and the way of the Indian people, whose ancestors were the masters of the land before the arrival of the European colonists.

As argued above, no fixed political system can forever lay claim to political virtue, morality, or *tiandao*. *Tiandao* can only be realized in the dynamic and rotating pattern of the three interconnected systems. In comparison, political virtue and legitimacy can only be constituted in a timely fashion *between* or *among* cyclic systems, instead of being locked within one system. No political system is good or virtuous by itself, but must instead demonstrate its goodness through opportune relations and tensions with others. For this reason, an SDC, in a broader sense, is essential for the manifestation of *tiandao* in this world.

Notes

1. See Zhang Xianglong 张祥龙, *Rujia wenhua baohu qu huo tequ* 儒家文化保护区或特区 (Providing an asylum for Chinese ancient culture [is] endangered: A suggestion for establishing a Protected District of Confucian Culture), *Xiandai jiaoyu bao* 现代教育报 (Modern Education News), July 20, 2001, p. B1.

See also by Zhang Xianglong: (1) " 'Rujia Wenhua Baohu Qu' yiweizhe shenme?" " '儒家文化保护区' 意味着什么？ " (What does it mean to establish a "Protected District of Confucian Culture"?), *Kexue Zhongguo ren* 科学中国人 (Chinese scientist) 10 (2001): 33–35; (2) *Sixiang binan: Quanqiu hua zhong de zhongguo gudai zheli* 思想避难：全球化中的中国古代哲理 (Refuge for thought: Chinese ancient philosophies in [an age of] globalization) (Beijing: Peking University Press, 2007), chap. 2; and (3) *Fu jian tiandi xin: Rujia zai lin de yun yi yu daolu* 复见天地心：儒家再临的蕴意与道路 (Showing the heart of Heaven and Earth by restoration: The implications and ways of Confucian revival) (Beijing: Dongfang Press, 2014), chaps. 8 and 9.

2. Mou Zongsan 牟宗三, *Xin ruxue lunzhu ji yao·daode lixiang zhuyi de chongjian·bian xu* 新儒学论著辑要·道德理想主义的重建·编序 (A selection of works on the reconstruction of Neo-Confucian moral idealism), ed. Zheng Jiadong 郑家栋 (Beijing: Zhongguo Guangbo Dianshi Chubanshe 中国广播电视出版社, 1992), p. 20; English translation here by Zhang Xianglong.

3. Jiang Qing 蒋庆, "Ru jiao chong jian: Zhuzhang yu huiying" "儒教重建：主张与回应" (Reestablishing Confucianism as a religion: Proposals and responses), in vol. 1 of *Rusheng wen cong* 儒生文丛 (Collected essays of Confucius), ed. Ren Zhong 任重 and Liu Ming 刘明 (Beijing: People's University Press of China, 2012), pp. 5–7.

4. What this section presents is discussed more concretely in chapter 8 of my book *Showing the Heart of Heaven and Earth by Restoration* (see note 1 above).

5. See Zhu Xuntian 朱循天, *Wang Fengyi nianpu yu yulu* 王凤仪年谱与语录 (Wang Fengyi's chronicle and sayings) (Beijing: Zhongguo Huaqiao Chubanshe, 2010), and Zhang Xianglong 张祥龙, "Wang Fengyi xueshuo de rujiaxing: Dui qi kaiwu tiyan de jiexi" 王凤仪学说的儒家性—对其开悟体验的解析 (The Confucian nature of Wang Fengyi's thought: An analysis of his enlightenment experience), in *Zhongwai renwen jingshen yanjiu* 中外人文精神研究 (Studies on the Chinese and foreign humanistic spirit), vol. 6, ed. Liu Muyu 刘牧雨 and Du Liyan 杜丽燕 (Beijing: Renmin Chubanshe, 2013), pp. 42–53.

6. The *Great Learning* (*Daxue* 大学), in *The Book of Rituals* (*Liji* 礼记).

7. See Roger T. Ames, *Confucian Role Ethics: A Vocabulary* (Hong Kong: Chinese University Press, 2011).

8. Translated by J. R. Hightower in *Classical Chinese Literature: An Anthology of Translations,* vol. 1, *From Antiquity to the Tang Dynasty,* ed. John Minford and Joseph S. M. Lau (New York: Columbia University Press; Hong Kong: Chinese University Press, 2000), p. 515.

9. "Poetry is the expression of earnest thought; singing is the prolonged utterance of that expression. The notes accompany that utterance, and they are harmonized themselves by the pitch pipes. In this way the eight different kinds of instruments can all be adjusted so that one shall not take from or interfere with another, and spirits and men will thereby be brought into harmony" (James Legge, *The Chinese Classics,* vol. 3, *The Shoo King* [Taipei: SMC Publishing Inc., 1994], p. 48).

10. John A. Hostetler. *Amish Society,* 4th ed. (Baltimore: Johns Hopkins University Press, 1993).

11. Donald B. Kraybill, Karen M. Johnson-Weiner, and Steven M. Nolt, *The Amish* (Baltimore: Johns Hopkins University Press, 2013), chap. 2.

12. Ibid., pp. 71–72.

13. Ibid., p. 72.

14. Ibid.

15. Ibid., p. 203.

16. Ibid., pp. 194, 203.

17. Ibid., p. 196.

18. Ibid., p. 203.

19. Ibid., p. 3.

20. Ibid., p. 51.

21. Ibid., p. 42.

22. Ibid., p. 43.

23. Hostetler, *Amish Society,* p. 18.

24. Kraybill, Johnson-Weiner, and Nolt, *The Amish,* p. 168.

25. Ibid., p. 44.

26. Ibid., p. 163.

27. Ibid., p. 315.

28. Ibid., p. 41.

29. Ibid., p. 46. "Beachy" refers to the "network of churches" that began under the leadership of Moses M. Beachy (1874–1946) (ibid.).

30. Ibid., p. 325.

31. Ibid., pp. 275–276.

32. Ibid., pp. 277–282.

33. Ibid., pp. 284–288.

34. Ibid., p. 316.

35. Ibid., pp. 324, 328.

36. Ibid., p. 334.

37. Ibid., pp. 15–17.

38. Ibid., p. 279.

39. Ibid., p. 280.

40. Ibid., p. 281.

41. Zhang Xianglong 张祥龙, "Xiaoyishi de shijian fenxi" "孝意识的时间分析" (An analysis of the consciousness of filial piety through time), *Beijing Daxue xuebao* (*Zhezue shehui kexue ban*) 北京大学学报 (哲学社会科学版) (*Journal of Peking University* [*Philosophy and Social Sciences edition*]) 1 (April 2006): 14–24.

See also by Zhang Xianglong: (1) "An Analysis of the Consciousness of Filial Piety through the Perspective of Time," in *Moral Life: Reclaiming the Tradition,* ed. David Solomon, Ping-Cheung Lo, and Ruiping Fan (Heidelberg, London, and New York: Springer, 2012), pp. 105–118; (2) "Xiangxiangli yu lishijiyi: Neishijian yishi de fenceng" 想象力与历时记忆—内时间意识的分层 (Imagination and episodic memories: The level-division of inner time consciousness), *Xiandai zhexue* 现代哲学 (Modern philosophy) 1 (2013): 65–71; and (3) "The Time of Heaven in Chinese Ancient Philosophy," in *Contemporary Chinese Thought* 30, no. 4 (1999): 44–61.

42. *Book of Changes, tuan* interpretation of the 49th hexagram (*Ge* 革); my own translation from the Chinese edition of the *Zhouyi jije cuan shu* 周易集解纂疏 (The interpretations of the collected annotations of the *Book of Changes*), by Li Daoping 李道平, ed. Pan Yuting 潘雨廷 (Beijing: Zhonghua Shuju, 1994; reprint, 2012), pp. 437–438.

43. *The I Ching or Book of Changes,* the Richard Wilhelm translation rendered into English by Cary F. Baynes (Princeton: Princeton University Press, 1967, 1969), Commentary on the Decision, "49. Ko/Revolution (Molting)," p. 636.

44. Cited from the biography of Confucius, "Kongzi shijia" 孔子世家, in the *Records of the Historian* (*Shiji* 史记), authored by Sima Qian 司馬遷.

45. Kraybill, Johnson-Weiner, and Nolt, *The Amish,* pp. 50, 415.

46. Ibid., p. 416.

47. Ibid., p. 385.

48. Ibid., p. 416.

49. Ibid., p. 418.

50. Ibid.

51. Dong Zhongshu, *Luxuriant Dews of Spring and Autumn,* chap. 23.

PART II

Different Confucianisms

CHAPTER 5

Why Speak of "East Asian Confucianisms"?

Chun-chieh HUANG

PRIOR TO THE TURN of the twenty-first century, very little research had been conducted on "East Asian Confucianisms" in Chinese academia.[1] However, in 2000, a team from National Taiwan University initiated the "Research Project on the Interpretation of Confucian Classics in Early Modern East Asia," which served as the first stage of research until 2004. This East Asian research project has been developing in stages, and since 2011 it has been conducted as the "Program of East Asian Confucianisms" and was set to continue until 2019. This initiative has ushered into the field a steadily growing number of scholars. Meanwhile, National Taiwan University Press had begun publishing a number of series of books on East Asian Confucianisms and East Asian culture, most notably Studies in East Asian Confucianisms, Research Materials in East Asian Confucianisms, and Studies in East Asian Civilizations. Nearly two hundred books have been published by National Taiwan University Press, and many have been reprinted in simplified-character editions in the People's Republic of China. Japanese and Korean scholars have also begun to conduct studies on Confucianism from a regional East Asian perspective, and even some mainland Chinese scholars are beginning to write books on East Asian Confucianisms.[2]

The theoretical foundations and future prospects of this new field of East Asian Confucianisms still await deep and extensive scholarly deliberations. In 2003, the methodological problems that would form the initial dialogue for these deliberations were examined in my article "How Is East Asian Confucianisms Possible [as a Field of Study]?"[3] The present essay examines the related question "Why Is East Asian Confucianisms Necessary?" The next section discusses the special features of East Asian Confucianisms, and the subsequent section considers the prospects of East Asian Confucianisms as a new field in the present academic world, providing the foundation for a new humanistic spirit for the twenty-first-century age of globalization. The final section concludes the study.

What Is "East Asian Confucianisms?"

The content and special features of "East Asian Confucianisms" can be viewed from a variety of perspectives, the most significant of which are: (1) the interaction between part and whole, and (2) the contrast between form and content.

With regard to the interaction between part and whole, the term "East Asian Confucianisms" is intended to stress that within the rich diversity of the Chinese, Japanese, Korean, and Vietnamese cultures and traditions, and within their differing Confucianisms, lies a common core of shared intellectual and ethical factors. This special feature of East Asian Confucianisms has several dimensions.

First, "East Asian Confucianisms" refers to the impact of Confucian values as manifested in indigenous thought and culture. The diversity of localized formations of Confucian thought and culture across East Asia is not a mere mosaic of these localized manifestations. As a matter of fact, the Confucianisms of the countries of East Asia have influenced one another through exchanges and interactions for centuries. Just as "Christendom," featuring a plethora of distinctive localized forms, was formed through religious and cultural exchanges and interactions across Western Europe, a similar sort of "Confuciandom" took shape across East Asia. The use of the term "Confuciandom" underscores the fact that despite the rich variety of localized manifestations of East Asian Confucianisms, there is a distinctive regional wholeness of intellectual and ethical factors that are held in common.

Next, the regional wholeness of East Asian Confucianisms does not exist as an abstraction over and above the concrete exchanges and interactions going on among the Confucian traditions of the East Asian countries. Rather, it exists—while growing and developing—right in the midst of these exchanges and interactions among these diverse East Asian Confucian traditions. The watchword here is "in the midst of." Again, this wholeness is not to be regarded as something "over and above."

Furthermore, since East Asian Confucianisms exist in the midst of, and not over and above, the cultural exchanges and interactions among the countries of East Asia, it cannot be regarded as a single, fixed, and unchanging intellectual form that originated and was rigidly defined over 2,600 years ago on the Shandong Peninsula in China. Rather, we must appreciate that it has undergone a continuous and ongoing process of development for over two thousand years across East Asia. Not only have East Asian Confucianisms progressed over time; they have adapted to suit each different locale they have encountered so that the manifestations of Confucian tradition in each locale seamlessly reflect the special features of that place while still instilling the central core values of Confucianism.

As mentioned above, the special feature, the wholeness, of East Asian Confucianisms exists in the midst of and not over and above the cultural and intellectual exchange activities among the respective East Asian countries. Consequently, they must be regarded as a sort of continuously evolving family of intellectual traditions. Although this sort of temporal and continuously evolving family has historical roots in the pre-Qin Confucian school, as soon as the downward and outward flow of Confucianism encountered different cultures and societies of other times and places, distinctive Confucian trademarks of each place were formed and set. We must appreciate that while Zhu Xi learning is very different from the humanist school of Neo-Confucianism, the difference between Chinese, Japanese, and Korean Zhu Xi learning is even greater. Therefore, research in East Asian Confucianisms cannot countenance such theoretical presuppositions as "orthodox versus heterodox" or "center versus periphery." It absolutely cannot be assumed that Chinese Confucianism is the highest form of Confucianism, which should serve as the vital standard for assessing the correctness of the various manifestations of Japanese, Korean, and Vietnamese Confucianisms. Such an assumption would turn Chinese Confucianism into the Procrustean bed of ancient Greek myth—such that the other East Asian Confucian traditions would have to be forcibly stretched or trimmed in order to fit the standards everyone conforms to. On the contrary, we should endeavor to grasp the history of the Confucian traditions of each East Asian country as part of the unfolding of its respective national cultural subjectivity. Simply stated, one must understand that the so-called "single thread" of East Asian Confucianisms exists and develops only as a burgeoning tapestry through the ongoing manifold developments going on in this rich diversity of peoples and cultures in order to grasp its creativity and emotional knowledge.[4]

As to the contrast between form and content, the modes of Confucian intellectual and cultural transmission across East Asia were not at all uniform; they were highly diverse. For example, while the transmitters of Confucian values in China were scholars or scholar-officials, in Tokugawa Japan they were commoner intellectuals, and in Joseon Korea (1392–1910) they were the *yangban* (feudal power holders). The transmitters of Confucian values in these three countries occupied very different positions in society and had highly different relations to political power.[5] However, despite these differences, commonalities remained among the Confucian traditions of China, Japan, and Korea. To wit, despite the different levels and scopes of Confucian transmitters (the form) in the politics and societies of these three countries, they all shared the same core Confucian values (the content).

The core Confucian values shared by Confucians in the various East Asian countries include, at the very least, the following two. First, Confucians in all of the East Asian countries firmly believe that the foundation and starting point of Confucianism lay in a self-cultivation process that involves extending sympathy—proceeding along a continuum from self, to family, to society, to state, then on to world. East Asian Confucians all hold, in effect, that the transformation of self is the starting point of transforming the world. Consequently, East Asian Confucian masters all passionately devote themselves to developing deeply profound theories of self-cultivation. Fundamentally, East Asian Confucian philosophies are constituted as practical philosophies of self-cultivation approaches and family ethics. Because the movement in cultivation from the self to family, society, state, and world is not sporadic and ruptured but rather forms a continuum, the practical philosophies of East Asian Confucian traditions all offer responses to the core problem in political philosophy concerning the possibility of getting from individual humane heartedness to general humane governance.

The second core value shared in common by the Confucians of each East Asian country and tradition is Confucius' teaching of *ren* 仁, rendered variously in English as "humanity," "humaneness," "humane heartedness," "benevolence," and "authoritative personhood." The term *ren* appears 105 times in fifty-eight chapters of Confucius' *Analects* (*Lunyu* 論語). Taking *ren* as the core value on which to arrange and construct the empire, the early Confucian masters and students dreamed of realizing a Confucian utopia. Han dynasty Confucians continued along the tracks laid down by the pre-Qin Confucian schools. For example, Dong Zhongshu 董仲舒 (ca. 179–104 B.C.E.) said, "The *ren* approach lies in loving others, not in just loving oneself."[6] In the Tang dynasty, Han Yu 韓愈 (768–824) (also known as Han Tuizhi 韓退之) said, "Broad [encompassing] love is called *ren*."[7] In other words, they explained *ren* directly in terms of love.

In the Northern Song, Zhang Zi 張載 (1020–1077) composed the *Western Inscription* (*Ximing* 西銘),[8] which implicitly presents *ren* at a lofty, cosmic level. Next, the Southern Song Neo-Confucian synthesizer Zhu Xi 朱熹 (1130–1200) (also known as Huian 晦庵) composed the masterpiece, *Treatise on Humanity* (*Renshuo* 仁說), which gives *ren* a metaphysical foundation as well as a cosmological function, thereby enhancing *ren*'s cosmic loftiness in the subsequent tradition. After Zhu Xi's new account of *ren* was transmitted northeast to Japan, it stirred up a hornet's nest of discussions and disputes among Zhu Xi's supporters and critics there, with his critics in the majority, as metaphysics did not sit well with the pragmatically minded Japanese. Itō Jinsai 伊藤仁齋 (1627–1705),[9] Ōta Kinjo 大田錦城 (1765–1825),[10] Toshima Hōshū 豐島豐洲

(1737–1814),[11] and Asami Keisai 淺見絧齋 (1652–1711)[12] all wrote original essays of their own on the meaning and significance of *ren* and the cultivation of *ren*. It was not only the Tokugawa Japanese Confucians who paid special attention to *ren* as a core value of Confucianism; Joseon Korean lords and ministers always discussed problems related to humane governance (*renzheng* 仁政). As Yang Rubin (1956–) points out, "The development of the concept of *ren* in East Asia is just like the unfolding grand epic of a heroic righteous war."[13] The East Asian Confucians were all bards of this grand heroic historical epic.

In general, from the seventeenth century, Confucians all over East Asia shared the core Confucian values. We could say that the East Asian Confucian community had quietly taken shape by the seventeenth century. Examples of this sort of common Confucian consciousness appeared in every East Asian country. It was manifested in Edo Japan in 1600 when Fujiwara Seika 藤原惺窩 (1561–1619), an early follower of Zhu Xi, called on Tokugawa Ieyasu 德川家康 (1543–1616), who ruled as Shōgun from 1603 to 1605. It was also manifested in the seventeenth century when another Korean follower of Zhu Xi, Yi Hwang 李滉 (1502–1571) (also known as Toegye 退溪) compiled *Zhu Xi's Essential Writings* (朱子書節要) for the edification of his students. It became even more apparent in nineteenth-century Japan during the popular general education explosion in society when many scholars enthusiastically began to offer public lectures on the *Analects* of Confucius.

Why Is "East Asian Confucianisms" Necessary?

We are now in a position to consider the fundamental question, "Why is 'East Asian Confucianisms' necessary?" This question can be approached from two angles.

First, we can view the rise of the field of East Asian Confucianisms on the new stage of scholarship in the twenty-first century as a reaction to the form of Confucian studies conducted in the Chinese-language academia of the twentieth century. For example, twentieth-century Chinese New Confucian philosophers tended to view Confucianism narrowly as a segment of their national and ethnic identity, especially as bound up with the vast and far-reaching historical traumas and transformations of the early twentieth century. With regard to methodology, they tended to be highly critical of programmatic May Fourth scientism and narrow-minded Qing dynasty empirical studies. Culturally, they staunchly supported cultural ethnocentrism and turned Confucian studies into a sort of mission to renew and recharge the national spirit. In a word, twentieth-century Chinese New Confucians took the promotion of a Chinese cultural renaissance as their existential responsibility.

In the twentieth century, through a series of important writings, the New

Confucians extended traditional Confucianism's spiritual resources as their raison d'être. Under the adverse conditions of twentieth-century China, these devoted scholars carried on with their studies and reflections, and made truly great contributions to Confucian culture and scholarship. However, since they accepted the limitations of a rigid national ethnocentrism, twentieth-century Chinese Confucian writings today come across largely as part of a national ethnic discourse. In fact, Japanese Confucian studies were also deeply imbued with cultural nationalism; as Yoshikawa Kōjirō 吉川幸次郎 (1904–1980) pointed out, the fundamental mission of Tokugawa era (1603–1868) Japanese Confucian scholarship was to "Japanize" Chinese Confucianism. Well into the twentieth century this scholarship was highly charged with nationalism.[14] During the 1930s, the early stage of World War II, Japanese scholars even reinterpreted the first chapter of Confucius' *Analects* on "learning and practicing what one has learned" in terms of the Japanese emperor's imperial edict directing education.[15]

Against this twentieth-century background, an important function of the new field of East Asian Confucianisms is that it involves actively purging Confucian studies of the limitations—and prejudices—of ethnocentrism to ensure that Confucian studies will never again be confined within state-centrism. This results in freeing Confucianism to be more broadly conceived and extending its spiritual mission to new heights in the twenty-first-century age of globalization. As the *Doctrine of the Mean,* chapter 28, anticipates:

致廣大而盡精微，極高明而道中庸。

[The superior man is] penetrating the furthest reaches while exhausting the most subtle essentials; attaining utmost loftiness and perspicacity while practicing the utmost propriety.

Freed of the twentieth-century nationalism and ethnocentrism that has characterized each East Asian country, scholars who actively pursue studies on East Asian Confucianisms will be able to debunk the limiting binaries of "center and periphery" and "orthodoxy and heterodoxy." Moreover, they will be freed from examining classical texts solely in the light of the history of their single country. Furthermore, scholars in East Asian Confucian studies will be able to undertake open-minded analyses of the interactions and fusions of Confucianism, and the societal and cultural traditions of each host country and locale around East Asia. Indeed, the developmental vantage of Confucianism in each East Asian country could be said to be a seamless reflection of the developmental process of cultural subjectivity in each of these countries.

Second, the necessity of advocating "East Asian Confucianisms" as a distinct field is a proactive intellectual response to the predilection of those twentieth-century East Asian academcians who have interpreted the East according to the West. In this sense, East Asian Confucianisms manifests the vital mission to revisit the Confucian core values as the mainstream of East Asian cultures that might be expanded to provide the foundation of a new Humanism for the age of globalization.

On the heels of the development of globalization and the rise of Asia, intellectuals worldwide are more and more starting to feel that the Humanism that arose out of the Enlightenment of eighteenth-century Europe is too strongly colored by special European sources and characteristics, which make it ill equipped to respond to the needs of the multifaceted demands of the twenty-first-century age of globalization. Therefore, it is necessary to undertake reviews, as well as to research and develop the alternative "other" humanistic resources contained in the treasures of non-European cultural traditions.[16] In the process of establishing a new Humanism in this age of inter-civilizational dialogue, the reinterpretation of the lost treasures of East Asian Confucian culture would indeed be a most worthwhile academic mission to undertake.

Can Confucianism Transcend the East Asian Sphere?

"East Asian Confucianisms" is constructed from the terms "East Asia" and "Confucianisms." However, once these terms have been combined to form "East Asian Confucianisms," two considerations immediately arise. First, during the twentieth century, the people of East Asia, including the Japanese, wrote East Asian history with their own blood, sweat, and tears. The expression "East Asia" in the term "East Asian Confucianisms" genuinely carries too many sad and horrific twentieth-century memories of imperialism. For example, the memory of imperial Japan's announcement of its ambition to establish a "Greater East Asia Co-Prosperity Sphere" in 1933,[17] now understood as Japan's pretext for invading East Asia, causes deep, gut-wrenching pain to the peoples of East Asia, particularly in China and Korea. Consequently, down to the present, the term "East Asia" is heavily burdened with historical baggage.[18] With the rise of China at the beginning of the twenty-first century, memories of the historical Chinese empire have begun to engage the attention of the academic world.[19] It is a historical fact that "East Asian Confucianisms" arose on the Shandong Peninsula some 2,500 years ago, and some scholars suspect that if China develops into a superpower in the twenty-first century then the advocacy of the values of "East Asian Confucianisms" in China would simply lead to an atavistic revival of "national" Chinese learning and culture in the twenty-first century. For this reason, the term "East Asia" that appears in the expression "East Asian Confucianisms" should be understood as a methodology rather than as a reality, in order to avoid its being subverted into an illicit new-imperialist discourse.[20]

Second, since the term "East Asian Confucianisms" presents Confucianisms on the platform of East Asia, we might wonder whether and how Confucianism could transcend this platform of East Asia and become a source of universal values for the age of globalization.

The two above-mentioned considerations touch upon two problems that warrant deeper discussion: (1) the problem of the conflict between political and cultural identity faced by Confucians in all of the East Asian countries, and (2) the problem of how the cultural subjectivity of Confucians in each East Asian country can manifest itself in shared universal values.

The core of the first problem lies in whether Confucian studies can transcend the confines of the state. The answer to this question is twofold. Viewed from the perspective of political identity, since the seventeenth century, after the rise of a regional East Asian national identity, Confucian scholars have found it extremely difficult to escape from the nationalistic platform of their respective countries. During the seventeenth century, from the time when Yamazaki Ansai 山崎闇齋 (1618–1682) posed the hypothetical question to his students, "What if Confucius and Mencius were to lead a mounted army of several ten thousands to attack our realm,"[21] until the Tokugawa Confucian scholars Yamaga Sokō 山鹿素行 (1622–1685), Asami Keisai 淺見絅齋 (1652–1711), Kōtsuki Sen'an 上月專庵 (1704–1752), Sakuma Taika 佐久間太華 (d. 1783), and Satō Issai 佐藤一齋 (1772–1859) reinterpreted *Zhongguo* 中國 as a political term,[22] they all manifested a national political identity, and it would have been difficult for them to transcend it. However, from the perspective of cultural identity, Confucians in each of the East Asian countries also shared the Confucian core values of *ren* and self-cultivation. Hence, these Confucian common core values ultimately transcended national boundaries and can be regarded as values that might be shared by all of humankind.

On the basis of the foregoing discussion, we may argue that, at root, Confucianism is a unique theory of self-cultivation, and it is also a collection of values of cultural identity. In this sense, Confucianism certainly could transcend the nationalistic confines of each country in East Asia. As these countries enter the twenty-first century, memories of past wars and other horrors are gradually fading away. However, both postwar economic competition and recent struggles in the East China Sea and the South China Sea are driving the continuing ethnocentrism of the East Asian people, and war clouds are beginning to form overhead. In light of this situation, the widespread adoption of the cultural identity of East Asian Confucianisms should be regarded as a matter of paramount importance.

Again, many of the doubts concerning the term "East Asia" in the expression "East Asian Confucianisms" arise because of the historical burden carried by imperial Japan from the 1930s and 1940s. Facing this problem, we are in complete agreement with the opinion of Wu Zhen 吳震, who said,

The "East Asia discourse" of imperial Japan is a relic of history. It is a matter that Japanese scholars in particular are responsible to investigate. Likewise, however, it is not suitable for Chinese scholars to treat East Asian Confucian studies as a linear or monolithic body of discourse. At the same time, it must be admitted that the Japanese scholars' troubled consciousness regarding that era and [the need to develop a] critical consciousness certainly merits our close attention. Their critical suggestions regarding the problem of the term "East Asia" certainly should inspire our deep reflection.[23]

Finally, the question remains: Can Confucianism shed its regional "East Asian" platform to provide truly universal values to be accepted by humanity around the world in this age of globalization? I consider the answer to this question to be in the affirmative.

The "universal values" of today, such as democracy, freedom, liberty, and human rights, all arose during the past 250 years in Europe and North America. Ironically, the Western powers were controlling and ruthlessly exploiting colonies in Asia, Africa, Latin America, and elsewhere at the very time that they were developing and promulgating such "universal" values. The Confucian traditions that arose and developed over time in East Asia, with their loftiness, breadth, and depth, naturally can be reinterpreted through "interpretive, bridging, and normative"[24] approaches and will certainly emerge as the source of truly universal values for the twenty-first-century age of globalization, most notably their shared core values of *ren,* self-cultivation, and the kingly way (*wangdao* 王道). In the civilizational dialogue of the new age, these values can offer new inspiration and new meaning.

This essay has explored several problems regarding East Asian Confucianisms as a new field of study. The second section explored how the Confucian traditions that arose in various East Asian countries—China, Japan, Korea, and Vietnam—shared a common thread, or tapestry, of core values in the midst of the exchanges and interactions among Confucian scholars in these different countries, but certainly not as a definite and fixed consciousness over and above each country's Confucianism. For this reason, as an ideology East Asian Confucianisms has advanced and diversified in accordance with the times, and has constantly adapted to suit local intellectual traditions and trends. Although the Confucians of each country in East Asia definitely hold different specific values and have widely differing attitudes and practices, they continue to share several fundamental core values, such as *ren* and self-cultivation.

In the third section above it was pointed out that the field of East Asian Confucianisms provides a relatively broad intellectual prospect. It involves the commitment to shed the confines of the narrow nationalistic ethnocentrism advocated in the twentieth century by each of the East Asian countries, and moreover to adopt its broad purview to observe the development process of cultural subjectivity in each East Asian country and locale. The very idea of a field of East Asian Confucianisms should stir scholars to rectify the "reflexive Orientalism" of twentieth-century scholars in each East Asian country and anticipate that scholars in the twenty-first century will reexamine this East Asian cultural mainstream and its core values.

The political identity of Confucians in each East Asian country should completely remove the limitations of their nationalistic ethnocentrism, and cause each to bear in mind that the Confucian world of thought is an even more fundamental cultural homeland. In the twenty-first-century age of globalization, the field of East Asian Confucianisms and its common core values, which originated and developed in East Asia, hold tremendous potential for offering a platform on which to host cross-civilizational dialogue in the new century.

Notes

1. Yu Ying-shih 余英時, "Dai Zhen yu Itō Jinsai" 戴震與伊藤仁齋 (Dai Zhen and Itō Jinsai), *Shi huo yuekan* 食貨月刊 (Shi huo monthly) 4, no. 9 (December 1974): 369–376; Huang Chun-chieh 黃俊傑, "Dongya jinshi ruxue sichao de xindondxiang—Dai Dongyuan, Itō Jinsai, yu Ding Chashan dui Mengxue de jieshi" 東亞近世儒學思潮的新動向－戴東原、伊藤仁齋與丁茶山對孟學的解釋 (The new tide of modern East Asian Confucianisms: Dai Zhen, Itō Jinsai, and Ding Chasan on the interpretation of Mengzi), *Han'guk hakbo* 韓國學報 (Korea journal) 1 (April 1981), later collected in Huang Chun-chieh, *Ruxue chuantong yu wenhua chuangxin* 儒學傳統與文化創新 (Confucianism and cultural creativity) (Taipei: Dongda Press, 1983), pp. 77–108. This article has also appeared in Korean; see Chung Inchai 鄭仁在, trans., *"Dong-a geunse Yuhak sajo ui sin donghyang— Dae Dongwon, Itō Jinsai, wa Dasan ui Maenghak e deahan haeseok"* 東亞近世儒學思潮의 신동향—戴東原「伊藤仁齋와다산의 孟學에 대한 해석, *Dasan hakbo* 茶山學報 (Seoul: Dasanhak Yeon'guwon), no. 6 (1984).

2. Cf. Chen Lai 陳來, *Dongya ruxue jiulun* 東亞儒學九論 (East Asian Confucianism: Nine essays) (Taipei: Sanlian Press, 2008); Guo Qiyong 郭齊勇, ed., *Dongya ruxue lunji* 東亞儒學論集 (East Asian Confucianisms: Collected essays) (Changsha: Yuelu Publishing House, 2011).

3. Huang Chun-chieh 黃俊傑, *"Dongya ruxue ruhe keneng?"* 東亞儒學如何可能？ (How is East Asian Confucianisms possible [as a field of study]?), *Qinghua xuebao* 清華學報 (Tsing Hua journal) 33, no. 2 (December 2003): 55–68, reprinted in Huang Chun-chieh 黃俊傑, ed., *Dongya ruxue: Jingdian yu quanshi de bianzheng* 東亞儒學：經典與詮釋的辯證 (East Asian Confucianisms: Dialectics of classics and interpretations) (Taipei: National Taiwan University Press, 2007), pp. 29–56.

4. I agree with Kan Huai-chen's account of this. See Kan Huai-chen 甘懷真, "Cong

ruxue zai Dongya dao Dongya ruxue: Dongya ruxue yanjiujihua de xingsi" 從儒學在東亞 到東亞儒學：東亞儒學研究計劃的省思 (From Confucianism in East Asia to East Asian Confucianism: Reflections on the research project on East Asian Confucianisms), *Dongya guannian shi jikan* 東亞觀念史集刊 (Journal of the history of ideas of East Asia) 1 (December 2011): 381–400, esp. p. 393.

5. Hiroshi Watanabe, "Jusha, Literati and Yangban: Confucians in Japan, China and Korea," in *Japanese Civilization in the Modern World V: Culturedness,* ed. Tadao Umesao, Catherine C. Lewis, and Yasuyuki Kurita, Senri Ethnological Studies 28 (Osaka: National Museum of Ethnology, 1990), pp. 13–30.

6. Su Yu 蘇輿, *Chunqiu fanlu yizheng* 春秋繁露義證 (Corroborated meaning of the *Chunqiu fanlu*), ed. Zhong Zhe 鐘哲 (Beijing: Zhonghua Book Company, 1996), "Ren, Yi, Fa 仁義法 no. 29," p. 50.

7. Han Yu 韓愈, "Yuan dao" 原道 (Inquiry into the Way). See Dong Dide 董第德, *Hanji jiaoquan* 韓集校詮 (Han Yu's collected writings with annotations) (Beijing: Zhonghua Book Company, 1986), vol. 1, chap. 11, p. 400.

8. Zhang Zai 張載, *Ximing* 西銘 (Western inscription), included in Okata Takehiro 岡田武彥, ed., *Zhouzhang quanshu* 周張全書 (Collected writings of Zhou [Dunyi] and Zhang [Zai]), *Heke yingyin jinshi Hanji congkan* 和刻影印近世漢籍叢刊 (Modern Chinese photo-engraved series), vol. 1 (Taipei: Kuangwen Book Company; Kyoto: Chubun Shuppansha, 1972), pp. 261–274.

9. Itō Jinsai 伊藤仁齋, "Jinsetsu" 仁說 (Treatise on humanity), in *Kogaku sensei shibunshū* 古學先生詩文集 (Collected literary works of ancient masters), in Kinsei Juka bunshū shūsei 近世儒家文集集成 (Harvest of early modern Confucian literature) series, book 1 (Tokyo: Perikansha, 1985), vol. 3, pp. 60–61.

10. Ōta Kinjo 大田錦城, "Shushi jinsetsu" 洙泗仁說, in *Nihon rinri ihen* 日本倫理 彙編 (Collected books on Japanese ethics) (Tokyo: Ikuseikai, 1901), vol. 9, 折衷學派の部, pp. 456–472.

11. Toshima Hōshū 豐島豐洲, "Jinsetsu" 仁說, Nihon Jurin sōsho 日本儒林叢書 (Japanese Confucianism book series) (Tokyo: Ho Shuppan, 1978), book 6, pp. 5–6.

12. Asami Keisai 淺見絅齋, "Kijinsetsu" 記仁說, *Keisai Sensei bunshū* 絅齋先生文集 (Literary anthology of Mr. Keisai), *Kinsei Juka bunshū shūsei* 近世儒家文集集成 (Anthology of early modern Confucian literature), book 2 (Tokyo: Perikansha, 1987), vol. 6, pp. 124–125.

13. Yang Rubin 楊儒賓, "Ren yu Lunyu de Dongya shijie" 仁 與 論語的東亞世界 (*Ren* and the East Asian world of the *Analects*), *Taiwan Dongya wenming yanjiu xuekan* 臺灣東亞文明研究學刊 (Taiwan journal of East Asian studies) 5, no. 1 (July 2008): 253–256, esp. p. 255.

14. Yoshikawa Kōjirō 吉川幸次郎, *Wode liuxueji* 我的留學記 (My journey of studying abroad), trans. Qian Wanyue 錢婉約 (Beijing: Guangming Daily Press, 1999), p. 4.

15. Itō Tarō 伊藤太郎, *Nihon tamashi ni yoru Rongo kaishaku gakuji daiichi* 日本魂 による論語解釋學而第一 (Interpretation of the first volume of the *Analects* based on the Japanese soul) (Tsu City: Rongo Kenkyūkai, 1935), table on pp. 34–35.

16. Since 2009, Jörn Rüsen has co-edited with others the series *Der Mensch im Netz der Kulturen—Humanismus in der Epoche der Globalisierung* = Being Human: Caught in

the Web of Cultures—Humanism in the Age of Globalization (Bielefeld: Transcript Verlag, 2009–). Since 2012, he has started editing with others another series, *Reflections on[/in] Humanity* (Göettingen and Taipei: V & R Unipress and National Taiwan University Press, 2012–).

17. *Daitōa kyōdō sengen* 大東亞共同宣言 (Greater East Asia joint declaration) (Tokyo: Shinkigensha, 1946).

18. Ironically, the Japanese imagined themselves as "Other" than East Asia due to their island status and their affinities with Europe. (If this seems odd, the United Kingdom often likes to imagine itself as unique and different from Western Europe.)

19. Charles Horner, *Rising China and Its Postmodern Fate: Memories of Empire in a New Global Context* (Athens: University of Georgia Press, 2009).

20. Koyasu Nobukuni 子安宣邦, *Dongya ruxue: Pipan yu fangfa* 東亞儒學：批判與方法 (East Asian Confucianism: Critique and method), trans. Chen Wei-fen 陳瑋芬 (Taipei: National Taiwan University Press, 2003), pp. 17–18. Wu Zhen 吳震 pointed out, "The Japanese used the expression 'East Asia' to oppose the realization and unification of East Asia. They in effect treated 'East Asia' as their 'Other' and 'Methodologized' it according to their plans." This is a shrewd and penetrating insight. See Wu Zhen 吳震, "Shishuo 'Dongya ruxue' heyibiyao" 試說 "東亞儒學" 何以必要 (The necessity of East Asian Confucianisms), *Taiwan Dongya wenming yanjiu xuekan* 臺灣東亞文明研究學刊 (Taiwan journal of East Asian studies) 8, no. 1 (June 2011): 301–320, esp. p. 306.

21. Hara Nensai 原念齋, *Sentetsu sōdan* 先哲叢談 (Collected anecdotes of former philosophers), vol. 3 (Edo: Keigendo 慶元堂, Yomando 擁萬堂, 1816), pp. 4–5.

22. See Huang Chun-chieh 黃俊傑, *Dongya wenhua jiaoliu zhong de rujia jingdian yu linian: Hudong, zhuanhua yu ronghe* 東亞文化交流中的儒家經典與理念：互動、轉化與融合 (The Confucian classics and concepts of cultural exchange in East Asia: Interactive, transformation, integration) (Taipei: National Taiwan University Press, 2012), chap. 4, pp. 85–98.

23. Wu Zhen 吳震, "Guanyu 'Dongya ruxue' de ruogan wenti" 關於 "東亞儒學" 的若干問題 (Questions concerning "East Asian Confucianisms"), *Rujia wenhua yanjiu* 儒家文化研究 (Studies in Confucian culture), vol. 6, *Zhongguo zhexue yu haiwai zhexue yanjiu zhuanhao* 中國哲學與海外哲學研究專號 (Special issue on Research in Chinese philosophy and overseas philosophy) (Beijing: SDX Joint Publishing Company, 2013), p. 442.

24. Robert Neville has said that contemporary Western scholars who investigate Chinese philosophy and Confucianism proceed by "interpretive, bridging, and normative" paths. See Robert Cummings Neville, *Boston Confucianism: Portable Tradition in the Late-Modern World* (Albany: State University of New York Press, 2000), pp. 43ff.

CHAPTER 6

The Formation and Limitations of Modern Japanese Confucianism

Confucianism for the Nation and Confucianism for the People

NAKAJIMA Takahiro

IN CONSIDERING THE FORMATION and development of modern Confucianism in Japan, it would be useful here to keep two key concepts in mind. The first is "Confucianism for the nation," a school of thought that existed for the purpose of creating the Japanese nation; the second is "Confucianism for the people," another body of teachings, rooted in commoner society, that was separate from and transcended the bounds of nation-making. The modernized teachings of Wang Yangming (hereafter referred to as Yōmei-gaku, as it is designated in Japanese) are what allowed these two Confucianisms to take shape in tandem. It must be noted that this modern Yōmei-gaku was an exceedingly unique interpretation of the Ming dynasty teachings that it referenced. It was greatly informed by the experiences of early modern and modern Japan—that is, from the end of the eighteenth century to the start of the Meiji period and after.

This chapter synthesizes prior research and details the process by which these two Confucianisms emerged as twins. Furthermore, it examines one aspect of the thought of Ishizaki Tōgoku, who established the academic society called the Osaka Yōmei Gakkai, as an important example of Confucianism for the people. Following that, it seeks to uncover a potential path toward another set of universalities within Confucianism for the people that are different from those sought after by Confucianism for the nation.

The Popularization of Confucianism in Early Modern Japan

Zhu Xi (1130–1200) was a philosopher of the Song dynasty who revitalized Confucianism in the wake of the pervading influence of Buddhism. By introducing *li* 理 (principle), and *qi* 氣 (vital force), he renewed the possibility of fully explaining this world without referring to some transcendent deity like the Buddha. Wang Yangming (1472–1529) followed Zhu Xi with a critical attitude toward the latter's teachings. He criticized Zhu's investigation of *li* as often resulting in a reading of the canons that was too complicated and separated from human practical experience. Instead Wang emphasized the importance of the unification of knowledge and action. His philosophy influenced the then-rising middle class, which included rich merchants and farmers.

After the Kansei Edict was issued in 1790 in Japan, *Zhuzixue* 朱子学 (Zhu Xi's philosophy) began to spread throughout the country. It became an ideology in support of the system for recruiting civil servants. Along with *Zhuzixue, Yangmingxue* 陽明学 (Wang Yangming's philosophy) was also taught. Japanese Confucianists in the Edo period learned both at the same time, but *Zhuzixue* was of much greater importance.

In the Meiji period, when Japan started its program of modernization, *Yangmingxue* was regarded as a guiding ideology of modernized Confucianism. It contributed to the creating of a modern notion of interiority in the individual through its emphasis on *xin* 心 (heart/mind).

As a part of the modernization that began during the Meiji period, Confucianism contributed greatly to the making of the Japanese nation. What made this possible was the popularizing of Confucianism, which progressively spread to the various regions of Japan from the end of the eighteenth century. Miyagi Kimiko describes it thus:

> During the *Bakumatsu* period [the last period of the Tokugawa shogunate], the Kansei Edict enriched the Confucian temple [Seidō] and simultaneously facilitated an increase in the establishment of domainal schools in each domain, which led to the implementation of the *gakumon ginmi* system as a means of clearing the way for the employment of lower-level *samurai;* with these elements, a feverish enthusiasm for Confucian education gestated across the land. It spread to commoners who were wealthy peasants and merchants, who studied Confucianism with an eye toward acquiring warrior rank, and thus was Confucian learning popularized. In other words, the learning undertaken by warriors of lower rank and commoners under the old shogunate government was Confucian learning; regardless of one's status or family background, it was the one narrow road that had to be trod in order for one to establish oneself.

As such, Confucianism for these commoners did not constitute learning chosen of their own free will. Instead it was something they learned as a historical given, a decision prone to becoming part of an unconscious structural paradigm.

Moreover, the Meiji government that eventually confronted them used this popularized Confucian learning as a tool of national education on the one hand, but aspired to European-style modernization flying the flag of "civilization and enlightenment" [on the other]. Under a Meiji government thus engaged, these men faced the destiny of having to take on the various problems of Japan's modernization in their capacity as intellectuals trained in Confucianism. While they were living out this destiny, what they inherited from the previous era undoubtedly formed the locus of opposition to the Meiji government.[1]

The Kansei Edict was a statute issued in the fifth month of 1790 by the *rōjū* (senior councilor) Matsudaira Sadanobu to Hayashi Nobutaka, the *daigaku-no-kami* who served as head of education at the shogunate. The disciples of the Hayashi family prohibited the learning of alternate Confucianisms exemplified by the Kobunji-gaku and Kogaku (Ancient Learning) of Itō Jinsai and Ogyū Sorai, respectively, and attempted an enforced conversion to the teachings of Zhu Xi (hereafter Shushi-gaku 朱子学). But this all begs the question of what the purpose of this reform was. According to Miyagi, Matsudaira was worried that Confucian teachings had become mere academic debates between scholars, making this knowledge irrelevant to political affairs. The reform was, thus, in order to promote a so-called "'unity of governance and education,' to realize a situation where government officials were also Confucianists."[2] Given this situation, how, then, was this "unity of government and education" to be enacted? The answer was to enlist fresh talent equipped with Confucian education into the government. This led, in the ninth month of 1792, to the promulgation of the *gakumon ginmi,* a system modeled on the Chinese civil-service examinations by which men of merit were appointed to political office. These examinations utilized the commentaries of Zhu Xi, a practice that resulted in the predominance of Shushi-gaku.[3]

The crucial point here is that in this way the system of recruiting talented men to office in the shogunate government spread to the various domains, causing an increase in domainal schools, where the practice of appointing officials by examinations was implemented. Thus, the enthusiasm for Confucian education spread even further to the commoners; a growing number of rural schools and private academies were opened, and these became the basic infrastructure of Confucian learning in commoner society. Miyagi terms this phenomenon "the popularization of Confucianism."[4] Moreover, as striking examples of "rich

peasants and merchants [who came] from [among] the commoners" who successfully gained autonomy through studying Confucian teachings, Miyagi lists,
among others, Bitō Jishū, Rai Shunsui, Fujita Yūkoku, and Yamada Hōkoku.[5]

Within this group, the most attention has been given to Yamada Hōkoku
(1805–1877). Hōkoku was a peasant in the Bitchū-Matsuyama domain, an area
now known as Okayama Prefecture, who plied his trade in the plant-oil extraction industry. When he was five years old, he entered a private academy run by
one Marukawa Shōin located in the neighboring Niimi domain. Shōin had studied Shushi-gaku at the famous Kaitokudō in Osaka, and had been sounded out
by Matsudaira Sadanobu himself as a candidate for the post of official instructor
to the Confucian temple. Hōkoku later studied in Kyoto, and also went to Edo
to become a pupil of Satō Issai, head instructor of the Shōheikō, the official academy of the *bakufu*. Between his stints in these two places, he studied Yōmei-gaku
in addition to Shushi-gaku, and ended up being so favorably disposed toward the
former that he began criticizing the latter. However, just as Satō Issai adopted a
stance of "Zhu in public, Wang in private"—a position also called "The *yang* of
Zhu and the *yin* of Wang"—Hōkoku, as the official Confucianist of the Matsu-
yama domain, based his pedagogy on Shushi-gaku at the domainal school, while
treading carefully with teaching Yōmei-gaku. In addition, though Yōmei-gaku
actually constituted the true ideal for Hōkoku, he himself possessed even stronger views that went beyond the Yōmei school of learning.[6]

In this way, within the "popularization of Confucianism" that followed the
Kansei Edict's ban of heterodox Confucianism, Shushi-gaku was not the only
school of learning that was valued; it is certain that Yōmei-gaku also exerted
influence at the same time. But this is not to say that Yōmei-gaku was directly
involved with the Meiji Restoration.[7] Nonetheless, during the formation of
modern Yōmei-gaku, a discourse circulated that it was Yōmei-gaku that actually
constituted the real spirit of the Restoration.

Forming Modern Yōmei-gaku: Connections from the Bakumatsu to Meiji Eras

The interpretation of Yōmei-gaku as the true spirit of the Meiji Restoration
spread widely, and this became the understanding shared even by modern Chinese intellectuals. Ogyū Shigehiro sums it up in the following manner:

> After Japan's war with Qing China [in 1894–1895], the Qing imperial
> government, in imitation of the Meiji Restoration, enacted policies of
> modernization, and many Chinese exchange students traveled to Japan.
> Moreover, exiled officials and revolutionaries also made Japan a base
> for their activities. Liang Qichao, Zhang Binglin, and even Sun Wen

[Zhongshan/Yat-sen] were examples of such figures. They "discovered" the Yōmei-gaku then popular in Japan at the time, and carried [with them back to China] the understanding that Yōmei-gaku constituted the motivating force of the Restoration.[8]

Moreover, Ogyū casts the Yōmei-gaku of modern Japan that the Chinese exchange students "discovered" in terms of a political discourse that is profoundly nationalistic, saying that "it was a 'modern' Japanese thought started anew in the midst of modern Japanese nationalism in the second decade of the Meiji era, a growing flourish of resistance to the governmental policies of Europeanization since the founding year of Meiji. Furthermore, it was a political discourse intentionally constructed to comprise the contemporary assertions of the Meiji era."[9]

Following this assessment, Japan's modern Yōmei-gaku can be seen as represented by two works published in the same year: Tokutomi Sohō's *Yoshida Shōin* (Minyūsha, 1893) and Miyake Setsurei's *Ō Yōmei* (Wang Yangming) (Seikyōsha, 1893). In addition, there was the magazine published by the Tekka Shoin company in 1896 called *Yōmei-gaku* (discontinued in 1900) and its successor serials, the *Ō-gaku zasshi* (Meizen Gakusha, 1906–1908) and the *Yōmei-gaku* (Meizen Gakusha and Yōmei Gakkai [from issue 2], 1908–1928). Each of these publications positioned Yōmei-gaku as the foundation of "national morality."[10]

One of the most important works was Inoue Tetsujirō's *Nihon Yōmei-gakuha no tetsugaku* (Japanese philosophy of the Yangming school) (Fuzambō, 1900), followed by *Nihon Kogakuha no tetsugaku* (Japanese philosophy of the Kogaku [Classical Study] school) (Fuzambō, 1902) and *Nihon Shushi-gakuha no tetsugaku* (Japanese philosophy of the Zhuzi school) (Fuzambō, 1905)— a trilogy of books that examined Edo-period Confucianism. The first of his works in this series, as mentioned above, was the treatise on Yōmei-gaku. In this volume, Inoue delineates a genealogy of Japanese Yōmei-gaku scholars, starting with Nakae Tōju and Kumazawa Banzan, moving on to Satō Issai, Ōshio Chūsai [Heihachirō], Yamada Hōkoku, and Kasuga Sen'an, and concluding with Saigō Takamori, Yoshida Shōin, and Takasugi Shinsaku. It is of deep interest that Katsu Kaishū of the shogunate camp is the final personage that Inoue presents at the end of this genealogy. In short, Inoue attempts to connect the Bakumatsu-era Yōmei-gaku with the Meiji Restoration by giving this idea an erudite lineage.

Inoue's understanding of Japanese Yōmei-gaku as official learning was shared not only by Chinese intellectuals who studied in Japan; in fact, even men of a stance foreign to Inoue's who challenged his outlook were part of that same paradigm.

Christianity and Yōmei-gaku: Uchimura Kanzō and Nitobe Inazō

For example, let's consider the Christian scholar Uchimura Kanzō. During the ceremonial reading of the Imperial Rescript on Education in 1891 at the First Higher School, Uchimura had refused to make the expected deep bow and received the label of being "disrespectful." Inoue Tetsujirō critiqued this incident as a "clash between education and religion." This same Uchimura penned a tract titled *Representative Men of Japan* in 1908, beginning it with an analysis of Saigō Takamori and ending with one of Nichiren, and lauding Saigō—a central figure in the Meiji Restoration—as the bearer of a Yōmei-gaku kind of spirit. Uchimura described Saigō as follows: "only for the lack of Puritanism, he was not a Puritan."[11] Yet this comparison of Saigō, a scholar of Yōmei-gaku, with a Christian believer suggests another possible avenue for understanding Yōmei-gaku, one that differs from Inoue's vision of it as a bastion of official learning:

> His [Saigō's] attention was early called to the writings of Wang Yang Ming, who of all Chinese philosophers, came nearest to that most august faith, also of Asiatic origin, in his great doctrines of conscience and benign but inexorable heavenly laws. Our hero's subsequent writings show this influence to a very marked degree, all the Christianly sentiments therein contained testifying to the majestic simplicity of the great Chinese, as well as to the greatness of the nature that could take in all that, and weave out a character so practical as his....
>
> ... So unlike the conservative Chu philosophy fostered by the old government for its own preservation, it (Yang Ming philosophy) was progressive, prospective, and full of promise. Its similarity to Christianity has been recognized more than once, and it was practically interdicted in the country on that and other accounts. "This resembles Yang-Ming-ism; disintegration of the empire will begin with this." So exclaimed Takasugi Shinsaku, a Chōshu strategist of Revolutionary fame, when he first examined the Christian Bible in Nagasaki. That something like Christianity was a component force in the reconstruction of Japan is a singular fact in this part of its history.[12]

On reading this passage, it becomes clear that Uchimura was trying to connect Christianity to Japan via Yōmei-gaku by means of his reading of Saigō as a Christian-like adherent of Yōmei-gaku. But even so, it must be remembered that this reading was undertaken in Inoue's paradigm of Yōmei-gaku as a motivating force of the Meiji Restoration. It then follows that even Uchimura's deep understanding of Christian teachings cannot overturn the framing of Yōmei-gaku as official learning.

Kojima Tsuyoshi offers a concrete example of this that involves the relationship between Inoue and Nitobe Inazō, who was a Christian scholar and a close friend of Uchimura. The stage for this episode occurred at a meeting of the Yōmei Gakkai, an academic society, and it was hosted by the publishers of the aforementioned serial, the *Yōmei-gaku* (Meizen Gakusha and Yōmei Gakkai [from issue 2], 1908–1928). The Yōmei Gakkai's first lecture event was held on March 21, 1909; both Inoue Tetsujirō and Nitobe Inazō attended and co-lectured on the topic of "A Nonprofessional View of Yōmei-gaku":

> Nitobe actually ascended to the same lectern as Inoue Tetsujirō. At the time, Nitobe had already assumed the post of principal of the First Higher School [its official appellation from 1894 onwards, which he held from 1906 to 1913]. The same school that had ousted Uchimura for "disrespect" ended up appointing his close friend and fellow Christian as its head. The previous year, Nitobe's *Bushidō* had been translated into Japanese by Sakurai Ōson, and it is thought that this was why he had been invited to speak at this lecture event. It is unclear when he joined the Society, but it is certain that he was a member in good standing of the Yōmei Gakkai.[13]

After the Russo-Japanese War, Christianity became incorporated into the religious policies of the Meiji government, and Inoue, perhaps softening his own stance toward Christian thought, did not take Nitobe's lecture to be a critique of Yōmei-gaku as official learning.[14]

Assuming that was indeed the case, distinctions like the ones drawn by Yamashita Ryūji in the following excerpt are not necessarily admissible:

> This same Inoue used Yōmei-gaku in the manner of an explanatory manual for the Imperial Rescript on Education. He praised the notion of "national morality," offering the view that Yōmei-gaku's practical approach could be useful for the purpose of controlling the influence of various kinds of European-style philosophies and ideologies and guiding the nation toward "moral practices." This carried the premise that statist ethics allowed no criticism, and resulted in Yōmei-gaku's inherently anti-authoritarian and anti-official tendencies to be abstracted away. The face-off between Inoue and Uchimura over the Imperial Rescript on Education was also a contest over how to interpret Yōmei-gaku. It was a contest between a statist ethical perspective and an individualist ethical perspective, a contest between the ethical interpretation and the religious interpretation, and also a contest between Japanism and cosmopolitanism. And it goes without saying that Inoue's stance became the orthodoxy in the Yōmei-gaku research that followed thereafter.[15]

Yamashita saw what he terms "Yōmei-gaku's inherently anti-authoritarian and anti-official tendencies" in Uchimura Kanzō, and considered these tendencies to have been oppressed by Inoue Tetsujirō's "statist ethics"—a conclusion that manages to ignore how Uchimura, in fact, shared the paradigm of Inoue's thought. Moreover, the situation gets even more complicated, because Inoue himself actually read "anti-authoritarian and anti-official tendencies" into Yōmei-gaku.

Confucianism for the Nation and Confucianism for the People as Twins

On the one hand, Inoue positioned Yōmei-gaku as Confucianism for the nation, which existed in order to create the nation of Japan; on the other, he thought that Yōmei-gaku stemmed from commoner society. Let us look at the preface to his *Nihon Yōmei-gakuha no tetsugaku*:

> If one desires to understand what the national morality of our country is like, he must reach comprehension of the spirit of the moral teaching [Confucianism] that has smelted and fired our national mentality. Thus, since this treatise is a place to describe the philosophy of Japan's Yōmei-gaku, it also tries to contribute to that end. If one would certify the manifestation of our national morality by realities occurring before our eyes, they only have to observe the actions of our army in China. What indeed is that which, amidst the united forces of the various nations, radiates so conspicuously? That which refrains from arbitrary plunder, from wanton violence, keeping strict observance of military discipline, and [is] never motivated by the desire for private gain—what indeed is it, if not the manifestation of our national morality?[16]

This preface is inscribed with the date of September 24, 1900. Here Inoue argued that Japan's Yōmei-gaku was in fact what had forged modern Japan's "national morality," and spoke proudly of how it was clearly displayed by the actions of the Japanese army, fighting in the Eight-Nation Alliance, to suppress the Boxer Rebellion that had taken place in June of the same year. Furthermore, the preface closes with the statement that "our national morality is nothing but the universal virtue of mind, and the universal virtue of mind can be said to be precisely the essence of Oriental morality."[17] For Inoue, Japan's Yōmei-gaku possessed universality through having a character for the nation.

Nonetheless, at the same time Inoue could also say that Yōmei-gaku differed from Shushi-gaku in that it was something wielded by "commoner scholars," and that it was "for the most part a doctrine for the commoners [平民主義]." Moreover, this work proclaimed its intention to "break the gloom" that had shrouded Yōmei-gaku's two hundred and fifty years of existence, and that its existence constituted "an excellent thing":

> Because Shushi-gaku was the educational ideology of the government, Yōmei-gaku was primarily promoted by commoner scholars; it produced a distinction between official and commoner learning, and made Yōmei-gaku for the most part a doctrine for the commoners. The teachings of Zhu and Wang were originally different in their ideas, constituting different standpoints between official and commoner spheres. This distinction could not be stopped in the discord between them. Facts demonstrate why this should be so. Yōmei-gaku was ostracized by government authority, and thus fell into a state of gloom where it could not expand its horizons. Now we have forged ahead into a world of free thinking. In this age, it is an excellent thing for the scholarly world to research the historical development of Yōmei-gaku, and to break the gloom that has shrouded it for two hundred and fifty years.[18]

Here, the important point in Inoue's thinking—as if to tear apart the distinction that Yamashita attempted to make—is that Inoue saw the "doctrine for the commoners" that Yōmei-gaku constituted as Confucianism for the people was potentially shifting toward Confucianism for the nation. Confucianism for the nation and Confucianism for the people were born as twins. That is precisely why, right after Kōtoku Shūsui had been executed in January 1911 for his involvement in the Great Treason Incident of 1910, Inoue had been able to speak of how Yōmei-gaku was connected to socialism.[19]

In one sense, this was only to be expected: if, like Inoue, one affirmed the revolution enacted by the Meiji Restoration and saw Yōmei-gaku as its philosophical pillar, then Yōmei-gaku could only be viewed as a revolutionary ideology. The problem here is that this view deviates from the trajectory of the nation created in the age of Meiji, and cannot be contained in the conceptual scope of "national morality." Within modern Japanese Yōmei-gaku, the potential for Confucianism for the people to transcend the bounds of nation-making is found elsewhere—in the Osaka Yōmei Gakkai established by Ishizaki Tōgoku.

The Osaka Yōmei Gakkai and the "Popular Foundation"

Ishizaki Tōgoku (1873–1931) established an academic society in June of 1907 under the official name of the Senshindō Gakkai (after the private academy set up by Ōshio Chūsai [Heihachirō]), before changing its name to the Osaka Yōmei Gakkai in December 1908. Its flagship magazine, *Yōmei,* was serialized from July 1910 and its name changed to *Yōmei-shugi* in 1919.[20]

The December 5, 1911 issue of *Yōmei* commemorated Nakae Chōmin, and carried a photo of him on its cover along with a citation from chapter 6 of his *Minyaku yakkai* (a translation of Jean-Jacques Rousseau's *Social Contract*); the comment honoring him ran as follows:

> It has been a full ten years since the passing of Master Nakae Chōmin, the Meiji scholar of Yōmei-gaku, who for fifty-five years fought so well for society and humanity. December 13 of this year marks the anniversary of his death. Our association cannot help but admire the master's character, particularly from the vantage point of today's society, and we have thus put together this commemorative volume.[21]

From the start, it had never been intended for this 1911 issue simply to commemorate the tenth anniversary of Nakae Chōmin's death (December 13, 1901). During the Great Treason Incident of the previous year (1910), Kōtoku Shūsui and Okunomiya Kenshi (the son of Okunomiya Zōsai, with whom Chōmin had studied) had been hauled off to prison; regarding this, Tōgoku had written about Chōmin saying, "this desolation is unbearable" (July 29, 1910), which was regarded by Inoue Tetsujirō as a dangerous idea.[22] Moreover, two full pages of the *Shinmin sekai,* a tract written by Chōmin from the position of being a "new commoner [*shinmin*]," the Meiji name for those born into outcaste communities (*hisabetsu burakumin*), were carried in this issue. Tōgoku stridently asserted that the Yōmei-gaku that he believed in belonged to the genealogy established by Chōmin.[23]

Ogyū Shigehiro offers the following synthesis of the situation:

> The same Society (the Osaka Yōmei Gakkai), from its inception, had been labeled by Inoue Tetsujirō as a "dangerous ideology" that "ostensibly assumed to attend the conscience while covertly promoting socialism"; instead, it began vending its flagship magazine externally on the occasion of the Great Treason Incident, and while on the one hand it cast Nakae Chōmin and Kōtoku Shūsui in the genealogy of Meiji-era Yōmei-gaku, it criticized the Yōmei-gaku of Inoue and his ilk as [leaning toward] "government education" and "official learning," which deviated from the essence of Yōmei-gaku, conducting its activities while struggling upstream against the tide of the times.[24]

Ogyū draws out the possibility for the Osaka Yōmei Gakkai to be understood as Confucianism for the people. He says, "It took the 'problems of life' of the masses as its foundation, and cast it in the logic of an international pacific solidarity that transcended the nation-state, reviving itself in modern fashion."[25]

Quite apart from the universality sought after by Inoue Tetsujirō, it revealed the other universality based on a "popular foundation":[26]

> In closing, although he declared that he was cutting ties with the movement to revive Chinese learning [Kan-gaku 漢学: a government-sanctioned movement aimed at molding the morality of the nation], I wish to ascertain whether Tōgoku continued to value the spiritual connection with the Confucianism of the Edo period. Along with his companions in the Osaka Yōmei Gakkai, modern heterodox thinkers such as Iwano Hōmei, Matsumura Kaiseki, and Miyatake Gaikotsu, he supported regional scholars who partook of Bakumatsu-style Confucian learning. And it is especially interesting that the most left-wing member of the Osaka society, who positioned himself as stridently against Chinese learning and caused the society to be divided over his criticisms of Takase Takejirō, was none other than Ikeda Shisei, the step-grandchild of Ikeda Sōan, the Bakumatsu-era Yōmei scholar also known as the "sage of Tajima." Against the new forces of modern Yōmei-gaku espoused by men like Inoue [Tetsujirō] and Takase, who had been educated in the intellectual vein of the modern West, traditional learning was brought into the modern Yōmei-gaku of the people, suggesting a kind of "universal" characteristic that runs to this present day.[27]

In other words, the Osaka Yōmei-gaku inherited the mantle of a "popularization of Confucianism" from the Bakumatsu period; unlike the universality of Confucianism for the nation, which was based in the nation-state, it can be said to have aimed for a kind of earthly universality based on a popular foundation.

Earthly Universality

Let us review, from a different angle, the potential in Ishizaki Tōgoku for a Confucianism for the people that transcends the bounds of nation-making. In his *Yōmei-gakuha no jinbutsu* (1912), Tōgoku's very first chapter is titled "Master Yangming and Master Nichiren." This means he was attempting to interpret Nichiren as Japan's Wang Yangming.

Upon reading Tōgoku's autobiography, *The Path by Which I Entered Wang Yangming Studies* (*Yo no Ō-gaku ni irishi keiro*), it seems that he encountered Buddhism when he traveled to Takamatsu at the age of twenty-six:

> If pressed to explain the change in my thoughts, it was here in this origin point of Kōbō Daishi [Kūkai] that I made some acquaintance with reli-

gion; however, I became a follower of Nichiren's Hokke rather than of
Kōbō Daishi's Shingon.[28]

It is deeply interesting that Tōgoku mentions his decision to convert to Nichiren Buddhism instead of Kūkai's Shingon Buddhism. Tōgoku, in "Master Yangming and Master Nichiren," saw an overlap between Wang Yangming, who succeeded Lu Xiangshan instead of Zhu Xi, and Nichiren, who succeeded Saichō
instead of Kūkai.[29] Based on this, in contrast to how Zhu Xi and Kūkai "simply
figured out how to appeal to vulgarity and built up a fleeting popularity in their
times," Yangming and Nichiren "spurned vulgarity and presented [themselves]
as beneficial role models who contributed greatly to the improvement of society and the human heart-mind."[30] Tōgoku evaluated Yōmei-gaku and Nichiren Buddhism in tandem because he felt that both schools of thought had frequently intervened in social problems.

This is clearly borne out in Tōgoku's autobiography. On this note, he
moved from Takamatsu to Osaka, and Ōshio Heihachirō's Yōmei-gaku and
Nichiren were connected along with the "new commoners":

> Religion surfaced when there was an insight that social problems could
> not be solved by material things alone. The religion that appeared for me
> was Nichiren, which I had encountered during my time in Takamatsu.
> As if by chance, the fifth Exhibition [the fifth National Industrial Exhi-
> bition of 1903] was held in Osaka, which was also the home of the new
> commoners, and a fraternization event called the Congress of New Com-
> moners was also organized in the same year [in 1903 they formed the
> Dai Nihon Dōhō Yūwa Kai in Osaka]; I devoted myself to this congress
> and offered all kinds of assistance to it. As a result, while researching the
> new commoners, it came to me that Nichiren had been a new commoner
> himself as well as a religious reformer, and that Ōshio had helped the new
> commoners to raise an army against all odds.[31]

For Tōgoku, Yōmei-gaku amounted to a religion that could solve "social problems." His later crystallization of the concept of a "Yōmei sect" (Yōmei-shū)
stems from this interest in the religious dimension.

At this juncture it is probably necessary to say a few words about the relationship of Yōmei-gaku with Nichirenism in modern Japan. As we have already
seen, Uchimura Kanzō, in his *Representative Men of Japan,* mentioned Nichiren
as one of the five great figures. He also concluded his text by declaring that
"Nichiren *minus his combativeness* is our ideal religious man."[32]

Regarding this I wish to make just one observation. It is well known that
Miyazawa Kenji (1896–1933) converted from Pure Land Buddhism to Nichi-

ren Buddhism, then in 1920 joined the Kokuchūkai—a lay association of Nichiren headed by Tanaka Chigaku—and then later left it. According to Pullattu Abraham George, it was the teachings of the *Lotus Sutra* that enabled the reincarnation into Paradise through one's own chanting of the Buddha's name, while the salvation of every being was guaranteed by the practice and effort of the individual in this world.[33]

On the one hand, the Nichirenism of modern Japan actively intervened in and lent a helping hand to alleviate the social problems in this world, rather than in the afterlife; on the other hand, it thereby fell into a tendency toward statism such as found in the Kokuchūkai. Tōgoku, too, had periods during which he failed to gauge his own distance from the state.[34] However, both Tōgoku and Kenji ultimately turned toward the people.

After Kenji left the Kokuchūkai and returned to Iwate, he established an association called the Rasu Earthly Men Association (Rasu Chijin Kyōkai) in 1926 in the city of Hanamaki. "Earthly Men" (*chijin*) denotes farmers, but in a broader sense it might also refer to people who live on the earth. This activism did not last long, but Kenji attempted to lecture these "earthly men" on science and the arts. Part of his efforts included trying to teach Esperanto. In fact, Tōgoku also tried to publish the Osaka Yōmei-gakkai flagship magazine in Esperanto, but failed. Even so, both Kenji and Tōgoku, via Nichirenism and Esperanto, tried to aim for what I have called here an earthly universality rooted in the people.

Confucianism for the nation and Confucianism for the people as conceived in modern Japan were nourished from the same roots, but their aims stood in contrast to each other. Should Confucianism look to the nation-state? Or should it look to the people? This chapter has examined one part of that complicated process. However, when Confucianism itself was erased from social experience in Japan after the Second World War, it might seem as if studying these debates over Confucianism holds little meaning. Yet even so, insofar as modern Yōmei-gaku in Japan was deeply involved in the formation of Japan's modernity, failing to examine it critically presents the risk of falling into the same trap of historical understanding. Moreover, we would overlook the potential once held by Japan's modernity. Ultimately, the question is how we can talk about "earthly universality" today—an issue that we have surely been tasked to engage.

Notes

This chapter was translated into English by Shi Lin Loh and has been reviewed by the author.

1. Miyagi Kimiko, *Bakumatsu ki no shisō to shūzoku* (The thought and customs of the Bakumatsu period) (Tokyo: Perikansha, 2004), p. 24.

2. Ibid., p. 26.

3. Ibid., pp. 26–27.

4. Ibid., p. 27.

5. Ibid., p. 28.

6. The following is Miyagi Kimiko's summary: "Hōkoku's consistent philosophical motif is to reject 'constitutional artificiality,' deliberate intentionality, and utilitarian calculation, which the 'rational principle' of Shushi-gaku unexpectedly exposes, while emphasizing 'natural sincerity'; in his pursuit of genuine 'naturalness,' Hōkoku was criticizing even the 'constitutional artificiality' so bound up with Wang Yangming thought" (Miyagi, *Bakumatsu ki no shisō to shūzoku,* p. 127).

7. Sawai Keiichi, on the purported "absence of Yōmei-gaku" from the Bakumatsu to the initial period of Meiji, has observed: "During the latter stages of the early modern period it is true that many people interested in Yōmei-gaku appeared, but of the thinkers and activists that succeeded these people, only Kasuga Sen'an can be said to have been actually involved in the political movement called the Meiji Restoration" (Sawai Keiichi, "Kindai Yōmei-gaku' no tanjō" [The birth of modern Yōmei learning], UTCP [University of Tokyo Center for Philosophy] Lecture, May 5, 2014, p. 4).

8. Ogyū Shigehiro, *Kindai, Ajia, Yōmei-gaku* (Modernity, Asia, Yōmei learning) (Tokyo: Perikansha, 2008), p. 400.

9. Ibid., pp. 354–355.

10. Ibid., p. 356.

11. Uchimura Kanzō, *Representative Men of Japan,* vol. 2 of *The Complete Works of Kanzō Uchimura* (Tokyo: Kobunkwan, 1972), p. 38.

12. Ibid., pp. 14–15.

13. Kojima Tsuyoshi, *Kindai Nihon no Yōmei-gaku* (The Yōmei learning of modern Japan) (Tokyo: Kōdansha, 2006), pp. 115–116.

14. Ibid.

15. Yamashita Ryūji, "Min-dai shisō kenkyū wa dō susumeraretekita ka" (How has research into Ming thought progressed?), in *Nagoya Daigaku Bungaku-bu kenkyū ronshū* (*Tetsugaku*) (Nagoya University Literature Department research essays [Philosophy]) 12 (1964): 59–60.

16. Inoue Tetsujirō, *Nihon Yōmei-gakuha no tetsugaku* (Japanese philosophy of the Yangming school) (Tokyo: Fuzambō, 1900), p. 3.

17. Ibid., p. 6.

18. Ibid., pp. 2–3.

19. Kōtoku Shūsui had been a disciple of Nakae Chōmin; Nakae had studied with Mishima Chūshū, a bastion of Meiji-era Yōmei-gaku. The rest of this paragraph references the previous work by Kojima Tsuyoshi. Cf. Kojima, *Kindai Nihon no Yōmei-gaku,* pp. 123–125.

20. See Ogyū, *Kindai, Ajia, Yōmei-gaku,* p. 405.

21. *Yōmei* 2, no. 6 (December 5, 1911): 1.

22. Ibid., p. 13.

23. Tōgoku's self-affiliation with Chōmin's genealogy and his affirmation of a Yōmei-gaku that was an ally of the "new commoners" remained constant, as seen in his

Yōmei-gakuha no jinbutsu (Figures in the Yōmei School) (Osaka: Maekawa Shoten, Taishō 1 [1912]), which he published the following year. There he described Chōmin as "one of the Yōmei-gaku scholars I revere second only to Ōshio Chūsai" (p. 94), and further that "the revolutionary thought of the Yōmei-gaku scholars has been secretly indoctrinated" (p. 94). However, even saying this, the assertion that "Master Chōmin was actually a Yōmei scholar cultivated in the Okunomiya [Zōsai] academy" (p. 95) cannot be accepted at face value. Okunomiya Zōsai, father of the aforementioned Okunomiya Kenshi, was a Yōmei scholar on close terms with Ōshio Heihachirō. It is true that Chōmin received tutelage from Zōsai, but he never forgot his debt to his other teacher of Yōmei-gaku, namely Mishima Chūshū of the Nishō Gakusha. Chūshū was a stalwart of the Yomei Gakkai in Tokyo, and also instructed the Taishō Emperor on Yōmei-gaku for twenty years. Nonetheless, when considering the fact that Chūshū was a disciple of Yamada Hōkoku, earlier mentioned as the domainal Confucianist of the Bitchu-Matsuyama domain, it can be said that Chōmin was indeed connected to the genealogy of scholars in the vein of Confucianism for the people.

24. Ogyū, *Kindai, Ajia, Yōmei-gaku,* p. 406.

25. Ibid., p. 409.

26. Ibid., p. 411.

27. Ibid., pp. 409–410.

28. Ishizaki, *Yōmei-gakuha no jinbutsu,* p. 174.

29. Ibid., pp. 29–34.

30. Ibid., p. 35.

31. Ibid., p. 175.

32. Uchimura, *Representative Men of Japan,* p. 177.

33. Pullattu Abraham George and Komatsu Kazuhiko, eds., *Miyazawa Kenji no shinsō—Shūkyō kara no shōsha* (The deep structure of Miyazawa Kenji: Irradiation [i.e., Radiance] from religion) (Tokyo: Hōzōkan, 2012), p. 6.

34. Ishizaki, *Yōmei-gakuha no jinbutsu,* p. 173.

CHAPTER 7

Historical and Cultural Features of Confucianism in East Asia

CHEN Lai

ALTHOUGH IT ORIGINATED in China, Confucianism has spread far and wide across the East Asian Sinosphere. In the long process of its historical and cultural development, due to different geographical, historical, and social conditions, and to the different dispositions of each country, Confucianism in China, Japan, and Korea has formed its respective features. Generally speaking, compared to Chinese Confucianism, Korean Confucianism in theory is more internal and abstract (e.g., in the distinction of the Four Sprouts [*siduan* 四端] and the Seven Emotions [*qiqing* 七情]), while Japanese Confucianism shows more external and concrete features.[1] However, what I am concerned with in this chapter are the following questions: What, respectively, was the ethos of Confucianism in China, Japan, and Korea before the nineteenth century? And connected with this, what were their respective axiologies? Or, what are the value principles that predominated in each of these Confucianisms?

Among the comparative Asian cultural studies in recent years, especially those on East Asian Confucianism, the research of Mizoguchi Yūzō demands our special attention. Not only was he familiar with the contemporary thought of both Chinese and Japanese, but his writings also evidence broad views and deep insights in his own thinking. His thought shows a universal axiological concern that greatly enlightens those of us in comparative Confucian studies.[2] The main arguments of the present chapter are, briefly, as follows. Among the virtues that are advocated by Confucianism, viewed from the value orientation of social life, we can say that Chinese Confucianism emphasizes consummate persons/conduct (*ren* 仁), while it is appropriateness (or *yi* 义) that is emphasized in Korean Confucianism and doing one's utmost or showing loyalty (*zhong* 忠) in Japanese Confucianism. Or, taking a closer look, we can say that Chinese Confucianism emphasizes putting oneself in the other's place (*ren* and *shu* 恕), while it is appropriateness and temperance (*jie* 节) in Korean Confucianism and loyalty (*zhong* 忠) and bravery (*yong* 勇) in Japanese Confucianism. These differences in emphasis in the different countries are not only axiological but also cultural. The conclusions we might draw in East Asian cultural comparative studies not only emerge at the level of canonical literature and philosophy, but also from studies in sociology and anthropology.

I

The idea of *renai* 仁爱 ("consummate persons/conduct" or "benevolence and love") lies at the core of ancient Chinese Confucian cultural ideals. It can be traced back to the early idea of "protecting the people" in China. The *Shangshu* says, "Deal with them [the people] as if you were protecting your own infants, and the people will be tranquil and well."[3] Not only is this a political idea, but it also has ethical and axiological import. The *Shangshu* especially attaches great importance to protecting the old, the weak, the orphaned, and the young. It is said in the *Shangshu,* "Do not despise the old and experienced, and do not make light of the helpless and young."[4] Also it is said that one should "not dare to treat with contempt widowers and widows."[5] This special concern for old widows and widowers, and orphans as well, is the initial expression of a Chinese humanism. Actually, the true meaning of filial piety (*xiao* 孝) should be understood from this perspective. Filial piety is the cherishing of, and repaying of affection to, one's parents. It is the root not only of *ren* but also of its practice. This is why Cheng Yi 程颐 (Yichuan 伊川) says, "To practice *ren* one should start with *xiao* 孝 and *ti* 悌 ['filial piety' and 'love of one's elder brothers']. *Xiaoti* is one important event (*shi* 事) in the practice of *ren*."[6]

For Confucius, the most significant meanings of *ren* are expressed as follows: "Loving people"; "consummate persons wishing to be established themselves seek also to establish others; wishing to be enlarged themselves they seek also to enlarge others"; and also "Do not do to others what one would not wish done to oneself."[7] For Confucius, *ren* has become a universal ethical principle. Hence, the *Spring and Autumn Annals* reports that Confucius values *ren,* and Mozi values undiscriminating love.[8] Confucius takes *ren* as the highest ideal principle while Mozi takes undiscriminating love as the highest principle. Even Laozi raised similar ideas. He states, "I have three precious things that I prize and hold fast. And the first of these is *ci* 慈."[9] *Ci* means compassion and love. In this sense we can say that these three important early Chinese thinkers all affirmed the significance of *renai* in different ways.

In the Warring States period, Mencius proposed the idea of loving the people and things (*renmin aiwu* 仁民爱物). Zhuangzi's Huizi went further and evoked the idea of "overflowing in love for the ten thousand things, and becoming one body with the heavens and earth,"[10] an idea that has had a great influence on later Confucianism. This is why *ren* has risen to the most important position in Confucianism since the Tang dynasty. Han Yu 韩愈 said, "Broad love is *ren*";[11] Zhangzai 張載 stated that "the people are my siblings and things are my friends";[12] and Cheng Hao 程顥 claimed that "consummate persons are one with the heavens and the earth and the ten thousand things."[13] Cheng Yi once pointed out that "The primordial source of the four virtues is the *ren* of the five constant virtues (*wuchang* 五常). Specifically, *wuchang* refers to the virtue of *ren* itself; generally speaking, *ren* can include the other four virtues."[14] Zhu Xi also maintained that the *ren* of the four virtues (*ren* 仁, *yi* 义, *li* 礼, and *zhi* 智) can "include everything," and that "the heart-mind of compassion runs through everything."[15] These are all explicit examples that *ren* has been taken as the predominant principle of Confucianism. Even in the 1980s Li Zehou still used "studies of *ren*" (*renxue* 仁學) to reference Confucianism.[16]

As we have seen above, the Neo-Confucianism of the Song and Ming dynasties used *ren* to unify and designate the four virtues. In fact, in Chinese Confucianism, *ren* has a special connection with the values of love (*ai* 爱), harmony (*he* 和), generosity (*shu* 恕), and impartiality (*gong* 公), which taken together constitute the dominating axiology of Chinese Confucianism. These values have formed a dynamic correlation with the social regime in history, and are embodied in the everyday conduct of the people.

In his significant sociological work titled *Essentials of Chinese Culture,* Liang Shuming points out that *ren* is an ethical sentiment whereby people express concern for others, while with desires there is only concern for oneself. He states, "In short, what an ethical society values is respect for others.... Moral relations are deontological relations, in which one seems not to exist for oneself but rather for one another."[17] Liang therefore summarizes Confucian ethics as "valuing one another." This is a conclusion that emanates from his social practice of rural reconstruction. It can also be viewed as a development of the Qing Confucian Ruan Yuan's interpretation of *ren* as respect for each other (*xiang/renou* 相人偶). According to Liang, after the Duke of Zhou and Confucius proposed the moral ideal of *ren,* China was gradually transformed from a feudal society into an "ethical society."

This change can be illustrated by the following example. Consider two brothers growing up following their natural sentiments in one family with the same parents. One might wonder what would be the difference in their rights to inheritance. In feudal society, however, once they grew up and came to inherit the property of their parents, they would each face a different treatment. The elder brother would inherit both the official titles and the property while the younger brother would get nothing.

With respect to the origins of primogeniture, Henry Sumner Maine once pointed out a principle in his work *Ancient Law* that whenever the inheritance system has to do with the political system, primogeniture necessarily emerges.[18] Generally speaking, feudal structure and patriarchal order are established according to the political and economic needs of the time. Yet the community life of a super-family has such great power in suppressing family affections that even when it is unnecessary to hold on to primogeniture it nonetheless exists as before within the tradition. Before World War II, I went to visit some Japanese villages and saw something called "primogen-school." Puzzled, I asked the local people and was told that the rural fields are inherited only by the first son, and no one else can claim them. The other sons usually go to the urban centers to make a living, while the first sons stay in the countryside, giving rise to different educational needs. This phenomenon shows that their culture is not far removed from the feudal society and that the old customs still prevail. In fact, this custom was also preserved in European countries up until modern times.

Only China is different. In China, the inheritance was evenly split among all sons. According to Liang Qichao's *History of Chinese Culture,* the fact that this inheritance system lasted for almost two thousand years is not a minor matter, nor was it merely accidental. Its consequence was to dissolve the unnatural feudal order by bringing out the natural emotions and sensibilities of the human being. This is a salient example of morality replacing feudality.[19]

Seen from Liang Shuming's perspective, the emergence of *ren* represents the "reasonable early maturity" of Chinese culture. The reason I talk about this here is that it is similar to Max Weber's "axiological rationality." Not only has it greatly influenced China's social regime but it has also helped to direct the overall trajectory of Chinese history.

II

The anthropologist Ruth Benedict, famous for her studies in Japanese culture and axiology, held that *ren* never gained the high position in Japan that it has had in China. In her studies of the idea of gratitude (*baoen* 报恩) toward the emperor and one's parents, she points out that this gratitude is an infinite, unconditional obligation, and that it is more absolute compared to the Chinese idea of duty to one's country and filial piety to one's parents. Although both ideas of loyalty (*zhong* 忠) and filial piety (*xiao* 孝) come from China, they are not unconditional in China: "A virtue dominating all others is established in Chinese thinking. That is *ren*."[20] She remarks that the rulers in China have to practice *ren* or else they legitimate rebellion against the throne. However, "This

Chinese moral idea has never been accepted by the Japanese. In fact, in Japan *ren* has been excluded from the ethical system, holding no lofty position as it does in China."[21]

Robert Bellah believes that in premodern Japan the idea of loyalty to one's superior has dominated all other moral ideas and was viewed as the core value and first virtue during the Edo period:[22]

> As we see, in Japan the idea of loyalty has permeated the whole society and become the ideal of all classes, although in China it is even difficult for it to be applied to the scholar class (*shi* 士). It only applies to the officials.[23]

According to this theory, the dominant value and principle in premodern Japanese Confucianism and Japanese culture was loyalty (*zhong* 忠), under which a person's commitment to some specific system or group trumped his or her commitment to universal values (e.g., justice, expansive love, and so on).

Actually, what needs to be stressed here is that this value orientation that was formed during the Edo period was tightly connected with the social structure of Japan at that time. The most important two points are as follows. First, Japan during the Edo period was a feudal society, similar to China's Spring and Autumn Period, when loyalty was the ethical embodiment of this type of society. Second, the Samurai class was the social foundation during the Edo period. This was completely different from the Chinese and Korean political structure with the literati (*shi* 士) as the social foundation. Although the Samurai class was the ruling class during the Edo period, Samurai nonetheless had no land of their own. So it was crucial for them to be loyal to their lord. While practicing Confucianism, the Samurai class formed the Confucian value orientation unique to the Japanese.

Because his research centered on sociology and history, Mizoguchi Yūzō was not interested in pure philosophical analysis. Mizoguchi had deep insights into the axiological principles of China and Japan. As he points out, Darwin's theory of evolution and Spencer's theory of social evolution in the West have been developed into Yan Fu's *Tian yanlun* 天演论 (theory of evolution) in China, generating a strong impact on modern Chinese intellectuals, for whom the competition for existence, "the survival of the fittest," "natural selection," and "the law of the jungle" are the principles of progress. However, China has had to undergo a fundamental change in its worldview in order to accept this "law of the jungle." This is because the world of *ren* (benevolence), *yi* (appropriateness), *li* (rituality), and *zhi* (wisdom) has been viewed as the world of humanity in China ever since the Song dynasty, while the "law of the jungle" is viewed as representative of the world of animals. In ancient China, property is evenly distributed, vocations are not inherited, the communal fields (*yitian* 义田), and communal villages (*yizhuang* 义庄) are everywhere, and communal life is viewed as virtuous. Accordingly, the established principles that dominate both the ethics and social structure of China are anathema to the "law of the jungle."[24]

Mizoguchi also underlines the fact that there is a big difference between Japan and China. Japan during the Edo period was a hierarchical society based on the right of primogeniture. For this reason the sense of private property and class consciousness were developed at that time and became the ground for adopting the principles of competition. On the other hand, when Confucianism was adopted by the Samurai class during the Edo period, bravery (*yong* 勇) was already accepted as an important virtue on a par with *ren*. Yet at the same time in China, both Chen Chun's *Beixi ziyi* and Dai Zhen's *Commentaries on Mencius* did not mention the virtue of bravery (*yong*), while in Ogyū Sorai's *Distinguishing Names* the virtues of bravery (*yong*), valor (*wu*), firmness (*gang*), strength (*qiang*), and fortitude (*yi*) were listed. This, Mizoguchi thinks, is why

> Japan has fertile ground for accepting the law of the jungle concerning its philosophical and ethical tradition. On the contrary, China not only has no such ground but rather has a contrary ground of principles.[25]

Indeed, loyalty, valor, and fortitude were significant virtues for the Samurai Confucians in Japan, which reflects the characteristics of the social structure and the needs of the Edo period. Even though there were scholars such as Yamazaki Ansai 山崎暗斎 and Itō Jinsai 伊藤仁斎 who underscored *ren,* they nevertheless emphasized only personal moral practice, and denied *ren* as a universal principle and thus its transcendental nature. For this reason, concerning their respective orientation of values, it is a simple fact that Japanese Confucianism cannot be summarized as the study of *ren* as it is in China.[26]

III

The ethos of Korean Confucianism is closely connected with the development of Korean history. The constant literati purges of the Joseon dynasty had great influence on the morale of Korean Confucians. These purges (in 1498, 1504, 1519, and 1545) led to great political persecution and the slaughter of Confucians—a rare phenomenon in other East Asian countries. The *shilin* school formed by the Confucians called for social reform and advocated social justice, and had thereby fallen into conflict with the *jiuxun* school, which represented the interests of the nobility. However, the tragic deaths of these famous Confucians subsequently served to fire the unyielding *daoyi* 道

义 spirit of Korean Confucianism. In the words of Zhao Guangzu, "Without regard for personal danger, dedicated to the public enterprise, this is the spirit of true literati." Thus, we can say that "righteousness" or "appropriateness" (*yi* 义) is the basis for the spirit and principle behind Korean Confucianism. As Liu Chengqiang has pointed out, "the *daoxue* school's spirit of justice (*yi*) illuminated through the literati purges and sacrifices reveals the specific feature of Korean Confucianism."[27]

Yi is the persistence of moral convictions. Confucianism in the Joseon dynasty strictly distinguished appropriateness (*yi*) from inappropriateness (*buyi* 不义), and appropriateness from selfish interests (*li* 利),[28] and this has a lot to do with Korea's history of constantly being invaded by other countries. For example, during the Goryeo era Korea was invaded by the Khitans and the Mongolians, and during the Joseon dynasty by the Japanese and then by the Manchus. In 1592, Toyotomi Hideyoshi attacked Korea. With the Confucians as their moral center, Koreans organized military volunteers, and this further inspired a spirit of loyalty (*chunghyo jeongsin* 忠孝精神) among the Korean people. In the course of this national battle many Confucians sacrificed their lives for their country, demonstrating a strong spirit of loyalty and righteousness (*zhongyi* 忠义) and patriotism, and thus earned the praise of the people. In 1636, Emperor Huang Taiji led a large army in an attack on Korea, and the latter was forced to sign a treaty surrendering to the Qing dynasty and breaking off with the Ming. Korean Confucians opposed to the surrender were executed. This opposition exemplifies how invasions from other countries have aroused the spirit of justice among Korean Confucians.

In this way the emphasis on justice and loyalty has set the tone for Korean Confucianism. Concerning its intellectual resources, Korean Confucianism was able to take the idea in the *Spring and Autumn Annals* of "distinguishing the great *yi*" and develop it into a national spirit of rebellion against injustice and resistance to aggression. This spirit of Korean Confucianism has become the main characteristic of the Korean national spirit. Here we need to bear in mind that Zhuxi studies, which was the leading ideological foundation of the Joseon dynasty, had undoubtedly fostered this strong and at times dogmatic cultural ethos. The Zhuxi school has to a large degree formed the basis of the cultural identity of the Korean literati for over five hundred years.

Professor Jin Zhonglie from Korea University, who for many years studied those places where the Chinese language was of great importance, offers the following observation:

> Before the impact of Western culture, China, Korea, Japan, and Vietnam were all part of the Sinosphere; all used Chinese characters, studied ancient Chinese canons like the *Four Books* and the *Five Classics,* and

were educated in Confucian morals such as *ren* (benevolence), *ai* (love), *xiao* (filial piety), *ti* (respect for elder brothers), *zhong* (loyalty), and *xin* (keeping promises). In this sense we can say that these countries used the same language. Despite their different natural environments and minor differences in lifestyle, the ideas formed by Confucianism—for example in cosmology, view of life, and cultural view—were roughly the same. However, although equally Confucian, the aims pursued by the respective countries as well as their social customs could be very different. The people cultivated by [the educational system in] these countries differed greatly in their ideologies, politics, and life views, largely due to differing national aims.

Jin also notes,

> Generally speaking, Chinese Confucianism emphasizes the personal moral life. Filial piety and respect for elders define what one should do. There is a strong atmosphere of modesty and generosity. But the sense of loyalty and patriotism is not very strong. There has always been some distance between the individual and the nation. As for Korean Confucians, they firmly believe that the three principles (三纲) are the root of heaven, earth, and human conduct. Korean Confucianism focuses on filial piety, and only regards one's own family's interests [as important]; thus there is a lack of public morality, even [to the extent of] bearing the foul [taint] of exclusiveness....Japan, as we have said above,...holds national aims and national interests above all else, and lays all the moral values on the foundation of loyalty to the monarch and patriotism. Diligence [in devotion] to [their] organization, loyalty to their monarch and nation, [oblivious] of their own and others' lives, they pursue only their national aims and interests. The so-called Japanese spirit is the very product of monarchism, which requires that people abandon personal interests, concentrating [their] efforts on yielding to the state.[29]

According to Confucian texts, this discourse is not a mere philosophical analysis; rather it has both sociological and anthropological significance. Due to the fact that he was reflecting on his own nation, Jin Zhonglie did not underline or praise the patriotism of Koreans, although his insights into the society are of great value for us.

The Confucian values represented by the five constant virtues are advocated by the Confucianisms found across China, Japan, and Korea. Restricted by their respective socio-historical traditions, not only are the Confucian dispositions different, but each society's value orientation and dominant principles are different as well, causing a different ethos to develop within each nation's form of Confucianism. Although appropriateness (*yi*) and loyalty (*zhong*) are also advocated by Chinese Confucianism, it is the way of putting oneself in another's position (*ren* and *shu*) that is emphasized. In the case of Japanese Confucianism, although *ren* and *yi* are also encouraged, it is loyalty (*zhong*) that is stressed. As for Korean Confucianism, although the five constant virtues are all advocated in theory, it is appropriateness (*yi*) that is highlighted.

Now these differences are also reflected in the modernization process of each country. Chinese Confucianism, taking *ren* and *shu* as its principle, is apt to confirm a kind of universal value in its principles. However, it has cast much doubt on modern Western civilization. Facing the colonialism and imperialism of the modern West, it has been difficult for Chinese Confucianism to admit its backwardness, and this has resulted in the slow pace of modernization in China. Although the emphasis of Japanese Confucianism on loyalty (*zhong*) and bravery (*yong*) is limited by its exceptionalism, it encountered fewer impediments while accepting modernization. It stepped rapidly into modernity—but payed the price for its exceptionalist ethics. Korean Confucianism, imbued with the spirit of justice (*yijie*), has given rise to the strong national subjectivity of Korean culture. Although it holds on to some of the cultural values from the past, it has nevertheless fostered the development of Korea as a modern national state. Now the principle of harmony included in *ren,* the principle of justice embodied by *yi,* and the principle of order demonstrated by *zhong* are all necessary for the continued vitality of each modern East Asian country. In the twenty-first century, the three countries should try to understand one another, learn from one another, and unite to establish a harmonious future.

Notes

1. For example, see the natural theory of Kaibara Ekken 貝原益軒 and the political theory of Ogyū Sorai 荻生徂徠.

2. Mizoguchi Yūzō 沟口雄三, *Riben xian jieduan de Zhongguo yanjiu ji 21 shiji de keti* 日本现阶段的中国研究及21世纪的课题 (Contemporary Chinese studies in Japan and themes in the 21st century), Guoji ruxue yanjiu, di er ji 国际儒学研究, 第二辑 (International Confucianism studies, 2nd series) (Beijing: Zhongguo Shehui Kexue Chubanshe, 1996).

3. *Shangshu* 尚書 (Book of Shang), "Kang Gao" 康誥, 6; adapted from the James Legge translation. Translations are my own unless otherwise cited.

4. *Shangshu* 尚書 (Book of Shang), "Pan Geng I" 盤庚上, 7; adapted from the Legge translation.

5. *Shangshu* 尚書, "Kang Gao" 康誥, 2; adapted from the Legge translation.

6. *Yichuan Yizhuan* 伊川易傳 (Cheng Yi's commentary on the *Yijing*), vol. 1.

7. *Analects* 6.30 and 12.2.

8. *Spring and Autumn Annals,* "Bu Er."

9. *Daodejing,* chap. 67.

10. *Zhuangzi,* chap. 33.

11. *Yuan Dao* 原道 (The origin of *dao*), in *Han Yu wenji* 韩愈文集 (Collected works of Han Yu).

12. *Zhangzi quanshu* 張子全書 (Collected works of Master Zhang [Zhang Zai 張載]), "Xi Ming" 西銘.

13. *Er Cheng quanshu* 二程全書 (Collected works of the Cheng Brothers), vol. 2.

14. *Yichuan Yizhuan* 伊川易傳 (Cheng Yi's commentary on the *Yijing*), vol. 1.

15. *Zhuzi quanshu* 朱子全集 (Collected writings of Master Zhu), vol. 67, "On *Ren*."

16. Li Zehou 李泽厚, *Zhongguo gudai sixiangshi lun* 中国古代思想史论 (On the history of Chinese ancient thought) (Beijing: Renmin Chubanshe, 1985).

17. Liang Shuming 梁漱溟, *Zhongguo wenhua yaoyi* 中国文化要义 (Essentials of Chinese culture) (Taipei: Liren, 1980), p. 90.

18. See Henry Sumner Maine, *Ancient Law: Its Connection with the Early History of Society and Its Relation to Modern Ideas* (London: Forgotten Books, 2012).

19. Ibid., p. 119.

20. Pan Nai De 潘乃德 [Ruth Benedict], *Juhua yu jian: Riben minzu de wenhua moshi* 菊花與劍：日本民族的文化模式 (The chrysanthemum and the sword: Patterns of Japanese culture) (Zhejiang: Zhejiang Renmin Chubanshe, 1987), p. 100.

21. Ibid., p. 108.

22. Robert Bellah, *Tokugawa Religion: The Cultural Roots of Modern Japan* (Oxford: Oxford University Press, 1957), pp. 7, 22, 26.

23. Ibid., p. 200.

24. Mizoguchi, *Riben xian jieduan de Zhongguo yanjiu ji 21 shiji de keti,* p. 129.

25. Ibid.

26. See Huang Junjie, "The Resonance of Zhuxi on *Ren* in Tokugawa Japan," paper presented at Taibei Zhuzi Forum, October 2011.

27. Liu Chengguo, *History of Confucianism in Korea,* trans. Fu Jigong (Taipei: Taiwan Shangwu Press, 1989), pp. 115, 133.

28. Ibid., p. 125. See also Huang Bingtai [Hwang Pyŏng-t'ai] 黄秉泰, *Ruxue yu xiandaihua: Zhong ri han ruxue bijiao yanjiu* 儒学与现代化：中日韩儒学比较研究 (Confucianism in modernization: Comparative studies on Confucianism in China, Japan, and Korea [Beijing: Shehui Kexue Wenxian Chubanshe, 1995], chap. 4).

29. Jin Zhonglie, "The Common Ethic of Confucianism: The Way of Zhongshu," in *Examining and Prospecting Chinese Culture* (Singapore: Bafang Culture Press, 2001), pp. 511–512 (quotation slightly modified).

CHAPTER 8

Animism and Spiritualism

The Two Origins of Life in Confucianism

OGURA Kizo

THE JAPANESE HAVE MAINTAINED a profound interest in the teachings of Confucius, especially the *Analects* (論語—*Rongo* in Japanese and *Lunyu* in Chinese). The popularity of the *Analects* has never withered, whether in the "modern" times of imperialistic aggression and postwar economic recovery, or in the "postmodern" times when the nation was captured by manga cartoons and animation products. If we think of other great Asian classical teachings such as the *Mencius,* the extraordinary popularity of the *Analects* in Japan leads us to an inquiry into the deep-seated issues and problems in the study of Confucianism in Japan.

In this chapter, I approach this subject by analyzing a core concept of Confucian thinking: life, or *anima* in Latin. My central argument is that the essential understanding of life in the thought of Confucius is animistic while that of Mencius is spiritualistic. I think that these two divergent understandings render "two origins" of conceptualizing "life" in the East Asian philosophical tradition.

In Japanese tradition, especially during the Tokugawa period, there were many "deconstructive" interpretations of the philosophy of Confucianism—for example from Ogyū Sorai, Itō Jinsai, Dazai Shundai, Motoori Norinaga, and Hirata Atsutane. I think this is because scholars in Tokugawa Japan tended to have non-moralistic and non-universalistic worldviews. Therefore, in Japanese tradition there were many interpretations that were unorthodox and deviant from the orthodox Neo-Confucian point of view, and they tended to criticize orthodox Neo-Confucianism. I am not a follower of the former; rather I would like to think through another path into the Confucian tradition.

Animism and Spiritualism

The *Analects* has been read by numerous scholars and followers in East Asia, producing numerous definitions and interpretations of the same Confucian terms in Confucian thinking. Thus, after thriving for twenty centuries, the *Analects* still remains in the realm of ambiguity, and this ambiguity has given life to a multitude of philological and philosophical variants and schools.

What explains this ambiguity? The answer can be diverse and complex. Yet I find a main reason in the very way in which we conceive of Confucius himself. In other words, in China, Japan, and Korea we might be still mistaken about the true identity of Confucius after all these centuries.

Who, then, was the true Confucius? I believe that he was a thinker who represented one of the two fundamental views on the interpretation of life. One is animism, and the other is spiritualism. And Confucius stood for the former, not the latter.

In order to understand animism properly, let me define spiritualism as the antonym of animism.[1] Here, I define spiritualism as a worldview according to which one spirit pervades the entire universe. Spinoza's pantheism can be interpreted as a typical example of spiritualism in our context. It carries conceptual elements similar to the view concerning *qi* 氣 in East Asian philosophical thought. *Qi* here does not merely mean "matter" or "material"; it means "spiritual matter," which connotes the substance of life. As such, we can approach the conceptualization of *qi* in Daoism as well as Confucianism in the context of spiritualism.

Animism and Shamanism

Now let me turn to animism. Among the scholars of Asian philosophy, there has been a robust view that the life of Confucius and the notion of the *ru* 儒 (the original term for Confucian scholar) in his times were deeply related to shamanism. This view is based on the observation that Confucius' mother was a shaman herself and that the Chinese character for *ru* 儒 originally referred to the rain-calling ritual of the ancient agrarian society of which the lead performer was the shaman.

I refute this view for analytical reasons. It is important to note that the life and thought of Confucius as a philosopher was in this regard unrelated to his mother's calling. His views and conceptions were close to animism, not shamanism. The widespread misunderstanding of this relationship stems from the superficial similarity between shamanism and animism. Yet a close examination reveals that they are entirely different.

Shamanism is rooted in a worldview that believes in the transcendent being known as Heaven. All essential values exist only in Heaven, and Heaven exercises dominion over all the world by imparting its essential values to the Earth. In this epistemological system, the shaman, who mediates between Heaven and Earth, resides in a position of rulership over the Earth. As the representative of Heaven, the shaman therefore has absolute authority and embodies the ultimate values of the universe on behalf of Heaven.

Confucius indeed criticized this shaman-centered worldview in several places in the *Analects*. For instance, there is the following statement:

子曰、君子上達、小人下達. (14.23)

Kanaya Osamu, one of the leading researchers in the field in Japan, translates this phrase into Japanese as follows:

君子は高尚なことに通ずるが、小人は下賤なことに通ずる。

The gentleman is good at refined matters; the small man is good at trivial matters.[2]

I believe this is one example of the misguided interpretations of Confucian thinking. "The gentleman" (*junzi* 君子) here refers to a learned man who possesses an animistic epistemology and belief system, while "the small man" (*xiaoren* 小人) is the one who has a shamanistic worldview. The small man deduces everything from the universal value of Heaven and tries to apply it to the secular world. In other words, he believes the value of Heaven to be universal and transmits it down to Earth, aggressively and authoritatively. This kind of deductive epistemology is referred to as "transmitting it down" (*xiada* 下達), which implies a vertical vector from up above to down below.

The Confucian gentleman is not consumed by a blind belief in universal, transcendent values. On the contrary, he searches for the true meaning of every worldly thing and fact around him. By doing so, he induces their validity as a way of reaching toward an understanding of the Order of Heaven. The very phrase "proceeding from below to above" (*shangda* 上達) implies this inductive epistemological methodology. Confucius' scholarly endeavor of over fifty years to reach the Order of Heaven was nothing but a tireless process of inductive reasoning, not research into shamanism.

Now, why is this inductive epistemology of "proceeding from below to above" of the Confucian gentleman animistic? In order to have a valid understanding, we need to clarify the true meaning of animism.

Animism is generally interpreted as a worldview that everything in the world has life (or *anima* in Latin). According to this view, a natural thing such as tree or rock has *anima,* often personified. But is this true?

Let us take the example of animism in Japanese parlance. The teachings of Japanese Shintoism say there exist eight million gods (*yaoyorozu no kami* 八百萬の神). And the term "eight million gods" can be mistaken to imply "everything in the world." Yet a true meaning of the term is the notion of the innumerability of kami (gods) in the world. Therefore, each and every "thing" in the world cannot be identified as a kami in the worldview of Japanese Shintoism.

There are a myriad stones on earth. Some can be worshipped as kami, and others can at the same time be kicked aside as worthless things. Both are stones, but the former is kami, while the latter is not kami. In the Japanese animistic worldview, there could be more than eight million kami. The point is that we should not be falsely bound by the face value of the terms of "eight million" and "kami." In this regard, this animistic worldview is not compatible with pantheism, spiritualism, or shamanism.

Then what is kami and what is not kami? The determining factor is not the transcendence itself of Heaven. If many members of a human community, be it a village or a country, perceive some indication of life or anima in a stone, it can be called kami, not because the stone's godly validity descends from Heaven but because the people recognize its kami-ness on the grounds that they share certain subjective but common feelings or an acknowledgment of the inductive recognition of Heaven, that is, "from below to above." This type of worldview is identified as the very notion of animism, which I emphasize throughout this chapter in order to distinguish it from the general usage of the term.

The Gentleman and the Small Man

We can assume that Confucius inherited some degree of shamanistic worldview from his mother. Nevertheless, what was more important for him was the philosophy that had sustained the ruling system of the Zhou dynasty. He was born in the state of Lu, which had inherited the glory of the Zhou, while his family lineage can be traced back to the Yin dynasty.

For this reason, Confucius thought that *li* 禮 (ritual) was the most important factor in the Zhou dynasty's political and social order. *Li* was a system of customs, rules, and cultures through which men in the traditional clan society managed their life properly. Confucius believed that *li* was not formed deductively from transcendent or metaphysical values. On the contrary, *li* was formed inductively, little by little, within the constraints of indigenous environments and conditions over the long history of the community. In Confucius' view, a man can only elevate the status and quality of his being within his community to the highest level as he acts in perfect accord with *li*.

However, the culture of the Zhou dynasty had already deteriorated in the mundane world of Confucius' times. Instead, the hegemony-seeking social groups that upheld universally applicable values were coming to dominate the world. They adopted universal values, among other things, in an attempt to eradicate all conventional values that had been accepted in the traditional societies. And it was the "small man" (xiaoren 小人) that had played the key role in this process of destruction and re-orientation.

The gentleman, then, was the one who took the opposite position against the new, universal worldview pursued by the small man. He attempted to guard the animistic worldview that adhered to the proper ways of living in the society of the ancient clan. His thinking in this regard was expressed in the following famous sentence:

子曰、君子和而不同、小人同而不和。

The Master said: The true gentleman is conciliatory but not accommodating. Common people are accommodating but not conciliatory.[3] (13.23)

The gentleman, the sentence reads, is capable of maintaining harmony in defending the animistic li of the traditional society, yet not of equating all things to universal values. In contrast, the small man equates all things to universal values and therefore does not seek harmony and tends to struggle against conservative opponents.

Confucius, rooted in a belief in animism, was very sensitive in perceiving and absorbing facial expressions, demeanor, appearance, and the atmosphere around human beings as well as figures, colors, and the sounds of natural objects. There is one instance where we are allowed to peek into Confucius' attachment to animism. He married his daughter off to Gong Ye Chang 公冶長, who was said to be able to communicate with birds. This discussion leads to another famous passage:

子曰、巧言令色、鮮矣仁。

The Master said, "Clever talk and a pretentious manner" are seldom found in the Good.[4] (1.3 and 17.17)

This passage says that a globalist person who embodies universal values and has an exquisite ability to conduct deductive communication with a pretentious face is seldom compatible with ren 仁 (the life of between-ness), which is inherently a central value of the local clan society. This small man is able to update his knowing of "truth" or value promptly from globalist groups and bring them to the community; he then applies them in the vertical way, that is, from above to down below (xiada 下達) as the shaman always does.

The knowledge of the small man was oriented toward the narrow end of constructing a global empire, and hence, to that end, he had the power to convince people to obey. As such, the small man was equipped with an excellent intellectual capability and efficient solutions, all of which proved valuable for the person who was in a position to exercise global power. But the nature of his knowledge was only strategic or tactical, after all. The gentleman was remote from the small man in terms of mundane knowledge.

Confucius was obviously aware of this knowledge gap and feared that the tremendous power of the small man would destroy the old values of the animistic clan community. His vocal and consistent criticism of the small man stems from this background. If we consider this, it is easy to reason that the stature of the small man was not as trivial as described by Neo-Confucian thinkers. On the contrary, small men formed a global elite group that had an open mindset that could cross over the borders of old cultures, customs, and traditions. On the other hand, the gentleman intentionally disregarded the new trends of the global world and chose to be stuck in the value system of the good old traditional community.

In light of this, until now there might have been a misunderstanding about Zai Yu 宰予, a disciple of Confucius, in the long history of Chinese thought. Zai Yu was infamous for sleeping during the daytime. Confucius is said to have criticized him for this:

子曰、朽木不可雕也、糞土之牆、不可杇也、於予與何誅。

The Master said, Rotten wood cannot be carved, nor a wall of dried dung be trowelled. What use is there in my scolding him any more?[5] (5.9)

Zai Yu had received two opposite evaluations. On the one hand, he was often scolded by Confucius, as just shown. On the other hand, he was praised for his outstanding ability in speech.

Why did he sleep during the daytime and why did Confucius scold him so severely? A careful reading of this chapter reveals that Confucius did not criticize him to his face. Instead, Confucius made critical remarks when Zai Yu was absent. In short, Confucius disclosed his dissatisfaction about Zai Yu deliberately in front of other disciples.

Confucius' act should be interpreted in light of the fact that Zai Yu was a very competent, globally minded member of the elite and had rich connections to diverse sources of the latest information about the world. We may presume that he continued to update his pool of information and knowledge by meeting with well-informed people who moved around the country. The meetings took place in the evening, and this affected his sleep.

I assume that Confucius was keenly aware of Zai Yu's activities, which put Confucius in a dilemma. A wanderer himself, Confucius was in need of the information and knowledge Zai Yu had for the purpose of finding valuable work. However, Zai Yu was a person who should be categorized as a small man. This dilemma might have led Confucius to share his negative views of Zai Yu with his disciples during Zai Yu's absence.

We can find a reference to a rather exaggerated situation in the *Mencius,* which depicts the scenes where Zai Yu and Zi Gong 子貢 make great efforts and use their speaking talents to promote Confucius as a greater sage than Yao 堯 and Shun 舜 (by Zai Yu) or even as the greatest sage in the history of humankind (by Zi Gong). Confucius was definitely ambivalent about Zai Yu.

The Third Life

What did the Confucian gentleman uphold to provide protection for his traditional community and the society at large? In order to answer this question, some conceptual clarifications will be required.

Here I wish to introduce the notions of the first life, the second life, and the third life. These may sound awkward, but they are crucial in my interpretation of East Asian philosophy.

Humankind has learned that there are two types of life. One is physical, and the other is meta-physical or spiritual. The physical life is perceived and sustained in our daily living, which depends on natural processes for well-being and continuity. Yet, this life is doomed to perish or be destroyed for a variety of reasons. The human being cannot but accept this law of nature with a fundamental sorrow and despair.

In order to relieve sorrow and despair, the human being finds comfort and rescue in religious notions about life. Statements such as "Even after the body has perished, the spiritual life continues eternally" and "Even though this physical being is limited, the spiritual life given by God is absolutely immortal" have been around for a very long time. The religious view of nature and life exemplified by these statements has had great influence throughout human history.

The former and the latter types of life I refer to here as the first life and the second life, respectively. Between and within each of these two types of life there are a number of variations. Even though we have conducted a deep search into these variations, they basically reside within, and not beyond, the two notions of life.

Now I would suggest a further notion: the third life. In essence, it is neither biological nor spiritual; it is animistic. A good example of this third life can be found in the Japanese conception of a natural being such as a stone or tree acquiring "life" as a kami. This third life can only appear when members of the human community have a shared perception of the life-ness (or *Aura* in German) and accordingly recognize it as kami.

Not being biological or spiritual, the existential mode of the third life is accidental, unpredictable; it may or may not emerge in any particular relationship between or among the entities of the world. This third life may sound illusive or superstitious, as humankind has not yet fully recognized it. But I argue that this third life exists around our daily life although it is not perceived.

In sum, we can attempt to conceptualize and compare the three modes of life as in table 1.

It is important to note that the third life is not unique to the Japanese notion of animism. A careful reading of the Confucian literature indicates that the notion of *ren* has profound logical connections to the "life-ness" between and among social entities. This notion breaks the boundary of the conventional socio-ethical understanding of *ren* in terms of "benevolence" or "love of humanity."

Confucius' *ren* at its core refers to the life of between-ness. This notion is rooted in Confucius' peculiar worldview that life is not a universal phenomenon, but an accidental, coincidental, adventitious one, which can only be recognized between and among the members of the community who happen to share certain common sensibilities. This is the kernel of the Confucian view of the third life. Whether a stone or a tree is perceived to be alive or not is not a concern of deductive reasoning through universal values. It is recognized and sanctioned by the members of the community who happen to share a certain inductive awareness or perception about the said concern. In this sense, animism can be understood as a worldview in a new context that is non-physical (non-first) and non-spiritual (non-second) in its mode of existence; it may or may not penetrate all modes of intersubjective relations of the world.

Table 1. Three Modes of Life

	THE FIRST LIFE	THE SECOND LIFE	THE THIRD LIFE
Nature, essence	Physical, biological	Religious, spiritual	Awareness, recognition of between-ness
Locus	Individual, human body	Universal	Inter-subject (nature-human, human-human)
Mode of existence	Visible and tangible in this world	Transcendent, transpersonal	Accidental, illusive, apparition
Scope of concern	Human needs, desires	Everything	Contingency
Contents	Substantial	Absolute truth	Aesthetic, sensuous

Ren as the Third Life

It is a common understanding that one of the core concepts of the *Analects* is *ren*. Yet it is not easy to come up with a handy definition of *ren* as discussed in the *Analects*. The difficulty stems from the fact that Confucius did not give a clear-cut definition of *ren* and instead mentioned it here and there in fragmented fashion in the *Analects*. This difficulty became ever more serious as the readers of the Confucian literature attempted to grasp some consistent meaning out of the heterogeneous, fragmentary words of Confucius. Captured by the image or prejudice of Confucius as a "great sage," the general reader presumes that there must be a logically coherent set of meanings among such fragmentary words. This is where we fail to obtain the true meanings and implications of *ren*.

In order to overcome this habitual thinking, among all things we need to realize that there is no consistent definition or meaning of *ren* in Confucius' thought. It is important to realize that *ren* is not supposed to be assigned a particular consistent definition if we recall Confucius' animistic views of life, society, and the world. Logically speaking, the animistic worldview cannot offer any universal, deductive, and consistent definition of life, let alone *ren*.

Ren becomes manifest and realized in coincidental and unintended ways. This is why disciples of Confucius always wanted to ask about *ren* while Confucius did not want to discuss it at great length. If there were any clear definition of *ren,* Confucius could lay it out once and for all, instead of taking up the topic time and again with his disciples. The very ambiguity of *ren* led Confucius to characterize it as something unclear, situational, and random, which his disciples were not up to swallowing.

For example, when Confucius says

克己復禮爲仁.

He who can himself submit to ritual is Good.[6] (12.1)

we should not conceive of this as a general definition of *ren*. This sentence means that if we can ourselves submit to ritual, there might appear an accidental life called *ren*. *Ren* is coincidental rather than entirely accidental. There is regularity and predictability to some extent; *ren* may or may not materialize according to a gentleman's experiences and intentions. In order to make certain this regularity and predictability, people should learn and practice *li* 禮 (ritual) as the reinforcing system for promoting the status of their being.

When Fan Chi 樊遲 asked about *ren* (12.22), Confucius answered that it is "to love men" (樊遲問仁、子曰愛人). However, this should not be considered anything close to a definition. Confucius' answer should not read as "To love men is *ren*." Instead, when he provided this answer, he might have meant that when a gentleman loves men, a new form of life-like between-ness called *ren* might appear in that particular coincidental interface between the gentleman and the men.

But we need to be reminded of the matter of regularity. When the gentleman loves a human, *ren* might materialize, but we do not definitely know whether or not *ren* materializes at each interface between the gentleman and the human.

When Confucius said "He who can himself submit to ritual is *ren*" to Yan Hui 顏回 and "to love men" to Fan Chi, he might have thought that *ren* would appear only to some specific persons under some specific situations. And all these incidents of *ren* must be recognized from shared subjective perspectives. This explains why there exists a variety of meanings and connotations of *ren*.

Having discussed the preceding, we can understand that *ren* is neither benevolence nor "human-heartedness" (as in Fung Yu-lan),[7] nor is it morality. Instead, it is life. To be more precise, *ren* represents a form of life in the way it involves the interface and interrelatedness of social entities. In other words, it is the life of between-ness, which is anchored in the power of inter-entity consciousness.

Life and Time

Ren is not eternal. It can be momentary, transitory, and ephemeral, because it is the third life. This is why Confucius thought that timing was the most important factor for the gentleman:

> 子曰、學而時習之、不亦説乎、有朋自遠方來、不亦樂乎、人不知而不慍、不亦君子乎。

> The Master said, To learn and at due times to repeat what one has learnt, is that not after all a pleasure? That friends should come to one from afar, is this not after all delightful? To remain unsoured even though one's merits are unrecognized by others, is that not after all what is expected of a gentleman?[8] (1.1)

The key word in this chapter is "time." The Master did not say "To learn and to repeat what one has learnt"; he said "To learn and at due times to repeat." Here, the phrase "at due times" is not to mean some points in time where some duty or obligation is implied. The repeating could be incidental; yet the final outcomes of the unplanned or unintended incidents would prove that the legitimate timing had been exercised. A gentleman neither prepares nor plans nor aims at a certain time deliberately. Instead he is cultivated to grope for the very best moments, which appears to be coincidental to the beholders.

However, we should be cautious about the "coincidental" nature of this revelation. It is because a lot of practice, training, and rehearsal are demanded for one to be able to catch the perfect timing. It is not guesswork. It is not a deliberate work either. In a natural stream of consciousness, a gentleman gets to catch the moment accurately as though he had planned it perfectly. This is the very meaning of "at due times." And it is at this very moment that the third life materializes in the form of pleasure and benefits all members of the group.

In a similar vein, the phrase "有朋自遠方來" should not be read as "from afar (遠方) friends come." Instead we should read it as "from afar (遠) at the very right moment (方) friends come." The reason is that Confucius is talking about timing here, too. He says here that at the very moment that friends come from afar, the third life, paraphrased as "delight," appears between the two persons. The timing may look coincidental, but the two true gentleman friends realize that the right timing is a manifestation of their shared perception.

From this animistic point of view, we can read the third sentence as follows: At the very moment when one remains unsoured (or not disappointed) even though his merits are unrecognized, the third life appears in the form of gentleman-ness.

A logical corollary is that the gentleman here is not a specific object that has an unchanging identity; it rather is a perception or recognition. The gentleman here implies a phenomenon or incident that can enlighten the life, and, for him to do so, timing is crucial. Even if the gentleman can enlighten life once, we should not presume that his gentleman-ness might last forever. In the next moment he can become the small man since the gentleman-ness does not stand for an unchanging, constant entity but a plastic, performative agency.

The following chapter proposes quite a challenge in figuring out the animistic nature of Confucius' writing:

色斯舉矣、翔而後集、曰、山梁雌雉、時哉、時哉、子路共之、三嗅而作。

[The gentleman] rises and goes at the first sign, and does not "settle until he has hovered." (A song) says: The hen-pheasant of the hill-bridge, Knows how to bide its time! Bide its time! When Tzu-lu made it an offering, it sniffed three times before it rose.[9] (10.18)

It is hard to comprehend this chapter clearly unless we understand the special importance of timing in Confucius' thinking. In my animistic point of view, this chapter must be interpreted as follows.

When Confucius and his disciples went on a journey, a hen-pheasant flying in the atmosphere about them rose and settled on a tree after hovering for a while. The Master said, "The hen-pheasant of the hill-bridge knows the time, it knows the time!" After listening to these words, Zi Lu (Tzu-lu) 子路 gave food to it, but the bird only sniffed three times and rose.

Confucius praised the hen-pheasant because it knew the timing. This statement corresponds completely to the opening chapter of the *Analects*. In the beginning there is the Chinese character *xi* 習, which portrays a young bird flapping its wings trying to fly.

Now in the last chapter of Book 10 (actually this book was the last volume of the ancient version of the *Analects*), this young bird has become the hen-pheasant (the gentleman) and is flying high (*xiang* 翔) after a lot of learning, practice, and experience in order to give life to everything. In the beginning, a little infant bird did practice the third life awkwardly, but through a long process of training it became able to display the third life without rational reflective knowledge. This is why Confucius emphasized what has happened by yelling out "Timing, Timing!"

That the hen-pheasant sniffed three times at the food Zi Lu gave it and then rose in fact represents the practice of ritual (*li*). Book 10 is a textbook description of Confucius' daily demeanors and bearings. The compiler of this book wanted to say that every move Confucius made represents the *ren* that gives life to everything. Acquiring the life of *li, ren,* and being a gentleman, the hen-pheasant now bows down low three times following the traditional ritual, as described in detail here:

（君召使擯、色勃如也、足躩如也）:揖所與立、左右其手、衣前後襜如也、趨進翼如也。

(An extremely elegant bird emerged as the gentleman here as though): "When saluting his (her) colleagues he (she) passes his (her) right hand (wing) to the left, letting his (her) robe (tail feathers) hang down in front and behind; and as he (she) advances with quickened step, his (her) attitude is one of majestic dignity."[10] (10.3)

And it is as though the bird has gracefully soared high up into the sky when Confucius says,

（賓退、必復命曰、）賓不顧矣。

"The guest is no longer looking back."[11] (10.3)

In all these situations, time and life are closely interrelated, for the third life emerges always "at due times." Confucius puts emphasis on timing in the daily practice of letting the third life emerge in the community.

Rising of the Second Life

This specific worldview of Confucius is based on a particular perspective on life. It recognizes life as a phenomenon that only occurs in a particular community or in a group that shares feelings, and not as a universal phenomenon. This is an animistic worldview in itself. Whether a stone or a tree is living or not is not to be decided deductively by a universal standard. It should be decided inductively by the collective feelings of the people or multitude that observe and listen to the stone or the tree.

However, this animistic worldview had been thoroughly destroyed in the process of dissolution of the traditional society while a powerful empire with a centralized government was establishing itself in the post-Confucian era, especially during the Zhanguo 戰國 (Warring States) period.

The global powers detested the old-fashioned animistic worldview of Confucius and adopted the opposite side's universal and shamanistic worldview. This saga is depicted in the genealogy from the Daoists to Mencius to Xun Zi 荀子 of the Legalist school. Daoists were a philosophical group who thought that it was not animistic life but Dao, the ultimate spiritual being, that was the ruler of the universe. Since Dao is universal, everything derives from and goes back to it; there are no mediating mechanisms such as customs, rules, or cultures between Dao and individual things. This completely brand-new school of thought was intimately understood in particular by the newly emerging global powers, whose intention was to destroy the old clan societies.

The following episode from Book 18 provides a vivid description of the nuanced relationship that Confucius and the early Daoists had with each other.

長沮桀溺耦而耕、孔子過之、使子路問津焉、長沮曰、夫執輿者爲誰、子路曰、爲孔丘、曰、是魯孔丘與、對曰是也、曰是知津矣、問於桀溺、桀溺曰、子爲誰、曰爲仲由、曰是魯孔丘之徒與、對曰、然、曰滔滔者天下皆是也、而誰以易之、且而與其從辟人之士也、豈若從辟世之士哉、耰而不輟、子路行以告、夫子憮然曰、鳥獸不可與同群也、吾非斯人之徒與而誰與、天下有道、丘不與易也。

Ch'ang-chu and Chieh-ni were working as plough-mates together. Master K'ung, happening to pass that way, told Tzu-lu to go and ask them where the river could be forded.

Ch'ang-chu: Who is it for whom you are driving?
Tzu-lu: For K'ung Ch'iu.
Ch'ang-chu: What, K'ung Ch'iu of Lu?
Tzu-lu: Yes, he.

Ch'ang-chu: In that case he already knows where the ford is.

Tzu-lu then asked Chieh-ni.

Chieh-ni: Who are you?

Tzu-lu: I am Tzu-lu.

Chieh-ni: You are a follower of K'ung Ch'iu of Lu, are you not?

Tzu-lu: That is so.

Chieh-ni: Under Heaven there is none that is not swept along by the same flood. Such is the world and who can change it? As for you, instead of following one who flees from this man and that, you would do better to follow one who shuns this whole generation of men.

> *And with that he went on covering the seed. Tzu-lu went and told his master, who said ruefully, One cannot herd with birds and beasts. If I am not to be a man among other men, then what am I to be? If the Way prevailed under Heaven, I should not be trying to alter things.*[12] (18.6)

This chapter introduces the picture of the primitive Daoists, Chang Ju (Ch'ang-chu) and Jie Ni (Chieh-ni), who were not mere hermits. They were ploughing their field without exchanging words. Daoists did not need words, while Confucius' group always needed a lot of words to communicate with each other. Nevertheless, Chang Ju and Jie Ni were not ignorant men; they knew everything in the world including the fact that Confucius and his disciples would come to them on that day. Since they always had the newest information concerning the whole world through the spiritualistic network of primitive Daoists, the meeting between them and Confucius was in fact not at all coincidental, and there seemed to be no surprise in this seemingly "accidental" encounter. The Daoists had all the information even though they hardly move around.

Chang Ju and Jie Ni were not perfect Daoists, but they understood the world in terms of universal spirituality and wanted to unite themselves to the One, escaping from an artificially segmented society.

This episode provides a window through which we can look at a situation where Confucius and his disciples were looking for the "right path" in a disorderly world. But from the perspective of Chang Ju and Jie Ni, Confucius' worldview was completely wrong. The reason is as follows. Confucius thought that he was going to cross over to a certain land when he came to a river, and he looked for a ford. This turned out to be a perfectly wrong understanding of the world. At the time, there was no land at all in the eyes of Chang Ju and Jie Ni. Everywhere the country was under water, and no one could distinguish land from river. So it was futile to look for a ford. Jie Ni said, "Under Heaven there is none that is not swept along by the same flood. Such is the world and who can change it?" This deductive recognition is the perfect expression of the primitive Daoist and spiritualist worldview. Everyone was drowning in the same moving flood of universal water, but no one could realize this except for the believer in the second life.

From Mencius to Neo-Confucianism

Mencius is widely believed to have been a successor of Confucius. However, he may in fact have been influenced by primitive Daoists and did bring about great changes in Confucianism. Mencius discarded the inductive methodology of Confucius and instead developed boldly the deductive methodology learned from primitive Daoists.

Mencius intended to destroy the profit-oriented (*li* 利) worldview of the hegemony-seeking global powers through righteousness (*yi* 義). Needless to say he was Confucian in this regard, but his perception of life was completely different from that of Confucius. Mencius might have been a successor to the Daoist concept of life, which approaches life in terms of spiritual matter (*qi* 氣). As I have mentioned, this is a typically spiritualistic worldview that believes all things in the universe are made of *qi*.

Confucius had never explained human nature by employing universalistic or deductive discourses. But Mencius explained it deductively in terms of universal morality and the metaphor of moving water spreading all over the world. This indicates a stark difference between the two thinkers.

After Mencius, Confucius' animistic notion of life on the one hand and the spiritual notion of life by Daoists and Mencius on the other came to be in competition with each other. Over the course of time Confucius' out-of-fashion notion of animistic life was forgotten, and his words in the *Analects* became incomprehensible all too soon. In this way, the interpretations of the *Analects* have all become out of focus because of their tendency to understand Confucius in terms of the second life. Thus, Confucius became a spiritual Divine Sage with absolute perfection.

The complete version of the notion of spiritual life in Chinese philosophy lies in Neo-Confucianism. According to the Neo-Confucian worldview, animism or the third life ought to be held in disdain as a lower-level or "vulgar" notion of life. The thorough extermination of the animistic way of thinking from the public sphere in China and Korea can be understood as a Neo-Confucian crusade in the name of civilization.

On the other hand, the animistic worldview was well preserved in a country that was relatively less civilized, that remained "barbaric" from a Neo-Confucian point of view, and that lacked a strong, centralized governing authority: Japan.

This offers a sharp contrast with China and Korea, where strongly centralized power existed that was highly civilized from the Neo-Confucian point of view. Japanese *waka* 和歌 and *haiku* 俳句 are just two illustrations of the animistic form of artistic expression that serves to realize and give form to the ephemeral third life.

The Japanese cherish the momentary aura in these forms of literature and strive to grasp the ephemeral yet eternal quality of "life" (*inochi* いのち) that is inherent in them. Japanese Shintoism is also animistic in its worldview and was not absorbed into shamanism or spiritual religion or formal thought until the Meiji era. The reason is that "vulgar" animism had widely penetrated to the far corners of the country, and the love of the Japanese for the *Analects* may be due to the very animistic atmosphere of the literature, instead of the spiritualism emphasized by a moralistic Neo-Confucianism that deviated from the original Confucian teachings.

Notes

1. In this chapter "animism" will be taking on a new meaning, to be elaborated below.

2. Kanaya Osamu 金谷治, trans., *Rongo* 論語 (*Analects*), Waidoban Iwanami Bunko series (Tokyo: Iwanami Shoten, 2001), p. 286.

3. Arthur Waley, trans. and annot., *The Analects of Confucius* (New York: Random House, 1989), p. 177.

4. Ibid., p. 213.

5. Ibid., p. 109.

6. Ibid., p. 162.

7. Fung Yu-lan, *A Short History of Chinese Philosophy,* ed. Derk Bodde (New York: Free Press, 1976), p. 42.

8. Waley, *Analects of Confucius,* p. 83.

9. Ibid., pp. 151–152. Where Chinese personal names occur in passages that are quoted from Waley's translation, his original Wade-Giles romanization has been retained.

10. Ibid., p. 146. I have inserted the parenthetical (her), (she), and so forth in order to explain the actions of the hen-pheasant.

11. Ibid.

12. Ibid., pp. 219–220. There are no line breaks in the original translation by Arthur Waley. I have rewritten this passage in a playscript style for readability.

CHAPTER 9

The Noble Person and the Revolutionary

Living with Confucian Values in Contemporary Vietnam

NGUYEN Nam

AT A CONFERENCE in Hanoi in 2012 on research methods for studies on Confucianism, a couple of papers were presented on President Hồ Chí Minh and Confucian teachings. During the discussion on this topic, a participant brought to the audience's attention the case of the well-known medical doctor and political activist Nguyễn Khắc Viện, who was seriously criticized in North Vietnam in the 1960s for figuring out, in an essay, Confucian elements in Hồ Chí Minh's thought. Rereading Viện's essay, titled "Confucianism and Marxism in Vietnam," together with his notes added to the text later in 1984, we can retrieve some traces of a downturn period for Confucianism in the Democratic Republic of Vietnam (DRV). Examining how the essay and its author have been treated throughout different phases of recent history, we can see the changing attitudes toward Confucianism, the opposing public points of view on it as part of socialist leadership, and the diverse standpoints of Vietnamese intellectuals under the influence of prevalent sociopolitical discourses.

Equally interesting is Nguyễn Khắc Viện's analysis of passages cited from Hồ Chí Minh's handbook *Let's Change Our Methods of Work*. The citations comprise a set of moral values put under the name of "Revolutionary Virtues," and they are unquestionably the modifications of Confucian cardinal moralities. Thus, these "revolutionary virtues" epitomize the revolutionization of Confucian pivotal virtues, which makes them more effective for and suitable to new revolutionary tasks. Through Hồ Chí Minh's revolutionization of Confucian moral values, it is not hard to see an enduring of Confucianism in his ideological foundation, and this is a universal feature shared by East Asian leaders, no matter which ideology they are pursuing. Furthermore, the core of Confucian virtues remains as a powerful force to unite people around a leadership that skillfully employs it in East Asian society. All these arguments will be justified through the scrutiny of Hồ Chí Minh's Confucian foundation and his cardinal revolutionary moral values as explained in *Let's Change Our Methods of Work*.

Introductory Remarks

In 1962, the French journal *La Pensée,* a quarterly review of "modern rationalism" founded in Paris, published a feature essay titled "Confucianisme et Marxisme au Vietnam" (Confucianism and Marxism in Vietnam) (*La Pensée,* no. 105 [October 1962]) by Vietnamese pediatrician and political activist Nguyễn Khắc Viện (1913–1997). It was later translated into English in 1974,[1] and subsequently became Viện's most widely read work. Ironically, however, it was not available in Vietnamese translation until 1993, more than three decades after its initial publication[2] and about seven years after the implementation of Đổi Mới (Renovation) policy in Vietnam.[3] The 1993 Vietnamese edition included a short but significant note from the translators, who observed that the essay "has been translated into many languages. That year [1962], the Sự Thật Publishing House[4] in Hanoi translated it into Vietnamese, but did not publish it."[5] Although the translators offered no explanation for the three-decade delay in publication, Nguyễn Khắc Viện himself offered a few hints in an appendix to the 1993 volume. The appendix, which Viện had drafted during the 1980s, proposed "to review a few crucial points from the previous essay before discussing other issues." Viện first restated the main argument that he had advanced in 1962, and acknowledged that his thesis had provoked controversy:

> Confucianism paved the way with auspicious conditions for the introduction of Marxism [into Vietnam]. This is an argument that has caused many "waves and winds." The main argument is that unlike other religions, [the aim of] Confucianism is to direct human beings' thought completely into social life; therefore it stands on the same page with Marxists. If we are able to convince a Confucian that Marxism can realize all the social ideals that he has ever thought of, this Confucian should be willing to decline Confucianism and accept Marxism. Meanwhile, socially persuading a Christian, a Buddhist, or a Muslim remains insufficient, because persuasion cannot provide them with an answer about the transcendental afterlife. Like Marxists, Confucians do not raise such a question.[6]

As a way of defending his argument, Viện identified two main historical aspects of Confucian thought. The first and most foundational aspect was
the essentially humane quality of Confucianism, which emphasized the ideal
of human social improvement. The second and far less appealing aspect of
Confucianism had to do with its recasting as a bureaucratic ideology of governance. Viện summed up this difference as follows: "one is the mandarin's
Confucianism, and the other the scholar's." According to Viện, the first aspect
of Confucianism—its fundamental humanity—was particularly apparent in
the Confucian background of Communist Party founder Hồ Chí Minh. Viện
argued that this claim regarding Hồ's affinity for Confucianism had been the
main reason that his essay had not previously been published in Vietnam.

Due to their lack of awareness of these two trends, a number of people
have blotted out the historical role of Confucianism, upholding that since its
beginning, Confucianism has only played a negative role antithetical to the so-
called folk-thought. Armed as these people are with such a prejudice, whenever
they hear someone asserting the proximity between Confucianism and Marxism, or, more seriously, mentioning some Confucian elements in President Hồ's
thought, they will treat [these allegations] as "heresies" or "insubordinations."

To back up his claims about Hồ's embrace of Confucianism, Nguyễn Khắc
Viện also cited at length a few passages from a 1948 handbook authored by
Hồ titled *Sửa đổi lề lối làm việc* (Let's change our methods of work). In this
text, Hồ undertook to transform pivotal Confucian values into revolutionary
moral concepts. An investigation of Viện's essay, coupled with an analysis of
Hồ's handbook, reveals some of the ways in which Vietnamese intellectuals and
political elites undertook to adapt core elements of Confucian morality into a
revolutionary ethical system.

Nguyễn Khắc Viện and His Essay

According to the autobiographical account in his book *Đạo và đời* (The way
and life), Nguyễn Khắc Viện was born into "a laureate family."[7] His father
Nguyễn Khắc Niêm (1889–1954) passed the imperial examination at a very
young age in 1907, with the title of Metropolitan Graduate with Honors, and
then served as a mandarin of the Nguyễn dynasty, but did not want his son
to follow in his footsteps. Viện was sent to a Franco-Vietnamese elementary
school, and later attended high school in Vinh, Huế, and Hanoi. After studying in Hanoi's Medical School for three years (1934–1937), Viện continued
his study in Paris. Having earned his medical degrees in pediatrics and tropi-
cal diseases in 1940 and 1941, respectively, he became active in the politics of
the overseas Vietnamese community in France. Suffering from tuberculosis,
Viện had to undergo seven surgeries between 1943 and 1948: eight of his ribs,

the entirety of his right lung, and one-third of his left lung were removed, and doctors warned him that he had at most two years to live. But instead of surrendering to this miserable fate, Viện consulted various "books on Eastern and Western philosophies," and finally adopted the technique of "breathing with the stomach" as a treatment for his aliments. In 1949, as Viện was recovering, he joined the French Communist Party. This was a significant political landmark in Nguyễn Khắc Viện's life, and he would later describe himself as "rooted in Confucianism but equipped with [the] experimental science that is liberal democracy and Marxism."[8]

As the secretary general and Communist Party secretary of the Overseas Vietnamese Federation in France from 1952 to 1963, Nguyễn Khắc Viện was a leader of the Vietnamese liberation movement in France, and contributed to notable French journals such as *La Pensée, La Nouvelle critique, Démocratie nouvelle,* and *Europe.* His essay "Confucianism and Marxism in Vietnam" was written during this time, coincident with the construction of "the initial foundation of socialism" in North Vietnam and "the struggle against [the] U.S. neocolonialism regime" in South Vietnam.[9] Recalling the causes and conditions of his essay's composition, Viện writes:

> On the occasion of a discussion with writer Albert Camus, I raised the question on the relationship between Confucianism and Marxism in Vietnam. I presented a few arguments. First, Confucianism actually had two trends; one was humane/anthropocentric [*nhân bản* 人本], and the other feudal [*phong kiến* 封建]. Second, although differing from one another, Marxism and Confucianism share a common point [in] that [each] directs human thought toward the improvement of social organization, and the construction of relationships among people, but makes no claims about where the soul goes after death, whether [to] heaven or hell. Hence, if persuaded, those who follow Confucian teaching can accept Marxism. Based on these observations, I wrote an essay printed in the journal *La Pensée* in 1962. This work received a lot of attention from the public within and outside Vietnam because the way it posed questions was not as rigidly dogmatic as the style favored by many Party authors during that period. Some brothers from Sự Thật ["Truth"] Publishing House also suggested that the work be translated and published, but they could not obtain permission and had to abandon the idea.[10]

In addition to reiterating his main point about the basic compatibility of Confucianism and Marxism, Nguyễn Khắc Viện also specified the adaptability and relevance of Confucianism in a new society founded on Marxist philosophy. Trained with the anthropocentric and collectivistic spirit of Confucianism, Vietnamese Confucian scholars, according to Viện, saw no conflict in their transition from the teaching of Confucius to the doctrine of Karl Marx. Viện's bifurcation of Confucianism into "humane/anthropocentric" versus "feudal" traditions was designed to legitimate it in the new socialist Vietnam. Yet it was the very distinctiveness of the essay's claims that had triggered the negative reactions against it.

Due to his antiwar activities, Nguyễn Khắc Viện was expelled from France and returned to Vietnam in 1963. Around the same time, the Ninth Plenum of the Vietnam Worker's Party passed a Resolution on "The International Situation and the Party's International Duties," which called on the Party to fight against opportunism, revisionism, dogmatism, and sectarianism.[11] Viện later described the political atmosphere in North Vietnam at that time as fraught with tension and suspicion:

> When I returned [to Vietnam], people in the country were conducting a course on learning Resolution Nine against revisionism. Since I had just come back, I did not yet fully understand the Party's internal situation. [The transfer of] my Party membership was also not yet accepted. [Vietnamese] members of the French Communist Party who had returned to Vietnam before 1960 only needed to complete a couple of formalities, and quickly joined the Vietnamese Party. However, as there occurred the problem of fighting against "revisionists" starting from 1960, European parties were regarded as "revisionist," and consequently Party members coming home from European countries had to endure a trial period [to verify if they were qualified to join the Vietnamese Communist Party]. The political situation of 1963 was truly quite complicated.[12]

Although Nguyễn Khắc Viện did not explicitly link the suppression of the Vietnamese version of his essay to the 1960s domestic context in North Vietnam, such a political situation was evidently unfavorable for the publication of his work.[13]

After his return, Viện eventually gained admission to the Party and was placed in charge of the Foreign Language Publishing House in Hanoi, where he became "an interpreter of Vietnamese history, culture, and the Vietnamese struggle to the many intellectuals, militants, and journalists sympathetic to Vietnam who visited Hanoi during the Vietnam War, from 1965 to 1975." In this role, he was "one of the Vietnamese scholars who did most to interpret Vietnam for the West."[14] Although he rejoiced at the end of the war and the reunification of the country in 1975, Viện remained critical of whatever was detrimental to the development of the nation. During the period from 1976 to 1993, he submitted about thirty recommendations, comments, and letters discussing various critical issues of the country and calling for reforms to leaders of the Party, the National Assembly, and the Government. These documents were not released to the public at the time, and only a portion of them was recently published.[15] In 1992, in keeping with the implementation of the Đổi mới policy, the Party's General Secretary Đỗ Mười had several meetings with various audiences, assuring them that the Party would welcome divergent ideas from the people.[16] It is probably not coincidental that in the following year, 1993, Thế Giới Publishers (formerly Viện's Foreign Language Publishing House) printed the Vietnamese translation of his essay together with some of his other writings in a book titled *Bàn về đạo Nho* (On Confucianism).

The publication of Nguyễn Khắc Viện's book *On Confucianism* in 1993 should be examined in relation to the broader reappraisal of Confucianism in connection with its alleged contribution to the rise of the "Four Asian Tigers" (alternatively, "Four Asian Little Dragons")—Hong Kong, Singapore, South Korea, and Taiwan. As early as 1974, Edwin O. Reischauer attributed the economic success of Japan, South Korea, Taiwan, Hong Kong, and Singapore to a number of key traits easily linked to Confucian values.[17] In his "1984's Supplemental Notes," Viện mentioned *en passant* that "a Japanese scholar[18] has also formed the argument that Confucianism has helped nations like Japan, Taiwan, [and] Korea easily move toward modernity."[19] In the same vein as these observations, *Le Nouveau monde sinisé* (The new sinicized world) by French scholar Léon Vandermeersch was translated into Vietnamese in 1992, reconfirming the appreciation of Confucianism within an Asian framework.[20] More than thirty years after he first wrote it, Viện's essay seemed to be reaching Vietnamese readers at a propitious moment. Four years later, in 1997, its author passed away at the age of eighty-four.

In a section of the 1962 essay called "Confucians and Marxists," Nguyễn Khắc Viện painted a picture of Vietnam's first Marxists. In most cases, these revolutionaries were "petty intellectuals," educated in the Franco-Vietnamese education system but "forced to end their studies before taking their baccalaureate exams." In other cases, they were "village teachers, often at private schools, just like the scholars of old."[21] Having grown up in the Confucian tradition, these Vietnamese Marxist cadres often appreciated and integrated Confucian principles of political morality into their revolutionary lives:

> The notion that leaders should exemplify high moral standards was deeply engrained in Confucian countries.... [Today's Marxists] still recite Confucian sayings: "Do not be corrupted by wealth," "Do not succumb in the face of adversity," "Do not bow your head before demonstrations of force."[22]

To support this contention, Viện quoted long passages from a handbook called *Sửa đổi lề lối làm việc* (Let's change our methods of work) that was employed as a main material for the Party's cadre training during the national liberation war in the late 1940s. Although Viện did not mention the identity of the writer of the handbook, Hồ Chí Minh (under the pen name of X.Y.Z.) is widely known to have been its author. And even though the reason why the author's name is omitted remains unknown, the cited passages in Viện's essay clearly showed how Hồ had transformed pivotal Confucian moral values into key virtues required for the revolutionary. Before examining their transformation in detail, let us do a quick review of Hồ Chí Minh's attitude toward Confucianism.

The Issue of the Noble Man and the Revolutionary

A number of Vietnamese scholars have written about Hồ Chí Minh and Confucianism since the 1990s.[23] The opening of a 1993 essay titled "Nguyễn Ái Quốc—Hồ Chí Minh với Nho giáo" (Nguyễn Ái Quốc—[also known as] Hồ Chí Minh and Confucianism) by Nguyễn Đình Chú points out that

> There exists something strange in the following case: Confucianism had had a predestined affinity with Nguyễn Ái Quốc since his childhood, and followed Hồ Chí Minh to the end of his life; and although the discipline "Hồ Chí Minh Studies" was founded and has been developing for about thirty years, the recognition of Confucian influence on Nguyễn Ái Quốc—Hồ Chí Minh—was officially promoted only three years ago (1990), on the occasion of the commemoration of the centenary of his birth. Perhaps the title of "Cultural Personality" that the world offered him on the occasion of this commemoration[24] plus the atmosphere of renovation started after the Sixth National Plenum of the Communist Party of Vietnam have helped us to overcome that abnormal thing.[25]

The Confucian background of Hồ Chí Minh has recently been lauded as a key part of his commitment to patriotic tradition. According to an official biography of Hồ Chí Minh (announced on the website of the Ho Chi Minh Museum), Hồ "was born into a *family of patriotic Confucian scholars,* and grew up in a locality that had a patriotic tradition of valorous fighting against aggression."[26] Thus, we may wonder what Hồ Chí Minh himself thought of Confucianism.

In a conversation with Russian poet and essayist Osip E. Mandelstam (1891–1938) in Moscow in 1923, Nguyễn Ái Quốc (the future Hồ Chí Minh) offered an understanding of Confucianism framed within a Vietnamese context:

I was born into a Vietnamese Confucian family.... The youth from those families often studied Confucianism. Comrade, you must know that Confucianism is not a religion but a science of moral experience and conduct. Based on this foundation, one puts forward the notion of the "Great Unity."[27]

Mandelstam recorded these words in an interview-like essay under the title "Visiting an International Communist Warrior—Nguyễn Ái Quốc." For Mandelstam, the view of Confucianism as "a science of moral experience and conduct" plus the Confucian goal of the "Great Unity" in Nguyễn Ái Quốc's narrative were highly suitable to communist ideals.

Hồ Chí Minh regarded Confucianism as part of his life. In a speech presented at the ceremony to celebrate the National Unity Front (Liên hiệp quốc gia) organized by the Buddhist Association for National Salvation (Hội Phật giáo cứu quốc) on January 5, 1946, Hồ claimed that " As Buddhists believe in Buddha, [and] Christians believe in God, *we believe in the teaching of Confucius.* Those are the most venerated to whom we entrust."[28] Later, during an interview with Vasidev Rao of Reuters in May 1947, when asked whether Hồ Chí Minh's government would include members of all social classes and parties in order to reach a political solution for a Vietnamese-French relationship, Hồ asserted that "*Hồ Chí Minh may pursue Marxism, or follow Confucianism,* but the Vietnamese government still comprises representatives of all parties and even those who belong to no party at all."[29]

Among the extant writings collected in *Hồ Chí Minh: The Complete Works* (*Hồ Chí Minh toàn tập*), there survives a short article titled "Confucius," published in 1927.[30] This article expressed Hồ's reaction to the Chinese Nationalist Government's decision "to henceforth abolish all ceremonies commemorating Confucius as well as projected expenses for those rituals, and to use all temples of Confucius as public schools." Hồ's reaction in this particular case was based not only on his political standpoint, but also on his general understanding of Confucius and Confucianism. According to the article, the Chinese Nationalist Government's official order was issued on February 15, 1927.[31] Hồ Chí Minh (also known as Ly Thuy around that time) wrote the article in Guangzhou—the former seat of the Nationalist Government, and commented on the abolition of the ceremonial ritual clearly from a communist perspective. The Nationalist Government's order discussed in Hồ's article was the beginning of an ideological policy that would be widespread in China in the next few years, pinpointing Confucius' political shortcomings, and reevaluating the contributions of Confucianism to the development of China through history.[32] Ho's response to this policy was decidedly mixed. While he seemed prepared to accept the abolition of Confucianism as a political doctrine, he argued that it could and should be preserved as a system of moral values:

> With the abolition of rituals commemorating Confucius, the Chinese government has dropped an old institution that goes against the spirit of democracy. For us, the Vietnamese, let us perfect ourselves spiritually by reading Confucius' works, and revolutionarily reading Lenin's works is a must.[33]

Eighteen years later, as the provisional president of the Democratic Republic of Vietnam, Hồ Chí Minh had the chance to formally pay respect to Confucius and his teaching in a revolutionary spirit and style. As the head of the new state, standing against colonialism and feudalism, in David Marr's words "Hồ was quite selective when it came to participation in commemorations, reflecting the national persona he was crafting for himself."[34] Nonetheless, on October 21, 1945, President Hồ invited the former emperor, Bảo Đại, who had previously announced his abdication, and was currently serving as a "Supreme Adviser" to the new DRV, to accompany him to Hanoi's Giám Temple (also known as the Temple of Literature, dedicated to Confucius) and attend the Autumn Ritual commemorating the Sage. It was worth mentioning that not only Vietnamese government officers but also high-ranking Chinese officials took part in this annual commemoration. It was also noteworthy that Hồ Chí Minh played the role of the ritual host, and that the commemoration "was carried out with a specifically new spirit" through several reformed rituals, reflecting the "breaking with bad feudal practices to follow the path of revolutionary democracy."[35]

The fusion of Confucian and revolutionary values was prevalent indeed during the early years of the DRV. Perhaps the best evidence of this appears in the reworking of the concept of "noble person" (*junzi/quân tử* 君子) in official DRV discourse. Only about three weeks after the commemoration of Confucius hosted by President Hồ, the DRV's first university opened in Hanoi. As the General Director of the Higher Education Department and the Director of the École française d'Extrême-Orient, Professor Nguyễn Văn Huyên delivered the opening speech at the university's inauguration in the presence of President Hồ. Emphasizing the university's responsibility to train a new generation of Vietnamese intellectuals, Nguyễn Văn Huyên announced:

> We all feel responsible in training a number of people who possess good morals and the capability to guide the masses. Should you allow me to employ an ancient term with its ancient connotations from an Eastern civilization, [these people are] *quân tử,* who, on the one hand, know how to hone their knowledge to be able to evaluate any force of civilization,

and who, on the other hand, also apprehend how to process practically so that they can apply their wisdom in life, raising the national flag together with their brothers, sisters, and compatriots of different professions, even in thunderous storms, and in all international meetings on culture built on the glorious foundation of peace, justice, liberty, happiness, and universal love of human beings in the future.[36]

The *quân tử* (noble person) in this speech implicitly carried on the traditional Confucian values, yet was also a blend of both nationalism and internationalism. Although sometimes overlooked, the notion of the "noble person" always serves as the foundation for the construction of the ideal personality (colored with a specific political ideology) in countries influenced by Confucian culture. In his essay, Nguyễn Khắc Viện portrayed Hồ Chí Minh as "a Confucian scholar who changed from one philosophy to another,"[37] and "yet still retained his basic personality of a *'quan-tu.'*"[38] Peter A. DeCaro, in his study *Rhetoric of Revolt*, even dedicates a full-length chapter to a portrait of "Ho Chi Minh: The Chun Tzu [*junzi*]."[39] Just as he had reformed the rituals commemorating Confucius along revolutionary lines, Hồ Chí Minh would promote the new image of the revolutionary (and not the "noble man"), with redefined Confucian values, in his handbook *Let's Change Our Methods of Work*.

Let's Change Our Methods of Work

For a better apprehension of the handbook *Let's Change Our Methods of Work* (hereafter, "the handbook"), a brief review of its historical background is needed. Hồ Chí Minh completed the handbook in October 1947 under the penname of X.Y.Z. It was first printed by Sự thật ("Truth") Publishing House in 1948, and was subsequently reprinted several times in Vietnam.

During the short but tumultuous period from 1945 to 1948, the Vietnamese were fighting for their country's unity and independence from the Japanese and French occupiers. Taking advantage of the Japanese surrender at the conclusion of World War II, the Việt Minh (League for the Independence of Vietnam), under the leadership of Hồ Chí Minh, established the new state known as the Democratic Republic of Vietnam on August 28, 1945. A few days later, on September 2, Hồ proclaimed Vietnam's independence in Hanoi, opening his speech with Thomas Jefferson's declaration "that all men are created equal, that they are endowed by their Creator with certain unalienable rights, that among these are life, liberty, and the pursuit of happiness."[40] More than a year later, unwilling to lose its colony, France opened fire in Hanoi on December 17, 1946; shortly after that, on December 19, France issued an ultimatum, demanding the disarmament of the DRV's armed forces. Refusing the French demand, on December 20, as DRV President, Hồ appealed to the whole nation to stand up and join the national resistance against the colonial regime. The Việt Bắc, a mountainous region between the Sino-Vietnamese border and the Red River, then became "the very cradle of the resistance." In October 1947 the French secretly launched the Lea Campaign to "destroy the foundation of Vietnamese resistance" in the north; it was also at that time that the Central Party Committee's Standing Bureau decided to "destroy the winter march of the French army."[41] Hồ's resistance government not only fought against the French army, but also commenced building the foundation for a new ideology. David Marr succinctly describes the beginning of this long and complex process:

> From his mountain hideout during the Pacific War, Hồ Chí Minh promoted a mix of Confucian and modernist values to be assimilated by the [Indochinese Communist Party] members and then taught to followers.... The Propaganda Ministry under Trần Huy Liệu took responsibility for devising a comprehensive program of social transformation dubbed the New Life Campaign (Vận động Đời sống Mới).[42]

These were the historical circumstances under which the handbook was completed. Its targeted readership clearly included Party members and cadres who were striving for the nation's independence and governing part of the country's territory.

Revolutionary Virtues

Under the title "Revolutionary Virtues" (Đạo đức cách mạng), Hồ presents a concise account of the moral values that a cadre must display and embrace in order to transform himself into a revolutionary:

> It is not difficult for a cadre to become a real revolutionary if he wants to. Everything depends on his *heart-and-mind* [*lòng mình*]. If his sole interest is the Party, the country, and his compatriots, he will *gradually* become *totally just and selfless* [*chí công vô tư* 至公無私]. *As he has been just and selfless,* his personal faults will progressively decrease, and his virtues *described below* will become increasingly apparent each day. *In brief, the good* virtues are five in all: humanity [仁], *righteousness* [義], knowledge [智], courage [勇], and integrity [廉].[43]

This excerpt brings up a number of issues, including the origin of *chí công vô tư,* a phrase that would later become one of the foundational revolutionary moral values of the members and cadres of the Vietnamese Communist Party. It also illustrates Hồ's selective appropriation of certain Confucian virtues to form the list of five required norms of revolutionary virtue. The first chapter of the *Classic of Loyalty* (*Zhongjing* 忠經), titled "Heaven, Earth, and Gods" ("Tiandi Shenming" 天地神明),[44] begins with the following lines:

> A maxim from ancient times [states that] the only virtue for the above and the below to receive Heaven's favor is the way of loyalty. Overshadowed by Heaven, sustained by Earth, and followed by human beings, nothing is greater than loyalty. Loyalty means [standing at] the center, being *totally just and selfless*.[45]

Another dictum in the same chapter also reads, "Loyalty is what is described as 'being whole-hearted.'"[46] Thus, the notion of being "totally just and selfless" and the importance of the *heart-and-mind* in self-training to become "a real revolutionary" asserted in Hồ's handbook seem to have been inspired by this classical text. Although Hồ did not cite the *Classic of Loyalty* explicitly, the circulation and popularity of the classic in Vietnam can be confirmed by the local reproduction of this work now preserved at the Han-Nom Research Institute in Hanoi.[47]

At first glance, the five good virtues of the revolutionary are reminiscent of the "Five Constants" (*wuchang* 五常) originally advocated by Dong Zhongshu 董仲舒 (179–104 B.C.E.). Indeed, three of Hồ's five essential revolutionary virtues apparently were taken directly from the "Five Constants": benevolence (*ren* 仁), righteousness (*yi* 義), and knowledge (*zhi* 智). Hồ opted to replace the other two of the five, ritual (*li* 禮) and trustworthiness (*xin* 信), with courage (*yong* 勇), and integrity (*lian* 廉). However, a further reading of the *Analects* shows another group of three fundamental virtues of the noble man:[48]

> The Master said, "The way of the superior man is threefold, but I am not equal to it. Virtuous [*ren*], he is free from anxieties; wise [*zhi*], he is free from perplexities; bold [*yong*], he is free from fear."[49]

> The Master said, "The wise are free from perplexities; the virtuous from anxiety; and the bold from fear."[50]

The *Doctrine of the Mean* (*Zhongyong* 中庸) also gathers *ren, zhi,* and *yong* into a trio called *dade* 達德 ("universally binding virtues"): "Knowledge, benevolence, and courage, these three are the universally binding virtues" (*Zhongyong* 20).[51] Hence, following this approach, one may treat Hồ's revolutionary virtue quintet as a combination of the *dade* trio and two additional elements (righteousness and integrity). However, due to the quintet format of the essential revolutionary moral values, they were apparently grouped together according to the model of the "Five Constants." The choice and use of these Confucian moral concepts was reminiscent of the New Life Movement in China of the early 1930s, which emphasized the roles of the old Confucian virtues of ritual (*li* 禮), righteousness (*yi* 義), integrity (*lian* 廉), and knowledge (*zhi* 智) as a means to reinforce nationalism and modernization.[52]

In his essay titled "Virtues of *Junzi*," Antonio S. Cua tries to distinguish the basic interdependent/complete virtues of *ren* 仁 (benevolence, humaneness), *li* 禮 (rules of proper conduct, ritual, rites), and *yi* 義 (rightness, righteousness, fittingness) from dependent/partial virtues such as *kuan* 寬 (magnanimity), *xin* 信 (trustworthiness), and *yong* 勇 (courage). According to Cua, the cardinal virtues of *ren, yi,* and *li* are "relevant to all situations of human life as our actions have always effects on others," whereas the partials have their "application to circumstances," and, furthermore, their ethical value "depends on connection with the . . . cardinals."[53]

The emphasis on certain moral values reflects specifically temporal sociopolitical demands, even as the modification of the connotations of the selected moral concepts reveals the efforts to make them fit well in new social contexts. Although the handbook does not specify any reasons for its particular choices from the Confucian repertoire of moral concepts, reading its interpretation of the five highlighted virtues can help to better understand why Hồ selected them.

HUMANITY

Humanity (*ren*) is the first virtue to be interpreted, and its interpretation also paves the way for the representation of the remaining virtues. The handbook explains:

> The virtue of humanity consists of loving deeply and wholeheartedly assisting one's comrades and compatriots. That is why the cadre who displays this virtue wages a resolute struggle against all those who would harm the Party and people. That is why he will not hesitate to be the first to endure hardship and the last to enjoy happiness. That is why he will not covet wealth and honor, nor fear hardship and suffering, nor be afraid to fight those in power. Those who want nothing are afraid of nothing and will always succeed in doing the right thing.[54]

In this explanation of "humanity," readers can identify at least two Confucian writings that have been reworded and altered for a better fit into the handbook's new context. First, there is Fan Zhongyan's 范仲淹 (989–1052) oft-quoted motto from his "Memorial to Yueyang Tower" (*Yueyang Lou ji* 岳陽樓記): "Be the first in all under heaven to bear hardship, be the last in all under heaven to enjoy happiness."[55] Moreover, Fan's thought is followed by a slight modification of Mencius' definition of "the great man" (*dazhangfu* 大丈夫). A passage in the *Mencius* reads:

> To be above the power of riches and honors to make dissipated, of poverty and mean condition to make swerve from principle, and of power and force to make bend—these characteristics constitute the great man.[56]

For Hồ, the ideal revolutionary was obviously close to the Confucian "great man." At the same time, Hồ departed from classical precedents in subtle ways. As described by the handbook, the "virtue of humanity" comprises *honestly* loving (*thật thà thương yêu*) and *wholeheartedly* assisting (*hết lòng* giúp đỡ) "one's comrades and compatriots." Here, humanity also requires sincerity (*cheng* 誠) and full devotion of one's heart-mind (*jinxin* 盡心) to realize one's object of commitment. Unlike the Confucian "great man," the revolutionary "wages a resolute struggle against all those who would harm the Party and people." Thus, for Hồ, loyalty (*zhong* 忠) was directed first and foremost to the Party and the people while love was clearly class-oriented.

RIGHTEOUSNESS

As for righteousness (*yi* 義), the handbook writes:

> Having a sense of duty means uprightness—not having ulterior motives, doing nothing unjust and having nothing to hide from the Party. It also means not being preoccupied by personal interests in conflict with those of the Party.[57]

The distinction between "just" and "unjust," the individual's transparency in front of the Party, and the harmonization between the individual's and the Party's interests here are clearly based on a subset of class-based moral values that the revolutionary must follow strictly. The distinction between "right" and "wrong" of course requires the involvement of knowledge/wisdom.

KNOWLEDGE

According to the handbook, selflessness plays a crucial role in the display and application of knowledge (*zhi* 智):

> Since one's conscience [*zhi/trí*] is not clouded by personal interests, clarity of purpose can be easily maintained. It becomes easier to reason and find the right way. One can judge men and investigate matters. Useful projects can be accomplished, while interests harmful to the Party can

be avoided. For the sake of the [Party's] just cause, people of value will be promoted while vigilance against crooks is maintained.[58]

Often rendered into English as "knowledge" or "wisdom," *zhi/trí*, as Henry Rosemont has observed, "is the philosophically significant most frequently occurring term in the *Analects*."[59] Having examined this concept in various contexts of the *Analects*, Rosemont concludes that "[*Zhi*] is perhaps best defined as *a sense of what it is most fitting to do in our interactions with our fellow human beings, understanding why, performing those actions, and achieving a sense of well-being from so doing*."[60] Hence, there is another translation suggested by Roger Ames for this Confucian concept: the term "realize" can serve well here, for "it is epistemically as strong in English as 'know' with respect to truth conditions."[61] Moreover, since "realize" also means "[making] real" it simultaneously carries the meaning of "[putting] into practice" with the proper stances and feelings toward what one is making real in one's conduct. Through Confucius' teaching on *zhi/trí*, Rosemont finally sees it as "religious or spiritual instructions for how to live a meaningful life."[62] The handbook's description of this concept also reflects this spirit, but redefines it on the basis of the interests of the Party and the people.

COURAGE

For Hồ, the introductions of *nhân, nghĩa,* and *trí* prepared the way for the fourth moral virtue, "courage" (*yong* 勇):

> Having courage means carrying out what one believes is right. It means not being afraid to correct one's faults, to endure suffering, and to face hardship. It means not hesitating to reject honors and ill-gained wealth. If necessary, it means the sacrifice of one's life for the Party and country without qualm.[63]

The premise on which Hồ understands *yong* is clear: it must be carried out on the basis of daring to realize "what one believes is right" (*gặp việc phải có gan làm*).[64] This principle is in agreement with Confucius' sayings in the *Analects*, where the Master emphasizes the critical need of righteousness in improving personal courage:

> To see what is right and not to do it is want of courage.[65] (2.24)

> Zilu said, "Does the superior man esteem valor [courage]?" The Master said, "The superior man holds righteousness to be of superior importance. A man in a superior situation, having valor without righteousness,

will be guilty of insubordination; one of the lower people, having valor without righteousness, will commit robbery. (17.23)

According to the *Analects,* courage must be guided by righteousness, and in its turn righteousness must be based on humanity/benevolence as indicated by Confucius: "Men of humanity are sure to be bold, but those who are bold may not always be men of humanity" (14.5).[66] Based on the *Analects'* accounts, one scholar has described the interrelationship among humanity, righteousness, and, implicitly, courage as follows:

> Hence, a *ren* person must be a righteous (*yi*) person. If this reasoning is correct, the relationship between *ren* and *yi* has to be that *ren* determines both *yi* as the rightness of an action and *yi* as the righteousness of the agent.[67]

Noteworthy is that courage is often linked to other virtues in the *Analects,* such as the love of learning: "There is the love of boldness without the love of learning; the beclouding here leads to insubordination" (17.8).[68] Bravery must follow propriety/rites (*li* 禮) to avoid chaos—"Boldness, without the rules of propriety, becomes insubordination" (8.2)[69]—and this is why Confucius hates those who "have valor merely, and are unobservant of propriety" (17.24).[70] In the handbook, since the "propriety/rites" of the Five Constants are not listed among the five required virtues of the revolutionary, the absence of the link between this moral value and courage is understandable. However, as we have seen in the elucidations of the previous three moral values of benevolence, righteousness, and knowledge, loyalty to the Party and the people stands out as the pivotal criterion that defines every single virtue essential for the revolutionary's self-cultivation. This trend of thought was first promoted in 1946 in the educational system of the Democratic Republic of Vietnam, and became an essential moral norm of the Vietnamese state.[71] Hồ Chí Minh would later crystallize this loyalty in his oft-cited motto, originally written in 1955:

> Revolutionary virtue can be summarized as clearly distinguishing right from wrong, persevering with class position, wholeheartedly being loyal to the country, and unreservedly practicing filial piety toward people (*tận trung với nước, tận hiếu với dân*).[72]

Nine years later, in 1964, he proclaimed another version of the motto:

> Our army is loyal (*trung* 忠) to the Party, and practices filial piety (*hiếu* 孝) toward the people, being ready to fight and sacrifice their lives for the independence and freedom of the fatherland, and for socialism.[73]

"Being loyal to the country/the Party and practicing filial piety toward the people" has been regarded as one of Hồ Chí Minh's fundamental ideas. The textbook *Tư tưởng Hồ Chí Minh* (Hồ Chí Minh's thought), prepared for college students, observes this principal virtue:

> Hồ Chí Minh introduces new revolutionary contents into a new concept, namely "being loyal to the country and practicing filial piety toward the people." This is the most important moral criterion. Moving from being loyal to the king and practicing filial piety toward parents to being loyal to the country and practicing filial piety toward the people is a revolution in moral conception. Hồ Chí Minh reverses the old Confucian concept, and constructs new morality as if "a man firmly stands on his feet, and raises his head toward the sky."

> In Hồ Chí Minh's view, the country is the people's country and the people are the country's owner. Hence, "being loyal to the country and practicing filial piety toward the people" is the expression of responsibility toward the enterprise of nation-building-and-defending and the development path of the country.

> The core content of loyalty to the country is that within the relationships of individuals, community, and society, one must give the foremost priority to the interests of the Party, Fatherland, and Revolution.[74]

The common thread that traverses the first four revolutionary moral values of humanity, righteousness, knowledge, and courage has been summed up in Hồ Chí Minh's mottos and clarified in the commentaries: as the representative of the country and the people, the Party deserves the top priority, and loyalty to the Party assures the perfection of the five fundamental revolutionary virtues highlighted in the handbook. Reading the handbook in its original context when the Party was taking the lead in the fight against feudalism and the resistance against French colonialism, one can straightforwardly understand why courage was one of the five desired moral values for the revolutionary.

INTEGRITY

As a Confucian moral value, depending on the contexts in which it emerges, *lian* 廉 has been rendered into various English equivalents, such as "grave reserve,"[75] "self-denying purity,"[76] or "upright, honourable, integrity and character."[77] However, the most common equivalent is "integrity," which also appears in Nguyễn Khắc Viện's citation from the handbook:

Having integrity means not coveting status or wealth, not seeking an easy life or *not willing to be flattered by others.* That is why one can be lucid and generous and avoid self-degradation. *There exists only one type of eagerness—that is the eagerness to study, work, and make progress.*[78]

In the Vietnamese original of the citation, the term *tham* ("coveting" 貪) stands for different English rewordings, such as "seeking" or "willing." The quote ends with the eagerness for self-cultivation, and this reminds us of a saying from the *Analects*: "When his desires are set on benevolent government, and he secures it, who will accuse him of covetousness?" (20.2).[79] Having a rhetorical structure similar to Confucius' cited assertion, the handbook defines "integrity" as the avoidance of any temptations that lead to self-degradation, and the enthusiastic striving for self-improvement.

Two years later, in 1949, writing under the pseudonym of Lê Quyết Thắng, Hồ Chí Minh revisited this moral concept in a series of four newspaper articles on diligence (*cần* 勤), frugality (*kiệm* 儉), integrity (*liêm* 廉), and straightforwardness (*chính* 正),[80] and discussed *liêm* in great detail:

> *Liêm* means purity, without greediness. In the past, under feudalism, mandarins who did not squeeze money from the people were called *liêm,* but it has only a narrow meaning. Our country is now the Democratic Republic; and the term *liêm* has a broader meaning. Everyone must practice *liêm.* Similarly *trung* is to be loyal to the Fatherland, and *hiếu* means to practice filial piety toward people. We love our parents, but we must also love others' parents, and inspire the love for parents in all human beings.
>
> *Liêm* must be accompanied by *kiệm.* Correspondingly, *kiệm* must be paired with *cần. Kiệm* is the premise for the practice of *liêm,* because lavish spending begets greediness.
>
> …Our nation is carrying out the war of resistance and structuring the country, building the New Life in our new Vietnam. Not only do we need to be diligent and frugal, but we must also keep our purity/integrity (*liêm*).[81]

Here, as in the earlier handbook, Hồ sought to redefine Confucian key moral values in the context of revolutionary Vietnam in the 1940s. An examination of some Confucian classics, such as the *Analects, Mencius, Liji* (Classic of Rites), and *Xunzi,* to name but a few, shows that *liêm* has various connotations, and as a moral value it can be universally practiced without restriction to any social class.[82] Like Hồ's elucidations of the other Confucianism-based moral values, his interpretation of *liêm* is positioned within the framework of the war of resistance and nation-building led by the Communist Party.

WHY ARE PROPRIETY AND TRUSTWORTHINESS MISSING?

The absence of two Confucian constants, propriety (*li* 禮) and trustworthiness (*xin* 信), from Hồ's set of revolutionary virtues cannot be easily overlooked. Given its status as a cardinal virtue, the exclusion of "propriety" from the list is particularly striking. As we will see, the logic of the omission of "propriety" helps explain Hồ's decision to leave "trustworthiness" off the list. Having reviewed extant documents relevant to Hồ Chí Minh and Confucian morality, Hoa John Le Van concludes:

> As a son of a Vietnamese mandarin-scholar, [Hồ Chí Minh] was trained early in the Confucian heritage. The five cardinal virtues of compassion, righteousness, ritual, knowledge, [and] integrity, perhaps except for ritual, were part of [Hồ]'s personal life.[83]

Nonetheless, Hồ Chí Minh himself did not stipulate why he left "propriety" out of the repertoire of revolutionary virtues. Various scholars have endeavored to fill in the gap, rationalizing any possible reason that might have caused Hồ to pass over "propriety." The following is a line of reasoning articulated by a Vietnamese academic:

> Whenever talking about human beings' virtue, Confucians often link it with *li/lễ* of the Five Constants (*ren, yi, li, zhi, xin*). Based on the explanation from the *Shuowen jiezi* [說文解字, Explanation of patterns, elaboration of graphs], the principle of *li* is "stable steps, respecting the spirits, and seeking happiness,"[84] reflecting the relationship between human beings and spirits. [*Li*] is combined with theocracy, and developed into the distinction between superior and inferior, rich and poor, closeness and distance, that is founded on a strict aristocratic ranking system. Therefore, in the *Zuozhuan,* the account of Zhanggong's [莊公] eighteenth year says, "As fames and positions vary, rituals are also different." ... Thus, *li/lễ* stands for the social status of the feudal hierarchy. Among the dominant classes, *li/lễ* also cannot escape from it. *Li/lễ* becomes a powerful political tool, and an effective method for controlling the realm and people in the feudal monarchical age. Thus, in *Hồ Chí Minh: The Complete Works* (ten volumes with 7,053 pages in total), Uncle Hồ never mentions the term *li/lễ* from the Five Constants of feudal Confucians.[85]

The passage starts with a definition of *li* (unfortunately, inaccurately translated) from the *Shuowen jiezi* to suggest that *li* was originally deployed as an instrument to enhance the unequal relationships between human beings and spirits. It then takes the next step of identifying *li* as a feudal social practice, a claim that appears to confirm the class-based nature of this moral concept and reveal it as a "powerful political tool, and an effective method for controlling the realm and people in the feudal monarchical age." Although Hồ Chí Minh never endorsed such an understanding of *li/lễ,* it seems to be widely accepted in Vietnam, as the phrase *lễ giáo phong kiến* ("feudal proprieties") carries strongly negative connotations (especially of gender inequality). However, the author of the excerpt above seemingly overlooks a well-known dictum of Confucius in the *Analects:* "To overcome oneself and restore the practice of proprieties is benevolent love."[86] Since *ren* (benevolence) is the ground of *li* (rules of propriety), and *li* must be in accord with *ren,* "customs, rituals, regulations, and rules eventually should be regulated by *ren.*"[87] In other words, rules of propriety are the vehicle for realizing and strengthening benevolence. When discussing the civility of the revolutionary policeman in a letter written in March 1948, Hồ Chí Minh reminds the reader that police must treat people with respect, etiquette, and moral standards (*lễ phép*).[88] Obviously, revolutionary benevolent love needs to be expressed through certain revolutionary rules of propriety. *Li/lễ* was omitted from President Hồ's writings possibly due to the fact that it was generally understood as "rites" or "rituals," and its hierarchical features had been prevalently associated with feudalism. However, as the set of rules of propriety or social conventions, *li/lễ* was unquestionably required and practiced in the Democratic Republic of Vietnam.

Although trustworthiness (*xin* 信) is not recorded in the handbook's list of moral virtues that the revolutionary must acquire, it occasionally emerges as a required virtue in a number of other writings by Hồ Chí Minh. In his speech given at the concluding ceremony of a complementary training course for mid-level cadres in 1947, Hồ declared:

A good cadre must have revolutionary morality. If one is well-trained in military affairs, but lacking revolutionary morality, it is difficult to succeed. In order to acquire revolutionary morality, one must possess the following five elements: *Trí* [智], *Tín* [信], *Nhân* [仁], *Dũng* [勇], [and] *Liêm* [廉]. I now clarify them.

Trí means clear-headedness, knowing both the enemy and ourselves; recognizing good people and supporting them; identifying bad ones and not employing them; being aware of our goodness and improving it; identifying evil and avoiding it.

Tín means [that] whatever is said must be trustworthy; assertions and practices must be in accordance with one another; we must try our best to earn people's and soldiers' trust.

Nhân means to possess universal love: loving our country, people, and soldiers.

Dũng means being forceful, decisive but not jeopardizing, having well-prepared plans and determinedly carrying them out straightaway, even if facing dangers. It also means to have bravery in any business.

Liêm means not to covet fame or position, not being excessively desirous of life, money, and sex. A cadre who dares to sacrifice his life for the fatherland, for his people, and for the just cause does not covet anything.[89]

The above-cited passage not only furnishes us with another chance to further comprehend Hồ's understanding of *trí, nhân, dũng,* and *liêm,* but also supplies us with his explanation of *tín,* another moral value. Hồ Chí Minh's notion of *tín* is basically in agreement with the Confucian notion of *xin,* which emphasizes verbal commitment with respect to one's deeds. This point can be illustrated through a couple of examples from the *Analects.* For instance, when asked about how a man's conduct can be appreciated by his fellows, Confucius replies, "Let his words be sincere and truthful, and his actions honorable and careful."[90] In another case, the Master places emphasis on the imperative concordance between words and conduct: "At first, my way with men was to hear their words, and give them credit for their conduct. Now my way is to hear their words, and look at their conduct."[91] Having examined the concept of *xin* in the *Analects,* Cecilia Wee comes to the following conclusion:

> *Xin* is concerned primarily with commitments in which verbal (or other) representations have been made, where trust can exist, and perhaps usually exists, against a background of unspoken social norms.[92]

Indeed, the agreement between words and deeds stands out as the foundational principle of *xin,* but it must be conducted against the "background of unspoken social norms." This background is spelled out in Hồ's discourse: as all means must serve revolutionary ends, the cadre must be trustworthy so as to win his people's and soldiers' hearts-and-minds. Hồ Chí Minh obviously did not treat the Confucian Five Constants as an entirety; he broke them down into individual entities and recombined them with other moral values into different clusters of five. Depending on his audience, Hồ selected a certain cluster to present to his targeted readers/listeners. Thus, even though *xin/tín* does not emerge among the "Revolutionary Virtues" discussed in the handbook *Let's*

Change Our Methods of Work, it remains as an essential quality of the revolutionary in other writings by Hồ Chí Minh.

The handbook in general and its five revolutionary moral elements in particular are in many ways reminiscent of Chinese Communist Party leader Liu Shaoqi's 劉少奇 *Lun gongchan dang yuan de xiuyang* (On the cultivation of Communist Party members).[93] First delivered as a series of lectures for CCP members at the Institute of Marxism-Leninism in Yan'an in 1939, Liu frequently invoked the Chinese concept of self-cultivation (*xiuyang* 修養), and therefore aligned his views with "Chinese tradition, most specifically with Neo-Confucian praxis based on the *Great Learning* [*Daxue* 大學], the *Mean* [*Zhongyong* 中庸], and self-examination through quiet-sitting." In this work, Liu cited several sayings from Confucian and Neo-Confucian sources, but these quotes "survive in the collective memory only as traditional sayings without awareness of their exact provenance."[94] Liu's work was translated into Vietnamese and also employed as training material for Vietnamese cadres in the late 1940s.[95]

Unlike Liu's indoctrination work, Hồ's handbook does not contain any direct quotations from the Confucian classics, although traces of those texts can be discerned in his text, as this chapter has shown. By rephrasing Confucian sayings in Vietnamese language, the handbook rhetorically presents them in a simple and easy-to-understand way, and consequently strips off the old-fashioned classical veneer of the original texts. This tactic is especially clear in Hồ's discussion of the Confucianism-inspired essential revolutionary virtues. The Confucian roots of these terms were instantly recognizable to Vietnamese elites trained in the Confucian educational system. And yet, as they were popularly employed and practiced in daily life, ordinary Vietnamese embraced them as common sense and as part of their culture, even though they were unaware of their classical provenance.

After examining several Confucian values as they were reinterpreted in Hồ Chí Minh's writings, Hoa John Le Van concludes:

> [Hồ]'s unique revolutionary contribution was his adaptation of Marxism to elaborate a new dimension of traditional Confucian values that had tightly bound Vietnamese society in ritual bondage. Earlier, we have noted that [Hồ] deliberately excluded [*lễ*, ritual] from the five basic Confucian virtues.[96]

That Hồ infused traditional Confucian values with revolutionary meanings is undeniable. However, based on the evidence presented here, it is hard to find any trace of Marxist theory in Hồ's adaptation of Confucian moral concepts. In addition to distilling and simplifying Confucian values, Hồ's revolutionary framework points his readers to the ultimate goal: service to the Party and the people, or, in Neil L. Jamieson's words, to "behave toward the party as if it were your family."[97]

Conclusion

Although there has never been any government-led campaign of "Criticizing Confucius" during the Democratic Republic of Vietnam era (1945–1975) or in the Socialist Republic of Vietnam period (1975 to the present), the treatment of Confucius and his doctrine has changed significantly over the decades. Often identified with pejorative suppressive feudalism, Confucianism has sometimes been targeted for eradication, even in countries where it enjoyed deep influence. Nguyễn Khắc Viện's essay "Confucianism and Marxism in Vietnam" serves as an example, showing an intellectual effort to acknowledge the positive aspects of "Confucianism of the scholars" of a Vietnam in transition. However, a number of his arguments, including his discussion of the relationship between Hồ Chí Minh and Confucianism, faced negative reactions and criticisms from contemporary readers. Only after the implementation of the Đổi mới (Renovation) policy, the international reappraisal of Confucianism due to the success of the four Asian Little Dragons, and the commemoration of Hồ Chí Minh as a "cultural personality" on the occasion of the centenary of his birth, did Viện's essay have the chance to reach its Vietnamese readers. Since the publication of the essay in Vietnam, numerous studies on Hồ Chí Minh and Confucianism have been carried out, revealing his skillful transformation of Confucian values to serve the nation's revolutionary cause. Cited in Nguyễn Khắc Viện's essay, the section "Revolutionary Virtues" from Hồ Chí Minh's *Let's Change Our Methods of Work* and other examples from Hồ's writings reveal how Hồ transformed pivotal Confucian moral values and reintroduced them as essential virtues required for the revolutionary. Simplified, Confucian values are rendered into new revolutionary contexts. The Confucian noble person is transformed into the ideal revolutionary and put forward to serve the revolution.

Appendix 1

1984'S SUPPLEMENTAL NOTES
by Nguyễn Khắc Viện[98]

Please allow me to review a few crucial points from the previous essay before discussing other issues:
We must clearly identify two trends of thought in Confucianism: one is

the original stream that is humane, and the other is a stream belonging to the ideology of the bureaucratic apparatus; one is the mandarin's Confucianism, and the other the scholar's.

Due to their unawareness of those two trends, several people have blotted out the historical role of Confucianism, asserting that since its beginning, Confucianism has only played a negative role in opposition to the so-called folk-thought. Of course, as they're armed with such a prejudice, whenever they hear someone asserting the proximity between Confucianism and Marxism, or, more seriously, mentioning some Confucian elements in President Hồ's thought, they will consider [these sayings] "heresies" or "insubordinations."

Also due to this type of prejudice, they believe that Nguyễn Trãi [阮廌] [1380–1442] has nothing to do with Confucianism, repudiating all Vietnamese patriotic Confucians as a whole, and treating patriotism merely as anti-Confucian. Someone even writes, "Patriotism is the *pathbreaking* light (let me emphasize the term 'pathbreaking') for the early naissance of a traditional and unique culture in Vietnamese territory."

Such statements reverse the historical process. There must first have been the establishment of a thriving and distinctive culture, and later from this foundation patriotism would gradually take shape. When the Bách Việt [百越, or "One-Hundred Viet] nations fought against the Qin-Han army, they were not motivated by patriotism; even in the time of the Trưng sisters [the rebellion against the Han military], there did not exist a true patriotism as it is understood in our time. People must have gone through a long historical process in which the resistance against foreign invasions was not the exclusive element that formed patriotism. One must include the following components:

Self-protection from natural disasters through the construction of
    embankment systems
The establishment of a centralized monarchical government
The construction of a national culture

Without the centralized monarchy with its mandarin machinery accountable for national duties based on a unified ideology, there could not exist the awareness of patriotism at an advanced level. Only when facing natural disasters and foreign invasions would commoners come to the recognition of transcending their local mentality, scholar gentry would be conscious of their duties to the nation, and everyone would be [unified] around the image of a king. Within a long historical evolution, being loyal to the king [*trung quân* 忠君] and being patriotic [*ái quốc* 愛國] would have remained inseparable from one another. Confucianism played a crucial role in the formation of patriotism. Nguyễn Đình Chiểu, Mai Xuân Thưởng, [and] Phan Đình Phùng were Confucians, and one cannot distort the truth by claiming that these patriots totally had no relationship with Confucianism.

Later, as history moved forward, there emerged more progressive regimes and ideologies. To return to Confucianism is reactionary, but to fully reject the role of Confucianism is really childish. Only the emergence of capitalist [thought] and proletarian thought could end the historical role of Confucianism. Nowadays it is easy to point out the weaknesses of Confucianism, but one has to relocate it back into its historical context to be able to see its multifacetedness.

Some have argued that people do not accept Confucianism because it arrived in our country together on "the hooves of invading soldiers." What a simplistic view! Some portion of the people will accept an ideology because of its contents, but not for its place of origin (let's consider the cases of Buddhism and Marxism!). In the early independent period, during the Lý and Trần dynasties, the centralized monarchical machinery had not reached an advanced level; although the warlords were gone, rice fields, estates, and the fiefs of royal nobles still existed. Confucianism and its unified mandarin apparatus were not accepted. The mandarin machinery employed Confucianism as its weapon to compete with Buddhism. During this period, Confucianism was progressive in comparison to Buddhism.

Others have also considered the Lý-Trần period with the dominance of Buddhism more progressive than the post-fifteenth-century Lê dynasty founded on Confucianism. To some extent, Buddhism was better than Confucianism, and the Lý-Trần regime more "likeable" than that of the Lê dynasty. However, examined within the nation's historical process, the Lê period achieved a higher level of unification of the kingdom. Newly independent, the Lý [and] Trần dynasties could only defend the northern borders of their realm; with a population still small, they could not fully explore the Red River Delta, and they had to confront two kingdoms, Champa and Khmer, without a decisive victory. The realm was always threatened by two-pronged attacks from the Northern and Southern frontiers. In the Lê dynasty, Đại Việt [大越, "Great Viet" = Vietnam] clearly gained more advantages: the Northern and Southern borders were secured for a long time, and the territory was expanded southward. This was a centralized monarchy with a mandarin apparatus working on a unified ideological foundation of Confucianism. In the historical context of that time, this regime was the most rational (in comparison to the Champa and Khmer kingdoms). Later on, Confucianism could not handle conflicts and had to concede.

Confucianism paved the way with auspicious conditions for the introduction of Marxism [into Vietnam]. This is an argument that has caused many "waves and winds." The main argument is that unlike other religions, [the aim of] Confucianism is to direct human thought completely into social life; therefore it stands on the same page with Marxists. If we are able to convince a Confucian that Marxism can realize all the social ideals that he has ever thought of, this Confucian should be willing to decline Confucianism and accept Marxism. Meanwhile, socially persuading a Christian, a Buddhist, or a Muslim remains insufficient, because persuasion cannot provide them with an answer about the transcendental afterlife. Like Marxists, Confucians do not raise such a question.

Recently a Japanese scholar[99] has also formed the argument that Confucianism has helped nations like Japan, Taiwan, and Korea more easily move toward modernity.

On this favorable land, Marxism sowed new seeds—science, democracy, and international proletarian spirit, which were completely new elements. However, like Confucianism, when the Party has held political power, the risk of the bureaucratization of Marxism is always threatening, and a Marxism bureaucratized in several aspects is very similar to Confucianism. Criticizing Confucianism is also helpful for the criticism of today's bureaucratism.

Appendix 2

CONFUCIUS[100]

Guangzhou, February 20, 1927

On February 15, the Government of the Republic of China issued a decree: henceforth to abolish all ceremonies commemorating Confucius as well as projected expenses for those rituals, and to use all temples of Confucius as public schools.

Confucius lived 2,478 years before our time. During the last 2,400 years, he had been worshiped by the Chinese people. All Chinese emperors called Confucius the head of sages, and offered honorific titles to his successors.

From ancient times, the Vietnamese people and Vietnamese kings highly respected this sage. Nevertheless, the Chinese government has just decided that from now on, there is no longer any official worship for Confucius. Is that truly a revolutionary action?

Let us first review who Confucius is, why kings and emperors venerated him so approvingly, and why the Chinese government now rejects such a sage who has been so greatly worshiped.

Confucius lived in the Spring-Autumn period. His virtue, scholarship, and knowledge have earned great admiration from his contemporaries and later generations. He studied tirelessly, and never felt shame when learning from his inferiors; being unknown to the masses did not bother him at all. His renowned formula "See what a man does. Mark his motives. Examine in what things he rests. How can a man conceal his character?"[101] reflects the profundity of his cleverness.

Nevertheless, in a setting twenty centuries ago, during the time when capitalism and imperialism did not exist, and nations were not oppressed as we have now experienced, Confucius' mind was never roused by revolutionary doctrines. His virtue is perfect but cannot accommodate our contemporary trends of thought. How can a round lid fittingly cover a square box?

Kings venerated Confucius, not only because he was not a revolutionary, but also due to the fact that he carried out a prevailing propaganda beneficial to them. They exploited Confucianism in the same way as imperialists are exploiting Christianity.

Confucianism is founded on three cardinal guides, namely [that] the king is the guide to his subjects, a father to his children, and a husband to his wife; and five constant virtues, namely benevolence, righteousness, courtesy, wisdom, and trustworthiness.

Confucius compiled the *Spring and Autumn Annals* to criticize "rebellious ministers" and "villainous sons,"[102] but did not write anything to indict the crimes of "evil fathers" and "parochial princes." In brief, he was obviously a speaker who defended the exploiters against the oppressed.

Judged by Confucian teaching, Russia, France, China, the United States, and democratic countries are nations in which moral principles are missing, and people who rise against the monarch are seditious. If Confucius lived in our time, and persistently kept those opinions, he would become a reactionary person. There could also be another possibility that this super-man would be able to cope with the situation, and quickly become a loyal inheritor of Lenin.

With the abolition of rituals commemorating Confucius, the Chinese government has dropped an old institution that goes against the spirit of democracy. For us, the Vietnamese, let us perfect ourselves spiritually by reading Confucius' works, and revolutionarily reading Lenin's works is a must.

Published in *Thanh niên* (Youth) newspaper, no. 80 (1927)
Translated [into Vietnamese] from a French translation

Notes

1. Nguyen Khac Vien, *Tradition and Revolution in Vietnam,* ed. David Marr and Jayne Werner; trans. Linda Yarr, Jayne Werner, and Tran Tuong Nhu (Berkeley, CA: Indochina Resource Center, 1974).

2. Nguyễn Khắc Viện, *Bàn về đạo Nho* (On Confucianism), trans. Đào Hùng and Trần Văn Quý (Hanoi: Thế Giới Publishing House, 1993).

3. This chapter employs the edition published by Trẻ Publishing House (Ho Chi Minh City, 1998).

4. Now known as Nhà xuất bản Chính trị Quốc gia (National Political Publishing House), this publisher belongs directly to the Party's Central Committee.

5. Nguyễn Khắc Viện, *Bàn về đạo Nho*, p. 1.

6. Ibid., p. 68. For a complete translation of the document, see Appendix 1 at the end of this chapter.

7. Nguyễn Khắc Viện, *Đạo và đời* (The way and life) (Hanoi: Social Sciences Publishing House, 2007), p. 7.

8. Nguyễn Khắc Viện, *Bàn về đạo Nho*, pp. 75–76.

9. Words used in the title of chapter 9 of Nguyễn Khắc Viện's book *Vietnam: A Long History* (Hanoi: Thế Giới Publishers, 1999).

10. Nguyễn Khắc Viện, *Ước mơ và Hoài niệm* (Wishes and yearnings) (Đà Nẵng: Đà Nẵng Publishing House, 2003), p. 143.

11. "Hội nghị lần thứ chính Ban chấp hành Trung ương Đảng khóa III, tháng 12–1963" (Ninth Plenum of the Party's Central Committee, Third Term, December 1963), accessed September 30, 2015, http://dangcongsan.vn/cpv/Modules/News/NewsDetail.aspx?co_id=30653&cn_id=65356.

12. Nguyễn Khắc Viện, *Tự truyện* (Autobiography) (Hanoi: Social Sciences Publishing House, 2007), pp. 4–105.

13. For the fight against revisionism in Vietnam, see Martin Grossheim, "'Revisionism' in the Democratic Republic of Vietnam: New Evidence from the East German Archives," *Cold War History* 5, no. 4 (November 2005): 451–477; "The Lao Động Party, Culture, and the Campaign against 'Modern Revisionism': The Democratic Republic of Vietnam before the Second Indochina War," *Journal of Vietnamese Studies* 8, no. 1 (February 2013): 80–129.

14. Elizabeth Hodgkin, "Obituary: Nguyen Khac Vien," *The Independent* (London), May 26, 1997.

15. Trung Sơn, "Nguyễn Khắc Viện và những 'di cảo' chưa công bố" (Nguyễn Khắc Viện and his unpublished 'Posthumous Manuscripts'), *Đại biểu nhân dân,* May 6, 2007, accessed September 30, 2015, http://daibieunhandan.vn/default.aspx?tabid=78&NewsId=13746; "Di cảo Nguyễn Khắc Viện: Vai trò của khoa học xã hội và dân chủ xã hội" (Nguyễn Khắc Viện's Posthumous Manuscripts: The roles of the social sciences and social democracy), *Sông hương* 294 (August 2013), accessed September 30, 2015, http://www.tapchisonghuong.com.vn/tap-chi/c289/n12315/Di-cao-Nguyen-Khac-Vien-vai-tro-cua-khoa-hoc-xa-hoi-dan-chu-xa-hoi.html.

16. "Vietnam" section in *Human Rights Watch World Report* 1992, accessed September 30, 2015, http://www.hrw.org/reports/1992/WR92/ASW-15.htm#P938_343433.

17. Edwin O. Reischauer, "The Sinic World in Perspective," *Foreign Affairs* 52, no. 2 (January 1974): 347.

18. This may refer to Morishima Michio and his book *Why has Japan "Succeeded"? Western Technology and Japanese Ethos* (Cambridge: Cambridge University Press, 1982).

19. Nguyễn Khắc Viện, *Bàn về đạo Nho*, p. 73.

20. Léon Vandermeersch, *Le Nouveau monde sinisé* (The new sinicized world) (Paris: Presses Universitaires de France, 1986); *Thế giới Hán hóa mới,* trans. Chu Tiến Anh and Hoàng Việt (Hanoi: Social Sciences Publishing House, 1992).

21. Nguyen Khac Vien, *Tradition and Revolution in Vietnam,* p. 45.

22. Ibid., pp. 47–48.

23. For instance, see Trịnh Khắc Mạnh and Chu Tuyết Lan, eds., *Thư mục Nho giáo Việt Nam = A Bibliography on Confucianism in Vietnam* (Hanoi: Social Sciences Publishing House, 2007), pp. 228–229. Some noteworthy works, just to name a few, are Lương Duy Thứ, "The Confucian Origin of Hồ Chí Minh's Ideas," in *Confucianism in Vietnam* (Ho Chi Minh City: Vietnam National University in Ho Chi Minh City, 2002), pp. 229–235; Hồ Sĩ Hùy, "Tư tưởng đạo đức Hồ Chí Minh với tinh hoa Nho giáo" (Hồ Chí Minh's moral thought and the quintessence of Confucianism), *Văn hóa Nghệ An Online,* accessed April 27, 2011, http://vanhoanghean.com.vn/goc-nhin-van-hoa3/nh%E1%BB%AFng-g%C3%B3c-nh%C3%ACn-v%C4%83n-h%C3%B3a/tu-tuong-dao-duc-ho-chi-minh-voi-tinh-hoa-nho-giao.

24. It is said that UNESCO conferred the title of "Cultural Personality" on Hồ Chí Minh. In fact, UNESCO adopted a Resolution on the commemoration of the centenary of the birth of President Hồ Chí Minh instead; see UNESCO's *Records of the General Conference: Twenty-fourth Session, Paris, 20 October to 20 November 1987,* vol. 1, *Resolutions,* pp. 134–135. However, in UNESCO's commemoration list of "Anniversaries of Great Personalities and Historic Events, 1990–1991," there are only three events listed for May 1990: the 100th anniversary of Labor Day (Federal Republic of Germany), the 100th anniversary of the birth of Portuguese poet Mario de Sa-Carneiro (Portugal), and the 100th anniversary of the founding of the National Theater (Costa Rica).

25. Nguyễn Đình Chú, "Nguyễn Ái Quốc: Hồ Chí Minh với Nho giáo" (Nguyễn Ái Quốc: Hồ Chí Minh and Confucianism), in *Tư tưởng đạo đức Hồ Chí Minh: Truyền thống dân tộc và nhân loại* (Moral thought of Hồ Chí Minh: National tradition and humankind), ed. Vũ Khiêu (Hanoi: Social Sciences Publishing House, 1993), accessed September 30, 2015, http://www.viet-studies.info/NguyenDinhChu_NguyenAiQuoc.htm.

26. Ho Chi Minh Museum, "Biography of Ho Chi Minh," accessed September 30, 2015, http://www.baotanghochiminh.vn/tabid/545/Default.aspx; emphasis added.

27. *Hồ Chí Minh toàn tập* (Hồ Chí Minh: The complete works), 2nd ed., vol. 1, *1919–1924* (Hanoi: National Politics Publisher, 2000), p. 476.

28. *Hồ Chí Minh toàn tập* (Hồ Chí Minh: The complete works), 2nd ed., vol. 4, *1945–1946* (Hanoi: National Politics Publisher, 2000), p. 256; emphasis added.

29. *Hồ Chí Minh toàn tập* (Hồ Chí Minh: The complete works), 2nd ed., vol. 5, *1947–1949* (Hanoi: National Politics Publisher, 2000), p. 373; emphasis added.

30. The time and location of this article's composition are quite clear as stated in the subtitle line "Guangzhou, February 20, 1927," but it remains unclear in which language the article was originally written. A few words added to the end of the article inform readers that it was published in a weekly newspaper called *Thanh niên* (Youth), and the current Vietnamese version is in fact a translation from another French translation (*dịch lại từ bản dịch ra tiếng Pháp*). In a report to the Comintern's Oriental Division dated June 1927, Hồ Chí Minh wrote: "Starting from November 1924, I was sent by the Oriental Division and the French Communist Party to Guangzhou to work for Indochina.... Although lacking time and money, thanks to the assistance of Russian and Vietnamese comrades, we were able to... publish three small weekly newspapers" (*Hồ Chí Minh toàn tập,* 2nd ed. [Hanoi: National Politics Publisher, 2000], vol. 2, *1924–1930,* p. 241). Thus, the newspaper in

question might have been one of the three publications printed in Guangzhou around that time.

31. This decree was issued during the transition of the Nationalist Government from Guangzhou to Wuhan, and only six days before the official inauguration of the Government in Wuhan on February 21, 1927. See Guo Tingyi 郭廷以, *Zhonghua Minguo shishi rishi* 中華民國史事日志, *1912–1949* (Daily record of historical events of the Republic of China, 1912–1949) (Beijing: Zhongyang Yanjiuyuan Jindaishi Yanjiusuo 中央研究院 近代史研究所, 1985), accessed September 30, 2015, http://fzr5185.blog.163.com/blog/static/15524088520111112913844968/.

32. See Zhang Songzhi 張頌之, "Kongjiaohui shimo huikao" 孔教會始末匯考 (Comprehensive research on the whole story of the Association for Confucian Religion), *Wen shi zhe* 文史哲 1 (2008): 68; Wang Shichun 汪士淳, *Ruzhe xing: Kong Decheng Xiansheng zhuan* 儒者行：孔德成先生傳 (A Confucian's practices: A biography of Mr. Kong Decheng) (Taipei: Lianjing, 2013), pp. 65–67.

33. For a complete translation of Hồ Chí Minh's article on Confucius, see Appendix 2 at the end of this chapter.

34. David Marr, *Vietnam: State, War, and Revolution (1945–1946)* (Berkeley and Los Angeles: University of California Press, 2013), p. 471.

35. "Ngày thu lễ đức Khổng Tử tại Đền Giám" (Commemorating Confucius in the Giám Temple on an autumn day), *Cứu quốc* 73 (October 22, 1945).

36. From Nguyễn Kim Nữ Hạnh, *Tiếp bước chân cha* (Following our father's footprint) (Hanoi: Thế Giới, 2003); the letter is accessible online at http://hnue.edu.vn/directories/Science.aspx?username=thanhvn&science=75.

37. Nguyen Khac Vien, *Tradition and Revolution in Vietnam,* p. 51.

38. Hoa John Le Van, "Cultural Foundation of Ho Chi Minh's Revolutionary Ideology" (Ph.D. diss., Northwestern University, 1989), p. 12.

39. Peter A. DeCaro, *Rhetoric of Revolt: Ho Chi Minh's Discourse for Revolution* (Westport, CT, and London: Praeger, 2003), pp. 51–86.

40. For a quick reference on Vietnamese independence movements, see Shelton Woods, *The Story of Việt Nam: From Prehistory to the Present* (Ann Arbor, MI: Association for Asian Studies, 2013), pp. 37–44.

41. Nguyễn Khắc Viện, *Việt Nam: A Long History,* 7th rev. and expanded ed. (Hanoi: Thế Giới Publishers, 2007), pp. 467–468.

42. David Marr, *Vietnam: State, War, and Revolution (1945–1946),* p. 536.

43. This is my revised version of the English translation from Nguyen Khac Vien, *Tradition and Revolution in Vietnam,* pp. 48–49. I also consulted the French original, "Confucianisme et Marxisme au Vietnam" and the Vietnamese translation of the essay "Bàn về đạo Nho" as references during my revision procedure.

44. The *Zhongjing* is attributed to Ma Rong 馬融 (79–166) of the Later Han period. This work is said to be commented on by Zheng Xuan 鄭玄 (127–200), a disciple of Ma Rong. For a study of the *Zhongjing,* see Judith Suwald, "*Zhong* 忠 und das *Zhongjing* 忠經" (Ph.D. diss., Ludwig-Maximilians-University of Munich, 2008).

45. 昔在至理，上下一德，以徵天休，忠之道也。天之所覆，地之所載，人之 所履，莫大乎忠。忠者、中也，至公無私。

46. 忠也者，一其心之謂矣。

47. For instance, the Han-Nom Research Institute has a copy titled *Trung kinh hiếu kinh tiết yếu* 忠經孝經節要, reprinted in 1852 (VHv.1006); accessed September 30, 2015, http://www.hannom.org.vn/trichyeu.asp?param=8833&Catid=248.

48. Scholars have recently tried to track the origin of the trio of knowledge, benevolence, and courage even further back than the *Lunyu*. See Peng Lin 彭林, "Cong 'San dade' kan Kongzi de shu er buzuo" 從 "三達德" 看孔子的 "熟而不做" (From "Three universally binding virtues," Reexamining Confucius' self-identification as "a transmitter and not a maker"), *Kongzi yanjiu* 孔子研究 5 (2012): 32–39.

49. 子曰：君子道者三，我無能焉：仁者不憂，知者不惑，勇者不懼 (*Analects* 14.28). Unless stated otherwise, this chapter employs James Legge's translation for all citations from the *Analects*, occasionally with slight modifications. See Confucius, *Confucian Analects, The Great Learning and The Doctrine of the Mean,* trans. James Legge, 2nd rev. ed. (Oxford: Clarendon Press, 1893; New York: Dover, 1971).

50. 子曰：知者不惑，仁者不憂，勇者不懼 (9.29).

51. 知仁勇三者，天下之達德也。

52. Jay Taylor, *The Generalissimo: Chiang Kai-Shek and the Struggle for Modern China* (Cambridge, MA: Belknap Press of Harvard University Press, 2009), p. 109.

53. Antonio Cua, "Virtues of *Junzi*," in *Confucian Ethics in Retrospect and Prospect,* ed. Vincent Shen and Kwong-loi Shun (Washington, D.C.: Council for Research in Values and Philosophy, 2008), pp. 10, 9.

54. Nguyen Khac Vien, *Tradition and Revolution in Vietnam,* p. 48. In this chapter, all excerpts of the handbook *Let's Change Our Methods of Work* are from Nguyen Khac Vien's work, pp. 48–49.

55. 先天下之憂而憂，後天下之樂而樂。

56. 富貴不能淫，貧賤不能移，威武不能屈。此之謂大丈夫 ("Teng Wen Gong II," 7, in *The Works of Mencius,* trans. James Legge [Taipei: SMC Publishing Inc., 1991], p. 265).

57. Nguyen Khac Vien, *Tradition and Revolution in Vietnam,* p. 48.

58. Ibid., pp. 48–49.

59. Henry Rosemont, *A Reader's Companion to the Confucian* Analects (Basingstoke: Palgrave Macmillan, 2013), p. 30.

60. Ibid., p. 32.

61. Ibid.

62. Ibid., p. 35.

63. Nguyen Khac Vien, *Tradition and Revolution in Vietnam,* p. 49.

64. Nguyễn Khắc Viện, *Bàn về đạo Nho,* cites it as "gặp việc phải *làm* có gan làm" (literally, "daring to do what one has to do"); here I follow *Hồ Chí Minh toàn tập,* vol. 5, p. 489.

65. 見義不為無勇也。

66. 仁者必有勇，勇者不必有仁。

67. Shirong Luo, "A Defense of *Ren*-Based Interpretation of Early Confucian Ethics," in *Taking Confucian Ethics Seriously: Contemporary Theories and Applications,* ed. Kam-por Yu, Julia Tao, and Philip J. Ivanhoe (Albany: State University of New York Press, 2010), p. 136.

68. 好勇不好學，其蔽也亂。

69. 勇而無禮則亂。

70. 惡勇而無禮者。

71. David Marr, *Vietnam: State, War, and Revolution (1945–1946)*, pp. 82–83.

72. From the article titled "Người cán bộ cách mạng" (The revolutionary cadre), published in *Nhân dân* (People) newspaper on March 3, 1955; see *Hồ Chí Minh toàn tập* (Hồ Chí Minh: The complete works), 2nd ed., vol. 7, *1953–1955* (Hanoi: National Politics Publisher, 2000), p. 480. A Chinese equivalent of *tận trung với nước, tận hiếu với dân* is *weiguo jinzhong, weimin jinxiao* 為國盡忠為民盡孝.

73. This citation is from a speech given on the occasion of the twentieth anniversary of the People's Army of Vietnam on December 22, 1964; see *Hồ Chí Minh toàn tập* (Hồ Chí Minh: The complete works), 2nd ed., vol. 11, 1963–1965 (Hanoi: National Politics Publisher, 2000), p. 351.

74. Mạch Quang Thắng, ed., *Giáo trình tư tưởng Hồ Chí Minh* (Hồ Chí Minh's thought: A textbook) (Hanoi: National Political Publishing House, 2005), pp. 160–161.

75. "The stern dignity of antiquity showed itself in grave reserve; the stern dignity of the present day shows itself in quarrelsome perverseness" (古之矜也廉，今之矜也忿戾) (*Analects* 17.16).

76. In his translation of the *Mencius*, James Legge also renders *lian* as "self-denying purity," in "Teng Wen Gong II," 15.

77. Patrick Kim Cheng Low and Sik Liong Ang, "Confucian Ethics, Governance and Corporate Social Responsibility," *International Journal of Business and Management* 8, no. 4 (2013): 32.

78. The original English translation reads, "becoming angered because of the actions of others" and "Our only aim should be to study, work and make progress," respectively.

79. 欲仁而得仁，又焉貪。

80. The four articles, titled "Thế nào là *cần?*" (What is "diligence"?), "Thế nào là *kiệm?* (What is "frugality"?), "Thế nào là *liêm?*" (What is "integrity"?), and "Thế nào là *chính?* (What is "honesty"?), were consecutively printed in the newspaper *Cứu quốc* (National salvation) from May 30 to June 2, 1949. Signing under the pen name Lê Quyết Thắng (Lê the determined-to-win man), Hồ Chí Minh opens the series with a rhetorical question, "Why does President Hồ promote the slogan *Diligence, Frugality, Integrity, Honesty?*" The answer is:

> Because Diligence, Frugality, Integrity, [and] Honesty are the foundation of *the new life (đời sống mới)*, and the cornerstone of *patriotic emulation (thi dua ái quốc)*. . . . From the success of the August Revolution (1945), and the establishment of the Democratic Republic of Vietnam, until these years of resistance, thanks to Diligence, Frugality, Integrity, [and] Honesty, our people have defeated many enemies such as flooding, illiteracy, colonialism, and famine. However, among our compatriots there are some people who comprehend those concepts, and others who still do not clearly understand them. There are some people who have practiced them well, and others who have rarely realized them. Hence, we must explain the concepts in question so clearly that everyone can apprehend and practice them. (See *Hồ Chí Minh toàn tập*, vol. 5, *1947–1949*, p. 1312)

81. *Hồ Chí Minh toàn tập*, vol. 5, *1947–1949*, pp. 1321, 1323.

82. In his translation of the *Mencius*, James Legge presents his understanding of this concept through different renditions, such as "moderation" in "Li Lou II," 51; "pure" in "Wan Zhang II," 10; or "disinterestedness" in "Jin Xin II," 83.

83. Hoa John Le Van, "Cultural Foundation of Ho Chi Minh's Revolutionary Ideology," p. 263.

84. The original reads, "*Li* is as if wearing shoes [i.e., being bound and following criteria], thus, worshiping the spirits and receiving blessings [from them]" (履也。所以事神致福也).

85. Lê Văn Quán, "Bước đầu tìm hiểu Bác Hồ với học thuyết của Nho gia" (Preliminary understanding of Uncle Hồ and Confucian doctrine), in *Thông báo Hán Nôm học 1996* (Sino-Nom Studies' reports of 1996), accessed September 30, 2015, http://hannom.vass.gov.vn/noidung/thongbao/Pages/baiviet.aspx?ItemID=176.

86. 克己復禮為仁 (*Analects* 12.1; English translation from Antonio S. Cua, ed., *Encyclopedia of Chinese Philosophy* [New York: Routledge, 2003], p. 941). In China, this renowned saying was severely criticized in the anti-Lin Biao, anti-Confucius campaign during the period from 1973 to 1976.

87. Bo Mou, *Chinese Philosophy A–Z* (Edinburgh: Edinburgh University Press, 2009), p. 84.

88. *Hồ Chí Minh toàn tập*, vol. 5, *1947–1949*, p. 875. The term *lễ phép* is, in fact, a Vietnamization of the Chinese *lifa* 禮法.

89. *Hồ Chí Minh toàn tập*, vol. 5, *1947–1949*, pp. 460–461.

90. 言忠信，行篤敬 (*Analects* 15.6; James Legge's translation).

91. 始吾於人也，聽其言而信其行；今吾於人也，聽其言而觀其行 (*Analects* 5.10).

92. Cecilia Wee, "Xin, Trust, and Confucius' Ethics," *Philosophy East and West* 61, no. 3 (2011): 529.

93. This text is also known as *How to Be a Good Communist* (see *Selected Works of Liu Shaoqi* [Beijing: Foreign Languages Press, 1984–], vol. 1), online version at http://www.marxists.org/reference/archive/liu-shaoqi/1939/how-to-be/index.htm; original Chinese version available at http://www.people.com.cn/GB/shizheng/8198/30513/30515/33955/2524494.html.

94. Wm.Theodore de Bary, ed., *Sources of Chinese Tradition* (New York: Columbia University Press, 2nd ed., 2001), vol. 2, pp. 427, 430–431.

95. According to Trần Đĩnh, Liu Shaoqi's book was translated into Vietnamese as *Bàn về tu dưỡng của người cộng sản.*" See Trần Đĩnh, *Đèn cù* (Lighted merry-go-round lantern) (Người Việt Books, 2014), p. 27.

96. Hoa John Le Van, "Cultural Foundation of Ho Chi Minh's Revolutionary Ideology," p. 269.

97. Neil L. Jamieson also has a brief comment on the handbook as follows, "A handbook used by Party militants defined the core values of tradition in contemporary terms. Nhan and nghia were still the core elements of the ethical system....This handbook for cadres might be summarized in a single sentence: behave toward the party as if it were your family." See Neil L. Jamieson, *Understanding Vietnam* (Berkeley and Los Angeles: University of California Press, 1995), pp. 217–218.

98. Nguyễn Khắc Viện, *Bàn về đạo Nho,* pp. 68–73.

99. This may refer to Morishima Michio and his book *Why has Japan "Succeeded"?*

100. *Hồ Chí Minh toàn tập,* vol. 2, *1924–1930,* pp. 456–458.

101. 子曰：「視其所以，觀其所由，察其所安。人焉廋哉？」(*Analects* 2.10).

102. 孔子成春秋而亂臣賊子懼 ("Confucius completed the Spring and Autumn, and rebellious ministers and villainous sons were struck with terror") (*Mencius,* Book 3, "Tengwen Gong II," part 2.9; English translation from Legge, *Works of Mencius*).

PART III

Clarifying Confucian Values

CHAPTER 10

The Ethics of Contingency

Yinyang

Heisook KIM

IN ORDER TO UNDERSTAND how Confucian culture is relevant to a changing world cultural order, we must allow this tradition to speak on its own terms. That is, we must appeal to its own philosophical vocabulary. The language of yinyang is pervasive in Confucian philosophy, from the *Yijing* in classical times down to the contemporary New Confucianism. What I want to do in this chapter is to bring clarity to this central idea, and then explore its philosophical implications and cultural expressions. The ethics of contingency that I try to draw from the doctrine of yinyang would be of significance especially in the age of contingency that we are living in.

The concept of yinyang in the East Asian philosophical context has worked as a core idea that explains changes, harmony, and unity in both the universe and the human world. Originally, yin and yang were two words referring, respectively, to the dark and to the light. Yin indicated the phenomenon of a cloud blocking the sun and yang that of the sun shining. But later they were combined to mean a complex quality (a pair of opposites) or function (a dialectical movement) of things or phenomena that displayed a dynamic feature of the world.

The concept of yinyang as a dialectical principle or as Dao is most perspicuously present in the *Yijing* 易經, or *Book of Changes,* which has had tremendous influence on Confucianism, ancient and modern. Even though "yinyang" is found in Daoist philosophy, the *Laozi,* and the *Zhuangzi,* but not in the four cardinal Confucian books (*Si shu* 四書), the Confucian metaphysics and cosmology developed in the Song dynasty cannot be discussed without it. Its influence on Confucian culture in general is even greater. The concept of yinyang, connected with that of the Five Phases (*wuxing* 五行) of Fire, Water, Wood, Metal, and Earth, has exercised great explanatory power in China since the Han dynasty (206 B.C.E.–220 C.E.) and was widely used among Han Confucians, especially by Dong Zhongshu, for political purposes. Since Song Neo-Confucianism developed a unique worldview by fully exploiting the *Yijing,* the doctrine of yinyang and *wuxing* has constituted a basic Confucian philosophical framework within which natural phenomena and human affairs could be explained. Its influence in Confucian culture is so extensive that we cannot fully understand its nature without recourse to it. In particular, the concept of yinyang defines a special aspect of Confucian reasoning: it is the ability to balance between two conflicting opposites through ways that are quite different from other ordinary ways of reaching equilibrium and from the way that Western dialectical reason works.

As the explanatory force of yinyang has been enormous, the range of its use has been wide to the extent that it has covered the areas of metaphysics, epistemology, logic, aesthetics, and ethics as denominated by the discipline of Western philosophy. The main reason for yinyang having such diverse and widespread use is that the history of its use is long and complex, generating multiple layers of meaning.

Risking oversimplification, I want to divide these layers into three categories.

1. Yinyang as *substances.* In a Neo-Confucian context, it is used to indicate two modes of *qi* 気. It is also not unusual to find contexts where yinyang refers to people or entities like male and female and heaven and earth.
2. Yinyang as the *properties of things.* It also refers to such properties of things as dark-light, soft-hard, feminine-masculine, and low-high.
3. Yinyang as a *principle of signification.* This refers to a function that generates contrasts and differences or a principle that makes changes in the world.[1]

For all of these equivocations, there is one essential aspect of yinyang: it is always concerned with the cyclic relation and the changing movement between contraries or opposites. They keep rotating without cessation. It is the *way* (*dao* 道) in which there is an eternal movement where yin follows yang and yang follows yin, as in the movement of bending and expanding, and in the change of day and night. This relation includes interdependence, in which opposites are interfused and intermingled so that they cannot exist on their own even though they keep their own identities in the sense that one cannot be reduced to the other or be defined by the other. The exact nature of the relation, however, cannot be manifested in clear terms or concepts. In the appended remarks of the *Book of Changes,* we find this passage: "The unfathomable in the operation of yin and yang is called spirit (*shen* 神)."[2] Throughout the history of the development of Confucianism, we may find different types of yinyang relations: (1) There is yinyang as a *successive* relation, where a yin phase follows a yang phase as in an ebb and flow. (2) There is yinyang as a *simultaneous* relation, where yin grows and yang shrinks simultaneously. In this type, yin and yang always come together, overlap, and interpenetrate. And (3) there is yinyang as a *stimulus-response* relation in order to make a unified whole. My concern in this chapter is to think about the ethical implication of the principle of yinyang characterized in type 2.

The Superposition of Yinyang and Its Moral Implications

The *Book of Changes* consists of judgments and comments on sixty-four symbolic hexagrams, each consisting of double trigrams, and each one of these in turn consisting of eight trigrams having an iconic relation with an element of the universe. One of the governing concepts of the *Changes* is the intertwining of yinyang to the effect of yin existing in yang and yang in yin (陰陽錯綜). Here, Heaven (*qian* 乾), earth (*kun* 坤), water (*kan* 坎), fire (*li* 離), wind (*xun* 巽), thunder (*lei* 雷), mountain (*gen* 艮), and pond (*dui* 兌) are considered the basic elements of the universe. Each corresponds to a state of affairs or a quality such as being lofty, being low, being in adversity, being bright, bending, being in action, stopping, and being pleased. This accordingly yields various meanings piling up one upon another. A trigram consists of three lines, divided or undivided. The divided line represents yin and the undivided yang. The first, third, and fifth lines of a hexagram are considered to take yang positions, and the second, fourth, and sixth, yin positions. A divided yin line (*yinyao* 陰爻) may take either a yang or a yin position. In this way, yin and yang are always superposed in a hexagram yielding different judgments depending on the ways they are superposed.

The fact that opposites and contraries are always intertwined, interpenetrating, and interdependent has an ethical implication of great importance in the East Asian cultural context. There is nothing that is one hundred percent pure yang or pure yin. The hexagram *qian* 乾 consists of six yang lines representing the image of pure yang. But the second, fourth, and sixth lines are located in yin positions, which means that yang lines (*yangyao* 陽爻) are located in yin positions. There is yin force hidden even in *qian* as pure yang. Even when something looks like pure yang, it contains a moment that makes the transformation of it into the other phase possible. The negative moment penetrating into the purity of yang or yin is indispensable for a certain state of affairs to change into another phase. Everything categorized as yang or yin contains a moment of its own negation within it to make the alternation possible. All things in the universe change through the alternation of opposing forces, yin and yang. Everything comes and goes in a cyclic order of the universe. When a state of affairs is such that a thing reaches the utmost limit of its development, it is doomed to change into the opposite state (i.e., its annihilation). On reaching the utmost limit, however, there is already inherent in the thing a seed of downfall at the moment of change. The sage is that person who can examine the subtle emergence of the moment and foresee the turning of one phase into the next. The moment is so subtle that ordinary men cannot recognize it. The ethics of yinyang exhorts people to learn the wisdom of the sage who can see the phase of a thing within the process of its changes and thus within the totality of the vicissitudes of life. This is the way we understand *dao*.

A sage is a person who can see the superposition of yin and yang in all phenomena of the universe. By noticing a sign of fall in rising and a sign of rise in falling, for instance, a sage can see the superposition of fall and rise. All things appear in the twofold yin and yang. As there is neither pure yang nor pure yin, there is nothing that is absolutely good or evil in a moral context. Unlike the Western philosophical tradition, where one may find the concept of absolute substance, or the concept of the highest good (*summum bonum*), the Confucian tradition does away with the concept of absolute good and absolute evil. In the Christian tradition, evil has been posited as the other of the perfect good, God. Modern philosophers tend to internalize evil as something deeply rooted in human nature. Kant, for example, identified radical evil in human nature as the perversion of our will exposed in our desires and inclinations.[3] The contemporary political philosopher Hannah Arendt observed in her early work *The Origins of Totalitarianism* that radical evil is rooted in some original fault of human nature, even though she later claimed the banality of evil.[4] But in the East Asian Confucian tradition, what counts as evil is the inappropriate manifestation of moral feelings and values. Even if the moral feelings represented in the four sprouts (*si duan* 四端) are themselves purely good, they tend toward being evil when not being properly utilized. Evil in this context does not have a radical feature of being deeply rooted in human nature. In the Confucian context, it is not the case that human feelings and desires are bad on their own account. Only when they run against the principle of the middle and the rules of propriety do they become evil. But how do we know the middle and what is proper in all the variety of human situations?

The Middle as Not Fixed, but Situated

The moral ideal in the ethics of yinyang is not the removal of the bad, as it is in Kantian ethics, where one's moral will is free of desires and inclinations that follow the dictates of a practical reason that is absolutely independent of sense experience. As mentioned above, the *dao* that governs all the changes in the universe tells us that there is no eternal good or bad. Everything has its own limit containing the seed of its downfall. Thus, if you are experiencing bad fortune, then it means that good fortune will soon come. If you are on the apex, then you have to prepare yourself for the downward road. Even before you arrive at the highest point, you should already have prepared for the lowest, because the lowest is already present in the highest without being seen. By avoiding the ultimate and the final, you can control your desires at the proper level. You always have to stop before your desire is fully realized. Full realization or perfection is almost the same as excess and overflow. Being at the highest simply means being at the beginning of falling: the judgment on the top yang in the hexagram *Qian* runs, " 'A dragon that overreaches should have cause for regret': when something is at the full, it cannot last long."[5] The position of a noble man is not the top, but right below the top (the fifth line).

The principle of the middle, in a Confucian context, tells us to avoid standing on two ultimate ends of a line in all human situations. To determine the middle, we have to examine closely the situation we are in. As everything constantly changes, there cannot be a fixed middle point where the balance between the two opposing forces, yin and yang, can be achieved. In accordance with the time and position in which one is located, one can determine where the middle point is. But it is not easily found. Nor can we depend on our intuition, as may be proposed in ethical intuitionism. There is no such thing as a moral intuition by which one knows the middle once and for all. Only the wisdom of a sage may let us know where the middle is. Wisdom is based on a deep reflection on human experience, helping us to attain a fine sensibility that enables us to be in tune with the needs of the time and space of a particular situation (*shizhong* 時中).

Let us think about the example in the *Mencius* ("Jin Xin I" 盡心章句上, 26) where the difficulty of taking the middle is mentioned. Taking the middle is different from holding just one middle point while disregarding a hundred others. It is rather like holding the whole by holding one point, the middle as the center point of weight.[6]

Cheng Yi, in his commentary to the *Mencius,* says that the middle is the most difficult concept to understand, and thus we dare not talk about it but rather try to grasp it in quiescence, utterly focused using our inner eye (*mo shi xin tong* 默識心通): "It is most difficult to understand the word *zhong* (中). Thus you should try to know it through your inner mind in silence."[7]

The middle is always contextually determined depending on the perspective one takes. The wisdom of a sage is the wisdom that sees the balancing point in the fluctuation of things and the flexibility of truth in human affairs. But this wisdom is different from moral intuition, which is a priori given as the wisdom learned through experience and through trial and error. Everything has its own middle. It is therefore impossible to grasp the middle in general, or the truth in all human affairs, as Cheng Yi tells us:

> It is impossible to grasp the middle. If we knew the middle, then we would not have to wait to search for the middle in each case of human affairs and in every natural phenomenon. If there were a given middle, then it is not a real middle.[8]

To find the middle of something, we have to examine it in its particularity, that is, examine the specific situation within which it is located. The middle must be determined in each individual case. As a skilled surfer knows how to balance at every movement of the waves, so a sage knows how to be attuned to the needs of the times in human affairs. As every layperson can learn the skill of surfing only by participating in surfing, a common man learns the wisdom of the sage through experience. Learning involves knowing how and when to advance, to retreat, to preserve, to live, when to gain, and when to lose. Through regret and good fortune, one can learn lessons and come to know proper timing and the way to refrain from certain actions at inopportune times.

On the surface, Confucian ethics has much in common with moral intuitionism. The concepts of Mencius' four sprouts (*si duan*) and Wang Yangming's innate knowledge (*liangzhi* 良知) are often considered to advocate innate or a priori moral knowledge. But I think rather that they represent a moral ability or disposition inherent in every human being. Moral knowledge in Confucian contexts always comes through constant learning and self-cultivation simulating the wisdom of a sage. It is not a priori or intuitively given but rather is to be searched in every moment of our experience by taking care of the moment. To attain moral wisdom, it is important to ride the change and transformation of affairs, trying to view matters in the totality of unending change. Is this kind of ethical position to be assimilated into a situation ethics? In what follows, I would like to argue that the ethics of yinyang is not a kind of situation ethics that may result in ethical relativism or ethical nihilism.

Keeping Desire Subdued through Concerned Consciousness

It is important to note that the yinyang ethics proposed in a Confucian context is not opportunistic, the strong emphasis on timing and the strong blame for inopportune choice of action notwithstanding. Situation ethics does not accept universal moral principles or values that may hold in every human situation. All moral judgments depend on the situation one is located in at the moment of action. In contrast, according to Kantian ethics, telling a lie is morally bad in whatever situation one is placed. If everyone tells a lie, then a linguistic discourse itself, let alone the everyday communication among people, would not be possible. In Kantian ethics, a maxim cannot be a moral rule if it cannot pass the test of universality. Kant thought that the first core of morality is universality, which prescribes that we must all be the same human beings. When one tells a lie, therefore, one goes against the principle of humanity. Regardless of the situation, certain actions are not to be allowed.

But in the context of yinyang ethics, we cannot make a Kantian judgment on the act of telling a lie as such. In certain situations, the act could also be one of helping a dying person or saving another person's life. Moral goodness is not something inherent in actions and intentions. It can only be measured in the wider context of human actions. There is no fixed rule to define the scale of that context. It only depends on one's own moral sensibility finely developed through one's experience in society. This kind of contextual and situational attitude of yinyang ethics, however, does not result in ethical relativism because in all situations one should not take one's eyes off the *dao*, moral truth, and rectitude. In the ethics of yinyang, there is a strong belief in the way of things and the dictates of the inner nature of things. The indeterminacy of the middle only shows the subtlety of the way these dictates emerge.

Accepting the contingencies and vicissitudes of life does not necessarily lead one to a relativist attitude toward what is valuable and right. A relativist believes that there are many ways to be good or right and that it is not possible to determine one right way. But the moral attitude advocated in the *Book of Changes* is that of an inquirer ever searching at every turn of life for what is right and morally true. The truth is not of relative value. Even though the truth is not what we can easily find, being hidden in moving moments of time, it does exist. To find the truth, we need wisdom and sensitivity to the manifold of human affairs. Wisdom is attained through constant efforts to achieve rectitude and propriety. These efforts include learning to take care of what every moment of life requires, willingness to rectify faults, and keeping one's own person through all adversities (*jinshen* 謹身). Learning through experience with a humble mind will show the way to the truth.

To make the proper response in every moment, one has to adopt an alert and fearful attitude (*jieju* 戒懼) toward the contingencies of life. This attitude of caution does not result from calculating the advantages or disadvantages one may have from taking a certain course of action. It is the awareness of the contingencies of human lives where nothing lasts long that makes us humble and fearful. A yang state contains a yin element, and a yin state a yang element. Let's consider an example of a line statement of the third yang in *Qian,* that is, the top of the lower trigram located just below the upper trigram. Here, yang is in its proper position (the third, top being yang elements) but located in the lower trigram, which contains yin force. The statement says, "The noble man makes earnest efforts throughout the day, and with evening he still takes care; though in danger, he will suffer no blame." In the "Commentary on the Words of the Text," we find this paraphrased as follows:

> The noble man fosters his virtue and cultivates his task. He fosters his virtue by being loyal and trustworthy; he keeps his task in hand by cultivating his words and establishing his sincerity. A person who understands what a maximum point is and fulfills it can take part in the incipiency of the moment. A person who understands what a conclusion is and brings it about can take part in the preservation of righteousness.... Thus when he occupies a high position, he is not proud, and when he is in a low position, he is not distressed. To be at the top of the lower trigram is still to be below the upper trigram.[9]

Being alert and fearful is a moral attitude commonly exhorted in Confucian texts, and constitutes a core value that differentiates Confucian ethics from a situation ethics of a relativist vein. This attitude keeps one from overreaching a maximum point and from pursuing the full realization of one's desire. Concerned consciousness or caution is a precondition under which one searches for what is right at the moment of action. It is an attitude that accepts the contingencies of human lives. One who is alert and fearful sincerely pursues rectitude and sincerity at the moment of one's choice of action. This attitude is needed to discern subtle changes in the processes of the world. It is not an expression of hesitation or oscillation between relative values. Rather, it helps one to find truth hidden in myriad moments of time. If one masters this moral attitude without losing rectitude in all actions, then one would suffer no blame and no regret. Unlike a relativist, who does not believe in a moral truth, a Confucian person being alert and fearful strongly believes in the existence of moral truths that underlie the moments of time and that are only revealed to searching and reflecting minds.

From Personal Morality to Social Ethics

Texts in Confucian ethics are abundant with everyday norms and exemplary models mainly focused on building moral character and traits in an individual, usually a male noble person (*junzi* 君子). They prescribe various ways for a person to be a morally right person modeled on a Confucian sage. But the final goal in Confucian ethics is not simply the perfection of an individual mind, or the fulfillment of virtues allotted to a person in accordance with social and familial position, but the common well-being of a wider community. Individual moral fulfillments must converge upon the general well-being and order of a society, eventually producing harmony within it.

For example, there is a much cited a passage in the *Great Learning* to the effect mentioned above:

> The ancients who wished to manifest their clear character to the world would first bring order to their states. Those who wished to bring order to their states would first regulate their families. Those who wished to regulate their families would first cultivate their personal lives. Those who wished to cultivate their personal lives would first rectify their minds. Those who wished to rectify their minds would first make their wills sincere. Those who wished to make their wills sincere would first extend their knowledge. The extension of knowledge consists in the investigation of things. When things are investigated, knowledge is extended; when knowledge is extended, the will becomes sincere; when the will is sincere, the mind is rectified; when the mind is rectified, the personal life is cultivated; when the personal life is cultivated, the family will be regulated; when the family is regulated, the state will be in order; and when the state is in order, there will be peace throughout the world.[10]

In the Confucian tradition, the philosophical and political base of the state is the family. As is widely recognized, a state is considered a big family. It is quite natural, therefore, that Confucian ethics is much focused on ramifying the role of an individual within a family and on analogically extending personal morality to the public arena. Most fundamental to making a Confucian individual is establishing sincerity within that individual's mind through constant inquiry into what is true. I have argued in the previous section that what differentiates Confucian ethics from situation ethics is the keen awareness of the true and of rectitude. The emphasis on knowledge is more conspicuous in the Neo-Confucian tradition than in the Yangming school.

The political ideal of the nation as a big family no longer serves the contemporary world based as it is on principles and laws not known to a traditional Confucian society. Confucian ethics nowadays seems to be left within the boundary of an individual life. To develop it into a social or political ethics, we need to pay attention to the spirit of the ethics of yinyang as an ethics of contingency that sees human civilization in constant change where nothing ever lasts. The ethics of contingency, as I have examined in the previous sections, suggests to us that there cannot be an eternal winner or loser, and that there cannot be ultimate otherness. It tells us that when one phase prevails, the opposite phase will soon follow. To live through such an ever-changing world we should continue to be alert and fearful without losing rectitude. This attitude is good not only for helping individuals to keep their desires within certain limits, but also for helping the state to attain justice by keeping it from going to the extreme in making social policies and pursuing relations, political and economic, with other states. All, being interconnected and interpenetrating, are under the perennial changes and mutual influences in which we move toward an ideal goal of reaching balance and harmony. Based on the metaphysics and the ethics of yinyang, we may have to redefine the identity of an individual and a nation. We may also envision a world order in which it is the correlational and intercultural aspects that are most valued.

Notes

1. These diverse aspects of yinyang have been explored in my recent book; see Kim Heisook 김혜숙, *Sin eumyangnon: Dong Asia munhwa nolli ui haeche wa jaegeon* 新음양론: 동 아시아 문화 논리 의 해체 와 재건 (A new interpretation of yinyang: Deconstructing and reconstructing the logic of East Asian culture) (Seoul: Ewha Womans University Press, 2014).

2. *A Source Book in Chinese Philosophy,* trans. and comp. Wing-tsit Chan (Princeton: Princeton University Press, 1963), p. 266.

3. Cf. Immanuel Kant, *Religion within the Limits of Reason Alone,* trans. Theodore M. Greene and Hoyt H. Hudson (New York: Harper and Row, 1960), pp. 15–39.

4. Hannah Arendt, *The Origins of Totalitarianism* (New York: Harcourt, Brace and World, 1951), p. 469.

5. *The Classic of Changes: A New Translation of the* I Ching *as interpreted by Wang Bi,* trans. Richard John Lynn (New York: Columbia University Press, 1994), p. 138.

6. *Mencius,* "Jin Xin I" 盡心章句上, 26:

> Mencius said, "The principle of the philosopher Yang was: 'Each one for himself.' Though he might have benefited the whole kingdom by plucking out a single hair, he would not have done it. The philosopher Mo loves all equally. If by rubbing smooth his whole body from the crown to the heel, he could have benefited the kingdom, he would have done it. Zi Mo holds a medium between these. By holding that medium, he is nearer the right. But by holding it without leaving room for the exigency of circumstances, it becomes like their holding their one point. The reason why I hate that holding to one point is the injury it does to the way of right principle. It takes up one point and disregards a hundred others." (James Legge translation; see Chinese Text Project website at http://ctext.org/mengzi/jin-xin-i)

7. *Maengja jipju* 孟子集注 (Complete translation of the Mencius), trans. and annot. Seong Baek-hyo 懸吐完譯 (Seoul: Jeontong Munhwa Yeon'guhoe, 1996), p. 395.

8. Ibid.

9. See Lynn, *Classic of Changes,* p. 135, and *Maengja jipju,* p. 395.

10. Chan, *A Source Book in Chinese Philosophy,* pp. 86–87.

CHAPTER 11

Zhong in the *Analects* with Insights into Loyalty

Winnie SUNG

THIS CHAPTER ATTEMPTS to analyze the notion of *zhong* 忠 in the *Analects*. Since *zhong* is often translated as "loyalty" in the existing literature, it is tempting to read Confucius as placing emphasis on the importance of being loyal, and this will easily call to mind many negative connotations associated with loyalty such as blind submission, ungrounded favoritism, and the erosion of integrity. Such a strong association between *zhong* and loyalty might prevent us from fully understanding why *zhong* is valued. The aims of this chapter are to examine Confucius' use of *zhong* as recorded in the *Analects,* to articulate the early Confucian conception of *zhong,* and to extract ethical insights from such an early Confucian conception by juxtaposing it against the contemporary conception of loyalty.

Zhong is often hailed as one of the cardinal concepts in early Confucian ethics. In English translations, the early Confucian term *zhong* is often rendered as "loyalty." The same tendency is found in modern Chinese translations. For example, in his modern Chinese translation of the *Analects,* Yang Bojun uses a seemingly similar modern Chinese expression, *zhongxin* 忠心, which means loyalty, as a modern translation of "*zhong.*"[1] In addition, there is a tendency to take the early Confucian conception of *zhong* to mean loyalty to a ruler. With regard to the spread of Confucianism to Japan, scholarly interest in *zhong* has been focused predominantly on loyalty to the emperor or the state and on the potential tension between loyalty to the state and filial piety.

If *zhong* is understood as loyalty, this understanding not only potentially conflicts with other ethical attributes, such as filial piety,[2] but it also seems to be in tension with the early Confucian ethical system as a whole. Loyalty requires

175

one to have a special regard for someone. I give unwavering support to my friend, to whom I am loyal, because my friend stands in special relationship to me. However, even though early Confucians do emphasize special relationships, the ideal seems to be that ethical agents should eventually extend their care to everyone.[3] The emphasis on loyalty is a prima facie obstacle to the extension of care to other people in general. If the focus of *zhong* is more narrowly on one's loyalty to the ruler or state, there are further problems, such as whether one is justified in being loyal to a corrupt ruler or what one should do in practical cases where there is a conflict between one's loyalty and one's duty to the general public. This raises the worry that the Confucian idealization of loyalty is in tension with our current global dynamics. Chenyang Li, for example, points out that one of the main contemporary challenges faced by Confucianism is pressure from liberal-democratic value systems. While Confucianism emphasizes loyalty to one's country and family, liberal democracies tend to emphasize individual autonomy and freedom.[4]

Worries along this line are not unfounded. Indeed, the Confucian notion of *zhong* has evolved throughout the imperial period to mean something ever closer to loyalty to the ruler. As we look for resources in early Confucian thought that could contribute to resolving our current global predicaments, we certainly need to be wary of the failings of Confucianism over its long history. However, we should not let our reading of the early Confucian conception of *zhong* be colored by these later developments. As some scholars have already pointed out, in the early Confucian texts *zhong* does not always mean loyalty, especially not in texts earlier than the *Xunzi*.[5] What I attempt to do here is not to elaborate on the Confucian emphasis on loyalty but to salvage the early Confucian view on *zhong* by clarifying the concept of *zhong* in the *Analects*.

As the following analysis will show, if we discard the assumption that *zhong* means "loyalty" in the *Analects* and try instead to approximate the meaning of the term as it is discussed in the text, we can retrieve valuable insights from early Confucian thought that have contemporary relevance. In section two below, I seek to approximate what *zhong* means in the *Analects* without being guided by any contemporary understanding of loyalty. In section three, I articulate what I take to be the early Confucian conception of *zhong* based on the textual observations made in section two. In section four, I discuss the ethical significance of *zhong* by juxtaposing it with our contemporary conception of loyalty. I attempt neither to equate Confucius' conception of *zhong* with loyalty nor to defend loyalty. Whether or not *zhong* means loyalty does not affect the second and third parts of the present investigation. What matters for the fourth part is that we can retrieve some early Confucian insights on a psychological attitude that has to do with how we relate to others. This attitude has aspects that overlap with those we find appealing about the notion of loyalty, yet avoids some of the difficulties with the contemporary understanding of and emphasis on loyalty.

Zhong in the *Analects*

The term *zhong* appears in sixteen passages in the *Analects* and is used as either an adjective or a noun. As D. C. Lau aptly points out in the introduction to his translation of the *Analects*:

> Translators tend to use "loyal" as the sole equivalent for *zhong* even when translating early texts. This is a mistake and is due to a failure to appreciate that the meaning of the word changed in the course of time. In the later usage, it is true, *zhong* tended to mean "loyalty" in the sense of "blind devotion." But this was not its meaning at the time of Confucius.[6]

Lau himself translated *zhong* as "doing one's best" instead of "loyalty." Since the nature of Lau's work is translation, he did not have the space to go into detailed discussion of why "doing one's best" is more suitable than "loyalty." Nonetheless, his insightful remark certainly suggests the limitation of translating *zhong* as "loyalty" and alerts us to do justice to the nuances and complexities of *zhong*. The task of this section is to follow up on Lau's suggestion and investigate the usage of *zhong* in the *Analects*. There is, of course, a question about the extent to which the *Analects* is an accurate record or representation of Confucius' thought. Indeed, two of the important quotes about *zhong* come from Confucius' disciple Zeng Can 曾參 (also known as Zengzi 曾子), rather than Confucius himself (*Analects* 1.4, 4.15). Such ambiguity will not greatly affect the discussion, and I leave open the possibility that this is not necessarily what Confucius himself took *zhong* to mean. The goal here is to analyze the concept of *zhong* as it is presented in the text of the *Analects*. For convenience, I shall continue to use the name "Confucius" in my discussion to refer to the ideas expressed in the *Analects*.

Three main observations may be made about *zhong* in the *Analects*. First, *zhong* has to do with how one engages with others in general. Although later scholarship tends to understand *zhong* as a normative trait that ministers should embody or the proper attitude that ministers should have toward their superiors, there is no indication that Confucius thought that *zhong* pertains specifically to ministers or any hierarchical relationship. In the *Analects* there is one instance where it is said that ministers should serve the lord with *zhong* (3.19) and another where a minister is described as *zhong* (5.19). But even in these two instances there is no conclusive reason to think that *zhong* is a specific ethical trait of ministers or an attitude that someone in a lower hierarchical position should assume toward those who are superior.[7] This observation is in line with those made by Satō Masayuki, who conducted a detailed textual analysis that traces the development of *zhong* in the Spring and Autumn period and argues that the concept of *zhong* at the time of Confucius broadened from an ethical attribute of the leaders to an ethical attribute of individuals in general.[8] A piece of positive evidence suggesting that *zhong* is about how one relates to people in general is *Analects* 13.19. When Fan Chi asks Confucius about *ren,* Confucius says:

> 居處恭，執事敬，與人忠。

> While at home hold yourself in a respectful attitude; when serving in an official capacity be reverent; when dealing with others be *zhong.*

It is worth nothing that the emphasis in this passage is that one has to be *zhong* in interacting with others or with people in general (*ren* 人).[9] There is no suggestion that one can only be *zhong* with someone who stands in special relation to oneself.

In a similar vein, one of the things Zengzi reflects on daily is whether he has failed to be *zhong* to others:

> 曾子曰，吾日三省吾身，為人謀，而不忠乎，與朋友交，而不信乎，傳不習乎。

> Zengzi said, "Every day I examine myself on three counts. In my planning for others, have I failed to be *zhong?* In my dealings with my friends have I failed to be trustworthy in what I say? Have I failed to practise repeatedly what has been passed on to me?"[10] (*Analects* 1.4)

It is said in this passage that Zengzi would frequently reflect on whether he had been *zhong* with people and *xin* 信 (trustworthy) with friends.[11] It is interesting to note that Zengzi takes *xin* to be the appropriate attitude for one's interacting with friends and *zhong* the appropriate attitude for one's interacting with people in general (*ren* 人).[12] This suggests that the domain of relationships that *zhong* covers is not restricted to special relationships. Another point made about *zhong* in this passage is that *zhong* is concerned with planning on others' behalf.

This leads us to the second observation: *zhong* in the *Analects* is intimately linked to offering advice. As the passage above suggests, *zhong* is an idealized state in which we *mou* 謀 for others. *Mou* in early Chinese texts is often used to mean planning strategies, offering advice to others, or giving thoughtful consideration to how to help others deal with a situation.[13] The association between being *zhong* and one's planning for others deserves attention. Indeed, in about a third of the passages where "*zhong*" appears, *zhong* is concerned with speech. There is hardly any evidence that *zhong* has to do with doing.[14] According to Confucius, the superior person always keeps nine things in mind, and one of them is *zhong* in speaking:

> 君子有九思，視思明，聽思聰，色思溫，貌思恭，言思忠，事思敬，疑思問，忿思難，見得思義。

> There are nine things the gentleman turns his thought to: to seeing clearly when he uses his eyes, to hearing acutely when he uses his ears, to looking cordial when it comes to his countenance, to appearing respectful when it comes to his demeanor, to being *zhong* when he speaks, to being reverent when he performs his duties, to seeking advice when he is in doubt, to the consequences when he is enraged, and to what is right at the sight of gain. (*Analects* 16.10)

The "nine things" identified by Confucius all seem to be concerned with the appropriate attitudes one should strive to assume when one finds oneself in any of these nine circumstances. For example, in looking at something, one should aim at looking at it clearly; in having doubts, one should aim at raising questions.

Similarly, in saying things, Confucius thinks that one should aim at *zhong*. This suggests that *zhong* is a mental state or attitude toward which one should aim when saying things. This impression is further supported by *Analects* 15.6:

> 子曰，言忠信，行篤敬，雖蠻貊之邦，行矣，言不忠信，行不篤敬，雖州里，行乎哉。

> The Master said, "If in word you are *zhong* and *xin* and indeed single-minded and reverent, then even in the lands of the barbarians you will go forward without obstruction. If you fail to be *zhong* and *xin* or to be single-minded and reverent in deed, then can you be sure of going forward without obstruction even in your own neighbourhood?"

It is obvious in this passage that both *zhong* and *xin* are attributes of speech. In addition, *Analects* 12.23 discusses *zhong* as the manner in which one should offer advice:

> 子貢問友。子曰，忠告，而善道之，不可則止，無自辱焉。

> Zigong asked about how friends should be treated. The Master said, "Advise them in a *zhong* manner and guide them properly, but stop when there is no hope of success. Do not ask to be snubbed."

An important clue in this passage is the latter part where Confucius says that one should stop if there is no hope of success in convincing the friend. This implies that *zhong* advice is not necessarily something that the friend would want to listen to.

Commentator He Yan took *zhong* in this context to mean that one should say what it is that is right and what it is that is wrong. His comment is insightful and it helps us make better sense of *Analects* 14.7:

> 子曰，愛之，能勿勞乎，忠焉，能勿誨乎。

> The Master said, "Can you love anyone without making him work hard [alternative translation: without working hard]? Can you be *zhong* without saying something to correct them?[15]

Confucius' view here seems to be that if one is *zhong* toward someone, it is inevitable that one would want to say something to instruct and correct them (*hui* 誨). Both passages convey the point that being *zhong* has to do with telling others what is right—at least what the subject deems to be right. Confucius is probably aware that the hard truth might not be something that the other side can receive very well and therefore says in *Analects* 12.23 that one should stop if the friend does not listen, to avoid possible infringement of propriety.

The third observation is that what motivates one to make this kind of corrective yet potentially irksome advice is a concern for others rather than the self. The following passage gives us a glimpse into the kind of person whom Confucius considers as *zhong*:

> 子張問曰，令尹子文，三仕為令尹，無喜色，三已之，無慍色，舊令尹之政，必以告新令尹，何如。子曰，忠矣。

> Zizhang asked, "Ling Yin Ziwen gave no appearance of pleasure when he was made prime minister three times. Neither did he give any appearance of displeasure [yun 慍] when he was removed from office three times. He always told his successor what he had done during his term of office. What do you think of this?" The Master said, "He can, indeed, be said to be a man of *zhong*." (*Analects* 5.19)

Although this passage tells us very little about Ziwen, one striking characteristic of him according to this passage is that he is neither pleased nor upset by whether he himself holds office. Even when he was removed from office three times, what seems to be at the center of his attention is whether the office itself was handed over properly, rather than how his own standing was affected. It is worth noting that the term that is being used for displeasure here is *yun* 慍. While *yun* roughly means feeling irritated or upset, it seems to be a special kind of displeasure that arises from one's thinking that something should not have happened to oneself, and one thinks the situation should be rectified. As we can observe from the accounts in the *Guoyu*, a ruler would feel *yun* when he believes that he has been offended and he wants to rectify the situation by going into battle.[16]

A similar idea is found in *Analects* 1.1 when it is said that the superior person is not *yun* even when others fail to appreciate him. This suggests that, in Confucius' view, people will normally *yun* when they are not recognized, presumably because they think they deserve to be recognized. In *Analects* 5.19, not only did Ziwen not show signs of *yun;* he would even ensure that the office was handed over properly so that the next prime minister would know what needed to be done. This suggests that Ziwen's focus was not on whether he was treated the way he thought he deserved to be treated but on what would advance the interest of the state. This is probably also why he did not show any sign of pleasure when he was made prime minister, for what occupied his mind was how he could do his job well in order to advance the interest of the state rather than dwelling on how the appointment reflected well on himself. This brief account suggests that, for Confucius, the state of *zhong* is one in which the subject is preoccupied with considerations of how to advance the interest of others and has bracketed, or at least marginalized, considerations of how to advance the subject's self-interest.

The general shape of these observations on *zhong* in the *Analects* is in line with the uses of *zhong* in early texts before and around Confucius' time. Indeed, scholars have noted that *zhong* is hardly used as a normative concept before the *Analects*. As Qu Wanli notes, there is no mention of *zhong* in the judgments of the hexagrams in the *Zhouyi* 周易, the *Shangshu* 尚書, the *Shijing* 詩經, or the *Chunqiujing* 春秋經.[17] This suggests that *zhong* is not used to describe a concept, or, at the very least, thinkers before Confucius had not paid attention to the importance of *zhong*.[18] It is in the *Zuozhuan* and the *Guoyu* that we start to see relatively more frequent occurrences of *zhong*. Assuming that the composition of the *Zuozhuan* 左傳 and the *Guoyu* 國語 are roughly contemporaneous with the *Analects,* we may through these two texts get a sense of the linguistic context of Confucius' time.

In the *Zuozhuan, zhong* is also concerned with a relational attitude that one has in one's interactions with others, and this attitude has the character of being objective and looking at the facts of the situation. For example:

所謂道忠於民而信於神也上思利民忠也祝史正辭信也

What I call *Dao* is being *zhong* to the people and being truthful [*xin*] to the Spirits. When [the ruler] thinks about benefiting the people, it is called *zhong;* when [the priests'] words are all upright, it is called *xin*.[19]

Here, *zhong* is characterized as an attitude the ruler assumes when he relates to his subjects. This further reinforces the impression that *zhong* is concerned with benefiting, rather than obeying, others. In addition, *zhong,* as a relational attitude, is not restricted to one's relation to those superior to oneself.

In another instance in the *Zuozhuan,*

公曰 小大之獄 雖不能察 必以情 對曰忠之屬也可以一戰

[When] the Duke said, "In great and small matters of legal process, even though I cannot investigate them thoroughly, I must rely on the facts," [Cao Gui] replied, "This is a type of *zhong,* [and] with it you can go into battle."[20]

In Cao Gui's reply to Duke Zhuang, we again get the impression that *zhong* is taken to mean viewing the situation objectively without being colored by presumptions or biases.

In the *Guoyu,* we also see a tight connection between *zhong* and offering thoughtful advice. In "Jinyu" 3, we find the line

不謀而諫不忠

Remonstrating without planning—it is not *zhong.*

It is clear in this instance that what makes one *zhong* is not just giving any kind of advice. Rather, a *zhong* subject would need to plan thoughtfully (*mou* 謀).[21] The thought here is probably that it is not sufficient to credit someone with *zhong* if she just candidly speaks her mind; what is also required is that she has to hold herself responsible and be committed to the person with whom she is *zhong.* Since she is committed in such a way, she has to consider carefully the different factors at play, put herself in the other person's shoes, and devise the best strategy that she can offer.

Another relevant piece of textual evidence is in "Jinyu" 2:

除闇以應外謂之忠.... 今君施其所惡于人，闇不除矣

To remove dimness in order to respond to the external is called *zhong.* . . . Now that the ruler imposes what he dislikes on others, the dimness is not removed.

The metaphor of dimness here suggests that a person who fails to be *zhong* is obscured in a certain way. Whether it is selfish desires or a deficiency in cognitive understanding that is obscuring the subject, when the subject is in such a state of moral obscurity he will impose what he dislikes on others. Interestingly, this idea also echoes the parallel between *zhong* and *shu* in *Analects* 4.15:

子曰，參乎，吾道一以貫之。曾子曰，唯。子出，門人問曰，何謂
也。曾子曰，夫子之道，忠恕而已矣。

The Master said, "[Zeng] Can! There is one single thread binding my way together." Zengzi assented. After the Master had gone out, the disciples asked, "What did he mean?" Zengzi said, "The way of the Master consists in *zhong* and *shu*. That is all."

And *shu,* for Confucius, is about "not imposing on others what you yourself do not desire" (15.24). Even though we lack the information here to tell what it is that connects the points about being obscured, *zhong,* and imposing on others, we can at least infer that not being *zhong* and *shu* is, in some way, to disregard the interest of others.

The Early Confucian Conception of *Zhong*

In the preceding section, I tried to organize Confucius' ideas about *zhong*. In this section, I shall try to articulate my own interpretation of the early Confucian conception of *zhong* on the basis of the three textual observations above. The goal is to approximate a faithful interpretation of Confucius' view on *zhong*, but I submit that my discussion of *zhong* from this point onward might depart from the way the early Confucians initially thought about *zhong*. The hope is that we can extract from the textual observations above a line of thinking that is of interest to us in contemporary ethical discourse.

If we piece together the three observations about *zhong,* we start to get the picture that *zhong* is a state of mind in which one interacts with others, most often in the context of offering advice. A *zhong* person is someone who would offer this advice or strategic plans, even though she knows quite well that this is not something the recipient can comfortably accept. It might be easier for her to say something that is conveniently pleasing to the recipient, but a *zhong* person would choose to tell the hard truth because her concern is to advance the interest of others instead of her own. She would, of course, still observe the basic etiquette and behave with decorum (12.23), but this will not change the content of her advice if she sincerely thinks that the advice is right and will do the recipient good. If this picture is roughly what Confucius espouses, then we can probe further into this conception of *zhong* by analyzing the nature of *zhong* advice, the objects of *zhong,* and the motives *zhong* entails.

Let us first analyze the nature of *zhong* advice. For convenience, I will label the *zhong* person as Z and the recipient of the *zhong* person's advice R. As we have seen, a piece of *zhong* advice is not necessarily something that would please R. But since Z cares about R, she would want to correct the mistake that she sees R is making (*Analects* 14.7) or potentially making. In considering what benefits the other, the *zhong* person's sole focus is on what is the right thing for R to do. The characteristically Confucian assumption operating in the background is likely to be that there is a distinction between what is in fact good for the self and what satisfies self-regarding desires, and that there is identification between what is in fact good for the self and what is in accordance with ethical standards. Hence, when I say that Z is one who offers advice that advances R's interest, I do not mean that she tries to satisfy R's desires or help R obtain whatever it is that R wants; instead, I mean Z will try to tell R what is in fact good or, equivalently, what is in fact right for R to do. From Z's point of view, her advice to R is what she thinks will in fact advances R's interest, which is also to say that her advice is about what is in fact in accordance with ethical standards.

It is not necessary for Z in fact to be right about what R should do. What is necessary is that she tell R what she sincerely believes to be the right thing to do. She might in fact be wrong, but it will not affect her being *zhong*. We can imagine a particular cultural setting where it is believed that a woman has to be confined to bed for a year after giving birth or else there will be far-ranging negative effects on her health. Let us suppose this is a myth. It is possible that someone who comes from this cultural setting would advise her friend who has just given birth to stay in bed for a year because she sincerely believes that this is good for her friend's health. Even though she is mistaken in this case, she can still be considered *zhong* in offering what she sincerely deems to be the advice that accords with the right standards. This is probably why, in Confucius' view, *zhong* is still short of *ren* (*Analects* 5.19, 5.28), for it is still possible that one misjudges a situation and imposes bad advice on others.

Paul Goldin suggests that *zhong* in the *Analects* conveys the sense of "being honest with oneself."[22] It should, however, be emphasized that, in my interpretation, *zhong* is different from just offering one's honest opinion. Honesty is certainly important here, for I have to say what I take to be the case, but it is not the defining feature of *zhong*. A subject may be required to be honest under other ethical constraints; she can also be dictated by her natural temperament to say what she thinks is true. However, if she has not put serious thought into what furthers the interest of R, honest opinion alone cannot count as *zhong* advice. *Zhong* has the constraint of good cognitive judgment. Z does not simply report true beliefs to R but has to make the effort to work out the various factors at play in the situation and form a view about what is best for R.[23] The requirement for good judgment also implies that the subject must have her own view on what the ethical standards are and which ones are applicable in the situation.

Our analysis so far shows that it is the psychology of having someone's best interest at heart that is constitutive of *zhong,* and this psychology is often instantiated in the context of offering advice. One important feature of being in a *zhong* psychological posture is that the *zhong* person holds herself responsible for others' well-being. People sometimes undertake responsibilities by publicly entering into special relationships, such as politicians assuming duties at office and doctors taking patients. In these relationships, there is an external set of responsibilities that the subject is required to fulfill. If a doctor fails to advise the patient on the best treatment available because of certain self-regarding considerations, the patient can accuse the doctor of failing to be *zhong* because the doctor is supposed to be responsible for her health problem. However, it is not always the case that our responsibilities for others are clearly and formally defined. Coming to see someone as a friend, for example, is often a gradual process that is not formalized by a public act.

Also lacking is a set of clearly defined responsibilities between friends. Suppose Z and R are friends. It is conceivable that there are many circumstances under which it is ambiguous as to when R can hold it against Z for failing certain responsibilities and Z herself might well be aware of it. If there is some kind of psychology ensuring that Z will still have R's best interest at heart even if R cannot hold her responsible, then this psychology is not R's holding Z responsible, but Z's holding herself responsible for R. The upshot of this is that *zhong* does not necessarily require a mutual understanding or acknowledgment of the *zhong* person's responsibility. It is crucial to being *zhong* that one hold herself responsible and commit herself to promote the best interest of those with whom she is *zhong.* A failure of *zhong* is when Z fails to deliver on her responsibility, and it is possible that this kind of failure is only known to Z herself. For example, I would have failed to be *zhong* if I had advised my friend not to apply for a certain job partly because I myself wanted to apply for the job and saw her as a rival. Even if the advice actually turned out to be beneficial to my friend and she would never have found out that I had factored in my own selfish interest in my planning on her behalf, I would still have failed to be *zhong.*

Let us now turn to the kind of relationship to which *zhong* pertains. Recall from our first textual observation that the scope of the object of *zhong* is broad and covers other people in general.[24] Although there is no textual evidence suggesting that the object of *zhong* must be someone who stands in special relation to the subject, there are good reasons to think that, in practice, *zhong* is an attitude that usually pertains to special relationships. This is so because the circumstances that call for *zhong* are likely to be those that involve people with whom one is in some kind of special relationship. Suppose I were approached by a stranger on the street who happens to ask me for advice on whether she should quit her job; I think the intuition here is that I am not in a position to give advice because I do not know her. Hence, in order to be in a position to give *zhong* advice, the *zhong* person must be in a position where she has adequate knowledge of the other person, the circumstances she is in, and the different factors at play. In our everyday life, the latter position is usually attained in special relationships.

That *zhong* is more often called for in special relationships further explains why *zhong* is a difficult psychological posture to sustain. Since the interests of both parties in a special relationship are so intimately intertwined, it is both practically and epistemically more difficult to separate considerations of what is good for others from what is good for oneself. Sometimes considerations creep in without the subject's awareness. A finance minister, for example, might propose a tax reduction for vehicle purchases. It might be true that such a tax reduction is in fact good for the state, but she might have factored into her consideration that this policy would serve her own interest in purchasing a vehicle. There could also be cases where the subject is not so blatantly self-serving. From an external standpoint, the public might insist that the finance minister take advantage of her position to benefit herself, but from the finance minister's own point of view, she might sincerely think that she was only considering what is good for the general public.

There are even fussier cases where it is difficult to tell what the subject's intention is from both external and internal standpoints. A parent might know the temperament of her child so well that she knows what kind of advice would upset the child. It is very likely that this worry about her upsetting the child would bias her consideration, and it turns out that the advice she gave is the kind that does not upset the child. However, in both cases, from the finance minister's and the parent's point of view, they might sincerely believe that they are offering advice on what is in fact the right thing to do. We do not have to go so far as to suppose that there is something like self-deception or unconsciousness involved. It can simply be that the interests in special relationships are so tightly connected that it is a challenging epistemic task to separate and differentiate considerations of the two.

What will ensure that the *zhong* subject does not slide into considerations of her self-interest, then? It seems that what grounds the *zhong* subject's focus on others' welfare is not a cognitive appraisal of the situation, for, as we have seen, there are cases where even if one holds herself responsible and is committed to the welfare of others, her self-interest might be so bound up with that of her object that it is genuinely difficult for her to keep track of where one ends and another begins. My proposed understanding is that *zhong* is grounded in the subject's affective concern and care for others, which motivates the subject's entire psychological posture to shift from focusing on the self to focusing on others. It is by virtue of this affective concern for others that, even if the subject cannot cognitively discriminate between others' interests and those of her own, her entire attention is directed to others rather than herself. All the considerations and planning that a *zhong* person undertakes for others occur under a guiding light that is directed to others.

This interpretation also has the advantage of explaining the parallel between *zhong* and *shu*. While *shu* is about not imposing on others what one dislikes, *zhong* is about helping others to obtain what is good for them. What is common between the two notions is that both are grounded in the affective concern for others. At first glance, it might be tempting to understand *shu* as grounded in rational reflection. For example, it is convenient for me to shovel the snow in front of my house to my neighbor's side. But on reflection, my neighbors might shovel snow to my side, and this is something I would not want. However, if I know for certain that what I impose on others will not come back to me, what is it that holds me back from taking a free ride? If we take seriously the parallel between *zhong* and *shu*, a plausible explanation is that it is because I care about my neighbor that once I come to see on reflection that this is something that I myself will dislike, I would not want to do it to my neighbor. The reason I do not want to impose on my neighbor is not that I rationally reason that I would not want her to do the same to me but because I have an affective concern for her so that I do not want her to go through the feeling of discomfort that I would go through if it were imposed on me.

Zhong and Loyalty

In this section, I extract several ethical insights from the early Confucian conception of *zhong* outlined above and make it relevant to contemporary interests by juxtaposing it with loyalty. I do not want to suggest that *zhong* is the Confucian conception of loyalty. Even if the early Confucians did have in mind a certain idealized psychological posture that is akin to loyalty, it is unlikely that such a posture is exhausted by the concept of *zhong* alone. If there is some early Confucian conception of "being loyal" that we can model, such a conception must involve a broader cluster of related concepts, such as *jing* 敬, *cheng* 誠, *zhong* 忠, *yi* 義, and *xin* 信. My limited goal here is to show that *zhong* partially captures in some important ways the psychological terrain of loyalty, and this gives us a basis to think that early Confucians still have some important insights to offer to present-day discussions. It will also be shown how *zhong* can avoid some key difficulties with our contemporary understanding of and emphasis on loyalty. This should help us further appreciate the distinctive insights of early Confucian ethics. Since my purpose is to make relevant early Confucian insights to contemporary interests, the notion of "loyalty" under consideration is not a technical one but a colloquial one. In that regard, a dictionary definition of loyalty should suffice to capture what we mean by "loyalty." According to the *Concise Oxford English Dictionary,* "loyal" is defined as "giving or showing firm and constant support or allegiance to a person or institution."[25] Throughout my discussion of "loyalty" below, it is this commonsense view of loyalty that I have in mind.

Loyalty is not an outdated concept. People across cultures still value loyalty in many domains of our contemporary life, whether it is the loyalty of a friend, of a spouse, of a family member, of an employee, or of a citizen. In modern multinational corporations, for example, loyalty is still expected from employees. However, if the balance between loyalty and duty to public justice is not maintained properly, things done in the name of loyalty sometimes have unfortunate consequences, with large-scale impact on the public. The Ford Pinto case is an example wherein excessive emphasis on loyalty had disastrous consequences.[26] Between 1970 and 1977 there were about five hundred to nine hundred burn deaths resulting from explosions of the Ford Pinto model caused by a faulty fuel system. Records show that in the pre-production period, engineers had already discovered that the gas tank used in the Pinto was unsafe and seriously considered switching to a different kind of gas tank. However, the loyalty of many of these engineers had prevented them from speaking up to the executive vice-president of Ford or "blowing the whistle." In another case at the B. F. Goodrich plant, engineer Kermit Vandivier handed in a fraudulent report of a new brake design for LTV Aerospace Corporation against pressure from his supervisor and resigned. The resignation was supposed to take effect a few weeks later, but the chief engineer, citing Vandivier's "disloyalty" to the company, informed Vandivier that he would accept his resignation "right now."[27] In view of the tension between the demand of loyalty and the sometimes disastrous consequences that result from being loyal, let me briefly highlight how *zhong,* in three respects, preserves the appeal of loyalty and avoids its difficulties.

One prominent feature of loyalty that normally appeals to us is its emphasis on special obligations. There is usually a history that we share with people who are special to us, and these historical qualities make us think that we have stronger obligations to those who stand in special relationship to us. For instance, I have a stronger obligation to support my friend because she is the one who stood by me and helped me during a difficult time. There are also circumstances under which by entering into special relationships, like getting married, I also make a promise always to be supportive to my partner.

Failing to be loyal is also in some ways like breaking a promise. This prompts philosophers like Andrew Oldenquist to argue for the moral priority of special obligations over universal moral principles.[28] But once we take this route, there is the problem of grounding special obligations. As William Godwin puts it: "What magic is there in the pronoun 'my', that should justify us in overturning the decisions of impartial truth?"[29] One might adopt an "objective consequentialist" reply along the line suggested by Peter Railton,[30] arguing that the form of deliberation that puts special relationships first is in fact conducive to bringing about the best possible outcomes. An objectivist consequentialist should indeed cultivate the trait of being loyal even though traits like this might sometimes manifest themselves in acts that do not seek to maximize the good. Railton himself gives the example of a couple, Juan and Linda, who live apart.[31] Suppose Juan faces the choice of paying Linda a surprise visit to temporarily cheer her up or donating his money for travel to charity. The difficulty with this line of thought, however, is that it is unclear how a consequentialist agent can identify her consequentialist commitment with an agent-relative commitment. It seems that the commitments of the consequentialist agent are, after all, commitments that make reference to the commitment to the best outcome, rather than the well-being of a particular person. Even if the objective consequentialist is committed to the person, such commitment is still derivative.

By contrast, the notion of *zhong* preserves the emphasis on special relationships and circumvents the problem of grounding special obligations. *Zhong* is not grounded in special relationships. Instead, *zhong* is constitutive of special relationships.[32] If we really are friends, I will necessarily want to take your best interest to heart and sincerely tell you what I think is the best thing for you. If in offering advice to you I have always factored in my own interest or made sure your interest will not conflict with my own, it is questionable if there really is a relationship between us as substantial as friendship. Indeed, as I argued in the previous section, the early Confucian reply is that there should not be any "magic of 'I'" in consideration of *zhong* at all. What *zhong* requires is precisely that any consideration of "my X" will be out of the picture in one's deliberation of what is good for others without sliding into consideration of oneself. A mother who is a lawyer may advise her child to pursue a career in law as well. Whether or not this is a piece of *zhong* advice does not turn on how well her child ends up doing in her career but on whether, when she offered the advice, she was only thinking about what is in fact good for the child or was thinking that "because she is *my* child, she has to follow in my footsteps." The latter kind of thought would discount her advice as *zhong* even if the child turns out to enjoy her career in law. Since a *zhong* person's regard for others is not further defined in terms of a regard for something that is "mine," she will not let any consideration pertaining to herself affect her judgment of what really is good for others.

It is precisely because *zhong* does not focus on the "mine" component, *pace* Oldenquist, that it also extends to non-special relationships. A *zhong* subject holds herself responsible and is committed to looking out for others who are related to her by virtue of certain undertakings or social roles in a way that is in accordance with ethical standards. This means that the content of a *zhong* person's obligations is not derived from special obligations but is derived from ethical standards. The obligation of a doctor to work in the best medical interest of her patient, for example, is not derived from the special relationship the doctor has with the patient but from the ethical standards to which the doctor is subject.[33]

A second appealing feature of loyalty is the resoluteness or perseverance of a loyal subject,[34] who will remain committed to her object even when doing so might be disadvantageous to her own interest. For many loyal subjects, it is not that they do not have alternatives available to them. But because of their loyalty, they do not see the alternative options as available to them. Instead, they dedicate all their strength and will to serving the interest of their object. This resoluteness is especially valuable when a third party potentially rivals the object of loyalty, which is most often seen in soldiers' putting their lives on the line to protect their country. It is very tempting to think that there is something admirable in how a subject would unwaveringly put her object's interest above her own. The obvious worry with this kind of resoluteness is that it threatens integrity. The demand of loyalty might require the subject to willingly compromise or overlook her ethical standards, as we saw with engineers involved in the Ford Pinto case. Moreover, since loyalty requires one to follow and support the object of loyalty, some form of loyalty might even discourage the subject from forming a view about what matters to herself because it is always the object's interest that should be at the forefront of her mind. For example, for centuries women were discouraged from thinking for themselves about what matters to them because that could potentially conflict with the interest of their husband. Hence, in demanding loyalty there is the danger of reducing the subject to a servile state in which she has little self-respect.

The early conception of *zhong* also values resoluteness. One will offer whatever advice one sincerely believes is good for others, even if the consequence of doing so is costly to oneself. As we saw in the case of Ziwen (*Analects* 5.19), it is possible that a minister's *zhong* might result in his removal from office; however, this will not deter him from saying what he thinks is the right way to safeguard the interest of the ruler and the people. And even though Confucius says that one should stop advising when there is no hope of success (*Analects* 12.23), it is not far-fetched to surmise that Confucius would think, should the friend come back and seek advice again, that the subject would still be required to be *zhong*. Implicit in the notion of *zhong* is the expectation that the subject herself needs to have her own beliefs about and commitment to ethical standards. Since the subject sees herself as accountable to others, she will also endeavor to form a view of the situation and deliberate about the relevant ethical standards at issue. This is also why *zhong* advice is not just an honest opinion but has to be something that is thoroughly thought through by the subject. Hence, what makes a *zhong* person's concern for others resolute is her firm commitment to observe ethical standards because of the assumption that what is good for one must be what is in accord with ethical standards.

The emphasis on a consideration of others' interests in a way that is independent of self-interest in *zhong* might lead some to worry that the subject's own interest and self-respect are threatened. This worry stems from a conflation of seeing oneself as one factor in the situation and seeing self-interest as the objective of one's consideration. It is possible that the subject's is one factor at play in the situation, in which case she should also take that into consideration. When sage Shun married without his father's permission, he did not do so out of self-interest. Rather, he took himself into account when thinking about what would further the interest of his father. Since Shun thought it would in fact be good for his father if his father had descendants, he felt it would be best for himself to get married so that his father could have descendants (*Mencius* 4A26). With *zhong* there is no connotation of obedience, implying that there is no requirement in the concept of *zhong* for the subject to go along blindly with the demands of others. If *zhong* is primarily a mental attitude that concerns how we offer advice to others, there is also little reason to think that there can be conflicting *zhong* as in the case of conflicting loyalties. If I am loyal to Team A, the nature of my loyalty will prevent me from supporting any team other than Team A. But if I am *zhong* to person X, there is nothing in the structure of *zhong* that prevents me from offering my honest advice to person Y about what I take to be right for her. This does not preclude the possibility that there is something else in my relationship with X that prevents me from offering *zhong* advice to Y.

It is interesting to note that, for the early Confucians, the image of the *zhong* subject is almost the exact opposite of the village worthies (*Analects* 17.13). While a village worthy is always eager to please her audience so as to advance self-interest when she in fact does not have any view that can be called her own, the *zhong* subject is only concerned with thinking about what advances her audience's interest.[35] She will carefully form her own view of the situation lest her object is obscured and, in voicing her honest opinion when necessary, she is willing to risk offending her audience.

The third aspect of loyalty that we normally find appealing is the emotive aspect. Josiah Royce poignantly characterizes this aspect of loyalty as follows:

> The finding of one's rest and spiritual fulfillment even in one's life of toil itself—this state is precisely the state of the loyal, in so far as their loyalty gets full control of their emotional nature.[36]

The idea that one's loyalty is at least supposed to have some grip over one's affective state is implicitly accepted in our everyday understanding. Suppose one claims to be a fan of a certain sports team but never shows any excitement or disappointment when the team wins or loses. It is difficult to see how one is really loyal to the team, even if one attends every game just as a fan would do. Supposing this affective dimension of loyalty to be what makes loyalty valuable, it cannot be the particular kind of affective state that can sustain the loyal subject's perseverance and devotion.[37] At least it cannot be the fleeting or primitive kind that directly responds to stimuli in the environment. Then, what causes or sustains this kind of ongoing emotional state wherein the subject has "neither eyes to see nor tongue to speak" and will serve her object "with all [her] might and soul and strength?"[38] Royce's own answer is that if one has the need to glorify oneself it is only by devoting oneself to an object that one sees oneself as worthy. However, there is something paradoxical in this line of thought. If the starting point built into loyalty is a self-serving one after all, how can we attain the kind of wholehearted devotion to the other that is idealized in loyalty?

In a *zhong* state, even though the way one works toward the interest of another is regulated by ethical standards, this kind of psychological posture, which requires effort and is demanding to sustain, is grounded in an affective concern for others. This is not to say that the emphasis of *zhong* is affective concern as such. What it means is that the kind of resoluteness and strictness with oneself in doing what is ethically appropriate is grounded in affective concern. If this is correct, the proposed interpretation of *zhong* captures the necessity of both *ren* 仁 (benevolence) and *yi* 義 (propriety) in being *zhong*. While one has to be *yi,* that is, subjecting oneself to ethical standards, one's resoluteness in subjecting oneself to ethical standards is grounded in *ren,* an affective concern for others.

The question, then, is what causes one to have such affective concern for others in the first place. It is at this point that I also lack the textual evidence to speculate what Confucius' answer would be. The following passage perhaps gives us a clue:

季康子問使民敬忠以勸，如之何。子曰，臨之以莊，則敬，孝慈，則忠，舉善而教不能，則勸。

Ji Kangzi asked, "How can one get the common people to be reverent, *zhong,* and to be filled with enthusiasm?" The Master said, "Rule over them with dignity and they will be reverent; treat them with kindness and they will be *zhong;* raise the good and instruct those who are backward and they will be filled with enthusiasm." (*Analects* 2.20)

Confucius' response suggests that one's becoming *zhong* has to do with treating others with kindness. I surmise from this and my early observation about the affective dimension of *zhong* that, for Confucius, what causes one to be *zhong* is that one is being *affected* or feels a certain resonance. The subject is jolted into a *zhong* state not only because she values her ethical commitments at a cognitive level but also because her heart, so to speak, is moved at an affective level. If this is something close to what Confucius had in mind, then an implicit assumption or nascent idea underlying his conception of *zhong* is that human beings are beings that have the capacity for affective resonance. It is by virtue of this capacity that we are affected by others' kindness and thereby develop an affective concern that motivates an attitude of *zhong*.

The preceding analysis has sought to piece together fragments about *zhong* in the *Analects* and to use these as the basis for articulating an early Confucian conception of *zhong*. I hope I have approximated a picture, even if it is not a completely accurate representation of the original, that helps us retrieve certain early Confucian ethical insights that are of contemporary interest to us.

Notes

The first draft of this chapter was presented at the conference on Confucian Values and a Changing World Cultural Order, held at the East-West Center in Honolulu, Hawaiʻi, in October 2014. I thank the participants for their helpful comments and questions. I am particularly indebted to the following people whose comments prompted significant revisions of the chapter: Roger Ames, Nicolas Bommarito, Bernhard Fuehrer, Peter Hershock, Karyn Lai, Chenyang Li, Michael Nylan, Kwong-loi Shun, and George Tsai. A revised version of the chapter was presented at the Ancient World reading group at Yale-NUS, and I would like to thank the participants for their very helpful comments and suggestions.

1. See Yang Bojun 楊伯峻, *Lunyu yizhu* 論語譯注 (Beijing: Zhonghua Shuju, 1980). For references to the *Analects,* I have benefited from James Legge, trans., *Confucian Analects* (Whitefish: Kessinger Publishing, 2010 [1967]); and D. C. Lau, trans., *Confucius: The Analects* (Hong Kong: Chinese University Press, 2002 [1979]). I have also consulted *Lunyu jijie yishu* 論語集解義疏 in *Sibu yaoji zhushu congkan* 四部要籍注疏叢刊, 1998 ed. (Beijing: Zhonghua Shuju). References are to the volume, page, and line numbers. Unless stated otherwise, I follow D. C. Lau's translations of the *Analects* throughout, with some modifications, including the use of pinyin romanization.

2. See, for example, Heiner Roetz, *Confucian Ethics of the Axial Age* (Albany: State University of New York Press, 1993), pp. 93–100, for a discussion of the tension between loyalty and filial piety.

3. For example, in *Analects* 12.22, *ren* 人 (benevolence) is characterized in terms of loving people (*ai ren* 愛人), and in *Mencius* 1A7, Mencius emphasizes that the ruler should extend his bounty (*tui* 推) to all his subjects.

4. See Chenyang Li, "Five Contemporary Challenges for Confucianism," *Journal of East-West Thought* 21, no. 2 (2012): 58.

5. See Lau, *Confucius: The Analects*, p. xvi; Paul Goldin, "When *Zhong* (忠) Does Not Mean 'Loyalty,'" *Dao: A Journal of Comparative Philosophy* 7, no. 2 (2008): 165–174; and Satō Masayuki 佐藤將之, *Zhongguo gudai de 'zhong' lun yanjiu* 中國古代的「忠」論研究 (Taipei: National Taiwan University Press, 2010).

6. Lau, *Confucius: The Analects,* p. xvi n. 6.

7. I am not suggesting that *zhong* as a concept does not have political implications. My point is simply that there is no textual support in the *Analects* for us to think that the scope of *zhong* is restricted to certain qualities of the ministers.

8. See Satō, *Zhongguo gudai de 'zhong' lun yanjiu,* chap. 1, for a detailed discussion on this point.

9. I am indebted to Kwong-loi Shun for his insightful remarks on the use of *zhong* in the *Analects.*

10. I have modified Lau's translation of *mou* as "In what I have undertaken on another's behalf" to "In my planning for others" here because Lau's translation might create the impression that *mou* means doing something for others in a dutiful manner and is therefore evocative of what loyalty requires.

11. My translation of *xin* 信 as "trustworthy" is only tentative. In the *Analects, xin* is often discussed in association with *zhong.* In a majority of the passages where *zhong* appears (1.4, 1.8, 5.28, 7.25, 9.25, 12.10, 15.6), the term is used in connection with *xin.* It is clear that both *zhong* and *xin* are esteemed as ethical traits.

12. It is also interesting to note that in contemporary philosophical discussions, loyalty is often taken to be an attitude necessary for friendship. Here in the *Analects* it is suggested that trustworthiness (*xin*) is an attitude pertaining to friendship, whereas *zhong* encompasses the broader domain of relationships in general. For a recent discussion of the relation between loyalty and friendship see John Kleinig, *On Loyalty and Loyalties: The Contours of a Problematic Virtue* (Oxford: Oxford University Press, 2014).

13. See, for example, *Guoyu,* "Luyu shang" 魯語下; *Zuozhuan,* "Xianggong Fourth Year" 襄公四年; *Shijing,* "Huang huang zhe hua" 皇皇者華.

14. I thank Nicolas Bommarito for pressing me to clarify this point.

15. I have modified Lau's translation of *hui* 誨 here. Lau has translated *hui* as "educating." Since *hui* in early texts has the connotation of using words, I opted for "to say something to correct them" to capture the verbal dimension of *hui* although this is not an elegant translation.

16. For example, Xu Yuangao 徐元誥, *Guoyu jijie* 國語集解 (Beijing: Zhonghua Shuju, 2002), "Jinyu" 晉語 3, "Jinyu" 晉語 4, and "Wuyu" 吳語.

17. Cited in Satō, *Zhongguo gudai de 'zhong' lun yanjiu,* p. 37.

18. A few scholars have suggested that *zhong* 忠 is connected or may even be used interchangeably in the early texts with the phonologically indistinguishable term *zhong* 中, which has the connotation of impartiality or conformity to penal laws without bias. If this is really the case, it will further strengthen my interpretation; however, textual evidence seems inconclusive in showing that there is such a connection. Scholars who have made this observation tend to rely on annotations in the Han period that define 忠 in terms of 中 (see, e.g., Wang Zijin, "Zhong" *guannian yanjiu—Yizhong zhengzhi daode de wenhua yuanliu yu*

lishi yanbian "忠" 觀念研究——一種政治道德的文化源流與歷史演變 [Changchun: Jilin Jiaoyu Chubanshe, 1999]). The methodology of interpretations of early texts based on Han texts is disputable. Paul Goldin ("When *Zhong* [忠] Does Not Mean 'Loyalty'") reiterates this point about the connection between 忠 and 中, but it is not clear what substantial textual evidence Goldin has in thinking that the two terms are intimately connected in early texts other than that they are phonologically indistinguishable and he uses a passage in the *Zuozhuan* to suggest that the meaning of the passage will not change even if we replace 忠 with 中. See Satō, *Zhongguo gudai de 'zhong' lun yanjiu*, chap. 1.1.2 for a discussion of and references to studies of the connection between 忠 and 中 in early texts.

19. Yang Bojun 楊伯峻, "Huangong liu nian" 桓公六年 (Huangong sixth year), in his *Chunqiu Zuozhuan zhu* 春秋左傳注 (Beijing: Zhonghua Shuju, 2006 [1981]), p. 111.

20. Yang Bojun, "Zhuanggong shi nian" 莊公十年 (Zhuanggong tenth year), in his *Chunqiu Zuozhuan zhu,* p. 183.

21. The connection between *zhong* and *mou* is also found in *Guoyu,* "Jinyu" 8.

22. Goldin, "When *Zhong* (忠) Does Not Mean 'Loyalty,'" p. 170.

23. I am indebted to Jay Garfield for prompting me to address this point.

24. See Satō, *Zhongguo gudai de 'zhong' lun yanjiu.*

25. "Loyal," in *Concise Oxford English Dictionary* (Oxford: Oxford University Press, 2004).

26. This case is widely discussed in business ethics and is also cited by Marcia Baron in her discussion of loyalty. See Marcia Baron, *The Moral Status of Loyalty* (Dubuque, IA: Kendall/Hunt, 1984), pp. 2–3.

27. Cited by Baron, *The Moral Status of Loyalty,* pp. 1–2.

28. Andrew Oldenquist, "Loyalties," *Journal of Philosophy* 79, no. 4 (1982): 173–193.

29. William Godwin, *Enquiry Concerning Political Justice and its Influence on Morals and Happiness,* 3rd ed., photographic facsimile, ed. F. E. L. Priestley (Toronto: Toronto University Press, 1946 [1798]), vol. 1, p. 127.

30. See Peter Railton's distinction between "subjective consequentialism" and "objective consequentialism" in his "Alienation, Consequentialism and the Demands of Morality," *Philosophy and Public Affairs,* no. 13 (1984): 152.

31. Ibid., p. 150.

32. I rule out cases of defective special relationships here, such as one's relationship with an enemy.

33. I owe this example to Kwong-loi Shun.

34. For further discussion on this point see John Kleinig, "Loyalty," *Stanford Encyclopedia of Philosophy,* Fall 2013, ed. Edward N. Zalta, http://plato.stanford.edu/archives/fall2013/entries/loyalty/, Section 2.1.

35. For a discussion of village worthies in early Confucian thought see Winnie Sung, "*Xiang Yuan* 鄉原: The Appearance-only Hypocrite," *Dao: A Journal of Comparative Philosophy* 15, no. 2 (2016): 175–192.

36. Joshua Royce, *The Philosophy of Loyalty* (New York: Macmillan, 1908), p. 97.

37. Some philosophers like R. E. Ewin and Simon Keller exclude loyalty as a virtue because of the emotional dimension of loyalty. The reservation is that loyalty hinders or dis-

courages epistemic judgment. Since the overall concern is related to the earlier point about how loyalty can threaten integrity and self-respect, I will not rehearse that here. Even so, they do not deny that this emotional dimension is what makes loyalty valuable. See R. E. Ewin, "Loyalty and Virtues," *Philosophical Quarterly* 42, no. 169 (1992): 403–419, and Simon Keller, *The Limits of Loyalty* (Cambridge: Cambridge University Press, 2007).

   38. These are phrases used repeatedly by Josiah Royce in *The Philosophy of Loyalty*.

PART IV

Limitations and the Critical Reform of Confucian Cultures

CHAPTER 12

Whither Confucius? Whither Philosophy?

Michael NYLAN

BERNARD WILLIAMS' *Ethics and the Limits of Philosophy* registers two important observations: first, that philosophy had better not aim to give an account of moral knowledge like that expected in scientific fields, since that would be futile and inappropriate; and second, that ethical philosophy is at best a particularly imprecise form of philosophizing. Moreover, as Otto Neurath noted, "we repair the ship while we are on the sea."[1] If these observations are true, as I believe they are, discussions about the current and possible future growth of Confucian studies, here and abroad, had better focus on the specifics of present-day practices and beliefs, leaving behind the antiquated and highly contentious notions of the Daotong 道統 ("Genealogy of the Way"). With this in mind, my chapter is divided into three parts: (1) a brief summary of observations made by others about contemporary life, which tend to highlight stark contrasts between contemporary life and life in the pre-industrial societies that gave rise to the early Confucian masters; (2) a summary of the values that we can *usefully* import from early Confucian teachings for adaptation to today's world, East or West, encapsulated in ten words; and (3) a brief consideration of motivation in light of a perceived need to make certain early Confucian teachings more appealing to those not conversant with traditions in early China (a group that would include many Chinese today). After all, the *Shiji* 史記 tells us that it was Mencius and Xunzi who once made Confucian teachings "sexy and appealing" (*runse* 潤色)[2] to the "talking heads" of the fourth and third centuries B.C.E., the implication being that it is hardly likely that Confucius would have become a household name or "icon" today had they not done so.

The present chapter, in short, attempts to consider this world, a world in an admittedly perilous state, asking how we can move beyond the semi-fictive construct that we dub "Confucianism" and the scary calls for "harmony"[3] to retain some of the best features of the Confucius that we find in the *Analects* and in the writings of his early followers.

Contemporary Life as Exceptional

A number of features sharply distinguish the late twentieth and early twenty-first centuries ("contemporary life") from earlier, pre-industrial eras. Readers should note that I will not address many larger aspects of contemporary geo-political life (e.g., proliferating nuclear arms and the resurgence of backward-looking binary models in politics) that philosophy can hardly hope to ameliorate.[4] I confine my list below to the features of contemporary life that others have identified before me and that seem relevant to a discussion about ethics:

1. Contemporary life requires us, as a matter of course, to rely ever more substantially on relations and instruments of impersonal trust rather than those of personal trust (e.g., email, ATM machines, and Internet information).[5]

2. Contemporary life makes available to each educated person a radically expanded set of ethical beliefs, as compared with societies of even a century ago.[6] Darwin may have sounded one of the first modernist voices when he wrote, "Let each man hope and believe what he can." Certainly, I have read the complaints that students (especially those at elite universities) tend to be smart "sheep" lacking any moral compass,[7] but I myself see more feasting at an ethical smorgasbord than "careerist zombies." For example, I have Caucasian students who identify their "ultimate concern" as Israeli nationalism, Zen Buddhism, atheism, or Sufi-Catholicism.

3. Most of the technologies, slogans, and institutions of contemporary life promote isolation and competition between individual persons and groups. For instance, the destructive "clash of civilizations" rhetoric battens on ever-stronger ethnic and cultural identities, as well as deep divisions among sectarian religions. Meanwhile, physical isolation is ensured by a host of new technologies such as Facebook and headphones, and is then reinforced by the corporate calls for a more "self-reliant" and "flexible" globalized labor market—calls reiterated despite sharply *decreasing* socioeconomic mobility.[8] In this our purportedly "ludic century,"[9] in unwitting defiance of earlier sightings of *Homo ludens,* institutions of group solidarity seem to be fewer and weaker outside the far right, which likes megachurches and megastores. Union and professional memberships are sharply down, for instance. Up through the mid-twentieth century,

concern about neighbors' opinions exerted a strong influence on personal behavior, but there are growing indications that the "international elites" (a.k.a. the 1 percent, buttressed by the 10 percent who serve them) identify far more with the members of their own class than with compatriots living in close proximity.[10]

4. Apparently contemporary life is so sex-drenched that it curiously retains many of the anti-carnal sentiments inherited from Platonic idealism, Neoplatonism, and the Mediterranean monotheisms via Kantian and Marxist doctrines. What Roland Barthes, in reifying virtual life, called the new "civilization of the image"[11] fosters two sorts of conflicting conditions. The first can be called "carnal alienation," opposing the tactile experiences of love and friendship in-the-flesh, and the second an incapacity to enjoy being well and truly alone. For evidence of "being out of touch with the body," we have only to think of phone sex, pornography-as-substitute sex, computerized diagnosis and treatment of illnesses, or remote-controlled drone killings. With people never truly in the moment in time and space, "the touch screen replaces touch itself. The cosmos shrinks to a private monitor, each viewer a disembodied self unto itself."[12] At the same time, some experts (e.g., Sherry Turkle at MIT) trace the popularity of these demanding "always on, always on you" technologies directly to people's losing their capacity to be alone while increasing their desires for control.[13] Certainly, I know people who cannot sit through a short meal without checking their iPhones repeatedly.

5. Ever faster computing is apparently changing the ways that people habitually interact with one another and analyze materials. As noted in Nicolas Carr's *The Shallows: What the Internet Is Doing to Our Brains,* new scientific studies now suggest that heavy Internet usage actually reformats our neural pathways so as to decrease our attention spans. As of January 1, 2014, the average American attention span was eight seconds, or one second less than that of a goldfish.[14] As a result, heavy Internet usage is correlated with a stronger desire for speedy results and efficient sound bites, which then work harder *against* our impulses to take the time we need for deep reflection or for rewarding long-term commitments.[15] Authentic conversations and companionship (usually messy and invariably time-consuming) are the real losers in this race, as my undergraduates in a recent seminar on friendship remarked.[16] One by-product of reduced social exchanges may be an increased risk of detaching ourselves from other people, and then regarding those outside our immediate circle "as less human."[17]

6. One early ethical concern was to ascertain the common good, and urge people to seek it.[18] Contemporary life's turn to a relentless celebration of

"choice"—a concept mainly reduced to consumer choice—is misguided on at least two counts: it downplays the role of habit and unthinking responses in the construction of personal and social identities,[19] and it also tends to reduce the exercise of personal freedom to consumer choice.[20] In addition, the well-known phenomenon called "hedonic adaptation" usually prevents consumer purchases from leading to feelings of long-term well-being.[21] Therefore, the freedom to consume is not just partly to blame for the environmental degradation we see all around us; it may account as well for the growing dissatisfaction with the state of the world, a dissatisfaction steadily expressed via countless polls since the 1980s.[22]

7. Nearly all philosophical thinking, in Euro-America and East Asia alike, is predicated on the pernicious fiction that people (i.e., people of privilege, those thought to truly "count") are autonomous, rational individuals capable of identifying and reforming their own conditions by sheer acts of will (—the old Unmoved Mover resurfaces). The language of "human rights" consistently argues that all people and nations should aspire to realize this condition of legal autonomy,[23] despite the obvious fact that this construction ignores many, if not most, present-day realities. Neuroscientific findings on "free will"[24] problematize the very notion of "agency,"[25] for example. In addition, as Joseph E. Stiglitz has pointed out, "[Legal] justice has become a commodity, affordable only to the very few."[26] For these and other reasons, more ethicists are turning to consider the roles played by the emotions, including self-regard, in shaping perceptions and modes of existence,[27] while querying the hard-and-fast dichotomies dividing the cognitive and evaluative impulses,[28] though their work seldom has an impact on the public discourse.

Taken together, such "acids of modernity" are having a predictably corrosive effect on human relations.[29] Amelioration may be possible, but what forms should it take? Many used to the daily specters, if not the actual experience of violence,[30] suspect that the highest present good may simply be to be left alone, in the company of family and friends, to live at peace.[31] But the documentary film *Citizen Four* should remind us that we are not left alone; privacy is dead. And what is it about contemporary life that has left us begging for a mere non-aggression pact when humanity as *Homo faber* is capable of so much more?[32]

These are ethical questions not amenable to quick or certain solutions. There are precedents, however, as Bernard Williams remarked, for treating a philosophical account "as a destination not a route."[33] We might benefit from a few signposts rather than the imposition of extra rules, since all of us are finite, embodied, and historically situated agents, whose rational faculties employed in cost-benefit analyses seldom offer much guidance, given how frequently we act on auto-pilot, operate purely by habit, and try to maneuver through a web of obligations ringed round with emotions. I will argue below that the Ancients have provided us with a series of signposts in the form of "practical wisdom."

The Utility of the Ancients

For some time now, I have been thoroughly convinced that the Ancients have things to teach about what it means to be human, in large part because they inhabited a world that was less ruled by arid abstractions and also more cognizant of the need to depend upon long-term personal exchanges and commitments. They "saw things differently than we do—or rather, they *saw different things*," as one historian of early Rome put it.[34] I like to cite Bernard Williams' *Shame and Necessity* in this connection, where Williams is talking of the Ancient Greeks instead of the early Chinese thinkers:

> The ethical thought...[of these early thinkers discussed here] was not only different from most modern thought, particularly modern thought influenced by Christianity; it was also *in much better shape*...since this system of ideas basically lacks the concept of morality altogether, in the sense of *a class of reasons or demands which are vitally different from other kinds of reason or demand....*Relatedly,...the questions of how one's relations to others are to be regulated, both in the context of society and more privately, are not detached from questions about the kind of life it is worth living....[35]

Needless to say, the erection of strict barriers between moral and practical reasons in contemporary discourse, far from elevating the work of universities and ethicists, has made it that much easier to dismiss careful investigation into the human condition as either hopelessly "reality-based" (and hence lacking in moral fire or political swagger)[36] or the sorry product of "ivory tower" idealists who couldn't think their way out of a paper bag in real life. When citing Williams, I often recall Herbert Fingarette's first paragraph in his classic *Confucius: The Secular as Sacred*:

> Increasingly, I have become convinced that Confucius can be a teacher to us today—a major teacher, not one who merely gives us a slightly exotic perspective on the ideas already current. He tells us things not being said elsewhere; things needing to be said. He has a new lesson to teach.[37]

History and philosophy should let the dead live again on their own terms, as much as possible, so that we moderns may benefit from better acquaintance with unfamiliar thoughts.[38] But there are major flaws with Greek thought and its Western successors, especially those of the Kantian and neo-Kantian sort. Doubtless we can all name features of earlier societies that we would prefer not to emulate: the enslavement of human beings, the casual oppression of women and homosexuals, the resort to superstition, and so on.[39] More subtle is the propensity of Greek and later Western thought to be "incurably egoistic" (i.e., narrowly preoccupied with the inner life of the presumed self).[40] Furthermore, most Western philosophy identifies two main motivations for action (the pursuit of pleasure and the grim acceptance of duty), in the rather naive belief that moving beyond perceived self-interest will make it much easier to reconcile self and society.[41] A close comparison of early Greek with early Chinese thought illustrates the virtues of the Chinese thinkers: they are not "incurably egoistic"; they stipulate far less about the world and its inhabitants, they are inclined to distrust arid abstractions claiming universal applicability,[42] and ultimately, in elevating the Middle Way, they require less of the person while nonetheless upholding strict standards for "civilized" conduct. If philosophy is the therapeutic examination of belief and action (in the old sense),[43] then greater resort to early Chinese modes of thinking may well be a salutary exercise for all of us.

Please understand: I am no wild-eyed romantic railing against a loss of community or tradition, content to shill for Confucian learning in the hopes that blind adherence to older forms will miraculously usher in a "return" to an idealized past that never existed.[44] Rather I am a hardheaded historian who is acutely aware of the dangerous propensity to retroject anachronisms into presentist readings of history.[45] But I confess that cataloging a huge range of invented traditions has led me to wonder whether contemporary life might not profit from the selective reinvention of a few traditions designed to counter the motley (when not positively murderous) traditions we have inherited. Are we not enjoined, as ethical people of some imagination, to "warm up the old" (*wen gu* 溫故)? Our job is to ask not only "How are we to live?" (that being, of course, the question posed by Socrates and Confucius), but also "How are we to live so as to be more alive?"[46] Like the Ancients whom I study, I seek a design of life (not wholly "rational") that would reduce the power of fortune and fate through maximal appreciation for hard work in service of communal goods, the sort of life that would help myself and others from being "enslaved by things."[47]

Older wisdom texts are in general agreement that an ethical life begins with moving beyond narrow self-interest. As one contemporary thinker summarizes it:

> Imagine that each of us lives at the center of a set of concentric circles, the nearest being our own self, the furthest being the entire universe of living creatures. The task of our moral development is to move the circles pro-

gressively closer to the center, so that we regard our parents and children like ourselves, our other relatives like our parents, and strangers like our relatives.[48]

Noting that "we are least like anything else in the world when we do not treat each other like physical objects, as animals, or even as sub-human creatures to be driven, threatened, forced, maneuvered," Fingarette skillfully argues that we are conversely most sublimely and supremely human whenever we fuse personal presence to "(learned) ceremonial skill," making ceremonial acts "the primary, irreducible events" constituting our memorable experiences.

In that spirit, I volunteer two early slogans as signposts for contemporary life, slogans associated with the early Confucian teachings and with the *Zhuangzi,* a work in critical engagement with those same teachings. The two signposts are "Know what is enough" (*zhi zu* 知足) and "Treat [others] as honored guests" (*ru jian da bin* 如見大賓). The first slogan is typically (mis)labeled as Daoist, since it occurs in both the *Laozi* and the *Zhuangzi;* however, the *Xunzi,* the *Zhouli,* and the *Kongcongzi* use the exact same phrase in the same way, so this two-character phrase in classical Chinese is better characterized as prevailing "wisdom talk."[49] Likewise, the second slogan, best known from *Analects* 12.2, does not belong solely to any particular group. In several pre-Han and Han texts, including the *Lunheng* 論衡, exemplary figures are said to epitomize this or closely allied notions, this being the best possible way to "pay due heed to and communicate with others" (*jing tong ren* 敬通人), based on their knowledge of past and present social practices.[50] Helpfully, the second slogan is paired with a parallel injunction in the same *Analects* passage; the injunction equally enjoins members of the governing elite to demonstrate their care for "those below": "Employ the people [as carefully] as if officiating at a solemn sacrifice" (*shi min ru cheng da ji* 使民如承大祭).[51] Rough equivalents for these slogans could be found, no doubt, in many different parts of the world in their distinctive "wisdom books," suggesting that they can shed a kind of "global radiance," provoking deeper reflection,[52] without getting hopelessly mired in arguments over the so-called "universal principles" masking neoliberal and statist agendas.

"Learning by subtraction" (as in "Know what is enough") can serve citizens of postmodern societies touting "choice" as the highest freedom.[53] For if "it is the vice of the vulgar mind to be thrilled by bigness," contemporary society is stupendously vulgar. Whether we would address environmental degradation and global warming or protest the serene self-righteousness displayed by our most flagrantly corrupt organizations and leaders,[54] the mere repetition of this mantra may create a distaste for "more is better" and "shop 'til you drop." The same phrase, meanwhile, undercuts the emerging world of virtual reality "rife with delusions of omniscience, omnipresence, and omnipotence,"[55] insofar as it reminds us to identify our real needs as human beings, among them the need to be loved and physically touched and to maintain a measure of dignity.

As the advantages of "Know what is enough" seem unmistakable, let me tarry a bit longer on the second slogan, which urges us to treat others as honored guests, a slogan redolent with antique notions of hospitality and sanctuary. One line after another of the *Analects* reiterates some variation on this set of injunctions, which leads me to see this extension of exquisite courtesies to the lowly among us as the central task for any would-be Confucian,[56] then or now. We have all heard of the Golden Rule, but Confucius asks both less and more of us here.[57] On the one hand, we are not expected to love others as ourselves (something that may be quite impossible for those not graced with special gifts). On the other, we are enjoined to consider what words and gestures we find humiliating, demeaning, and condescending, and then avoid using those words and gestures with others. More pro-actively, we are instructed to treat others with the same exquisite courtesy we would render recognized dignitaries. This standard asks us not only to meet, but also to anticipate the needs of others, as we would happily do for important guests due to visit. It requires recurrently asking others what they would prefer, rather than presuming what they deserve and merit. When successful, this highly ritualized performance conveys via complex gestures a temporary self-effacement meant to honor the engrossing importance of another; thus it balances an acute awareness of one's own person in relation to the visitor(s) with a willing displacement of conscious focus on oneself.[58] It moreover asks us to regard those who are in our power as if they were a higher power, without conceding to worldly powers any power to harm ourselves or others.

But let us not ignore the flipside: to receive a dignitary well places the host in the gratifying role of the person conferring hospitality. The miracle is that somehow the great dignity residing in the one can be shared with another, with no diminution to either party. For hospitality given and acknowledged valorizes both sides' implicit claims to worth.[59]

Unless the host is blessed with stupendous luck, however, easy and affable treatment of the guest presupposes the host's prior acculturation to a range of enlivening sociable exchanges. Long before the guest arrives, she must, *as if by instinct,* have learned the art of "reading" people, even strangers. And there is more: she must evince a readiness to change course when advisable, in a kind of free-form, improvisational fugue or dance.[60] As with any art form, the course of training for a virtuoso performance is long and arduous; after all, by the moral mandate, the host does nothing less than open herself to fully experiencing the presence of another person (followed by another and another), equipped with the social insights and practices culled over time.[61] The ultimate goal: a kind of fluency that lends the mundane a sort of magic, thereby reacquainting us with the ordinary mysteries of life. Yet no part of this set of injunctions dictates a particular religious, philosophical, or patriotic creed about this life or the next; every part of it hearkens to local practices and individual idiosyncrasies.[62] Even to pose the question "what is enough?" is, like acting hospitably, to firmly refuse to subscribe to one or more universal rules, in that suitable adjustments will continually have to be made to assess "what is enough" and "goodly" under changing circumstances. Most importantly, perhaps, learning to aim for this set of injunctions moves us firmly away from the "main aspects of modern identity—that is, liberty, autonomy,... and...the subject's self-positioning or rational self-determination."[63]

There is no reliable way to calculate the long-term consequences of our actions, however well intended, nor can reason, custom, or experience resolve many puzzles of human existence.[64] I am willing to live with the Mystery.[65] Yet it is best to be as precise as possible when we talk, and speaking of "dignity" rather than "justice" seems a vast improvement, since no two figures in my readings in philosophy and history have ever arrived at a shared notion of justice. Some equate "justice" with utilitarianism and others with communitarianism, libertarianism, or God's will.[66] As one smart philosopher put it: "Justice is inescapably judgmental...an open invitation to narrow, intolerant moralisms."[67] By contrast, we all have a fairly good sense of what constitutes the sort of treatment we would accord dignitaries, those deemed to have dignity. Dignity is hard to make into an abstract quality, and therein lies its attraction for me as a grounding for life. I note in this connection that Wittgenstein's description of the ethical/religious is "a sense that we are absolutely safe."[68] Having members of a community preserve our human dignity—that's as close to paradise on earth as we are likely to get.

The legends about Confucius would have us understand that Confucius goes to his death believing himself a miserable failure, but ultimately he is hailed as an uncrowned king (and in some texts a virtual god), for his remarkable ability to turn personal misfortunes into blessings for others. If the main thrust of the Confucian *Analects* throughout remains the human imperative to accord others the same dose of dignity that we would gladly impart to an honored guest, the life of Confucius suggests that we may sometimes have to set aside our physical comforts and our most cherished mental constructs in order to clear a space wherein we may better observe the needs of others. As the *Analects* makes plain, we must not only adopt this way of operating in the world but make it a habit before we can possibly see any benefits accruing from this ritualized mode of operation. We must try it as an act of faith, in other words. The promise is that we are then likely to learn to feel at home in our own skins in our daily rounds. We may then derive pleasure (*le* 樂) from living in the simplest circumstances (*Analects* 6.11, 7.16), from seeking wisdom and acting compassionately (6.23), and from visits paid by friends and peers (1.1), all in the serene confidence that "to find it [this way] a pleasure is better than to know it or prefer it" (6.20), since secure "pleasure need not be licentious or [to] go to excess" (3.20). The early Confucian masters assure us that greater human happiness is to be found in connecting, communicating, and sharing than in gaining or asserting power over others. In doing so, they supply models for continual engagement with the world, rather than urging a hasty retreat from it.

I was deeply moved when reading one op-ed writer's recent summation of her "thought processes" in her younger days:

> You do things you regret or don't understand and then you make other choices because life keeps going forward. Or you do something out of love and then, through biology or accident, it goes inexplicably wrong, and you do what you can to cope. Or you do whatever you do, however you do it, for whatever reasons, because that's your experience.[69]

Doubtless, some people will deplore the lack of self-knowledge expressed here, but to me, at any rate, this looks a lot like life, and not even a particularly bad or unreflective sort of life. In *A Room of One's Own,* Virginia Woolf commented: "Life for both sexes...is arduous, difficult, a perpetual struggle"; "it calls for gigantic courage and strength," yet we usually go around "snubbed, slapped, lectured, and exhorted." To maintain courage in the face of this muddle, the key thing may be just to keep the image of our common (if failed) humanity front and center before us, refusing to go to a place where we grow numb.[70] To that end, I read and reread this set of questions posed in early China:

> In our world, is there such a thing as supreme pleasure or is there not? Is there something that may be used to make ourselves more alive or not?[71] In the present times, how are we to act? How are we to make a basis?...What are we to take pleasure in and what are we to deplore?[72]

This set of questions reminds us that a good life must bespeak plenitude (a "richness"), that boils down less to material resources and more to a life open to encounter new experiences every single day, thanks to a more capacious regard for the world.

Moral philosophy invites a second look at the early Chinese thinkers, who go beyond a few guideposts to speak of the sorts of human institutions that promote the "most alive" forms of being and acting, producing pleasures great and small. If we are looking for something that may help us find our way around, everyday experience usually suffices to reveal a startling amount of information that we need to know about ourselves and the world we inhabit, if we are to act wisely and well, even if that information is not liable to objective proof.[73] And, as a recent psychology experiment has shown, the only sure indicator of what we ourselves will end up doing in a particular moral dilemma is what we presume others in our community would do in precisely the same situation.[74] In short, if I wish to act well, I must conceive of the possibility that others will act well and then act upon that conception. (This is precisely what one Chinese Classic, the *Shujing* 書經 or *Documents,* advises.) But that is not all: I must know the members of my community well enough to be able to visualize what actions others might take in similar situations. Should I manage that, it should be less difficult to conceive of the potential benefits—intangible and unseen, as well as tangible—of cooperating with others, while conceding, too, that occasional feeling of being deceived or disappointed in others. That concession may be reckoned a small price to pay for the possibility of transfiguration, a sort of "rent" for living fully,[75] so that one is primed ("heartened" if you will) to embrace the rigors of contemporary life.

Confucian Teachings and Their Appeal

Confidence in our ability to improve contemporary conditions is half the battle. But, as Bernard Williams notes, "Confidence [in an ethical decision]…is basically a social phenomenon." He means, in general, that confidence relies on social confirmation; a society's support for a person's attitude tends to make him or her more conscious of holding certain convictions. Williams continues:

> Philosophy cannot tell us how to bring it [confidence in an ethical conviction] about. It is a social and psychological question what kinds of institutions, upbringing, and public discourse help to foster it.[76]

Williams may be right, but he then concludes—quite wrongly, I feel—that the business of philosophy is not to consider social and psychological questions, and hence not to think further about institutions. Apparently, he wishes for philosophy today to preserve or even harden its current conventional academic boundaries. I dearly wish, in return, to ask him why, for it seems to me that philosophy has been proposing social and psychological institutions for millennia now, at least since Plato and Confucius. How could an abnegation of our responsibility to plan for our own and future generations possibly lead to better philosophy? Surely the job of philosophy is to map, then ruminate upon, the many ways that human beings have sought to be human.

So, *pace* Williams, I feel we should be asking, "What mix of motives, instrumental and non-instrumental, is most likely to propel people to perform their tasks constructively and well, without summoning inadvertent disasters?"

A recent set of studies suggests that efforts to promote constructive activities should focus on the meaning and potential impact of these initiatives, rather than on their connection with conventional markers of "success," if we are to ensure good and lasting outcomes.[77] Xunzi made the same point centuries ago, in the essay "On Ritual,"[78] where he insisted that ritual shapes and channels people's disparate longings within a larger symbolic system that creates meaning. Yet too many self-styled Confucians today have forgotten what both Mencius and Xunzi knew: that people living on the margin of subsistence cannot be expected to be good candidates for moral development, and people rightly seek satisfaction in their social relations and in their work.

Were I in a position of power, such attention to economic and environmental conditions would require me to consider giving out cash grants to the poor, so as to ensure their minimum standard of living. Certainly this would be cheaper than our current patchwork of "social safety nets"—and nineteen major studies agree: only a very small proportion of the poor will waste the money (especially if women are the targeted recipients). If we let the poor "eat cash," then alcohol and tobacco consumption falls or stays the same, while drug counseling and anger management programs fare better. Why? People need food security if they are to feel that they merit other people's warm regard.[79] And, as Mencius bluntly puts it, "It is not worth the trouble talking to a man who has no respect for himself... or confidence in himself" (4A1).[80]

Mencius and Xunzi made Confucian teachings more glossy and appealing to a wide range of thinkers in a second way: both of these thinkers went far beyond the earlier teachings ascribed to Confucius to elaborate the pleasures that rest upon establishing a secure place in close communities. Book 1 of the *Mencius* details the conversation between Mencius and King Hui of Liang, where the King is asked to conceive of the pleasures that will accrue once he rests secure in the allegiance of his own subjects. A lesser moralist might have been inclined to score points by labeling the desires of this powerful man as flaws, faults, weaknesses, and shortcomings (*ji* 疾). Mencius tries quite another tactic: he focuses upon the common human desire to be held in high esteem, insisting that "all people share the same desire to be exalted," to be held in high regard in one's own estimation and in that of others. Nonetheless people often fail to appreciate the fact that every person has the wherewithal within the self to be exalted (6A17).[81] But so long as the person believes himself to be capable of acting morally, Mencius says, this basic compulsion to be admired can motivate constructive social action. So whenever power-holders seem unaware of their potential to become authoritative figures, they are to be given better teachers (6A9).[82] Reasoning in much the same way, Xunzi famously articulates the view that the fundamental human desires are not obstructions to morality, but rather the bedrock of morality.[83] Far from endorsing the popular slogans "reduce desires" (*shao yu* 少欲) or "eliminate desires" (*wu yu* 無欲), Xunzi argues that (a) desires are what people have, (b) desires make the world go around, and (c) wise policy-makers use these two facts to devise better institutions of governance and compelling models of cultivation (i.e., self-governance). These, in turn, ultimately promote the satisfaction of all bodies (and so the body politic itself), with the result that the imperial subjects eagerly learn to "manage their lives and their means of living" (*zhi sheng chan* 治生產).[84]

In the expansive view informed by Mencius and Xunzi, good governments utilize any and all methods that make it markedly easier to rule well—wanting good governance to be as easy as the proverbial "reeling in like skeins of silk," as natural as "the spokes of a wheel hub converging on the hub." The writings ascribed to Mencius and Xunzi, not coincidentally, share an unremitting focus on institutional matters, with both thinkers assuming that personal morality, with rare exceptions, can never be sustained for long in the absence of institutional props. Sumptuary regulations and regular community rituals (e.g., community banquets and well-defined marriage and mourning practices) are but two of the institutions they pushed to encourage the development of the basic sociable habits upon which super-civilization is to be built. I doubt that the United States will ever establish anything like sumptuary regulations, but that kind of willingness to countenance powerful destructive behavior may feed the Gordon Gekkos of this world.[85] So it is well worth asking, "What features of our current tax code truly benefit society by inducing real contributions to it?"[86] Put another way, what message does it send to society-at-large when Scientology, Princeton University, and charities set up for cats all get equal tax deductions under our code?

The early classicists and Confucians in China showed exceptional clarity in three areas: they insisted that economic security is a necessary, if not sufficient, condition for building good character,[87] they carefully delineated the pleasures to be had from living in more secure communities, and they urged reward structures to be put in place so as to encourage people to make more constructive contributions to their neighbors and peers, not to mention future generations. If the early Chinese thinkers exhibited such practical wisdom millennia ago, then one may well ask, "Why is it that Chinese thought and Chinese institutions have received such unrelentingly bad press in modern times?" Anthropologist Jack Goody offers a forceful analysis in his recent book *The Theft of History*.[88] According to Goody, long ago, in colonial days, Northern Europe and the United States gained the upper hand in discussions about human development, thanks to the master narrative of "Western civilization" (a shape-shifting siren, if ever there was one), so much so that, regardless of whether the discourse is Orientalizing or self-Orientalizing,[89] Euro-America is now credited with playing the central role in the evolution of all manner of desirable goods, ranging from "democracy" and "humanism" to, most astonishingly, "antiquity" itself. Consequently there is little left for China to claim but perceived "lacks" or "failures." Then, too, the spectacularly bad behavior of certain Chinese elites may have deterred those unfamiliar with Confucian ideas from undertaking quiet study of the good advice proffered by wise men long ago in China. That said, no time or place is ever free of cheats and sycophants and connivers.

In any case, that would be a discussion for another day. I cannot do better than end on a poem by a Han dynasty poet, Cui Yuan 崔瑗 (77–142 C.E.), that encapsulates some of the foregoing themes in a supremely artful way:

> One must not speak of others' faults,
> > Nor of one's own strengths.
> If you offer someone something, forget it later on.
> > If someone offers you something, never forget it!
> A reputation is not worth envying in another.
> > Only *ren* (humankindness) should become your rule and frame,
> Keep your person in the shadows, and then act.
> > Then how can slander and talk ever really harm you? . . .
> So long as all your actions be as constant as the day is long,
> > You will find yourself forever sweetly perfumed.

無道人之短。 無說己之長
施人慎勿念。 受施慎勿忘
世譽不足慕。 唯仁為紀綱。
隱身而後動。 謗議庸何傷？ . . .
行之苟有恆。 久久自芬芳。

Notes

This chapter is dedicated to Henry Rosemont, Jr., who can say everything better.

1. Otto Neurath, cited in Bernard Williams, *Ethics and the Limits of Philosophy* (Cambridge, MA: Harvard University Press, 1985), p. 113.
2. *Shiji* 121.3116.
3. Repeated calls for "harmony" in today's world often mean little more than "forced ethnic assimilation" and "obedience to the powers-that-be." An early Qing dynasty exchange suggests that this (mis)use of "harmony" is long-standing. Dorgon in 1645 defined "harmony" as "acting in concert to serve the ruling house and country (*guojia* 國家) and the people," as against "acting in concert to serve themselves, their families, or their selfish desires," which is said to be "conspiring." See Harry Miller, *State versus Gentry in Early Qing Dynasty China* (New York: Palgrave Macmillan, 2013), p. 25. Rosemont and Ames have insisted, quite rightly, on the importance of remonstrance functions in the early Confucian classics, including the *Xiaojing*.

4. A reduction of potential outcomes seems to be on offer with respect to the systems for contemporary politics and economics. In politics, for example, there have been put forward two main models for future emulation: (a) the Northern European "world of postmodern statehood," where roughly equal partners tend to tend their own gardens in considerable smugness, and (b) the model which says that only worlds dominated by a single superpower can ever enforce the peace. As Robert Kagan's 2000 essay "Power and Weakness" suggests, these two views have prestigious pedigrees, as they hearken back to Immanuel Kant and Thomas Hobbes. Incredibly, to my mind, the Northern European powers are increasingly adopting the American model in their cultural and political institutions.

5. For this distinction, see Steven Johnstone, A *History of Trust in Ancient Greece* (Chicago: University of Chicago Press, 2011).

6. Stephen Angle, *Human Rights and Chinese Thought: A Cross-cultural Inquiry* (Cambridge: Cambridge University Press, 2002).

7. William Deresiewicz, *The Miseducation of the American Elite and the Way to a Meaningful Life* (New York: Free Press, 2014) (see *New York Times,* September 20, Book Review, p. C1, for a review of this book). Deresiewicz describes the students he knew at Yale as trapped "in a bubble of privilege, heading meekly in the same direction, great at what they're doing but with no idea why they're doing it" (p. 3).

8. For the corporate origins of the "self-reliance" movements, designed to absolve corporations from many responsibilities toward their employees, see Barbara Ehrenreich, *Bright-Sided: How the Relentless Promotion of Positive Thinking Has Undermined America* (New York: Metropolitan Books, 2009). "Flexible" globalized markets are but another name for outsourcing and downsizing, which increase anxiety among most workers.

9. Eric Zimmerman of New York University has called this "the ludic century" (Eric Zimmerman, "Manifesto for a Ludic Century," online at http://ericzimmerman.com/files/texts/Manifesto_for_a_Ludic_Century.pdf). See Chris Suellentropoct, "Can Video Games Survive?" *New York Times,* October 26, 2014, Sunday Review, p. 1. For *Homo ludens,* see Johan Huizinga, *Homo Ludens: A Study of the Play-element in Culture* (London: Routledge and Kegan Paul, 1949).

10. The first time I saw this "unmooring" discussed was in 1990, in Anthony D. King's *Global Cities: Post-imperialism and the Internationalization of London* (London: Routledge, 1990). Counter-evidence may come from Erez Yoeli, Moshe Hoffman, and David Rand, "How to Prevent Summer Blackouts," *New York Times,* July 5, 2014, Opinion Pages, p. A19, which concludes, "Humans have faced public-good quandaries since the dawn of time, and we've developed since the dawn of time, and we've developed a powerful force to deal with them: our reputation in society."

11. See Barthes' essay in *Classic Essays on Photography,* ed. Alan Trachtenberg (New Haven: Leete's Island Books, 1980).

12. Richard Kearney (Boston College), "Losing Our Touch," in *New York Times,* "Opinionator," August 30, 2014.

13. Sherry Turkle (interview), "The Networked Primate," in "Special Evolution Issue: Humanity's Journey," *Scientific American* 311, no. 4 (September 2014): 82–85. This past summer's comedy hit titled "Her" (director Spike Jonze) plays with such fears, insofar as it depicts a man falling in love with his own operating system, which he nicknames "Saman-

tha"; before long, however, the male lead becomes insanely jealous because he discovers that his virtual lover is flirting with tens of thousands of other subscribers. Susannah Elm, my colleague at Berkeley, clearly struck a nerve in Germany when she remarked that master-slave relations in the Roman empire were perhaps more positive than her relation with her iPhone (she was interviewed by *Frankfurter Allegemeine* and four other newspapers).

14. See the National Center for Biotechnology Information, U.S. National Library of Medicine, report of January 1, 2014, which also reports a sharp decrease from the year 2000 (from an average of twelve seconds to eight). "Attention span" is the amount of time concentrated on a task without becoming distracted. Most educators and psychologists agree that the ability to focus attention on a task is crucial for the achievement of one's goals. Nicholas Carr, in *The Shallows: What the Internet Is Doing to Our Brains* (New York: W. W. Norton, 2011), speaks of the Internet "remapping the neural circuitry, reprogramming the memory," destroying our powers of concentration. "We don't see the forest when we search the Web," he writes. "We don't even see the trees. We see twigs and leaves" (p. 91). A 2008 study, reviewing 34 million academic articles published between 1945 and 2005, concluded that while the digitization of journals made it far easier to find this information, it produced a narrowing of citations, with scholars relying much more heavily on recent publications.

15. Carr, *The Shallows,* passim.

16. Evolutionarily, *Homo sapiens,* we are told, developed a competitive advantage due to its special capacity for engaging in the figurative "mind reading" of another person's thoughts and engagement in shared tasks, where the engagements required memory, touch, speech, and sight. See Gary Stix, "The 'It' Factor," in "Special Evolution Issue: Humanity's Journey," *Scientific American* 311, no. 4 (September 2014): 72–79.

17. Aaron Ben-Ze'ev, *The Subtlety of Emotions* (Cambridge, MA: MIT Press, 2001), pp. 259–260.

18. See Hans Sluga, *Politics and the Search for the Common Good* (Cambridge: Cambridge University Press, 2014).

19. Xunzi was a genius at explaining this role, but so is Herbert Fingarette in his *Self-Deception* (Berkeley and Los Angeles: University of California Press, 1969, 2000); cf. Anaïs Nin, "We don't see things as they are, we see things as we are" (*Seduction of the Minotaur* [Chicago: Swallow Press, 1961], p. 124), and Epictetus, "People are not moved by things, but the views which they take of them."

20. I recommend Adam Phillips, *Missing Out: In Praise of the Unlived Life* (New York: Farrar, Straus and Giroux, 2013). A review of that book by Sheila Heti (*New York Times,* January 20, 2103, Book Review, p. 12) says this: "We live in an age in which many of us no longer feel rooted in traditional systems of belief[, and] we know we are nothing special— 'on a par with ants and daffodils'—and so seek our satisfaction in the perpetual present of consumer capitalism, in which 'knowing ourselves' means 'simply knowing what we have to have.'"

21. Generally speaking, hedonic adaptation involves a happiness "set point," whereby humans maintain a constant level of happiness throughout their lives, despite events that occur in their environment. The process of hedonic adaptation is often conceptualized as a treadmill or thermostat, since one must consciously or mechanically work to maintain a certain level of happiness beyond a certain "set point."

22. "[T]he pursuit of happiness of modern (consumer) society is [one where]...the Utopian project is reduced in scale to the *individual,* into a modern mode of self-building aiming at completion within the boundaries of one's own self and one's own life," with "[consumer] goods as the building bricks" (Pasi Falk, *The Consuming Body* [London: Sage, 1994], p. 30). Some have called this contemporary Utopian project "consumutopia." See, e.g., Grant McCracken, *Culture and Consumption: New Approaches to the Symbolic Character of Consumer Goods and Activities* (Bloomington: Indiana University Press, 1990); Brian J. McVeigh, " 'Consumutopia' versus 'Control' in Japan," *Journal of Material Culture* 5, no. 2 (1990): 225–245.

23. Henry Rosemont, Jr., has led the way here in consideration of the enormous gap between the discourse of rights in China and in Euro-America. See, e.g., "Human Rights: A Bill of Worries," in *Confucianism and Human Rights,* ed. Wm. Theodore de Bary and Tu Weiming (New York: Columbia University Press, 1998). See his recent monograph, *Against Individualism: A Confucian Rethinking of Morality, Politics, Family, and Religion* (Lanham, MD: Lexington Books, 2015).

24. E.g., Michael Gazzaniga (University of California–Santa Barbara) argues, "Social constructs like good judgment and free will are even further removed, and trying to define them in terms of biological processes is, in the end, a fool's game." See "Decoding the Brain's Cacophony," *New York Times,* November 3, 2011; John Tierney, "Do You Have Free Will? It's the Only Choice," *New York Times,* March 21, 2011; Kerri Smith, "Neuroscience vs. Philosophy: Taking Aim at Free Will," *Nature* 477 (August 2011): 23–25.

25. Apparently, we smell differently and appreciate smells differently, depending upon our political orientations. See Arthur C. Brooks, "Smelling Liberal, Thinking Conservative," *New York Times,* October 5, 2014, Sunday Review, p. 5.

26. Joseph E. Stiglitz, "Is Inequality Inevitable?" *New York Times,* June 29, 2014, Sunday Review, p. 7; also Martha Bergmark (Executive Director, Voices for Civil Justice), *New York Times,* July 4, 2014, Opinion Pages response.

27. As Western society becomes more individualistic, a successful life has come to be equated with having high self-esteem, but paradoxically, people with high self-esteem tend to be less effective as social agents, since people don't really like self-enhancers very much (Steven J. Heine et al., "Is There a Universal Need for Positive Self-regard," *Psychological Review* 106, no. 4 [October 1991]: 766–794).

28. Memory does not correspond to a single brain site or function; it is a complex group of learning systems. For a review of such ideas, one may consult Ben-Ze'ev, *The Subtlety of Emotions,* esp. chaps. 2, 3, 6 (the last on "rationality" vs. "functionality"). Martha Nussbaum, among others, has been arguing for the inseparability of the emotions from reasoning. See, for example, her *Upheavals of Thought: The Intelligence of Emotions* (Cambridge: Cambridge University Press, 2003), which argues for the complex intelligence of emotions.

29. The phrase was originally that of Walter Lippmann, but it has been widely adopted in theological studies, including *The Cambridge History of Christianity,* vol. 8, *World Christianities c. 1815–c. 1914,* and vol. 9, *World Christianities c. 1914–c. 2000.*

30. See, e.g., http://www.apa.org/about/gr/pi/advocacy/2008/kunkel-tv.aspx, for the assertion that watching violence on TV, at the movies, or in video games affects us as deeply as violence in the flesh.

31. One woman explained to Sherry Turkle (Turkle, "The Networked Primate," p. 84) why she preferred a robot boyfriend to a real one: "Look, I just want civility in the house. I just want something that will make me feel not alone."

32. For *Homo faber,* see Richard Sennett, *Together: The Rituals, Pleasures, and Politics of Cooperation* (New Haven: Yale University Press, 2012), which is part of a larger project.

33. Williams, *Ethics and the Limits of Philosophy,* p. 55. Cf. Iris Murdoch, in her 1967 lecture "The Sovereignty of Good over Other Concepts": "Ethics should not be merely an analysis of ordinary mediocre conduct; it should be a hypothesis about good conduct and about how this can be achieved," in Iris Murdoch, *The Sovereignty of Good* (London and New York: Routledge Classics, 1970, 1971), p. 76.

34. Daryn Lehoux, *What Did the Romans Know? An Inquiry into Science and World-making* (Chicago: University of Chicago Press, 2012), p. 8.

35. Adapted from Bernard Williams, *Shame and Necessity* (Berkeley: University of California Press, 1993), pp. 20, 251 (italics mine). Williams speaks of the Ancient Greeks; I of those thinkers (nearly all of whom were policy advisors at court) writing in classical Chinese.

36. The sneering quotation condemning the Third Estate as a *"reality-based* community" (now widely attributed to Karl Rove) first appeared in an October 17, 2004 issue of the *New York Times.* The quotation juxtaposed people who rely upon faith, assumption, or ideology and those who naively "believe that solutions emerge from judicious study of discernible reality." Bush (or Rove?) reportedly continued, "That's not the way the world really works anymore.... We're an empire now, and when we act, we create our own reality."

37. Herbert Fingarette, *Confucius: The Secular as Sacred* (New York: Harper/Torchbooks, 1972), p. vii.

38. Samuel Moyn speaks of the "ethical value of the past," and also of "an ethical command to respect its alterity.... The past is not simply a mirror for our own self-regard" (Samuel Moyn, *Human Rights and the Uses of History* [London: Verso, 2014], p. xii). Arnaldo Momigliano posited another distinction, whereby the antiquarian gathers details to accumulate a store of facts, whereas the historian looks for patterns. By his definition, I would prefer to be a historian than an antiquarian. See his "Ancient History and the Antiquarian," *Journal of the Warburg and Courtauld Institutes* 13, no. 3/4 (1950): 285–315.

39. Williams' *Ethics and the Limits of Philosophy* shows that a position is idealist if what is ontologically primary in the position is something abstract. As a trained historian, I am more accustomed to the idea that truth is contingent and change constant. From the outside, philosophy seems much more stable in its objects of contemplation and models of inquiry. I have argued at some length elsewhere that the charge that "Confucians oppressed women" is muddle-headed.

40. Williams, *Ethics and the Limits of Philosophy,* pp. 15, 49. These broad generalizations ignore the huge gaps between Plato and Aristotle, just to name two classical Greek philosophers, which Williams and other classicists acknowledge. See Kearney, "Losing Our Touch," for a listing of some of these gaps.

41. One of the strengths of Kongzi in the *Analects* is that he allows that this is so only in some cases, not all.

42. Here I part company with Hans-Georg Moeller, whose book *The Moral Fool: A*

Case for Amorality (New York: Columbia University Press, 2009), passim, enjoins us to eschew universal injunctions universally, which is a logical contradiction in terms.

43. Leroy S. Rouner, ed., *The Longing for Home* (Notre Dame, IN: University of Notre Dame Press, 1996), p. 5. Cf. Pierre Hadot, *What is Ancient Philosophy?* trans. Michael Chase (Cambridge, MA: Belknap Press of Harvard University Press, 2002).

44. Sarah Hoagland says that "care ethicists" tend to underplay self-regard, thereby helping to maintain the existence of oppressive institutions; and besides, the reciprocity they ascribe to warm social relations is much overrated. See Sarah Hoagland, *Lesbian Ethics* (Palo Alto, CA: Institute of Lesbian Studies, 1988) and "Some Thoughts about Caring," in *Feminist Ethics,* ed. Claudia Card (Lawrence: University of Kansas Press, 1991). What I am discussing is not exactly "reciprocity," but rather what actions may lead to a better outcome.

45. Cited in Moyn, *Human Rights and the Uses of History,* p. xi.

46. See the opening lines of the "Zhi le" 至樂 chapter in the *Zhuangzi*.

47. On enslavement by things, no reading can surpass that of the *Xunzi* or chapter 129 of the *Shiji*. Sima Qian is particularly clear on the subject of "wage slavery," and the early Chinese thinkers generally regard "enslavement by things" to be harmful to a person's health and community. That hard work is "the epicenter of a good life" is suggested by the University of Michigan's Panel Study of Income Dynamics, which polls thousands of American families. See Arthur C. Brooks, "The Father's Example," *New York Times,* June 13, 2014, Opinion Pages, p. A25.

48. Ben-Ze'ev, *The Subtlety of Emotions,* p. 261. Note, too, that the foregoing ideal does not map neatly onto the "cascading logic of human rights" outlined by Lynn Hunt in her book *Inventing Human Rights: A History* (New York and London: W. W. Norton, 2007).

49. See *Xunzi*, chapter 18, "Zhenglun" 正論; *Kongcongzi*, chapter 7, "Juwei" 居衞; and *Zhouli,* chapter 2, "Da Situ" 大司徒. Cf. *Laozi,* sections 33, 44, 46, and *Zhuangzi,* chapter 18, "Rang Wang" 讓王.

50. See *Lunheng, pian* 38, "Bie Tong" 別通; please note that I translate *jing* as "pay due heed to," following the Han dynasty *Shangshu* commentaries. Cf. *Hanshu* 47, where a successful Overseer of the Han Capital invites potential candidates to office, treating them with the same ceremony accorded dignitaries (*jin jian ru bin li* 進見如賓禮). *Zuozhuan,* "Lord Xi," year 33, defines "respect" and "due attention" (*jing* 敬) as *xiang dai ru bin* 相待 如賓, as does the *Guoyu,* "Jin Yu," 4.53. This line is very much paired with *shi min ru da ji* 使民如大祭.

51. *Huainanzi* 19, "Xiuwu Xun" 脩務訓, has the sage-ruler Yao "employing the people as if they were sons and disciples" (much the same idea); *Fengsu tongyi* 風俗通義 8.1 has the Ancients employing the people as if they were "on loan."

52. Here I am mindful of Arthur Waley's remark that the Confucius of the *Analects* "contrived to endow compromise [i.e., the Middle Way] with an emotional glamour." See Arthur Waley, trans. and annot., *The Analects of Confucius* (London: George Allen and Unwin; reprint, New York: Vintage Books, n.d.), p. 37. I wonder if these two slogans do not have the same potential. On the propensity for major thinkers to be radical, however, see Lee Yearley, "The Perfected Person in the Radical Chuang-tzu," in *Experimental Essays*

on Chuang-tzu, ed. Victor H. Mair (Honolulu: University of Hawai'i Press, 1983), pp. 126–147.

53. The phrase is that of François Jullien, and it is cited by Martin Verhoeven in his article "Buddhism and Science: Probing the Boundaries of Faith and Reason," *Religion East and West* 1 (June 2001): 77–97.

54. We should not look to our leaders to offer profiles in courage. Throughout the twentieth and twenty-first centuries, American presidents, both Democrat and Republican, have repeatedly launched wars simply "to avoid appearing to be a coward," though their declarations of war have spouted high-minded principles. See the 2009 documentary *The Most Dangerous Man in America: Daniel Ellsberg and the Pentagon Papers,* directed by Judith Ehrlich and Rick Goldsmith (shown on PBS).

55. Verhoeven, "Buddhism and Science."

56. Cf. *Analects* 9.22: "Respect the young. How do you know that they will not be all that you are now?" or *Analects* 5.26: "In dealing with the aged, comfort them; with friends, be trustworthy; and with the young, cherish them."

57. Those who know their *Analects* well will have noticed that I do not suggest that we impose on others the much stricter standard of altruistic behavior found in *Analects* 14.45, where Zilu asks about the qualities of the noble person: "The person cultivates his or her person by comforting others." "Is that all?" "To cultivate one's person by comforting everyone else is something that even Yao and Shun found difficult."

58. Simone Weil wrote that beauty requires us "to give up our imaginary position as the center.... A transformation then takes place, at the very roots of our sensibility, in our immediate reception of sense impressions and psychological impressions." See her "Love of the Order of the World," in *Waiting for God,* trans. Emma Craufurd (New York: Harper and Row, 1951), p. 159. Iris Murdoch, in "The Sovereignty of Good over Other Concepts," says: "The Sovereignty of Good makes beauty the single best or most obvious thing in our surroundings which is an occasion for 'unselfing.'" By this Murdoch does not mean "self-forgetting," but something more interesting: that all the space typically devoted to protecting or promoting the self or its prestige seems now freed to be in the service of something else.

59. Ben-Ze'ev, *The Subtlety of Emotions,* p. 170, usefully distinguishes the function of the emotions from the functions of reflexes and physiological drives: reflexes allow human beings to interact with their environments in highly stereotyped ways (which often come at a high cost), and physiological drives serve a particular homeostatic need. Emotions differ from both reflexes and drives in "flexibility, variability, richness, and dependence upon the mental." Imagination allows us to refer to what is not actually present to the senses.

60. Here I think of the arguments put forward by Maurice Hamington, in his *Embodied Care: Jane Addams, Maurice Merleau-Ponty, and Feminist Ethics* (Urbana and Chicago: University of Illinois Press, 2004). I do not argue that the development of caring habits is instinctual; rather it demands a great deal of attention; still the bodies that human beings inhabit give everyone the potential to develop habits of imaginative care that integrate the epistemic and the ethical. Hamington writes, "Habits of care 'hold' knowledge of what it is to care, but the imagination is also present, because knowledge must be applied to new and unknown situations" (p. 66).

61. It is this way of conducting oneself that represents "full humanity"—the ability,

as Shakespeare said, "to feel what wretches feel" and also what artists, cooks, and massage therapists feel. Alexander Pope once said, "Drop into thyself, and be a fool!" See the last line of his philosophical poem "An Essay on Man" (ca. 1733).

62. Why would these slogans have a prayer of working, when so many pieces of antique "common sense" have failed? Perhaps because they do not particularly reflect any single tradition's assessment of the human condition and its relation to the extra-social world. Xunzi made this point when he argued ritual theory: the priority should be on inducing constructive behavior, not orthodox thinking, as did Rosemont and Ames, in their discussions of "role ethics" in their various publications on this topic. In life, Confucius or Zhuangzi may be a better model than Socrates, who was purportedly certain of a rash of highly questionable propositions, for example that deep reflection invariably leads to firm knowledge, and so on.

63. Monique Canto-Sperber, *Moral Disquiet and Human Life,* trans. Sylvia Pavel (Princeton and Oxford: Princeton University Press, 2008), p. 45.

64. *Analects* 13.24; 17.13; cf. *Nichomachean Ethics* I, 2, 1094b–1095a: "We do not seek or expect the same degree of exactness in all sorts of arguments…and because this is the nature of our premises, we must be satisfied [when discussing ethics or political science] with probabilistic conclusions of the same sort." It does not help us one bit to equate settled conventions or local norms with profound moral insights. See *Analects* 13.24. We routinely (mis)read recommendations and endorsements about the world as empirical statements about the world that are verifiable (thinking ethics to be a science).

65. John Rawls' *A Theory of Justice* (Cambridge, MA: Belknap Press of Harvard University Press, 1971) would demonstrate, if proof were needed, that no way exists to construct a theory of human morality with the certitude demanded in the evaluation of scientific theories.

66. Utilitarianism: minimize social harm; libertarianism: maximize personal freedom; communitarianism: cultivate civic virtue.

67. Michael J. Sandel, *Justice: What's the Right Thing to Do* (New York: Farrar, Straus and Giroux), p. 261. I am not convinced by the arguments lodged by Simone Weil and Iris Murdoch that say an experience of beauty prepares us to receive a sense of justice. They were responding, of course, to aesthetic theories that put the sublime above the beautiful—a silly dichotomy. See above for citations.

68. Ludwig Wittgenstein, "A Lecture on Ethics," part I of "Wittgenstein's Lecture on Ethics," *Philosophical Review* 74, no. 1 (1965): 3–12, at p. 8.

69. Merritt Tierce, "This Is What an Abortion Looks Like," *New York Times,* September 13, 2014, Opinion Pages, p. A19.

70. Dina Kraft, "By Talking, Inmates and Victims Make Things More Right," *New York Times,* Sunday, July 6, 2014, p. 13, on the "restorative justice" movement, where victims and offenders discuss how their lives were affected by crimes. One speaker, a longtime community activist, said that "Holding you in your humanity—it's how we hold each other accountable."

71. As Zhuangzi says, this means there are principles whereby one can attain happiness and keep oneself alive, but he doesn't know about others' propensity to choose or reject them.

72. This is the opening of the "Supreme Pleasure" ("Zhile" 至樂) chapter in the *Zhuangzi.*

73. One obvious candidate here is *bao* 報 (requital, return). While one is not invariably repaid for good deeds or bad in kind, more often than not there is a return.

74. Nicholas Epley and David Dunning, "Feeling 'Holier than Thou': Are Self-serving Assessments Produced by Errors in Self- or Social Prediction?" *Journal of Personality and Social Psychology* 79, no. 6 (December 2000): 861–875. Four studies cited here suggest that people hold overly charitable views of themselves and accurate impressions of their peers. Participants consistently overestimated the likelihood that they would act in generous or selfless ways, whereas their predictions of others were considerably more accurate (and the best indicator of what they would do themselves in the same situation). This work builds upon Anatol Rapoport's "Tit-For-Tat," where an account of this code appears in Rapoport's book, *General System Theory: Essential Concepts and Applications* (Tunbridge Wells, UK: Abacus, 1986).

75. Here, Confucius comes close to E. M. Forster's "Only Connect" in *Howard's End*: the Schlegel sisters call this "small price" a form of "rent" that must be paid, if one is not to descend into cynicism or paranoia.

76. Williams, *Ethics and the Limits of Philosophy*, p. 189.

77. "The Secret of Effective Motivation," in "Gray Matter," by Boaz Keysar and Albert Costa, *New York Times*, July 6, 2014. In 2009, researchers from the University of Rochester conducted a study tracking 147 recent graduates in reaching their stated goals; those with "intrinsic" goals (e.g., the aim is for enduring relations or satisfying work) fared much better on the "happiness scale" than those with "extrinsic" goals (e.g., to get ahead); the latter experienced much higher levels of shame, fear, and dissatisfaction.

78. I have in mind the lines where Xunzi says, not far into his essay "On Ritual" ("Lilun" 禮論): "Let the [would-be candidates for office] know...."

79. Christopher Blattman, "Let Them Eat Cash!" *New York Times*, June 30, 2014, p. A19, reporting on nineteen recent studies conducted by the World Bank economists tracking money grants given to countries in Latin America, Africa, and Asia.

80. I do not mean to imply that this idea is exclusively Confucian. The *Guanzi* "Mu Min" 牧民 chapter argues that "The granaries must be full first, before people can have an understanding of ritual principles, and clothes and food must be sufficient before people can develop a sense of shame."

81. All references in the text to the *Mencius* use the standard book, part, and chapter designations (e.g., "4A1," "6A17," 6A9," etc.).

82. This tactic works, as Mencius says, because "if one does not give one's whole mind to it, one will never master it" (D. C. Lau, trans., *Mencius* [London and New York: Penguin, 1970], p. 165). Conversely, if one devotes one's whole effort to something, one will master it.

83. In other words, Mencius and Xunzi see no necessary conflict between the "want" self and the "should" self, contra the Harvard Business School analysis offered by Ann E. Tenbrunsel, Kristina A. Diekmann, Kimberly A. Wade-Benzoni, and Max H. Bazerman, in their 2012 working paper "The Ethical Mirage."

84. *Shiji* 129.3259; the phrase is ascribed to Bo Gui. The phrase "managing their lives" occurs in *SJ* 129.3259, the story of Fan Li 范蠡.

85. Of course, this is the fictional character in the movie *Wall Street* who pronounces the slogan "Greed is good."

86. See Jane Mayer's article "Covert Operations" in the *New Yorker,* August 30, 2010, which argues that corporations are moving swiftly to the right, seeing regulation not as something that may "save" capitalism but as something that destroys their productivity.

87. Although David Brooks, columnist in the *New York Times,* usually enrages me, I agree with his basic analysis about character formation on the op-ed page of July 31, 2014, which associated character with four factors: habits, opportunities, exemplary models, and societal standards. The devil is in the details, of course.

88. Jack Goody, *The Theft of History* (Cambridge: Cambridge University Press, 2006).

89. Here the Confucius Institutes have played a big role in "essentializing" Chinese culture, reducing its marvelous complexity to politically safe topics.

CHAPTER 13

Euro-Japanese Universalism, Korean Confucianism, and Aesthetic Communities

Wonsuk CHANG

The Advent of European-Japanese Universalism since the Nineteenth Century

During the nineteenth century, core Western countries such as Great Britain, Germany, France, and Russia began to penetrate into East Asia, and the traditional East Asian tributary system centered on China was challenged. The consequence of war between Great Britain/France and China in the years between 1839 and 1860 demonstrated the ineluctable dominance of the main European powers over China.

It is interesting to note that until the eighteenth century Chinese civilization had served Europe as a model to be emulated, or at worst as a rival. China had a *lingua franca,* a centralized bureaucratic system, and sophisticated philosophies in the form of Confucianism and Buddhism. Yet suddenly, from the nineteenth century on, Chinese civilization came to seem increasingly ossified, straddled by serious and inherent defects that could only be remedied through the tutelage of Western modernity.

The images and the knowledge of East Asia produced by key Western countries in the course of the nineteenth century were based on a simple premise. Everything that had occurred to put Western countries in their current position had been inevitable, progressive, civilized, and universal; this included ideas and movements such as the rise of capitalism, liberal democracy, and the development of the natural sciences and industrialization. At the same time, whatever resisted these forces was feudal, barbaric, reactionary, and backward.

What is distinctive in this era in East Asia is the role of Japan as a late colonizer. In the wake of Perry's expedition to Japan, during the period 1868–1912, and under the slogan of "enrich the country, strengthen the military" (*fukoku kyōhei* 富國强兵), Japan transformed itself along the Western model of the aggressive nation-state. As a late colonizer, Japan presented two faces: inferiority regarding Western domination and superiority vis-à-vis its Asian neighbors. Japan defined itself as a paradox, part of a larger community of oppressed Asian nations standing against Western hegemony, while also being the most Westernized, civilized country among Asian nations.

As a late colonizer, Japan began to develop a knowledge of Korean Confucianism from both of these perspectives. Korean Confucianism was seen as the main source of Korea's backwardness: Korea was destined to fall because of its preoccupation with pedantic and unproductive debates, ignorance of the state of the people's welfare, and blind dependence upon the Zhu Xi school of Confucianism that was followed by the Korean literati. At the same time, Japan was developing a "Pan-Asian" theory of culture regarding the "yellow race" on the basis of which Japan claimed the exclusive right and "burden" to intervene in Asian countries. As an Asian country that had successfully adjusted to the Western model of an aggressive nation-state, Japan began to cultivate a kind of European-Japanese universalism, nurtured in the soil of racism and Pan-Asianism, and to introduce it into the neighboring cultures, including Korea, where it was combined with local Confucian beliefs and practices. In this way Japan was able to introduce European universalism along with selected elements of the Japanese tradition, including Japanese Confucianism, especially the Wang Yangming School (*Yōmeigaku* 陽明学) and the National Studies School (*Kokugaku* 国学).

Inoue Tetsujirō (1855–1944), philosopher and proponent of the theory of Eastern philosophy (*Tōyō tetsugaku* 東洋哲學)—as distinguished from Western philosophy (*Seiyo tetsugaku* 西洋哲學)—argued that Japanese philosophy was unique in that it combined the merits of both Eastern and Western philosophical traditions. Although today Inoue's arguments are seriously challenged, they were representative of the Euro-Japanese universalism that dominated the modern intellectual climate in East Asia at the time.

Some Forms of Orientalism and Occidentalism in Interpreting Korean Confucianism

Many intellectuals in late nineteenth-century Korea, including Yun Ch'i-ho (1864–1945), a Korean "enlightenment" intellectual educated at Emory and Vanderbilt Universities in the United States as well as in Japan, began to express a highly iconoclastic attitude toward Confucianism, viewing it as a shackling ideology of backwardness, oppression, hierarchism, laziness, and hypocrisy, and thereby incompatible with modern values such as individualism, tolerance, and freedom, which he felt the Korean people should be pursuing. Commenting on a situation where a Chinese teacher quit his position in his Western-style school without prior notice, Yun wrote:

> The more Confucianism a Chinaman has the less reliable he is in words. Shame on Confucianism! After having absolute control over the body, mind, and heart of a nation over twenty-five centuries the system has ever failed to make honest men and women of its worshippers.
>
> The maxims of Confucianism are simply beautiful. But what is the use of them? A system that has no power to make its believer practice its maxims is as bad as a Chinese proclamation full of fine things never intended to be carried out. A rule can't work without someone to work it. Confucianism is *powerless* and therefore *useless* because its foundation is no higher than filial piety. It contains the seeds of corruption in its doctrine of the inferiority of women, of absolute submission to kings, of its everlasting "go-backism." Its materialism makes men gross. It has no life and vitality in it to advance or improve. Now when a system of teaching has no power to make its professor a better man than he might be otherwise it is worse than useless.
>
> A Confucianist thinks he has reached the principle of virtues when he fulfills the prescribed rules of filial piety. With him this exceedingly commonplace virtue made uncommon covers every sin—licentiousness, revengefulness, lying, hatred, great dissimulation....[1]

More subtle forms of interpreting Confucianism in Korea according to an increasingly influential Euro-Japanese universalist perspective were developed by other Japanese scholars, including Takahashi Tōru (1878–1967).[2]

Attacking mainstream Neo-Confucianism for its political-factional conflicts that had no philosophical value, its dependency on China, its neglect of the people's welfare, and its general responsibility for Korea's backwardness, Takahashi reevaluated the statecraft of marginalized Confucian scholars, such as Chŏng Yag-yong, Yu Hyŏng-wŏn, and Chŏng Che-du, and the Wang Yang-ming School in Korea of the seventeenth through nineteenth centuries.

Takahashi's perception of the eighteenth-century "Confucian Statecraft School" (*Keirin no gaku* 經倫の學) as a failed forerunner of modernity came from his appreciation of Japanese Confucian statecraft studies, such as the Wang Yangming School or various other Confucian schools during the late Tokugawa period. This Confucian scholarship on statecraft is thought to be a key factor behind Japan's ability to achieve an aggressive nation-state status without being colonized. Takahashi's appraisal of Chŏng Che-du, a Wang Yangming scholar in Korea, also derives from a Japanese chauvinistic attitude because many of the participants in the Meiji Restoration, including the likes of Nakae Tōju, Kumazawa Banzan, and Yoshida Shōin, were perceived to be from the Wang Yangming School.[3] Presented with the model of Euro-Japanese universalism, Takahashi saw the statecraft of the Wang Yangming School in Korea as either very weak or absent altogether. In his view, because the Confucian tradition in Korea had become ossified, it could only achieve modernity through Japanese tutelage.

Interestingly, Korean nationalists also developed their reinterpretation of Korean Confucianism within the confines of a chauvinistic Euro-Japanese universalism. Chŏng In-bo (1893–1950), one of the scholar-journalists and founders of the *Chosŏnhak* 朝鮮學 (nationalist Korean studies) movement in the 1930s, brought back into the foreground of Korean national history such marginalized Korean traditions as Wang Yangming Learning and Practical Learning (*Sirhak* 實學), Confucian scholars like Chŏng Yag-yong, and even Tan'gun, the mythical founder of the Korean nation. Chŏng In-bo argued in his book *Extended Studies of Wang Yangming* (*Yangmyŏnghak yŏllon* 陽明學 演論) (1933) that while the Cheng-Zhu school had undermined traditional Korean society with its futile metaphysical debates between rival political factions, Wang Yangming Studies was able to encourage the Korean people to achieve modernity through practicality (Ch. *shixin* 實心; K. *shilshim*) and self-assertiveness (Ch. *zhuti* 主體; K. *chuch'e*).[4] As an ardent proponent of the idea of "practical learning," Chŏng was also one of the editors of the *Complete Works of Chŏng Yag-yong* (*Yŏyudang chŏnsŏ* 與猶堂全書), compiled with An Chae-hong and Kim Sŏng-jin during the period between 1934 and 1938. It is noteworthy that Takahashi Tōru and Yun Ch'i-ho joined the celebrations upon the publication of the work. In a predictable manner, Takahashi expressed his approval of *Yangmyŏnghak yŏllon* in his published review of it in 1955.

In the wake of the Great Depression of 1929, Japan became a national socialist regime in opposition to the Allies, adopting Pan-Asianism as an ideology and launching a series of military attacks: on Manchuria in 1931, China in 1937, and Pearl Harbor in 1941. Its ideology combined Shinto-Confucian elements with totalitarianism. Imperial Confucianism (*Kōdō Jugaku* 皇道儒學), supporting the national socialist regime in Japan and the ideology of unifying the five Asian races—Japanese, Korean, Manchu, Mongol, and Chinese—was a Confucian form of Occidentalism. In a 1931 article, Takahashi restrained his harsh criticism of Korean Confucianism with a more positive tone, lauding it as an exemplar of national education. Originally Takahashi was adamant in criticizing T'oegye (Yi Hwang) (1502–1571) as a mere imitator of Zhu Xi as follows:

T'oegye is the typical example of Korean Confucian thinking, more broadly representative of all Koreans' way of learning. Lacking in creativity and originality, he was just an authentic transmitter of Zhu Xi. In interpreting the Classics, he modeled himself after Zhu Xi's Collected Commentary without considering works prior to Zhu Xi. By contrast, Ogyū Sorai and Itō Jinsai, heroic Japanese Confucians, initiated the National Learning School, a civil school, rather than the Zhu Xi School, a bureaucratic school. This is the stark difference between Japanese and Korean Confucianism; there is an everlasting disparity between the two nations and schools.[5]

Yet, according to Abe Yoshio (1905–1978), one of Takahashi's disciples, this same T'oegye was elevated in 1944 beyond the level of practical scholar to that of creator:

> At the moment the peninsula [Korea], as part of imperial Japan, is committed to the construction of a moral world. It is worth reflecting on the practical thought of Yi T'oegye, the foremost educator-scholar of the Korean peninsula and the creator of the philosophy of moral national education. Thereby it is never insignificant for us to consider how best to act as loyal subjects of the emperor and train our spirits. Moreover, it is urgent and relevant for educators on the peninsula whose mission it is to transform the people.[6]

Colonial scholars such as Takahashi Tōru and Abe Yoshio had situated T'oegye, like Wang In, who was the putative transmitter of Confucianism from Korea to Japan in ancient times, as the creator of moral cultivation in Korea, which was then transmitted to Japan. Prior to 1930, T'oegye had seemed a quintessential Cheng-Zhu Confucian, responsible for the ossified Confucian tradition of Korea. Yet during the war period he was transformed into a model of national education, contributing to the ultra-nationalistic Imperial Confucianism headed by the Japanese emperor.

During the war, Confucianism was employed as part of the strategy of fundamental "otherness" vis-à-vis Western domination. Confucianism as a whole became a representative and inclusive culture of the "yellow races," antagonistic to the egoistic, hedonistic, dominant Western culture. According to Korean Confucian scholar Yi Myŏngse, American and British civilization, characterized by individualism, materialism, and utilitarianism, is inherently greedy and exploitative. To save the repressed yellow race from becoming the prey of the dominating West, Japan had a moral duty (*dōgi* 道義) to fight on behalf of the Asian peoples: "Our imperial army is invincible because we fight for benevolence and righteousness (*renyi* 仁義). The Sage's dictum that the benevolent do not have enemies proves this."[7]

A Critical Assessment of Modern Assumptions

THE PRACTICAL SCHOOL: WAS THERE A PRACTICAL
SCHOOL IN SEVENTEENTH- THROUGH NINETEENTH-
CENTURY CHOSŎN?

The colonialist Takahashi's interpretation of Korean Neo-Confucianism as being unproductive and that an anti–Zhu Xi Confucianism (i.e., a "practical" Confucianism, including the Wang Yangming School) emerged from the seventeenth to nineteenth centuries is still influential today. Nationalist as well as socialist historiographies have argued that there emerged a practical Confucian school, termed *Sirhak* 實學, whose characteristics were practical and whose emphasis was on statecraft, capitalist development, individualism, and evidence-based science.

It is interesting to see that in the history of the Confucian tradition, Neo-Confucians referred to their school as *Sirhak,* in contrast to the "unproductive" Buddhist studies (*Xuxue* 虛學). In this tradition, emerging Confucian schools, including Neo-Confucianism and the Wang Yangming School, have used this general term to refer to themselves. Yet Takahashi's idea of a practical school seems to derive from a Eurocentric perception of Asian history, because we can discern in the features of this "practical school" a mere collection of European "universal values" such as individualism, capitalism, empiricism, and rationality.

In fact, the idea of a practical school is closely related to the reorganization of the world of learning in nineteenth-century Europe, characterized by the nation-state-funded rehabilitation of the university and professional fields. During the nineteenth century, the European world of learning began to define itself as a concentration of professionals pursuing objective truth (the rise of positivism) between two extremes—reactionaries and radicals—for the betterment of the people and the nation-state. For example, the newly unified German Verein für Sozialpolitik (Social Policy Association), founded in 1873, was the operational organization for supporting a Bismarckian centrist social-program legislation that avoided both the liberal-economic circle and social revolutionaries. It is well known that the Prussian (German) model of the world of learning was the object of emulation by Japanese academics during the nineteenth century. One of these was Shiratori Kurakichi, the founder of Eastern History (Tōyōshi 東洋史) in Japan, who studied under Ludwig Reiss, himself a student of Leopold von Ranke. Enshrining positivism as an analytical and universal method, Shiratori established the particularistic and nationalist historiography of Eastern History. The aim of the Imperial universities in Japan was the teaching of arts and academics and the pursuit of in-depth research to meet the demands of the state. The Japanese construction of modern higher learning did not differentiate between the state and the people. It supported the ideal of objectivity and positivism as a method, and "practical studies" to meet the demands of the state.[8]

These days, an increasing number of Koreanists have found the term *Sirhak* or "Practical Learning" in seventeenth- through nineteenth-century Chosŏn to be not an indigenous term but one imposed by a linear-progressive view of history. Chŏng Yag-yong was not antagonistic to Zhu Xi but an admirer of Zhu Xi *and* a revisionist at the same time. The notion of self-interest was not advocated by "conservative" Confucians, nor was it by most *Sirhak* scholars.

Yet, at a deeper level, arguments about the emergence of the practical school in the early modern period are a product of the modern notion of time being linear and progressive. This teleological view, giving priority to a certain "end of history" toward which the deterministic historical route was fixed, is not congruent with postmodern sensibilities in the humanities, social sciences, and natural sciences, or with Confucian tradition. Non-linear and irreversible time as posited by Ilya Prigogine does not allow any teleological end to the historical process.[9] Rather, evolving systems have their internal times of birth and death, such as oscillations, cycles, progression, and the emergence of novelty, without any transcendent, deterministic sense of the beginning or ending of time. The idea of time (*shi* 時) in the *Yijing* is historicist, emphasizing the priority of process over causal or teleological agency. In such concepts of time, a universal standard or inevitable route of history dissolves into the shifting propensities (*shi* 勢) as alternating modes of centralization and decentralization, unification and diversification—that is, *yang* and *yin*.

CONFUCIANISM AND THE STATE: WAS T'OEGYE AN IMPERIAL TEACHER?

The dominance of Pan-Asianism from 1930 on was the basis for a strategy of "otherness," assuming there was that essential other called the "East" in opposition to the "West." As we have seen, as part of a Pan-Asian tradition, the Confucian tradition as a whole was interpreted in a more positive light than before, as in the aforementioned case of T'oegye. Yet, was Neo-Confucianism in Korea, including T'oegye's philosophy, supportive of central statism? There is much evidence to show that T'oegye's ideas were rather supportive of the domination of local elites in the Yŏngnam area, for example in his commitment to local education and community compacts, while sympathetic to the criticism of legalists and Wang Anshi, the state-led reformer of the Northern Song.[10] Many topics of his counsels to the King include the necessity of a self-effacing and deferential kingship. Dismissing the arrogance of the king, T'oegye said, "When there is no reciprocal trust, [no] agreement between ministers and kings in governing the country, benefits are not able to reach the people."[11] His family consisted of local landlords who owned large areas of land and slaves in the Andong area. Though the actual relationship between Confucian scholar-officials and the monarchy during the Chosŏn period is complex, the power of the kings in sixteenth-century Chosŏn was limited, and, relative to the period of Japanese imperial rule in Korea in the 1930s, Confucians and communities at the local level enjoyed autonomy. After denouncing Korean Confucians, Japanese colonialists invented the image of T'oegye as an imperial or national teacher and educator who supported highly centralized power.

On a deeper philosophical level, I argue that Occidentalism after 1930 was the reverse of the liberalism-Orientalism of the Taishō era, because both were based on a modernist epistemology of essentialism entailing interdependent notions of universalism and particularism. One strategy of this way of thinking is an assumption that a certain thing, person, or group—such as a race, nation, culture, or civilization—has an unchanging, abstract, and inherent essence. Yet, defining an entity in this way easily exposes it to historical and geographical contingencies. For example, when Occidentalists state that Asian people are inherently reticent and obedient, do they mean a person from eighteenth-century Andong? Third-century Shandong? Tenth-century Okinawa? Twenty-first-century Hong Kong?

One of the most insightful arguments against essentialist knowledge comes from the pragmatist John Dewey. According to Dewey, the most pervasive fallacy of philosophical thinking is the error of ignoring the historical, developmental, and contextualizing aspects of experience, something termed "the philosophical fallacy." It is the abstracting of one element from the organism that gives it meaning and sets it up as absolute, and then proceeds to revere this one element as the cause and ground of all reality and knowledge. In the same context, John Dewey mentioned the invalidity of the essentialist notion of the East or West in his congratulatory remarks in the inaugural issue of *Philosophy East and West*:

> I think that the most important function your journal can perform in bringing about the ultimate objective of the "substantial synthesis of East and West" is to help break down the notion that there is such a thing as "West" and "East" that have to be synthesized.... Some of the elements in Western cultures and Eastern cultures are so closely allied that the problem of "synthesizing" them does not exist when they are taken in isolation. But the point is that none of these elements—in the East or the West—is in isolation. They are all interwoven in a vast variety of ways in the historical-cultural process. The basic prerequisite for any fruitful

development of inter-cultural relations—of which philosophy is simply one constituent part—is an understanding and appreciation of the complexities, differences, and ramifying interrelationships both within any given country and among the countries, East and West, whether taken separately or together.[12]

Appreciating Uncommon Assumptions for a Viable Confucianism: Aesthetic Communities

Since the early twentieth century, assumptions of European universalism, such as universal values, nationalism-racism, scientism, a progressive view of history, capitalist economics, technological advancement, individual rights, citizenship and national sovereignty, and essentialism and objectivism, have all become objects of criticism by late-modern philosophers and Asian thinkers, and in the frontiers of some natural sciences. At the same time, cultural studies have dismissed the Western canons of white male European bias. Philosophers from the West have been urged to look within Western cultural elements, heretofore marginalized. We can observe a surging interest in pragmatism, hermeneutics, process philosophy, feminist philosophy, and postcolonialism. There is also an increased interest in non-Western philosophies, including Confucianism and Buddhism, distinctive cultural assumptions far from European universalism.

I believe we need imagination and a knowledge of viable Confucianism beyond Euro-Japanese universalism (Orientalism) and its antagonistic particularism (Occidentalism) because they have been neither philosophically coherent nor sound, and they have been historically catastrophic. It is tragic to realize that since the advent of European-Japanese universalism around 1875, the Korean people have had to endure two Sino-Japanese Wars, the Russo-Japanese War, colonization, the Japanese invasions of China, World War II, and the Vietnam War, and they are still technically fighting the Korean War. If war is the most horrible event that can befall the common people, Orientalism and Occidentalism, which have dominated the intellectual atmosphere over the last century in Korea, may be the primary sources and consequences of such tragedies.

According to Confucian philosophy, war, social conflict, sectarianism, and exclusion are the result of a failure of communication of shared experience—a lack, that is, of ritual propriety. We also need new ways to interpret Confucian philosophy and tradition that come without assumptions regarding essentialism and the linear notion of time, which are constituents of liberal ideologies.

I mentioned an essentialist strategy as one of the epistemological assumptions of European universalism. Debates over individualism and collectivism, the core concepts of modern political philosophy, are attempts to establish answers in this manner. They are conflicting answers to the same question regarding the identity of "the people." This became a focus of debates after the French Revolution, in which the sovereignty of the monarch was replaced by popular sovereignty. While the liberal answer has been that the people constitute a collection of "individuals" bearing rights, on the extreme other end of the spectrum it is said that the people constitute a single collective society. The issue is as follows: when many modern political philosophers deal with the relationship between the individual and society, they tend to use atomistic, essentialist, quantitative language that assumes there are two distinct entities in the form of a right-bearing individual and a general social will. As we have seen in the emergence of the modern *Yomeigaku* (Wang Yangming School) in nineteenth-century Japan, the controversy over the nature of the "people"—between the nationalist, state-oriented, right-wing idea of *kokumin* 國民 and the cosmopolitan, civic-oriented, left-wing idea of *heimin* 平民—was the East Asian form of the sovereignty debates in the modern nation-state.

However, it is hard for us to encounter the Leviathan as a personalized collective polity. Society as a whole, independent of process, is an abstraction from larger complex transactional processes. According to Ch'oe Han-ki, a nineteenth-century Korean Confucian scholar, if you achieve proper communication between self and others (in his words, the penetration of configurative energy), there is continuity between them, and relationships will be productive. In the same context, it is hard to assume a discrete self in our experience. Once you accept this abstract entity as reality, there are two contested entities, namely the discrete individual and the collective society. These entities, far from authentic experience, can become a source of the variety of social and ethical theories in which ideas regarding the individual or state compete with each other for priority. Individualism is closely related to liberalism and utilitarianism, in which individual rights, freedom, and autonomy are an end where government or communal purpose cannot intervene and rather are used as a means for the happiness of individuals. By contrast, collectivism is closely related to totalitarianism, which argues that individuals should be in the service of a greater good, such as the aims and interests of the nation-state. Seemingly contradictory, what they have in common is their view of the individual or community as a self-sufficient entity that requires others as a means to achieve its own ends.

Elsewhere I mentioned that we need to construct a viable Confucian philosophy without essentialist assumptions. Now we begin to focus on experience instead of abstraction. Experience is communal and aesthetic. The term aesthetic is derived from the Greek αἰσθητικός (aisthetikos), meaning "esthetic, sensitive, sentient," which is in turn derived from αἰσθάνομαι (aisthanomai), meaning "I perceive, feel, sense." I argue for the notion of "aesthetic communities" as conceptual sources for a viable interpretation of Confucianism without an essentialist assumption.

The self is not a discrete entity but an experiential or aesthetic field in the sense that the person has as many selves as there are others who recognize the person. This is also true for a variety of groupings, such as ethnicity, gender, sexual preference, one's own lived body, family, fraternity, religious community, nations, international communities beyond national boundaries, and so on. Fields are composites, vague and full of shared experience constituting their meaning. Ch'oe Han-ki thought it was configurative energy forming the emergence of the self and others as focus-field relations. This radical relatedness permits the self and others to communicate at a deep level and to achieve an associated humanity (Ch. *ren* 仁; K. *in*), penetration of the spiritual configurative energy (Ch. *shenqi tong* 神氣通; K. *shin'gi t'ong*), consensus (Ch. *yitong* 一統; K. *ilt'ong*), and impartiality (Ch. *gong* 公; K. *kong*) in shared experiences. This vagueness of shared experience is focused and made immediate through its embodiment by a particular focus, such as *this* communal exemplar, *this* mother, *this* leader of a fraternity, and *this* historical model. This is a performance of optimal signification (*yi* 義) by which the meaning of the group is made present in its exemplary personalities or symbols.[13]

Optimal signification of shared experience means responding to the world with our senses in meaningful, skilled, productive, active, and shared ways. It is the art of communities (*li* 禮) that allow humans to feel one with each other in a meaningful, rich, and productive way. The term art or aesthetic here denotes neither individualistic creativity nor a special domain outside the ordinary business of life. Art is an integral part of communal life (*li*). It includes facial expressions, calligraphic style, table manners, and quality human relations in the workplace and at memorial services, which are the source and expression of collaborative creativity.

Lastly, it seems worthwhile to think about democracy from a Confucian standpoint. As I mentioned, these days we may be entering a period of disintegration for European universalism, in which liberal democracy, capitalist economic systems, and technological progress lose their legitimacy and power. Yet democracy should not be thought of as the product of a European bias, but in fact as something in conflict with liberalist assumptions in general. John Dewey did not think democracy to be the product of the inevitable progress of Western civilization, nor possible with liberalist assumptions. Rather he presumed that democracy meant full participation and communication in many forms of communities. The interpretation of the Confucian idea as aesthetic communities may be a viable alternative to the European universalist interpretation of Confucianism as well as democracy. How can we reconstruct the idea of democracy and viable Confucianism without intellectual assumptions constructing the modern world? I believe this to be the direction of the collective discussions and research being conducted today worldwide by scholars interested in Confucian philosophy.

Notes

1. Yun Ch'i-ho 尹致昊, *Yun Ch'i-ho ilgi* 尹致昊日記 (Diary of Yun Ch'i-ho) (Seoul: Kuksa P'yŏnch'an Wiwŏnhoe, 1973), December 12, 1893; my emphasis.

2. Starting his career as a journalist in Japan, from 1903 Takahashi Tōru took up residence in Korea as teacher and colonial bureaucrat. From 1926 he was a professor of Korean language, culture, and thought at Keijo (Seoul) Imperial University. After World War II, he was one of the founders of Chōsen Gakkai 朝鮮学会 (Association for Korean Studies). He left behind extensive writings on Korean Confucianism, Buddhism, culture, and language, which had a profound impact on the next generation of Japanese, Korean, and American scholars of Korean Studies, including Edward Wagner.

3. Inoue Tetsujirō was one of the major scholars to view the Wang Yangming School as having contributed significantly to the activists of the Meiji Restoration, delineating the genealogy from Nakae Tōju to Katsu Kaishū, as he argued in his book, *Nihon Yōmeigakuha no tetsugaku* 日本陽明學派之哲學 (Philosophy of the Japanese Wang Yangming School), published in 1900. Yet many scholars today have found the notion of the Wang Yangming School as being behind the spirit of the Meiji Restoration to be incongruent with the historical facts and a deliberate creation of Inoue's. For example, Ogyū Shigehiro has argued that there were two conflicting ways of interpreting the sovereignty of the people in the nineteenth century: by commoners (*heimin* 平民) or by all the people of the nation (*kokumin* 國民). The Wang Yangming Learning discussed above that was transformed by modern ideas into *Yomeigaku* should be distinguished from the *Yomeigaku* that existed prior to the Meiji Restoration: "The idea that Wang Yangming Learning contributed to the Meiji Restoration was a thesis created by modern nationalists through the projection of their own ideas onto history" (see Ogyū Shigehiro 荻生茂博, *Kindai, Ajia, Yōmeigaku* 近代・アジア・陽明学 [Modernity, Asia, and Yangming Learning] [Tokyo: Perikansha, 2008]). For a partial English translation of this book, see Ogyū Shigehiro, "The Construction of 'Modern Yomeigaku' in Meiji Japan and its Impact in China," trans. with introd. by Barry D. Steben, *East Asian History* 20 (December 2000): 83–120.

4. Chŏng In-bo 鄭寅普, *Tamwŏn Chŏng In-bo chŏnjip* 薝園鄭寅普全集 (Collected works of Chŏng In-bo), vol. 2 (Seoul: Yonsei University Press, 1983), p. 114.

5. Takahashi Tōru 高橋徹, *Chōsen Jugaku taikan* 朝鮮儒學大觀 (General survey of Korean Confucianism), in *Takahashi Tōru Chōsen Jugaku ronshū* 高橋徹朝鮮儒學論集 (Collected articles of Takahashi Tōru on Confucianism in Korea), ed. Kawahara Hideki 川原秀城 and Kim Kwang-nae 金光来 (Tokyo: Chisen Shokan, 2011 [1927]), p. 31.

6. Abe Yoshio 阿部吉雄, *Ri Taikei* 李退溪 (Yi T'oegye) (Tokyo: Bunkyō Shoin, 1944), pp. 7–8.

7. Haruyama Akiyo 春山明世 [Yi Myŏngse], "Tōa Kyōeiken to Jukyō no yakuwari" 東亞共榮圈と儒敎の役割 (The [Greater] East Asia Co-prosperity Sphere and the role of Confucianism), *Judō* 儒道 (Confucian way) 1 (1942): 1, 38.

8. Imperial Ordinance No. 3 of 1886, Article 1 in the Decree of the Imperial University, Nakano Bunko, http://www.geocities.jp/nakanolib/rei/rm19-3.htm#帝国大学令(明治19年勅令第3号).

9. Ilya Prigogine in collaboration with Isabelle Stengers, *The End of Certainty: Time, Chaos, and the New Laws of Nature* (New York: Free Press, 1997).

10. In addition to reluctant service to the central government, for many years T'oegye also actively served local bureaucrats in Tannyang and P'unggi in promoting private local Confucian academies and community compacts. Regarding his hostile comments on Wang Anshi, see *T'oegye chip* (Collected works of T'oegye), book 4, "Petition to the King No. 2" (Seoul: Minjok Munhwa Ch'ujinhoe, 1988).

11. *T'oegye chip*, Book 7, "Lectures on the top line of the hexagram Qian" (Seoul: Minjok Munhwa Ch'ujinhoe, 1988).

12. John Dewey, "On Philosophical Synthesis," *Philosophy East and West* 1, no. 1 (1951): 3.

13. David L. Hall and Roger T. Ames, *The Democracy of the Dead: Dewey, Confucius, and the Hope for Democracy in China* (Chicago: Open Court, 1999).

CHAPTER 14

State Power and the Confucian Classics

Observations on the *Mengzi jiewen* and Truth Management under
the First Ming Emperor

Bernhard FUEHRER

DISCUSSIONS OF THE RELATION between state power and the Confucian classics tend to revolve around distinct events such as the infamous burn-
ing of the books, the central government's attempts to re-take possession of the
classics in the late medieval periods after the reunification of the empire that
led to the "correct meanings" (*zhengyi* 正義), regulations for prohibiting foreigners access to the classics, or the stocktaking-cum-censoring enterprise that
produced the *Siku quanshu* 四庫全書.

   Notwithstanding academic trends, China's intellectual history as well as
the distinctly political nature of discussions of this topic in the contemporary
context attest to the mere truism that the state's exercise of control over the
Confucian classics was—and still is—an ongoing project, not limited to discrete events. As ultimate authority governing intellectual discourse, the Confucian classics constituted not only a comprehensive and definitive intellectual
framework but also an instrument of state power to ensure continuation of
existing hierarchies of social status and political power, embedded in which
was the authority to define, disseminate, and enforce orthodoxy. Where the
interests of the supreme earthly powers required new interpretative norms and
directions, these changes tended to be set out by leading scholars under imperial
directives, on some occasions even through emperors directly engaging with the
classics as commentators.[1]

   The canon and its exegetical directives were enforced via education. From the Han onward the curriculum, with its focus on the classics and associated works—such as the *Analects* (*Lunyu* 論語) or, in later periods, the *Xiaojing* 孝經 and the *Mencius* (*Mengzi* 孟子)—functioned as the primary mechanism not only to shape the minds of the educated classes but also to control their intellectual pursuits. Despite the textually heterogeneous nature of the classics, they were traditionally perceived as an embodiment of the *dao* 道—which we read here as "the ultimate truth." At first glance, this textual embodiment of "the ultimate truth" seems to provide learners with basic ethics in a given environment, a method to better oneself, a procedure that ideally leads to the attainment of the highest level of self-cultivation, that is, to become an "accomplished person" (*junzi* 君子). But then, the classics and their state-sanctioned readings had another and—in our context here—far more significant function. They offered clear guidelines on how established hierarchies were to be maintained, and imperatives that—once internalized through educational indoctrination—demanded subordination by means of a philosophy of "knowing one's station" in society.

Of course, the primary corpus of the classics (*jing* 經) is not an eternally fixed textual body but has gone through various stages of complex canonization processes. But it seems perhaps more important that the real prowess of the classical canon lies in its interpretations and the way in which earthly authorities invested authority in their readings. Different periods showed different levels of tolerance toward divergent interpretations, some institutionalized interpretative diversity even in the highest educational bodies, and at other times some allowable co-existence of conflicting and sometimes even mutually contradictory readings. The degree to which the canonical texts are perceived as open texts often tends to coincide with periods of governance characterized by the ineffectiveness of the political mandate. In times when we observe strong central power, the authority's urge to take possession of the intellectual foundations of state power, namely the Confucian classics, tends to become preeminent. At the direction of emperors, scholar-officials set out to narrow the range of allowable readings. This standardization of readings of the canon aims at bringing out a particular version of "the ultimate truth," a process that renders the canonical texts serviceable in a specific historical and political context.

In this chapter I shall concentrate on Zhu Yuanzhang 朱元璋 (1328–1398; r. 1368–1398), the founding emperor of the Ming (1368–1644), his management of truth, and his attempts to ensure the serviceability of canonical writings. In pursuit of these aims, he applied various strategies.[2]

As he felt discontent with interpretations of the *Shujing* 書經 by Cai Chen 蔡沈 (1167–1230), Zhu Yuanzhang ordered his trusted advisor Liu Sanwu 劉三吾 (1312–1399) to revise the parts of Cai Chen's commentary that the emperor considered deficient or unsuitable.[3] Liu Sanwu, an erudite scholar who found favor in the eyes of the emperor at a very late stage in his life, revised over sixty passages in Cai Chen's *Shu jizhuan* 書集傳 (1210), parts of which carry glosses made by his former teacher Zhu Xi 朱熹 (1130–1200) shortly before his death.[4] After its completion in 1394, the *Shu zhuan huixuan* 書傳會選 by Liu Sanwu and his team of Hanlin scholars was promulgated to the empire until it underwent further revisions during the Yongle 永樂 period (1403–1425).[5] What we witness in this case is an emperor who challenges received norms and orders a revision of crucial explanatory material. In the *Shu zhuan huixuan* the transmitted *jingwen* 經文 ("main text") remains untouched. Nonetheless, the readings extracted from the *jingwen* as well as their implications undergo significant changes pontificated by the emperor. The new exposition of the canon is a redefinition of a classic by exegetical means, constructed through rectifications according to a new interpretative standard.[6] The newly established readings are promoted throughout the empire as standard for examinations. Non-adherence to this new standard simply means that the doors to any career as a scholar-official remain closed.

Zhu Yuanzhang also applied the classics to regulate and remedy hierarchies. His continuous revisions of various ritual prescriptions were aimed at keeping potentially treacherous members of the imperial family in check, and at making visible the envisaged hierarchies through the symbolic language of ritual performances. The revised ritual prescriptions and their points of reference stemmed from the venerated exegetical traditions in exactly the same way as the pre-reform prescriptions. While remaining within the multifaceted repertoire of exegetical traditions for ritual affairs, revisions of ritual prescriptions allowed the emperor to react to changing political situations. These revisions were confirmed in tandem with points of reference in the tradition, which consented—or could be explained as consenting—to changes implemented to address perceived new operative needs. The classics and their exegetical corpora served as a repository of glosses at the disposal of erudite literati, who, in accordance with the imperial directive, formulated codified credenda of governance.[7]

In *biji* 筆記 notebooks—which I perceive as highly valuable accounts that not only offer information otherwise not transmitted in official historical source material but provide us with an alternative historiography—Zhu Yuanzhang tends to appear primarily in an unfavorable light.[8] However, these sources contain interesting accounts of the first Ming emperor's elaborations on the readings of the classics. They tell us of his aversion to the contemplative interaction with canonical texts that was so fashionable during the Song (960–1279), and of the issues Zhu Yuanzhang had with Zhu Xi's readings.[9] Although *biji* authors may well aim at caricaturizing the first Ming emperor, the important point here is that some of the readings put forward by Zhu Yuanzhang do actually coincide with interpretations suggested by earlier scholars.[10] This is to say that the man who is widely perceived as the embodiment of an emperor with an educational deficit, and whose views on the classics are often in open disagreement with Zhu Xi's line of scholarship, which was elevated to the national standard during the Mongol period, arrived at readings shared with earlier scholarship.[11]

A particularly noteworthy case of manipulation of the classics by state power is Zhu Yuanzhang's short-lived suppression of substantial portions of the *Mencius*.[12] The Qing scholar Quan Zuwang 全祖望 (1705–1755) transmitted a short account of Zhu Yuanzhang faulting the *Mencius* for promoting insurrection and subversive teachings.[13] In 1372, so Quan Zuwang reports, the emperor set his mind on prohibiting the transmission of such outdated views.[14] But shortly after he had the tablet of Mencius removed from the Confucius temple, Zhu Yuanzhang saw himself forced to withdraw his order following the occurrence of an inauspicious omen.[15] In the same source we also learn of his rage over the warning given by Mencius to King Xuan of Qi (齊宣王) which Zhu Yuanzhang deemed entirely unacceptable.[16] The relevant passage in *Mencius* 4B3 reads:

> 君之視臣如手足，則臣視君如腹心；君之視臣如犬馬，則臣視君如國人；君之視臣如土芥，則臣視君如寇讎。[17]

> If the ruler looks upon subjects as [his] hands and feet, then the subjects look upon the ruler as [their] belly and heart. If the ruler looks upon subjects as dogs and horses, then the subjects look upon the ruler as a passerby.[18] If the ruler looks upon [his] subjects as mud and weeds, then the subjects look upon the ruler as a robber and enemy.[19]

With the office of prime minister abolished and the government reorganized in 1380, Zhu Yuanzhang's ministers thus expurgated from the *Mencius* the passages faulted by the emperor and produced an abridged version of the *Mencius* that, it would appear, became part of the reading list for civil examinations after the restoration of the examinations in 1384–1385.[20]

One decade and several serious episodes of political turbulence later, Zhu Yuanzhang ordered Liu Sanwu to cleanse the *Mencius,* once again, of material that he found objectionable.[21] In 1394 the *Mengzi jiewen* 孟子節文 was established by the Imperial Academy as the standard version of the *Mencius* in civil examinations.[22] Two decades later, Zhu Di 朱棣 (1360–1424; r. 1403–1424) abolished the version censored according to his father's wish and reinstated the full transmitted version of the *Mencius,* which—in the compendium of commentaries on the *Five Classics* and the *Four Books,* the *Wujing Sishu daquan* 五經四書大全 (1415), compiled by the Hanlin academician Hu Guang 胡廣

(1370–1418) and his staff—became part of the newly established reading list for civil examination candidates.[23]

In the introduction to his excerpts from the *Mencius,* Liu Sanwu endeavors to provide a rationale for censoring this book.[24] He states that during the time of Mencius, titled lords (*zhuhou* 諸侯) behaved without restraint, "valued their own profit most highly, and no longer knew of the existence of humankindness (*ren*) and sense of duty (*yi*)."[25] And with reference to the first section of the *Mencius,* that is, Mencius' encounter with King Hui of Liang/Wei, Liu Sanwu notes the philosopher's failure to grasp the actual threat that the king and his country faced from their mighty neighbors:[26]

> 仁義正論也。所答非所問矣。是以所如不合，終莫能聽納其說。[27]

> Humankindness and sense of duty are the correct teachings. [But Mencius] did not answer [the king's] question(s). Hence their destinations were not in accord, and in the end his suggestions could not/cannot be accepted.[28]

Liu Sanwu clearly agrees with the *Mencius* that, as a matter of principle, *ren* 仁 and *yi* 義 are the right measures.[29] Nevertheless, he—as well as Zhu Yuanzhang and others before them—came to consider his approach starry-eyed and thus unable to deal with the actual political situation. In their judgment the *Mencius* is deemed incapable of providing counsel that Zhu Yuanzhang would deem fit for his purpose.[30] Section 1A1 of the *Mencius,* which according to Zhao Qi 趙 岐 (d. 201) sets the main theme of the entire book, is subsequently taken out.[31] With *Mencius* 1A2 also deleted on similar grounds, the *Mengzi jiewen* begins with *Mencius* 1A3.

Where he spotted a need for censorial action, Liu Sanwu did not doctor sentences, words, or characters but deleted entire sections (*zhang* 章) and noted that these sections would no longer be included in examination questions and topics.[32] As a result, the *Mengzi jiewen* carries only about two-thirds of the sections transmitted in Zhu Xi's *Mengzi jizhu* 孟子集注 (1177).[33]

In the sections deleted by Liu Sanwu we observe a clear focus on the relationship between subjects and rulers, a crucial point in the Mencian political philosophy that Zhu Yuanzhang found particularly difficult to endorse. In his preface to the *Mengzi jiewen* the *realpolitiker* Liu Sanwu summarized his objections to the *Mencius* with reference to its historical environment. The current situation under the first Ming emperor, Liu argued, was fundamentally different from the Warring States (475–221 B.C.E.) environment in which the Mencian argument was situated. Strategies suitable then would thus not be applicable under the newly established regime. In his view, the Mencian strategies and postulates

...在當時列國諸侯可也。 若夫天下一君，四海一國， 人人同一尊君
親上之心，學者或不得其扶持名教之本意。[34]

...were allowable in those days of various states and titled lords. Nowadays there is one ruler of the "all-under-heaven," one state within the
four seas, and all men are united in their mind of honoring the ruler and
having affection for the supreme [emperor], [but] some scholars do not
grasp his genuine intention to support the venerated teachings [on Confucian morality and ethics].

In the reception history of the *Mencius,* Zhu Yuanzhang—and Liu Sanwu
with him—stands in an illustrious line of scholars who vented their skepticism
about or outright denial of the efficiency of core political concepts outlined in
the *Mencius.*[35] Though Zhu Yuanzhang and Liu Sanwu clearly paid lip service
to—or may even have agreed with—some of the more widely shared aspects of
its general ethics, the book *Mencius* and its commentarial traditions provided
no valuable perspectives for some of their more pressing lines of inquiry. From
an exegetical standpoint, the crucial task of interpreters, namely to take older
traditions and reinterpret them in light of their own situation, seemed impossible: the deficit of the *Mencius* could not be bridged; central portions of the
book were deemed to be "beyond repair." Rather than attempting to have the
message of the *Mencius* adjusted to Zhu Yuanzhang's needs through reinterpretation of the main text, he thus decided to repress the operative force of the
Mencian tradition.[36] With interpretative projections of meaning being rooted
in the situation of the interpreter, the sections expurgated by Liu Sanwu, which
can be divided into the following groups, offer insights into Zhu Yuanzhang's
political and social philosophy.[37] None of the following five topic areas was a
natural paradigm for the first Ming emperor to employ.[38]

1. Sections in which the *Mencius* proposes the people as the ultimate locus
   of political sovereignty: the Mencian hierarchy (in descending order:
   people, state, ruler) clashed with the emperor wielding power oppressively
   and striving at ruling with absolute power. This includes Mencian views
   on the prerogatives and duties of rulers, namely to serve and look after
   their people.[39]
2. Sections in which the *Mencius* explores its vision of an idealized relationship between ruler and subject: from the Northern Song (960–1127)
   onward, this had become an increasingly popular stance among officials.
   In Zhu Yuanzhang's view, the teachings of the *Mencius* led to unrest and
   lack of respect for the ruler; and he took decisive action wherever he
   encountered any signs of these.

3. Sections in which the *Mencius* discusses the possibility of dethroning a ruler and the conditions under which such an act would be legitimate.
4. Sections in which the *Mencius* hints at a certain degree of (intellectual) autonomy of members of the educated class, which, in the eyes of Zhu Yuanzhang, led to insufficient subordination and disputatious officials.
5. Sections in which the *Mencius* makes pacifistic statements or argues against the wars between titled lords that lead to nothing but suffering and destruction.[40]

Though Zhu Yuanzhang's attempts to eradicate Mencius from the Confucian pantheon were short-lived, the case of the *Mengzi jiewen* remains rather unique—so unique, in fact, that some challenged the historical truthfulness of accounts of the first Ming emperor's anti-Mencian activities.[41] Some go so far as to urge us to disregard entirely the *Mengzi jiewen* in our considerations and discourses. Because of—what he perceived as—a lack of reliable records, the eminent Qing scholar Zhu Yizun 朱彝尊 (1629–1709), among others, refused to regard accounts of Zhu Yuanzhang's censorship of the *Mencius* as trustworthy.[42]

What may have seemed most inconceivable in the traditional environment is the candid nature of Zhu Yuanzhang's management of orthodoxy. Whereas other rulers adjusted the classics—or had them adjusted—to their needs via exegetical procedures without major amendments of the venerated main texts (*jingwen*), Zhu Yuanzhang stands out in assigning to himself such authority over the main text of a classic as to be permitted to make significant editorial changes.[43] And in contrast to others who engaged in censorship and who made possession or dissemination of uncensored material a criminal offense, Zhu Yuanzhang allowed the unabridged version of the *Mencius* to remain in circulation. If the examination system is seen as a means to implement a new state orthodoxy, the decision to keep the uncensored version in circulation may be understood as a confident manifestation of imperial power that is—inter alia—formulated through and symbolized in the bold contrast between the old and the new *Mencius*.

The founding father of the Ming dynasty attributed great importance to education; his efforts to establish schools throughout the empire are well documented.[44] And the Confucian classics, which are traditionally presumed to elevate their readers out of their own lives to another reality with overriding purposes and concerns, played a prominent role in this education campaign: they were held as an indispensable requisite in every household.[45] Within this context of education, the expurgated version, that is, the *Mengzi jiewen,* was established as the only valid version of the *Mencius* in the compulsory reading list for examination candidates. Its main purpose was to make a claim on its readership so as to rein in potential criticism rooted in the political philosophy of the *Mencius*. As a function of the examination mechanism, education was the channel through which he promulgated and tried to enforce his "*Mencius light*," excerpts from one of the traditionally celebrated Confucian core readings cleansed of edges and potential points of reference for critical minds in an autocratic system.

Notes

I would like to take this opportunity to thank Ms. Liu Yangruxin and Ms. Eleanor Lipsey, both of the London School of Oriental and African Studies (SOAS), for their comments on earlier drafts of this chapter.

The following abbreviations are used for collectanea:

CSJC   *Congshu jicheng* [*chubian*] 叢書集成 [初編]. 3,999 vols. Shanghai: Shangwu Yinshuguan, 1935–1937.
SBBY   *Sibu beiyao* 四部備要. 100 vols. Beijing: Zhonghua Shuju, 1989.
SBCK   *Sibu congkan* [*zhengbian*] 四部叢刊 [正編]. 100 vols. Taipei: Taiwan Shangwu Yinshuguan, 1979.
SKJHSCK   *Siku jinhuishu congkan* 四庫禁燬書叢刊. 300 vols. Beijing: Beijing Chubanshe, 2000.
SKQS   *Siku quanshu* 四庫全書. 1,501 vols. Shanghai: Shanghai Guji Chubanshe, 1987.
SKQSCMCS   *Siku quanshu cunmu congshu* 四庫全書存目叢書. 1,298 vols. Jinan: Qi Lu Shushe, 1997.

  1. Though highly authoritative at the time they were issued, only a fairly limited number of commentaries made by or attributed to emperors remained part of the canonized readings of the Confucian classics over more substantial periods of time. The preface (*xu* 序) and the commentary (*zhu* 注) on the *Xiaojing* 孝經 (722; revised 743) by Li Longji 李隆基 (685–762), i.e., Emperor Xuanzong of the Tang 唐玄宗 (r. 712–756), which—through the subcommentary of Yuan Xingchong 元行沖 (653–729)—fed into Xing Bing's 邢昺 (931–1010) subcommentary in the highly authoritative *Thirteen Classics* of 1815/1816, may serve as an example here for an imperial reading that exercised considerable influence on the subsequent reception of this elementary teaching material. Li Longji brought together the conflicting commentarial traditions deriving from the works of Zheng Xuan 鄭玄 (127–200) and Kong Anguo 孔安國 (d. ca. 100). For the imperial commentary and preface see Li Shuchang 黎庶昌 (1837–1897) and Yang Shoujing 楊守敬 (1839–1915), *Guyi congshu* 古逸叢書 (Tokyo: Published by the compiler, 1882–1884), 5:1a–5b (preface) and 5:5b–25b (commentary). Cf. also Ruan Yuan 阮元, *Shisan jing zhushu* [*fu jiaokanji*] 十三經注疏 [附校勘記] ([1815/1816], 8 vols. (Taipei: Yiwen Yinshuguan, 1985), vol. 8.
  2. For further comments on Zhu Yuanzhang "rectifying the classics" see the notes by Zhu Yunming 祝允明 (1461–1527) under the heading "Zheng jing zhuan" 正經傳 in his

Qianwenji 前聞記, in Deng Shilong 鄧士龍, *Guochao diangu* 國朝典故, 3 vols. (Beijing: Beijing Daxue Chubanshe, 1993), vol. 2, pp. 1389–1390 (*juan* 62).

3. See the "Introduction" (*tiyao* 提要) to *Shu zhuan huixuan* 書傳會選, *SKQS* 61, 1a–4b, esp. 1b; cf. also Ming T'ai-tsu and Romeyn Taylor, "Ming Tai-tsu's 'Essay on the Revolutions of the Seven Luminaries and the Body of Heaven,'" *Journal of the American Oriental Society* 102, no. 1 (1982): 93–97, esp. p. 93. The *Shu zhuan huixuan* is also known as *Shangshu huixuan* 尚書會選. On some of Liu Sanwu's amendments to Cai's readings see the comments by Zhu Yunming in his *Qianwenji*, in *Guochao diangu*, vol. 2, pp. 1389–1390 (*juan* 62); cf. also Zhu Yunming, *Yeji* 野集, 4 *juan*, in *Guochao diangu*, vol. 1, pp. 496–497 (*juan* 31). Prior to this attempt to rectify and improve Cai's readings of the *Shangshu* 尚書, we observe a number of efforts to correct Cai's version, including Zhang Baoshu 張葆舒 (Yuan dynasty) in his *Cai zhuan dingwu* 蔡傳定誤; Huang Jingchang 黃景昌 (early fourteenth cent.) in his *Cai shi zhuan zhengwu* 蔡氏傳正誤; and, among others, the two *Shujing* commentaries by Chen Li 陳櫟 (1252–1334), namely his *Shu zhuan zhezhong* 書傳折衷 and his *Shangshu jizhuan zuanshu* 尚書集傳纂疏. See Yves Hervouet, *A Sung Bibliography* (*Bibliographie des Sung*) (Hong Kong: Chinese University Press, 1978), pp. 22–23. On Liu Sanwu and his works see L. Carrington Goodrich and Chaoying Fang, eds., *Dictionary of Ming Biography 1366–1644,* 2 vols. (New York: Columbia University Press, 1976), vol. 1, pp. 956–958.

4. Cai's *Shu jizhuan* was established as the standard commentary for civil examinations under Emperor Renzong 仁宗 (r. 1312–1320) of the Yuan (1279–1368). It was in circulation under a number of alternate titles including *Shangshu jizhuan* 尚書集傳 and *Shujing jizhuan* 書經集傳. For Zhu Xi's corrections on the chapters "Yao dian" 堯典, "Shun dian" 舜典, and "Da Yu mo" 大禹謨 see the "Preface" (*xu*) to the *Shu jizhuan* 書集傳, *SKQS* 58, 1a–2b. Later, the *Shu jizhuan* served as the primary base when Hu Guang 胡廣 (1370–1418) and others, again under imperial direction, compiled their *Shu zhuan daquan* 書傳大全 as part of the *Wujing daquan* 五經大全 (1415) project. And it served again as a base for the [*Qinding*] *Shujing zhuanshuo huizuan* [欽定] 書經傳說會纂 (1730) by Wang Xuling 王頊齡 (1642–1725) and others.

5. See Zhang Tingyu 張廷玉 (1672–1755) et al., *Mingshi* 明史 (1739), 28 vols. (Beijing: Zhonghua Shuju, [1974] 1987), 96:2352, 137:3942, 137:3955, and the various prefaces to the *Shu zhuan huixuan*. Cf. Goodrich and Fang, *Dictionary of Ming Biography,* vol. 1, pp. 362–363.

6. On competing orthodoxies from the Song to the Ming see Thomas A. Wilson, "The Ritual Formation of Confucian Orthodoxy and the Descendants of the Sage," *Journal of Asian Studies* 55, no. 3 (1996): 559–584, esp. pp. 560–563.

7. For more detailed investigations see Ho Yun-i, "The Organization and Functions of the Ministry of Rites in the Early Ming Period (1368–1398)" (unpubl. Ph.D. diss., University of Minnesota, 1976), and Ho Yun-i [He Yunyi 賀允宜], *The Ministry of Rites and Suburban Sacrifices in Early Ming* [*Ming chu de li bu ji jiao si* 明初的禮部及郊祀] (in English) (Taipei: Shuang-yeh Bookstore, 1980). I am also indebted to Dr. Zhan Beibei's research on changes in the official prescriptions for marriage rituals applicable to imperial princes under Zhu Yuanzhang; see Beibei Zhan, "Deciphering a Tool of Imperial Rule: A Case Study of the Marriage Rituals for Imperial Princes during the Hongwu Reign" (unpubl. Ph.D. diss., SOAS, 2015).

Cf. also Edward L. Farmer: "Social Regulations of the First Ming Emperor: Orthodoxy as a Function of Authority," in *Orthodoxy in Late Imperial China,* ed. Liu Kwang-ching (Berkeley: University of California Press, 1990), pp. 103–125, esp. pp. 107–111.

8. See the comments in Wolfgang Franke, *An Introduction to the Sources of Ming History* (Kuala Lumpur: University of Malaya Press, 1968), esp. pp. 98–118.

9. See, e.g., Li Xian's 李賢 (1408–1466) *Gurang zalu* 古穰雜錄 (1460s), *CSJC* 3962, p. 10.

10. For one such case see his reading of *Lunyu* 2.16, which coincides with explanations offered by Sun Yi 孫奕 (d. after 1205) in his *Lüzhai Shierbian* 履齋示兒編 (1205), *SBCK*, 5:15a (442); cf. Bernhard Fuehrer: "Did the Master Instruct His Followers to Attack Heretics? A Note on Readings of *Lunyu* 2.16," in *Reading East Asian Writing: The Limits of Literary Theory,* ed. Michel Hockx and Ivo Smits (London: RoutledgeCurzon Press, 2003), pp. 117–158.

11. Whereas it is well known that at the beginning of his enterprise Zhu Yuanzhang was rather undereducated, he later achieved a good command and knowledge of classical learning and literature; see Zhao Yi's 趙翼 (1727–1814) appraisal in his article "Mingzu wenyi" 明祖文義, in Zhao Yi, *Nian'er shi zhaji* 廿二史劄記 (1799), *SBBY* 51, pp. 387–388 (*juan* 32), and the references in Hok-lam Chan: "Xie Jin (1369–1415) as Imperial Propagandist: His Role in the Revisions of the *Ming Taizu Shilu,*" in *T'oung Pao* 91, nos. 1/3 (2005): 58–124, esp. p. 61.

12. With regard to the short period of its effectiveness, we note that the bibliographical chapter of the *Mingshi* as well as the magisterial *Siku quanshu zongmu* 四庫全書總目 (1782), 2 vols. (Beijing: Zhonghua Shuju, [1965] 1987) both fail to list the *Mengzi jiewen*. Though Zhu Yizun 朱彝尊 (1629–1709) records the *Mengzi jiewen* in his *Jingyikao* 經義 考, *juan* 235, he notes that he had not seen it; see Zhu Yizun: *Jingyikao* 經義考 (Beijing: Zhonghua Shuju, 1998), p. 1192. As it is absent from the important catalogs of private book collectors (for one of the rare exceptions see the reference to the *Dushu minqiu ji* in note 13 below) it would appear that copies were exceptionally rare during later Ming and Manchu times. This is also confirmed by a catalog entry on a Hongwu block print in Mo Boji's 莫伯 驥 (1878–1958) *Wushiwanjuanlou cangshu mulu chubian* 五十萬卷樓藏書目錄初編 (Tai-pei: Guangwen Shuju, 1967), p. 355, where it is noted that no recent prints of the *Mengzi jiewen* were available. For the short entry on the *Mengzi jiewen* in the more recent continuation of the *Siku quanshu* catalog see *Xuxiu Siku quanshu zongmu tiyao: Jing bu* 續修四庫全 書總目提要 • 經部, 2 vols. (Beijing: Zhonghua Shuju, 1993), vol. 2, p. 921.

13. The book collector Qian Zeng 錢曾 (1629–1701) has a somewhat different take on this and states that Liu Sanwu cleansed the *Mencius* text of "impurities" (*wei chun* 未醇), which Qian Zeng—with direct reference to Han Yu 韓愈 (768–824)—sees as a result of the *Mencius* text being put together posthumously by disciples of Mencius; see Qian Zeng, *Dushu minqiu ji* 讀書敏求記 (1726), *CSJC* 49, 1:13, and Han Yu, "Da Zhang Ji shu" 答 張籍書, in Ma Qichang 馬其昶, *Han Changli wenji jiaozhu* 韓昌黎文集校注 (Shanghai: Shanghai Guji Chubanshe, 1986), pp. 30–133, esp. p. 132. Similar arguments about the transmitted text as a twisted representation of Mencius' statements, and about these distortions being caused by the way in which the text of the *Mencius* came into being, have also been made by scholars such as Feng Xiu 馮休 in his *Shan Meng* 刪孟, 2 *juan,* and Sima

Guang 司馬光 (1019–1086) in his *Yi Meng* 疑孟, 1 *juan*. Though Sima Guang found the *Mencius* objectionable and considered it a fabrication of the Later Han (25–220) period, his own son (nephew?) Sima Kang 司馬康 (1050–1090) adhered to the orthodox reception and dominant evaluation of this book and its philosophy; see *Qingxi xiabi* 清溪暇筆, 2 *juan*, in *Guochao diangu*, vol. 2, p. 1451 (*juan* 63). On Sima Kang's father see the debate in Song Yanshen 宋衍申, "Sima Kang wei Sima Guang zhi qin suo sheng" 司馬康为司馬光之亲所生, *Guji zhengli yanjiu xuekan* 古籍整理研究学刊 1 (1986): 30–31; Zheng Bijun 郑必俊, "Dui 'Sima Kang wei Sima Guang zhi qin suo sheng' yi wen shangque" 对司马康为司马光之亲所生一文商榷, *Guji zhengli yanjiu xuekan* 1 (1987): 30–34; and Yan Zhongqi 颜中其, "Sima Kang wei Sima Guang xiong qinzi" 司马康为司马光兄亲子, *Guji zhengli yanjiu xuekan* 3 (1988): 53–57.

14. See also Liang Yi 梁億 (*jinshi* 1511), *Zunwenlu* 尊聞錄, in *Guochao diangu*, vol. 2, p. 1426 (*juan* 62), who records Zhu Yuanzhang reproaching Mencius for his irreverence (*bu xun* 不遜). The exact dating of this event provided in the sources differs but they agree insofar as that it reportedly took place during the first few years of the Hongwu period, namely between 1368 and 1372/1373. For the removal of Mencius from the temple and for his reinstallation a year after this event see also *Mingshi* 50:1296.

15. See Quan Zuwang 全祖望, *Jieqiting ji* 鮚埼亭集 (1804), *SBCK* 85, 35:3a–4b (370). Zhu Yuanzhang also considered removing the *Mencius* from the curriculum for civil examinations. On this and his attempts to remove the tablet of Mencius from the Confucius temple see also Tu Shan 涂山, *Mingzheng tongzong* 明政統宗 (1615 block print), *SKJHSCK, Shi* 2, 5:11a (215), and *Mingzheng tongzong* (1615 block print), 7 vols. (Taipei: Chengwen Chubanshe, 1969), vol. 2, 5:11a (497). Cf. also Ho Yun-i, *The Ministry of Rites and Suburban Sacrifices in Early Ming*, p. 80; Benjamin A. Elman, " 'Where is King Ch'eng?' Civil Examinations and Confucian Ideology during the Early Ming (1368–1415)," *T'oung Pao* 79, nos. 1/3 (1993): 23–68, esp. p. 44; and Goodrich and Fang, *Dictionary of Ming Biography*, vol. 1, p. 389. Though Zhu Yuanzhang later managed to remove the tablet of Mencius from the Confucius temple, the status of Mencius and his place in the Confucian pantheon were restored by Zhu's son Zhu Di 朱棣 (1360–1424) during the Yongle reign period. Cf. Zhu Honglin 朱鴻林, "Ming Taizu de Kongzi chongbai" 明太祖的孔子崇拜, *Lishi Yuyan Yanjiusuo jikan* 歷史語言研究所集刊 70, no. 2 (1999): 483–530. For other changes to the Confucian pantheon under Zhu Yuanzhang such as the removal of Yang Xiong 揚雄 (53 B.C.–A.D. 18) and the integration of Dong Zhongshu 董仲舒 (179–104 B.C.) in 1396 see Gu Yingtai 谷應泰 (*jinshi* 1647), *Mingshi jishi benmo* 明史紀事本末 (1658), *CSJC* (reprint of a 1879 block print) 3918–3927, vol. 2, p. 84 (*juan* 14).

16. See Quan Zuwang, *Jieqiting ji*, 35:3a–4b (370). This anecdote appears, with some modifications, in a number of sources. *Mingshi* 139:3982 records it in the biography of Qian Tang 錢唐 (1314–1394) and states that Zhu Yuanzhang considered the speech transmitted in *Mencius* 4B3 utterly inappropriate for any subject, and that he would regard those who argued in support of such thought (like Qian Tang) guilty of *lèse majesté* (*da bu jing* 大不敬). On this incident see also the discussion in Huang Yunmei 黃雲眉, *Mingshi kaozheng* 明史考證, 8 vols. (Beijing: Zhonghua Shuju, 1979), vol. 4, pp. 1189–1191. Qian Zeng relates that Zhu Yuanzhang's reaction to reading this passage in *Mencius* 4B3 was to order Liu Sanwu to censor the *Mencius*. The modern compilers of the *Xuxiu Siku quanshu zongmu tiyao: Jing bu,*

vol. 2, p. 921, also copied this anecdote into their entry on the *Mengzi jiewen* and describe it as the event that led to Liu Sanwu producing the *Mengzi jiewen*. Others see the narrative about Zhu Yuanzhang reading *Mencius* 4B3 as an earlier event that triggered an entirely separate attempt at dealing with perceived inadequacies in the *Mencius*. In his *Shuanghuai suichao* 雙 槐歲抄, 10 *juan* (1495), Huang Yu 黃瑜 (1425–1497) also reports on this event but does not relate it to the compilation of the *Mengzi jiewen;* see Huang Yu, 黃瑜 *Shuanghuai suichao* 雙槐歲抄 (Beijing: Zhonghua Shuju, [1999] 2012), *Lidai shiliao biji congkan: Yuan Ming shiliao biji congkan* 歷代史料筆記叢刊 : 元明史料筆記叢刊, pp. 12–13.

17. *Sishu jizhu* 四書集注 [Song block print] (Taipei: Xuehai Chubanshe, 1984), pp. 307–308 (*Mencius* 4B3).

18. The reading of the term *guoren* 國人 as "passerby" follows Zhu Xi's gloss; see *Sishu jizhu,* pp. 307–308.

19. For other translations see D. C. Lau, *Mencius* (London: Penguin, 1970), p. 128, and Bryan W. Van Norden, *Mengzi: With Selections from Traditional Commentaries* (Indianapolis: Hackett, 2008), p. 104.

20. The official account in the *Mingshi* does not seem to be particularly forthcoming on this: in the biography of Qian Tang it states: "but in the end [the emperor] ordered (a) Confucian minister(s) to prepare the *Mengzi jiewen*" (然卒命儒臣修孟子節文); see *Mingshi* 139:3982; cf. also Chen Jian 陳建 (1497–1567) (with additions by Jiang Xuqi 江旭奇), *Huang Ming tongji jiyao* 皇明通紀集要 [late Ming block print], *SKJHSCK, Shi* 34, 9:5b (120). With reference to this account Benjamin Elman seems to suggest that Qian Tang agreed to excise passages deemed insulting to the imperial authority (*bu jing* 不敬) from the *Mencius;* see Elman, "Where is King Ch'eng?" p. 44. However, no such early version of the *Mencius* cleansed (by Qian Tang?) of passages that Zhu Yuanzhang judged as an offense to his sovereign power has yet been identified or located. In the *Mingshi* as well as elsewhere, Qian Tang is portrayed as a dedicated defender of Confucius, Mencius, and the Cheng-Zhu orthodoxy who managed to change the emperor's mind on a number of occasions. In an earlier episode when the emperor restricted sacrifices to Confucius to celebrations at the master's old hometown (1369), Zhu Yuanzhang did not, at first, listen to Qian Tang's objections but only "followed his advice" (*yong qi yan* 用其言) after "a long time" (*jiu zhi* 久之) in 1382 when the nationwide sacrifices were reinstated; see *Mingshi* 139:3982. As the narrative of this incident (as well as accounts of other events) in the *Mingshi* jumps forward in time by a considerable number of years, we understand *zu* 卒 (in the end) in the reference to the compilation of the *Mengzi jiewen* as pointing to a much later event, namely the censoring of the *Mencius* under Liu Sanwu (1394). On the restoration of the civil examinations in 1384/1385 see Zhang Chaorui 張朝瑞 (1536–1603), *Huang Ming gongju kao* 皇明貢舉考 (1589), *XXSKQS* 828, 1:4a–4b (149).

21. Following the abolition of the post of prime minister in 1380, the status of the Hanlin Academy, an eminent locus in the interaction between imperial power and scholarship, was readjusted and transformed to formulate and implement imperially sanctioned doctrines and orthodoxies more efficiently. On the Hanlin Academy during the Hongwu period see Zheng Liju 郑礼炬, "Mingdai Hongwu zhi Zhengde nianjian de Hanlinyuan yu wenxue" 明代洪武至正德年间的翰林院与文学 (unpubl. Ph.D. diss., Nanjing Shifan Daxue, 2006), esp. pp. 49–78.

22. The *Mengzi jiewen* was the standard *Mencius* version for civil examinations between 1394 and 1411. With the *Mengzi jiewen* being submitted to the throne just a few months after completion of his *Shu zhuan huixuan* in 1394, it appears that although Liu Sanwu worked simultaneously on these two works for some time, he applied rather different strategies to ensure adherence to imperial directives; cf. the notes by Song Duanyi 宋端儀 (1447–1501) in his *Lizhai xianlu* 立齋閒錄, 4 *juan*, in *Guochao diangu*, vol. 2, pp. 913–914 (*juan* 39). The imperial order to compile the *Mengzi jiewen* was issued in 1390; see, e.g., Peng Sunyi 彭孫貽 (1615–1673), *Mingshi jishi benmo bubian* 明史紀事本末補編, 5 *juan* (*juan* 1), in *Lidai jishi benmo* 歷代紀事本末, 2 vols. (Beijing: Zhonghua Shuju, 1997), vol. 2, p. 1516. Cf. Liu Sanwu, "*Mengzi jiewen* tici" 孟子節文題辭, 3a–3b, in *Mengzi jiewen* 孟子節文 (1394), 1a–4b, in *Beijing Tushuguan guji zhenben congkan* 北京圖書館古籍珍本叢刊 (Beijing: Shumu Wenxian Chubanshe, 1988–) 1:955–1016, esp. p. 956, on Liu Sanwu working on the two projects at the same time. For a rounded discussion of the *Mengzi jiewen* and related issues see Zhang Jiajia 张佳佳, "Mengzi jiewen yanjiu" 孟子节文研究 (unpubl. M.A. diss., Qinghua Daxue, 2007), and Wolfgang Ommerborn, "Der Ming-Kaiser Taizu und das *Mengzi jiewen*," in Wolfgang Ommerborn, Gregor Paul, and Heiner Roetz, *Das Buch Mengzi im Kontext der Menschrechtsfrage,* 2 vols. (Berlin: LIT Verlag, 2011), vol. 1, pp. 419–439.

23. See the imperial preface to the *Sishu jizhu daquan* 四書集注大全, *SKQSCMCS,* *Jing* 170, 1a–11a (641–646), and Elman, "Where is King Ch'eng?" pp. 50–58. See also Pan Chengzhang 潘檉章 (1626–1663), *Guoshi kaoyi* 國史考異, 6 *juan,* in Chen Shoushi 陳守實 et al., *Mingshi kaozheng juewei* 明史考證抉微 (Taipei: Xuesheng Shuju, 1968), p. 113 (*Guoshi kaoyi, juan* 3, chap. 17), where Pan Chengzhang elaborates on the negative effects of the *Mengzi jiewen* on the orthodox transmission of the "wisdom of the ancient sages"; cf. *Guoshi kaoyi, XXSKQS* 452, 3:27b–29b (58–59). For the commentary versions of the *Five Classics* and the *Four Books* used in examinations during the reign of Zhu Yuanzhang see Zhang Chaorui, *Huang Ming gongju kao,* 1:4b–5b (149).

24. See Liu Sanwu, "*Mengzi jiewen* tici," 1a–4b (955–956).

25. Liu Sanwu, "*Mengzi jiewen* tici," 1a (955):... 以功利為尚, 不復知有仁義.

26. For *Mencius* 1A1 see *Sishu jizhu,* pp. 197–198; Lau, *Mencius,* p. 49; and Van Norden, *Mengzi,* pp. 1–2.

27. As indicated in the translation above, the last phrase of this passage carries some ambiguity. If read in relation to the encounter(s) between Mencius and King Hui of Liang, a reading such as "...and in the end [the king] could not accept his suggestions" seems appropriate. Where this is contextualized as part of Liu Sanwu's concluding statement regarding the preceding examples of expurgated passages, it may be perceived as part of his argument for censoring the *Mencius.* In this case, we observe a switch of focus that leads to a more general perspective: "...and in the end his suggestions cannot be accepted" by the emperor (Zhu Yuanzhang), Liu Sanwu (who carried out the imperial will), and indeed, by extension, anyone.

28. Liu Sanwu, "*Mengzi jiewen* tici," 1b (955).

29. *Mingshi* 135:3923, for example, records Zhu Yuanzhang's approval of humankindness (*ren*) and sense of duty (*yi*) as guiding principles, his verdict that it was the lack of these two virtues that led to Xiang Yu's 項羽 (232–202 B.C.) defeat, and his intention to not

make the same mistake as Xiang Yu. For Zhu Yuanzhang's views on humankindness (*ren*) as a strategic requisite in warfare see also *Ming Taizu shilu* 16:1b (vol. 1, p. 214).

30. On the wider perspective of Zhu Yuanzhang's limited commitment to a Confucian worldview and his selective approach to its teachings see Farmer, "Social Regulations of the First Ming Emperor," p. 108. For another interpretation of Zhu Yuanzhang's esteem for Confucius and the teachings attributed to him see Zhu Honglin, "Ming Taizu de Kongzi chongbai," pp. 483–530, whose arguments appear to be embedded in the contemporary discourse on a so-called renaissance of Confucianism. John D. Langlois, Jr. and Sun K'o-k'uan 孫克寬, "'Three Teachings Eclecticism' and the Thought of Ming T'ai-tsu," in *Harvard Journal of Asiatic Studies* 43, no. 1 (1983): 97–139, describe Zhu Yuanzhang as "a syncretist at heart" (quote, p. 97).

31. See Zhao Qi's 趙岐 note in his *Mengzi shisi juan* 孟子十四卷, *SBCK* 2, 1:1a (4). On this earliest extant commentary on the *Mencius* see Bernhard Fuehrer, "*Mencius* for Han Readers: Commentarial Features and Hermeneutical Strategies in Zhao Qi's Work on the *Mencius*," *Zeitschrift der Deutschen Morgenländischen Gesellschaft* 164, no. 2 (2014): 501–526.

32. See Liu Sanwu, "*Mengzi jiewen* tici," 3b (956). A close textual comparison of the *jingwen* in *Mengzi jiewen* and in Zhu Xi's version of the *Mencius* reveals a few minor textual discrepancies, none of which, however, has a major impact on the message. Liu Sanwu's approach to the text also means that in the context of Zhu Yuanzhang's literary persecution (*wenziyu* 文字獄), otherwise tabooed characters (such as *zei* 賊) remained unchanged in the *Mengzi jiewen*. On the literary persecution during the Hongwu reign see also the sources listed in Bernhard Fuehrer, "An Inauspicious Quotation or a Case of Impiety? Mr. Zhang and Literary Persecution under the First Ming Emperor," in *China and her Biographical Dimensions: Commemorative Essays for Helmut Martin,* ed. Christina Neder et al. (Bern: Peter Lang, 2001), pp. 75–82. Cf. also Hok-lam Chan, "Ming T'ai-tsu's Manipulation of Letters: Myth and Reality of Literary Persecution" [reprint from *Journal of Asian History* 29 [1995]: 1–60), in Hok-lam Chan, *Ming Taizu (r. 1368–98) and the Foundation of the Ming Dynasty in China* (Farnham, UK: Ashgate, 2011)]. For a discussion of the *Mencius* in civil examinations during the Ming see Benjamin A. Elman, *A Cultural History of Civil Examinations in Late Imperial China* (Berkeley: University of California Press, 2000), pp. 78–88. It seems noteworthy that although Liu Sanwu clearly confirmed that the expurgated sections of the *Mencius* would no longer be included in the exams, Huang Yu reports that, in fact, from 1384/1385 (Hongwu *jiazi* 洪武甲子) onward there was no fixed rule for selection of the three examination topics on the *Four Books,* and that some exams did not include the *Mencius;* see Huang Yu, *Shuanghuai suichao,* p. 91 (*juan* 5), and the quote of this passage in Zhang Chaorui, *Huang Ming gongju kao,* 1:5b (149). The omission of topics on the *Mencius* seems to indicate a certain disinclination of top scholars to fully implement the imperial directives via the examination system.

33. See Zhu Ronggui 朱榮貴, "Cong Liu Sanwu *Mengzi jiewen* lun junquan de xianzhi yu zhishi fenzi zhi zizhuxing" 從劉三吾孟子節文論君權的限制與知識份子之自主性, *Zhongguo Wenzhe jikan* 中國文哲研究季刊 6 (1995): 173–198, esp. p. 179. As the *Mengzi jiewen* carries 172 out of the 260 sections in the *Mengzi jizhu,* Liu Sanwu deleted a total of 88 sections from the *Mencius.* Cf. also Huang Jingfang 黃景昉 (1596–1662), *Guoshi*

weiyi 國史唯疑 (Taipei: Zhengzhong Shuju, 1969), pp. 32–33. (*juan* 1), who, like many others, follows Liu Sanwu's count of 85 omitted sections; see Liu Sanwu, "*Mengzi jiewen* tici," 3b (956).

34. Liu Sanwu, "*Mengzi jiewen* tici," 2b–3a (955–956).

35. These include early figures such as Xunzi 荀子 and Wang Chong 王充 (27–ca. 97), and a considerable number of Song scholars such as He She 何涉 (fl. 1041), Sima Guang, Li Gou 李覯 (1009–1059), Su Shi 蘇軾 (1037–1101), and so forth. For concise summaries on the anti-Mencian points of view in the wider political and philosophical context of the Song see Huang Chun-chieh (黃俊傑), *Mencian Hermeneutics: A History of Interpretations in China* (New Brunswick, NJ: Transaction Publishers, 2001), pp. 155–171, and Huang Junjie 黃俊傑, *Mengzi sixiangshi lun* 孟子思想史論 (Taipei: Zhongyang Yanjiuyuan, 1997), vol. 2, pp. 127–190.

36. In his *Mingshi jishi benmo bubian, juan* 1, Peng Sunyi notes that "all [passages] which do not focus on [the proper] respect for the ruler such as '[if the ruler] is remonstrated but does not listen, then [he] is to be removed from [his] position' [諫而不聽則易位] [*Mencius* 5B9] or '[the] ruler is the least important' [君為輕] [*Mencius* 7B14] and the like were all to be expurgated"; see *Mingshi jishi benmo bubian, juan* 1, in *Lidai jishi benmo,* vol. 2, p. 1516. The quote from *Mencius* 5B9 exhibits significant omissions; compare *Sishu jizhu,* p. 350; Lau, *Mencius,* p. 159; and Van Norden, *Mengzi,* p. 142. On *Mencius* 7B14 see *Sishu jizhu,* pp. 403–404; Lau, *Mencius,* pp. 195–196; and Van Norden, *Mengzi,* p. 187. On the passages quoted by Peng Sunyi see also Chen Jian, *Huang Ming tongji jiyao,* 9:6a (120). Cf. Huang Yunmei, *Mingshi kaozheng,* vol. 4, p. 1191, who emphasizes that the *Mengzi jiewen* contains only a small fraction of the "real spirit" of the *Mencius.* The excision of *Mencius* 5B9 and 7B14 is also mentioned in Liu Sanwu, "*Mengzi jiewen* tici," 2b (955). As Huang Jingfang, *Guoshi weiyi,* p. 32 (*juan* 1), draws our attention to the omission of *Mencius* section 2A2, we note that *Mencius* 2A ("Gongsun Chou: Shang") begins with section 5. The first four sections of this chapter are omitted.

37. On the *Mengzi jiewen* as a means of indoctrination and a document transmitting insights into despotism in action see Rong Zhaozu 容肇祖, "Ming Taizu de *Mengzi jiewen*" 明太祖的孟子節文, *Dushu yu chuban* 讀書與出版 2, no. 4 (1947): 16–21, esp. p. 18.

38. For the first four groups of topic areas see Zhu Ronggui, "Liu Sanwu *Mengzi jiewen,*" pp. 184–191. The last group follows a suggestion in Jiang Guozhu 姜国柱, "Wen-hua zhuanzhi de yi li: Zhu Yuanzhang de *Mengzi jiewen*" 文化专制的一例：朱元璋的孟子节文, *Liaoning Daxue xuebao* 辽宁大学学报 3 (1981): 17–19, esp. p. 18. Rong Zhaozu, "Ming Taizu de *Mengzi jiewen,*" pp. 18–21, identified a total of eleven doctrines eradicated from the Mencius.

39. Under the ninth moon of the fifth year of the Hongwu period, the *Ming Taizu shilu* 明太祖實錄, in *Ming shilu* 明實錄 (Taipei: Zhongyang Yanjiuyuan, 1962–1968), 76:4b (vol. 4, p. 1402), records that in his earlier years Zhu Yuanzhang followed the concept of the "people as the root/basis of the country" (*guo yi min wei ben* 國以民為本). And under the fourth moon of the third year of his reign, *Ming Taizu shilu* 51:8a (vol. 3, p. 1005) records his use of the analogy of the people as the water and the ruler as a boat. Further to this, Zhu Yuanzhang presented "himself in temples of Confucius in 1356 and 1360…, bestowed honors on the heirs of the sage…," and "granted special privileges to the descen-

dents of the disciple Yen Hui 顏回 and of Mencius 孟子" (quotes from Romeyn Taylor, *Basic Annals of Ming Tai-tsu* [San Francisco: Chinese Materials Center, 1975], p. 19). For a discussion of the source material regarding his attitude toward descendents of Confucius see Zhu Honglin, "Ming Taizu de Kongzi chongbai," pp. 504–513. Notwithstanding a few (possibly rhetorical) references to these political concepts during his later years, the sources seem to suggest a personal development that made it increasingly difficult for the emperor to subscribe to the political concepts outlined in the *Mencius*.

40. For Zhu Yuanzhang commenting on the negative consequences of prolonged fighting on agricultural production at the end of the Mongol period see *Ming Taizu shilu*, 22:1a (vol. 1, p. 313), and Taylor, *Basic Annals of Ming Tai-tsu*, p. 52.

41. See, e.g., Jia Naiqian 贾乃谦, "Cong *Mengzi jiewen* dao *Qianshu*" 从孟子节文到潜书, *Dongbei Shida xuebao* 东北师大学报 2 (1987): 43–50, esp. pp. 43–44. The *Ming Taizu shilu* deals with the *Mengzi jiewen* only cursorily, and Zhu Yuanzhang's other anti-Mencian activities such as the removal of Mencius from the Confucius temple do not seem to attract much of the compilers' interest.

42. See Zhu Yizun 朱彝尊, *Pushuting ji* 曝書亭集, *SBCK* 81, 69:8b–9b, esp. 69:9a (526). Zhu Yizun understands Zhu Yuanzhang as showing great respect for Confucius and therefore finds it inconceivable that such a man would censor the *Mencius*. Others who rejected the historical truthfulness of the so-called "Qian Tang incident" and of Zhu Yuanzhang's censoring of the *Mencius* include Tan Qian 談遷, *Guoque* 國榷, 6 vols. (Beijing: Guji Chubanshe, 1958), vol. 1, p. 478 ("Taizu Hongwu wu nian"); cf. Zhu Honglin, "Ming Taizu de Kongzi chongbai," pp. 483–530. For discussions of relevant material see Huang Yunmei, *Mingshi kaozheng*, vol. 4, pp. 1189–1191, and Zhang Jiajia 张佳佳, "*Mengzi jiewen* shijian benmo kaobian" 孟子节文事件本末考辨, *Zhongguo wenhua yanjiu* 中国文化研究, 2006, pp. 84–93.

43. As far as we can see from the extant copies, it appears that the *Mengzi jiewen* circulated in two versions: one that carries only the main text with no glosses or commentary and one that includes Zhu Xi's glosses, which seem to remain unaltered. With regard to amending the main text of the classics, and without going into the thorny question of what happened to the classics during the Han period, scholars throughout the imperial periods (especially during the Song) adjusted the main text of the Confucian classics (and associated works), but they aimed at rectifying the text so as to arrive at good readings. For examples of emendations of the classics made by Song scholars see Ye Guoliang 葉國良, *Songren yijing gaijing kao* 宋人疑經改經考, *Wenshi congkan* 文史叢刊, 55 (Taipei: Guoli Taiwan Daxue, 1980). Needless to say, these activities are fundamentally different from the way in which Zhu Yuanzhang carried out his censoring exercise.

44. On the status of Confucian learning in the educational policies of Zhu Yuanzhang see Chen Hanming 陈寒鸣, "Hongwu Ruxue jiaoyu yu keju bagu de xingcheng" 洪武儒学教育与科举八股的形成, *Zhongzhou xuekan* 中州学刊 5 (1993): 105–111, and Chen Hanming 陈寒鸣, "Zai lun Hongwu Ruxue jiaoyu" 再论洪武儒学教育, *Hebei xuekan* 河北学刊 5 (1997): 60–63. On Zhu Yuanzhang's efforts to reshape the educational infrastructure see Wu Han 吳晗, "Mingchu de xuexiao" 明初的學校, *Qinghua xuebao* 清華學報 15, no. 1 (1948): 33–61. Sarah Schneewind, *Community Schools and the State in Ming China* (Stanford: Stanford University Press, 2006), pp. 6–32, emphasizes the function of schools

as a means to uphold and enforce new state doctrines, and questions reports that suggest an efficient implementation of Zhu Yuanzhang's educational policies.

45. See Huang Pu 黃溥, *Xianzhong jingu lu* 閒中今古錄, 2b, in *Wuchao xiaoshu daguan* 五朝小說大觀 (1926), 6 vols. (Taipei: Guangwen Shuju, 1979), vol. 6, p. 2648. On the republication and dissemination of the *Five Classics* and the *Four Books* to schools at an earlier stage of Zhu Yuanzhang's career (1380–1381) see *Ming Taizu shilu*, 136:3b (vol. 5, p. 2154), and Taylor, *Basic Annals of Ming Tai-tsu*, p. 89. For the *Mengzi jiewen* and the *Shangshu huixuan* being distributed to schools throughout the empire see Liu Sanwu, "*Mengzi jiewen* tici," 3b (956), and the remark by Song Duanyi in his *Lizhai xianlu*, in *Guochao diangu*, vol. 2, p. 913 (*juan* 39).

CHAPTER 15

Striving for Democracy

Confucian Political Philosophy in the Ming and Qing Dynasties

WU Genyou

CONFUCIAN PHILOSOPHERS LAUNCHED a political philosophy movement from the late Ming dynasty (1368–1644) to the early Qing dynasty (1600–1700). The core idea of this movement was opposition to the royal tyranny that had lasted for over two thousand years. This movement promoted the idea of a division of political power and allowed more freedom for the people. Chinese Marxists early in the twentieth century called it the "Early Enlightenment," while Mizoguchi Yūzō and John King Fairbank both agreed that late Ming and early Qing Chinese society were trending toward modernization. I believe that this movement was in pursuit of political democracy, but I understand that "democracy" in modern English is quite different from *minzhu* 民主 in modern Chinese. In modern Chinese, democracy is the opposite of autocracy. Any expression of opposition to autocracy is regarded as democratic, although it may not include actual details about democratic institutions. In any case, with regard to these details, I do not think that the separation of powers practiced in the West should be the only model; any idea that promotes the limitation of royal power may be considered democratic. Therefore, I believe that there is a continuity of thought from the Ming to the Qing in the criticism by the literati of those times of any concentration of royal power. It may seem that the demise of the Ming and the establishment of the Qing were a direct cause of this movement, but it may be more accurate to say that it was a result of the transition to modernization in China. My reason for this claim is as follows. When the Qing government became stable and the whole society became politically and economically more developed than the previous dynasty, a few Confucian philosophers, such as Yuan Mei 袁枚 (1716–1797), continued to argue for the same political reforms. What Yuan Mei and other thinkers of the Qing period attempted to do was in part a continuation of what Gu Yanwu 顾炎武 (1613–1682), Huang Zongxi 黄宗羲 (1610–1695), and Wang Fuzhi 王夫之 (1619–1692) had been doing in the late Ming.

The central idea behind this movement was that the monopolization of power by the throne was the source of social and political turmoil. During that period in China's history this was a revolutionary idea. Philosopher Dai Zhen 戴震 (1724–1777) argued that "those who hold political position lack virtue and are good at deceiving people. They are a disaster for the people." Furthermore, he made the revolutionary claim that "Social chaos originates from the top, which hurts the people."[1] Historian Qian Daxin 钱大昕 (1728–1804) argued against this kind of despotism, saying that it was wrong to infer that loyalty to family was equivalent to loyalty to the government. He made a clear distinction between the private life of the family and public life, where loyalties were impartial, arguing that the filial piety valued in family life was not applicable to the relation between a subordinate and a superior in the affairs of state.[2] Public officials should be loyal to the people, rather than to an emperor. And emperors should not take away the rights of the people, such as the right to free speech. Qian's distinction between the public and private domains and between loyalty to the emperor and to the people was representative of the anti-despotism movement of the late Ming.

In this chapter I will discuss the political thought of four philosophers of the early Qing period: Gu Yanwu, Huang Zongxi, Wang Fuzhi, and Yuan Mei. I will argue that these four Confucian thinkers are consistent in voicing their opposition to despotism and calling for political reform and democracy.

Gu Yanwu's Idea of Political Reform and Democracy

Gu Yanwu proposes that "We should combine the feudalistic system of dukes with the system of counties."[3] He argues that the sharing of power among the feudal dukes implemented in the Western Zhou dynasty (1046–771 B.C.E.) could be duplicated by absorbing each feudal state into a centralized county system, which would enable the people to overcome the monopolization of power by the throne. Gu sees the feudal state system as what we today would call a "division of power," while the county system would be a "centralization of power." Combining the two systems would create a better system.

There were problems with each of the two systems in Gu's time. In the feudal state system, Gu points out, the dukes have more powers than county magistrates and easily become dictators of a region. In the county system, a county magistrate does not have enough power to oversee his district. Gu was concerned with the critical problems of the county system of his day. He claims that under this system, an emperor is always thinking that his territories are not large enough, that he does not trust his local officials, and that he wants to regulate every detail of local administration. Thus, there would be more paperwork and regulations. Then the local government agency would become too large to be run effectively, and local county magistrates would constantly be worrying more about whether they might break any rules than about how they might better serve the people. Gu believes that under this system, the people have become poorer and the state weaker. There is no way out of this dire situation without changing the system itself.[4]

According to Gu, the solution to this predicament would be to increase the power of the county magistrates by giving them the necessary financial support and administrative authority. For example, the emperor should give county magistrates the same authority to collect taxes and appoint lower-ranking government officials that is allowed in the feudal state system. Gu argues that the central government should abolish the government agencies that spy on local magistrates and also allow magistrates with exemplary records of achievement to pass their positions on to their competent descendants. Furthermore, in selecting magistrates there should be alternatives to accepting those who pass the national examinations.[5] All these measures would be justified by the argument that the division of power in the feudal state system could be introduced into the county system. Gu is confident that the emperor would endorse his view if the emperor wanted a powerful country.

Gu's understanding of the division of power is quite different from that of a liberal democracy. The system of checks and balances in modern democracy is best seen as a process on the horizontal level, but Gu's division of power is more vertical. In Gu's ideal, the regional governments share power with the central government. But on the horizontal level, there are no checks and balances among the local government agencies. Nonetheless, Gu's proposal is innovative and significant compared to the dominant county system in existence at that time. The following discussion explains why.

First of all, Gu's idea of a division of power is motivated by his view of human nature. Gu believes that humans are selfish; everyone works for him/herself. In contrast, the county system is based on the idea that everyone should work for the emperor, the representative of the public good. In the county system, the whole nation actually works for the royal family. For example, during the Tang dynasty the people worked for the Li royal family; during the Song dynasty they worked for the Zhao royal family; and during the Ming dynasty they worked for the Zhu royal family. Although these royal families established political order in the name of the national interest, in reality they only worked for their own family interests. They endorsed Confucianism, especially Mengzi's idea that human nature is basically good. They condemned the view that human beings by nature are selfish and that it is good to be selfish. But Gu argues that everyone should to some degree express love for their family and recognize that this is natural and even normative. Gu believes that the ancient sage-kings did not forbid or condemn this ideal but encouraged it. The sage-kings divided the land, awarded it to the dukes, and finally established the "sage-king government," which motivated the dukes to serve for the good of the nation by letting them pursue their own legitimate interests.[6] According to Gu, what the sage-kings did not do was teach people to be selfless. What motivates Gu's political reforms is a different theory of human nature from the one that underlies the county system.

Second, Gu's proposal for a division of power includes the distinction between the management of the local governments and the ownership of the central government. He proposes that a magistrate (*zhixian* 知县) should not only be given more managerial power and be promoted from the political rank of the seventh level to the fifth level, but also be given a new name: county commander (*xianling* 县令). Furthermore, every three years there would be an assessment of the achievement of any commander. Gradually, the commander would have managerial autonomy. Finally, the commander's position could be passed on to his capable descendants. It is believed that this tenure system could motivate the commander to be more responsible for the welfare of the public. The commander could lease mining rights, which would increase local revenue.[7] For Gu, the commander is in a political contract with the emperor. Gu's design definitely would cause new problems, such as unintentionally creating space that would allow separatist regimes to arise. Nonetheless, his design is meant to weaken the centralization of the county system.

Finally, these political reforms come with Gu's proposal to reform the imperial examination system. He suggests that the exams should not be the only way to select government officials. There should be alternatives, such as what was practiced during the Han dynasty (202 B.C.E.–220 C.E.); that is, candidates for political positions could be recommended by the people. Another alternative would be to select officials based on certain talents, such as public speaking, calligraphy, and legal knowledge—a method that was practiced in the Tang dynasty (618–907 C.E.).[8] Both alternatives would avoid the limitation of one single examination to determine eligibility for political office. Furthermore, this might motivate some scholars who did not have these talents to pursue other career tracks, such as teaching. If becoming an official were the only recognized career track for scholars, then it would be a wasted effort for those scholars who did not have the politically relevant talents to pursue this career.

Overall, I believe that Gu's proposal for political reform was meant to alleviate the monopolization of power in the county system. His proposal also implies a new political ideal, one that shares some similarity with modern liberal democracy, which recognizes the importance of the division of power. To some extent, Gu's proposal can be seen as a seventeenth-century Chinese appeal for liberal democracy.

Huang Zongxi's Political Ideal and the Prototype of Chinese Liberal Democracy

Compared to Gu's proposal for political reform, Huang Zongxi elaborates a more comprehensive and intensive criticism against monarchy. Huang is the first Chinese philosopher to propose a clear democratic ideal. He argues that promoting people's well-being should be the only aim of political activity. He further argues that the rise and fall of different dynasties has nothing to do with the aim or essence of politics.[9]

How is this political ideal different from the traditional idea that the people are the "root" of a country (*minben* 民本)? I believe that there are five differences.

First of all, Huang proposes a political arrangement that would establish a new type of relationship between the emperor and his ministers. From the standpoint of the division of power, the emperor and his ministers are equal. They all serve the people. However, the traditional idea that the people are the root of a country takes the people as the only means to keep the country at peace. The end is the stability of the country. The emperor and his ministers are not equal. The emperor has an absolute power that cannot be challenged by the ministers. However, Huang believes that since the country is so big and the population so large, one man cannot rule it all. A division of power is necessary.[10] Furthermore, Huang uses a metaphor to describe the relationship between the emperor and his ministers: all of them are working to pull a log forward. The only difference is in the division of labor.[11] Thus, Huang believes that the traditional metaphor of a father and sons is not an accurate way to capture the relationship. Huang perceives the relationship from the standpoint of serving the people. If a minister resigns from his position, then he is like a stranger to the emperor without any further duty to serve. If a scholar who holds a political position does not serve the public, then he is merely a servant of the emperor. However, if he is to serve the public, then he is either a teacher or a friend to the emperor.[12] What Huang proposes about the relationship between the emperor and the ministers is quite different from the traditional idea that people are the root of the country.

Second, Huang argues that there is a difference between public law and private law. Public law refers to law made by the people. Private law refers to law made by the emperor. Furthermore, Huang argues that public law should replace private law, and that public law should regulate the following aspects of life: farming, herding, schooling, marriage, and taxation. The spirit of the law does not show itself in private law. Huang offers the criticism that, since the establishment of the county system in the Han and later the Qing, there has been no real system of laws. All the laws practiced were made by and for royal families.[13]

Third, Huang proposes that a prime minister (*zaixiang* 宰相) should be reinstated to assist the emperor or even to substitute for the emperor. The reasoning is that since the purpose of an emperor is to manage the public affairs of the whole country, a responsibility that cannot be handled by just one man, additional positions should be established. Thus, various political positions are set up for deputies of the emperor. An emperor is only one public official among others. There is no barrier between him and other public officials. He can even be replaced. An emperor is more of a symbol of the highest power. Thus, in Huang's political design, a prime minister is different from the traditional official who must obey the emperor unconditionally. A prime minister should be equal to the emperor and be able to replace the emperor and carry out executive power if the emperor is incompetent.[14] Huang's political design is not compatible with the traditional idea that the emperor as the son of heaven has absolute power over everything.

In the historical context, when the founding emperor of the Ming dynasty abolished the position of prime minister, all officials reported to the emperor, which resulted in a monopoly of power in his person. Furthermore, in political practice the emperor was not able to manage the government by himself, and it was then possible for a few corrupt ministers or persons close to the emperor to seize power, as in the eunuch period of the Ming dynasty. Huang proposes that the prime minister should be given more authority so that power would not fall into the hands of royal relatives or royal servants. Since royal relatives and servants lack political knowledge or training, they would not be expected to act in the interests of the country. Rather, they would act in the interest of the emperor or even in their own interests. Thus, government becomes a tool for a group of people to gain benefits for themselves. Huang points out that if the prime minister can work with the emperor, the emperor does not need to deal with public affairs alone. To some extent, the power of the emperor is weakened or divided.[15] This political design is very similar to what happened in the constitutional monarchies of some early modern European countries.

Fourth, Huang argues that the function of schools should be expanded and that schools should also be made into places for training officials. Emperors and officeholders alike should be educated as culturally informed intellectuals. But what the emperor affirms is not necessarily right, and thus the emperor should leave judgments to places like schools, where scholars can discuss and debate.

Obviously, this design is very different from the reality in which the emperor determines what is right or wrong. Huang even suggests that the emperor should go to listen to the critics from the royal academy, and that officials should do the same.[16] This proposal can be traced back to the traditional idea that local schools should participate in local politics. But according to Huang, the political involvement of schools should be more extensive. This might strengthen the political function of schools, but it could also jeopardize the academic independence of the schools from politics, since schools are supposed to be politically neutral.

Fifth, Huang suggests that there should be different methods of selecting officials, that the royal examinations cannot be the only way; other methods such as recommendations should be included. Furthermore, the government should also employ those with special talents and a strong commitment to serve the country.[17]

Overall, Huang's political design is quite different from the traditional idea that the emperor alone should hold absolute power. Huang believed that the purpose of a government is to function for the good of the people.

Wang Fuzhi's "Gong Tian Xia" (The Good of the Country)

With regard to the criticism of monopolization of power in the county system, Wang Fuzhi shares a similar view with Gu Yanwu and Huang Zongxi. Wang criticizes King Wen of the Zhou dynasty (1152–1106 B.C.E.), who was well respected by Confucians. Wang points out that in both the Xia and Shang dynasties there was the position of prime minister. But starting with King Wen of the Zhou, the position of prime minister was abolished and absolute monarchy in China began.[18] Wang argues that the power of the emperor should henceforth be shared.

Wang proposes the political ideal of "*gong tian xia*" (the good of the country). His principle is that the well-being of the people is more important than the power of the royal family. This principle is similar to Huang Zongxi's idea that the well-being of a country depends on the life of the people rather than the power of the royal family. Wang also compares the county system with the feudal state system, arguing that the county system is much better for the country. However, Wang also points out that since the county system assumes the monopoly of power by the emperor, it is not good for the well-being of the people. Furthermore, the length of rule of a royal family has nothing to do with whether or not the people are well cared for. Wang believes that the first emperor of the Qin dynasty (259–210 B.C.E.) was overthrown because the royal family was interested only in passing the royal line to its descendants. However, afterward many royal families did not see this as the reason for the failure of the Qin royal family.[19] Wang argues that the good of the people should be the only criterion of political legitimacy.

However, regarding the best way to restrain the power of the emperor, Wang's view is different from Gu's and Huang's. Huang argues that the emperor and the ministers should share power and suggests that a senior minister can even exercise executive authority when the emperor is incompetent. Wang disagrees. He proposes that the position of the emperor should be more like a symbol of power and that a set of laws and regulations are the basis for government policies to be made and carried out. Wang even argues that the early sage-kings were humble and never used power to dominate others. They acted in accord with the spirit of Daoism, *wuwei* 无为, letting the ministers perform their duties according to the laws and regulations.[20] In this way are the political institution and the existing laws and regulations the key to good government.

Wang also proposes that there are three ways to transfer the power of the emperor: inheritance, recommendation, and revolution. He points out that when the security of the nation is at stake, those who can defend it should be leaders so that the nation does not fall into the hands of foreigners.[21]

With regard to how to achieve a balance of power, based on his research of Chinese political history Wang proposes that the emperor, the prime minister, and the counselors should form the core of the government. According to Wang, they have different duties. The duty of the emperor is to appoint the prime minister. If the prime minister is incompetent, then the emperor can determine whether to discharge him. And the counselors are supposed to point out the mistakes made by the emperor, rather than those by the prime minister. And the prime minister should weigh in on significant issues, such as national security and important appointments. Counselors can participate in the deliberation of less significant issues.[22] Thus, Wang's proposal is different from those of Huang and Gu with regard to the balance of power. Overall, the emperor appoints the prime minister, the prime minister appoints counselors, and the counselors evaluate the political performance of the emperor. Wang believes that this arrangement of the balance of power could keep the government stable.

Compared to Huang's proposal, Wang's idea of the balance of power is less radical. It is much closer to the traditional political setup in the Tang dynasty. Compared to Gu's proposal to balance power vertically by increasing the power of the county magistrates, Wang's idea is to balance power horizontally at the highest level. Nevertheless, the balance of power is the goal of both, and both are drawn to the spirit of modern liberal democracy. Their proposals present different alternatives for early Chinese democratic ideals. In fact, Gu and Huang did communicate with each other about their political ideals, but Wang did not participate. However, they all targeted the problems of the county system.

In addition to the balance of power, Wang also discusses the issue of land property rights. Wang argues that the right to land ownership should be protected; the replacement of one royal family by another one should not affect people's rights to their land since the land was not given to them by the new emperor.[23] Thus, people's property rights are immune from political change. This is a huge challenge to the idea that the land is owned by the royal government under the county system. This idea is similar to what modern philosophers hold concerning the legitimacy of private property.

Political Thought of the Middle Qing Period and the Modern Transformation of Confucian Political Thought

Even under the tight literary inquisition during the rule of the Qianlong Emperor in the Qing dynasty, philosopher Yuan Mei made a comparison of the county and feudal state systems and pointed toward the direction of modern democracy.

With regard to political reform, Yuan Mei's proposal is close to Gu's. Yuan argues that the county system does not carry out the ancient sages' idea of "the good of the country," and that the feudal state system does a better job. Here is Yuan's argument: as the ancient sages pointed out, since the emperor cannot govern the country by himself, in the feudal state system the dukes would share power with the emperor, and this would serve the country better. As there are many dukes, they would challenge and even overthrow any emperor who is incompetent and corrupt.[24]

Furthermore, Yuan argues for the feudal state system from the perspective of personal liberty. First of all, Yuan argues that the feudal state system would prevent a corrupt emperor from abusing power since the dukes share some of the power. A local riot against a duke would not jeopardize the stability of the whole country. But it would in the county system, as it did in the peasant riot against the Qin dynasty, which rapidly resulted in its overthrow.[25]

Second, under the feudal state system, scholars have more freedom. What Kongzi, Mengzi, and other early Chinese philosophers achieved occurred during the time of the feudal states. If a scholar was not welcomed or valued by one duke, he could move and make proposals to another duke, as Kongzi and Mengzi did in their times. However, under the county system, the standard examination was implemented nationwide. If a scholar failed this exam twice, he would not be given credentials to move to another county and find a job there. Therefore, under the feudal state system, scholars would have more space to exercise their capacities.[26]

Yuan shares many arguments with Gu. But Yuan has some distinct views of his own. For example, Yuan perceives the space for scholars to exercise their capacities as intrinsically valuable, and he believes that a diversity of professional skills is also good in itself. This view is compatible with the value given to diversity in modern society.

I believe that what Gu Yanwu, Huang Zongxi, Wang Fuzhi, and Yuan Mei each argue for, and sometimes disagree about, in their stated political ideals and designs is far from liberal democracy, but what I have tried to explain up to this point is something that has been ignored by many philosophers: they miss the significance of the anticipation by these four thinkers of political modernization in China. Gu, Huang, Wang, and Yuan should not be perceived as classical Confucians, such as the New Confucians during the Song and Ming periods. However, they are still Confucians and are inspired by Confucianism. Therefore, I believe that Confucian political thought has the potential to contribute to modernization in China today. During the seventeenth, eighteenth, and nineteenth centuries there was no Western political democracy in theory or practice that developed from the native Confucian tradition. However, this does not imply that during these three centuries that no Chinese political democracy, at least in theory, emerged from the Confucian tradition. Probably due to the influence of this newly emergent thought, many Confucian scholars during the transition from the Qing to the Republic endorsed Western political democracy. The political reform launched by Kang Youwei and Liang Qichao was an experiment that resulted from this endorsement. Even if it did not last long and ultimately failed, it marked the official beginning of the pursuit of real political democracy, an experiment that continues today.

Notes

1. Dai Zhen 戴震, "Yuan shan" 原善, in *Dai Zhen quanji* 戴震全集, vol. 2 (Beijing: Qinghua Daxue Chubanshe, 1999), p. 27.

2. Qian Daxin 钱大昕, "Yuan xiao" 原孝, in *Qian Yan Tang ji* 潜研堂集, vol. 2 (Shanghai: Shanghai Guji Chubanshe, 1989), p. 281.

3. Gu Yanwu, "Junxian lun yi" 郡县论一, in *Gu Tinglin shi wenji* 顾亭林诗文集 (Beijing: Zhonghua Shuju, 1983), p. 12. Hereafter, "feudalistic system of dukes" will be referred to as "feudal state system," and "system of counties" as "county system."

4. Ibid.

5. Ibid.

6. Gu Yanwu 顾炎武, "Yan si qi cong" 言私其豵, in *Ri zhi lu ji shi* 日知录集释, (Changsha: Yue Lu Chubanshe, 1994), p. 92.

7. Gu Yanwu, "Junxian lun yi."

8. Ibid., p. 17.

9. Huang Zongxi 黄宗羲, "Yuan Chen" 原臣, in *Huang Zongxi quanji* 黄宗羲全集, vol. 1 (Hangzhou: Zhejiang Guji Chubanshe, 1985), p. 5.

10. Ibid.

11. Ibid.

12. Ibid.

13. Huang Zongxi 黄宗羲, "Yuan Fa" 原法, in *Huang Zongxi quanji,* vol. 1, pp. 6–8.

14. Ibid., p. 8.

15. Ibid., p. 9.

16. Huang Zongxi, "Xue Xiao" 学校, in *Huang Zongxi quanji,* vol. 1, p. 10.

17. Ibid.

18. Wang Fuzhi 王夫之, "Shangshu yin yi" 尚书引义, in *Wang Fuzhi quanji* 王夫之全集, vol. 5, book 2 (Changsha: Yue Lu Chubanshe, 1996), p. 397.

19. Wang Fuzhi, "Du tong jian lun" 读通鉴论, in *Wang Fuzhi quanji,* vol. 1, book 10, p. 68.

20. Ibid., p. 474.

21. Wang Fuzhi, "Huangshu yuanji di yi" 黄书原极第一, in *Wang Fuzhi quanji,* vol. 1, book 12, p. 503.

22. Wang Fuzhi, "Song lun" 宋论, in *Wang Fuzhi quanji,* vol. 4, book 11, pp. 121–122.

23. Wang Fuzhi, "E meng" 恶梦, in *Wang Fuzhi quanji,* vol. 4, book 12, p. 551.

24. Yuan Mei 袁枚, "Shu Liuzi fengjian lun hou" 书柳子封建论后, in *Xiao Cang Shan Fang shi wenji* 小仓山房诗文集, book 3 (Shanghai: Shanghai Guji Chubanshe, 1988), pp. 1634–1636.

25. Ibid., p. 1636.

26. Yuan Mei, "Zai shu fengjian lun hou" 再书封建论后, in *Xiao Cang Shan Fang shi wenji* 小仓山房诗文集, book 3 (Shanghai: Shanghai Guji Chubanshe, 1988), p. 1638.

Contributors

ROGER T. AMES is Humanities Chair Professor at Peking University. He is Professor Emeritus of Philosophy at the University of Hawai'i and former editor of *Philosophy East and West* and *China Review International*. He has authored interpretative studies of Chinese philosophy and culture: *Thinking Through Confucius* (SUNY Press, 1987), *Anticipating China: Thinking Through the Narratives of Chinese and Western Culture* (SUNY Press, 1995), and *Thinking From the Han: Self, Truth, and Transcendence in Chinese and Western Culture* (SUNY Press, 1998) (all with David L. Hall), and most recently *Confucian Role Ethics: A Vocabulary* (Chinese University of Hong Kong, 2011). His publications also include many translations of Chinese classics: *Sun-tzu: The Art of Warfare* (Ballantine Books, 1993); *Sun Pin: The Art of Warfare* (SUNY Press, 1996) (with D. C. Lau); *The Analects of Confucius: A Philosophical Translation* (Ballantine Books, 1998) and the *Classic of Family Reverence: A Philosophical Translation of the* Xiaojing (University of Hawai'i Press, 2009) (both with Henry Rosemont, Jr.); and *Focusing the Familiar: A Translation and Philosophical Interpretation of the* Zhongyong (University of Hawai'i Press, 2001) and *Daodejing: A Philosophical Translation* (Ballantine Books, 2003) (both with David L. Hall).

WONSUK CHANG is Senior Researcher at the Academy of Korean Studies in Korea. His publications on comparative philosophy and East Asian philosophical traditions include *Confucianism in Context: Classic Philosophy and Contemporary Issues, East Asia and Beyond* (SUNY Press, 2010) (with Leah Kalmanson); "Ch'oe Han-gi's Confucian Philosophy of Experience: New Names for Old Ways of Thinking" (*Philosophy East and West* 62, no. 2 [2012]); "Reflections on Time and Related Ideas in the *Yijing*" (*Philosophy East and West* 59, no. 2 [2009]); "Gazing at the White Clouds: An Annotated Translation of Yulgok's Sŏnbi haengjang" (*Review of Korean Studies* 18, no. 2 [2015]) (with Lukas Pokorny); and "Mibunhwadoen migamjŏk yŏnsok, Tongyang ch'ŏrhak, kŭrigo Hwait'ŭhedŭ-pigyo ch'ŏrhagŭi pangbŏmnonŭl wihayŏ" (Undifferentiated aesthetic continuum, Asian philosophies, and Whitehead: For the method of comparative philosophy) (*Hwait'ŭhedŭ yŏn'gu / Journal of Whitehead Studies* [2013]).

CHEN LAI entered the Department of Philosophy at Peking University in 1978 as a graduate student in Chinese Philosophy. He received his Master's degree in 1981 and his Doctorate in Philosophy in 1985. In 1986, he became Associate Professor in the Department of Philosophy at Peking University and for the next two years, as a Visiting Scholar supported by the Henry Luce Foundation, conducted research at Harvard University. He has been a full Professor at Peking University since 1990, and is currently a professor in the Philosophy Department and Dean of the Academy of Chinese Learning (Guoxue) at Tsinghua University. Professor Chen has made important contributions to research in Confucian philosophy, especially Song-Ming Ru (Confucian) thought. His best-known writings include *Zhu Xi zhexue yanjiu* (Research in the philosophy of Zhu Xi) (1988), *Zhu Zi shu xin biannian kaozheng* (A chronological record of Zhu Xi's books and letters: Textual investigation and verification) (1989), *You wu zhi jing: Wang Yangming zhexue de jingshen* (Here and beyond: The spirit of Wang Yangming's philosophy) (1991), and *Song-Ming Lixue* (Song-Ming Neo-Confucianism) (1992), as well as numerous essays and articles. Dr. Chen is an honorary professor at eleven universities and is a member of the editorial boards of sixteen academic journals.

BERNHARD FUEHRER is Professor of Sinology at the Department of the Languages and Cultures of China and Inner Asia, School of Oriental and African Studies (SOAS), University of London. He received his B.A. from National Taiwan University (1990) and his Ph.D. from Vienna University (1994). He is the author of monographs on medieval poetics (1995, 2001), the history of Sinology (2001, 2011, 2016), and Southern Hokkien (2014). He has published volumes on musicology (1993), censorship (2003), reading (2005), and knowledge transfer (2014). He has also published extensively on traditional Chinese exegesis, reading traditions, and the reception history of the Confucian canon.

PETER D. HERSHOCK is Director of the Asian Studies Development Program (ASDP) and Education Specialist at the East-West Center (EWC) in Honolulu, Hawai'i. His work with ASDP over the past twenty years has centered on designing and conducting faculty and institutional development programs aimed at enhancing undergraduate teaching and learning about Asian cultures and societies. As part of the EWC Education Program, he has collaborated in designing and hosting international leadership programs and research seminars that examine the relationship among higher education, globalization, equity, and diversity. Trained in Asian and comparative philosophy, his main research work has focused on using Buddhist conceptual resources to reflect on contemporary issues of global concern. His books include: *Liberating Intimacy: Enlightenment and Social Virtuosity in Ch'an Buddhism* (SUNY Press, 1996); *Reinventing the Wheel: A Buddhist Response to the Information Age* (SUNY Press, 1999); *Chan Buddhism* (University of Hawai'i Press, 2005); *Buddhism in the Public Sphere: Reorienting Global Interdependence* (Routledge, 2006); *Changing Education: Leadership, Innovation and Development in a Globalizing Asia Pacific* (Springer, 2007) (edited with Mark Mason and John N. Hawkins); *Educations and Their Purposes: A Conversation among Cultures* (University of Hawai'i Press, 2008) (edited with Roger T. Ames); *Valuing Diversity: Buddhist Reflection on Realizing a More Equitable Global Future* (SUNY Press, 2012); *Public Zen, Personal Zen: A Buddhist Introduction* (Rowman and Littlefield, 2014); and *Value and Values: Economics and Justice in an Age of Global Interdependence* (University of Hawai'i Press, 2015) (edited with Roger T. Ames).

CHUN-CHIEH HUANG is the National Chair Professor and Director of the Program of East Asian Confucianisms at National Taiwan University. He served as President (now Honorary President) of the Chinese Association for General Education. He has received many awards including the National Award for Teaching Excellence in General Education, the Award for Lifelong Contribution to General Education, and the 55th National Academic Award and the 16th National Chair Professorship. Among his numerous publications, four books were recently published in English: *Taiwan in Transformation: Retrospect and Prospect* (Transaction Publishers, 2014); *Mencian Hermeneutics: A History of Interpretations in China* (Transaction Publishers, 2001); *Humanism in East Asian Confucian Contexts* (transcript Verlag, Bielefeld, 2010); and *East Asian Confucianisms: Texts in Contexts* (National Taiwan University Press, 2015).

HEISOOK KIM received her B.A. in English Language and Literature and her M.A. in Christian Studies from Ewha Womans University. She finished her Ph.D. in the Department of Philosophy at the University of Chicago. She has taught in the Department of Philosophy at Ewha Womans University since 1987. Her areas of interest range from epistemology/philosophical methodology to feminist philosophy within the cultural contexts of the East and the West. She has served as President of the Korean Philosophical Association.

LEE SEUNG-HWAN is a professor of Confucian and Neo-Confucian philosophy at Korea University, and the director of its Institute of Philosophy. He is the author of several social philosophical studies on Confucianism, including *Social Philosophical Re-illumination of Confucianism* (in Korean). His recent book *Horizontal Frame and Vertical Frame: Semiological Analysis of [the] Xing-*

Li Debate (in Korean) is recognized as the final settlement of a philosophical debate that lasted for more than four hundred years during the Chosun dynasty.

NAKAJIMA ᴛᴀᴋᴀʜɪʀᴏ is Professor of Chinese Philosophy and Comparative Philosophy at the Institute for Advanced Studies on Asia, the University of Tokyo, where he is currently Vice-Director. His publications include *The Chinese Turn in Philosophy* (UTCP, 2007); *The Reverberation of Chinese Philosophy: Language and Politics* (University of Tokyo Press, 2007); *Philosophy in Humanities* (Iwanami-shoten, 2009); *Zhuangzi: Telling the Hour of Dawn as a Hen* (Iwanami-shoten, 2009); *Deconstruction and Reconstruction: The Possibilities of Chinese Philosophy* (UTCP, 2010); *Praxis of Co-existence: State and Religion* (University of Tokyo Press, 2010); *Practicing Philosophy between China and Japan* (UTCP, 2011); and *Philosophy of the Evil: Imagination of Chinese Philosophy* (Chikuma-shobo, 2012).

NGUYEN ɴᴀᴍ is a lecturer and the former Chairperson of the Division of East Asian Studies (1994), and Division of Chinese Studies (2010–2012), at Vietnam National University in Ho Chi Minh City. He also served as the manager of the Academic Program of the Harvard-Yenching Institute (2004–2010). His research interests focus on comparative literature (dealing mainly with China and Vietnam), translation studies, and adaptation studies. He is currently an associate of the Harvard-Yenching Institute.

ᴍɪᴄʜᴀᴇʟ NYLAN writes: I have benefited from extraordinary teachers, including Michael Loewe, Liu Tzu-chien, Nathan Sivin, Henry Rosemont, and Paul Serruys (listed in the order of my acquaintance). I chose the early China field when it bordered on lunacy to do so, for no graduate program in the early 1980s existed in the U.S. to train me in that field. But I had developed a love of Han dynasty prose, a fascination with the new archaeological discoveries, and a strong sense that historians were still treating early China as if it were late imperial China. Clearly, there was work to be done, and above all, I did not want to specialize. Joseph Levenson, my first teacher in Chinese history, had instilled in me a love of the "amateur ideal," and besides, technocrats such as Robert McNamara were contentedly destroying the world. As the people I admire in the classical world crafted pieces subsumed under the academic disciplines of history, art history, archaeology, religious studies, and philosophy, my writing surveys topics as various as *Chang'an 26 BCE: An Augustan Age in China* (University of Washington Press, 2015) (edited with Griet Vankeerberghen); "Administration of the Family," in *China's Early Empires: A Re-appraisal*, (Cambridge University Press, 2010) (volume edited with Michael Loewe); and Yang Xiong's *The Canon of Supreme Mystery* (SUNY Press, 1993).

OGURA K I Z O was born in Tokyo and graduated from the University of Tokyo with a degree in German literature. He studied Confucianism and earned credits in the doctoral course of the Faculty of Philosophy (Oriental Philosophy) of the Graduate School of Seoul National University. He is currently a professor in the Graduate School of Human and Environmental Studies, Kyoto University. His academic interests include the structuring of East Asia based on Eastern thought, culture, and philosophy.

W I N N I E SUNG is an assistant Professor at Nanyang Technological University in Singapore. She received her B.A. in Philosophy from the University of Toronto and her Ph.D. from the University of New South Wales. Her primary research project is the thought of the Confucian thinker Xunzi, focusing in particular on interpreting and working through the implications of Xunzi's concept of *xin* (heart/mind). She is also interested in issues related to self-knowledge, emotions, and moral psychology. Her other research projects include self-ascription of belief, resentment, sympathy, and trustworthiness.

S O R - H O O N TAN is Associate Professor of Philosophy at the National University of Singapore. She is author of *Confucian Democracy: A Deweyan Reconstruction* (SUNY Press, 2004) and editor of *Challenging Citizenship: Group Membership and Cultural Identity in a Global Age* (Routledge, 2016) and *The Bloomsbury Research Handbook of Chinese Philosophy Methodologies* (Bloomsbury, 2016).

P E T E R Y. J. WONG is a graduate of the Philosophy Department at the University of Hawai'i with a focus on Chinese philosophy, especially Confucian thought. He is a Book Review Editor with the journal *Sophia*. An itinerant academic, he has taught at the University of Melbourne and Deakin University, and occasionally shows up at the odd philosophy conference. He is currently working on a manuscript dealing with the sense of religiousness in early Confucianism, which is non-theistic in nature.

WU G E N Y O U received his Ph.D. in philosophy from Wuhan University, where he is currently Professor of Philosophy. He works primarily in Chinese philosophy during the Ming and Qing dynasties, comparative philosophy, and political philosophy. He has published more than ten books, which include *Philosophical Issues in Chinese Philosophy of* [*the*] *Ming and Qing Dynasties; Between Deontology and Theory of Justice: On Comparative Political Philosophy* (in Chinese); and more than 160 journal articles which appear in *Asian Philosophy, Chinese Social Science,* and other peer-reviewed journals.

XIANGLONG ZHANG is a professor at both Shandong University and Peking University (retired). He received his Ph.D. at SUNY-Buffalo in 1992 and became a faculty member at Peking University the same year. He has research interests in phenomenology and Confucian philosophy, especially the philosophical meanings of *xiao* (filial piety), and has published a number of books and articles on these topics. He is a practitioner of *taiji* and finds it an aid to the understanding of ancient Chinese intelligence.

Index